Juvenile Corrections

Edited By

Rick Ruddell
Eastern Kentucky University

Matthew O. Thomas
California State University - Chico

Newgate Press

www.newgatepress.com
2009

Published by Newgate Press

Richmond, Kentucky
http:www.newgatepress.com

ISBN - 978-0-9796455-1-8

Printed in the United States of America on acid-free paper.

Contents

Chapters

FOREWORD

David W. Roush

A n effective practitioner in juvenile corrections is today's prized commodity. Many reasons contribute to this phenomenon, and a full discussion of these factors might prove beneficial at another time. It is sufficient to acknowledge that success in any area of juvenile corrections is extremely difficult.

The evidence of the problems in juvenile corrections continues to mount. While the tales of abuse, assaults, injury, and violence do not represent the majority of juvenile corrections programs, the systems failure in Texas and the in-custody deaths in Florida combine with an ever increasing number of news headlines to paint a picture for the public and for policy makers that appears frightening at times. In response, politicians have moved state and local juvenile corrections systems toward a more punitive, adult oriented, and paramilitary structure in the mistaken belief that prison-like construction, harsh discipline, and lengthy confinements will solve the problems of today's juvenile offender.

Some of the best information about the failures of juvenile corrections comes from findings letters from the U. S. Department of Justice's investigations of juvenile facilities under the Civil Rights of Institutionalized Persons Act (CRIPA). A review of several findings letters gives the impression that one could simply use the "replace" function on any word processing software to change the name of the particular institution to that of another without substantially altering the accuracy of the findings. Common themes exist in CRIPA findings letters: substandard conditions of confinement (overcrowding and unsanitary living conditions), an inadequate number of direct care staff, inadequate training for staff, inadequate programming for youth (education, recreation, mental health services, and social skills), and high rates of violence, physical restraints, room confinements, and injuries. More importantly, common problems portend common solutions, and jurisdictions that have responded well to CRIPA involvement, (e.g., the Kentucky Department of Juvenile Justice), can serve a model for reform.

Much can also be learned from states that have been slow to embrace reform. For example, Professors Ruddell and Thomas include references to the California and Ohio juvenile corrections systems. Again, similarities exist about "what doesn't work" in the forms of: (a) compartmentalization or the disconnect between services and security; (b) the need to overcome architectural problems (the N.A. Chadjerian Youth Facility in Stockton, California, and the Marion Juvenile Corrections Facility in Marion, Ohio, are two examples of the most inappropriate juvenile correctional facility design); (c) the failure of national accreditation to exert a mitigating influence on these problems; and (d) the negative influence the labor unions in the perpetuation of punitive institutional climates.

Having been dealt a difficult and less than optimistic hand, the challenge for today's juvenile corrections practitioner is how to play these cards. Skill is acquired through knowledge of the game and acquisition of concepts and principles from those who play the game well. For juvenile justice practitioners, success may depend on the ability to move adeptly between the worlds of academia and the institution, between theory and practice, and between research and applied behavior analysis. The successful juvenile corrections practitioner must understand what to do and how to do it. Given the complexity of today's juvenile offender, juvenile corrections cannot succeed by relying upon leadership from individuals who know paramilitary organizations or law enforcement agencies or adult corrections but who do not understand juvenile delinquency, adolescent development (especially the developmental differences between boys and girls), mental health disorders among adolescents, post traumatic stress disorders among adolescents, just to name a few.

Into this murky mix of challenges comes the sobering reality of a national economy that is going to ask juvenile corrections practitioners to move far beyond the old request of "doing more with less." The impending financial crises will require juvenile corrections practitioners to do "less with less" without allowing them a proportionate reduction in the expected outcomes of their facilities or agencies. In other words, the future of juvenile corrections dictates that practitioners must be able to work smarter and more effectively.

Two issues are required. The first is a change in direction. The adult model does not and has not worked for juvenile corrections, and we need to promote a community-based strategy. It is imperative to do this quickly, since some states will soon start to eliminate community-based programs as part of misguided costs cutting efforts. The second is the creation and expansion of a compendium of useful information about "what works." Practitioners need to have accessible resources that provide understandable concepts and strategies for producing successful outcomes with juvenile offenders in a variety of settings.

The strength of this text is its ability to address both issues.

David W. Roush, Ph.D.
Juvenile Justice Associates, LLC
5 Locust Court
Albion, MI 49224

INTRODUCTION

There is increasing interest in what occurs in juvenile correctional facilities: we know from media reports that there are assaults, murders and suicides, staff and resident misconduct, escapes, medical misadventures, unintentional injuries, and mismanagement. On the other hand, there are thousands of dedicated and hard-working staff members in these settings who enthusiastically work toward rehabilitating these young people. We are more likely to hear about problems in these placements than the successful interventions that occur each day as many youth return from these placements to the community and live crime free lives.

The Bureau of Justice Statistics reported that there were about 93,000 youth in detention or juvenile correctional facilities on December 31, 2006 (Sabol, Couture, & Harrison, 2007). We do not know, however, the number of juveniles held in privately operated residential facilities such as boot camps, community-based wilderness programs, or those placed in foster homes or psychiatric facilities. Some are incarcerated in adult jails or prisons: there were 2,639 prisoners who were less than 18 years of age in state prisons at midyear 2007 (Sabol & Couture, 2008) and another 6,837 juveniles incarcerated in local jails (Sabol & Minton, 2008)—although, prior to January 1, 2009, there were three states where juveniles become adults on their 16th or 17th birthdays. (Now, only two states consider persons less than 18 years of age as adults.)

Many of these youth pose incredible challenges for the practitioners who work with them. Some have been accused or adjudicated of serious and violent crimes, some are gang-involved, and others have histories of mental health or substance abuse problems. Others—especially girls—have sad histories of emotional, physical, and sexual abuse as well as neglect. Sometimes, their escape from these conditions places them on the streets with an increased risk of prostitution, gang life, substance abuse, and other self destructive behaviors (Chesney-Lind & Shelden, 2004). Furthermore, many of the youth admitted to correctional facilities today have serious mental health problems (Fazel, Doll, & Langstrom, 2008).

There has always been a tension in juvenile justice systems between acting in the best interests of the juvenile (e.g., their rehabilitation) contrasted against punishing them (also called "holding youth accountable" or "the interests of public safety"). Over the past three decades, most states increased the severity of sanctions for delinquent youth (Redding, 2008). In some jurisdictions, these legislative changes occurred after a single youth committed violent offenses (Singer, 1996). In other states, severe legal consequences for violent offenders were legislated as a response to increased violence and were often related to the intersection of drugs, gangs, and guns—especially in inner-city neighborhoods. In the 1980s and 1990s, rates of transfer to adult courts increased and thousands of juveniles found guilty were sent to adult prisons. In fact, the Equal Justice Initiative (2007) has reported that there are 73 youth serving life without the possibility of parole within the United States—all of them were 13 or 14 years of age at the time of their offenses (p. 20). Unless laws change, all of those persons will die in prison. Furthermore, until the U. S. Supreme Court's *Roper v. Simmons* decision in 2005, 16- and 17-year-olds were in jeopardy of the death penalty. Streib (2005) estimated that some 366 Americans were put to death after committing crimes as juveniles from 1642 to 2005.

Yet, rates of youth violence in the community have decreased over the past fifteen years. Snyder (2008b) reported that 1,310 juveniles were arrested for homicide in 2006 (p. 2), which was down from the 3,790 arrests in 1993 (Snyder, 2008a, p. 1). Along with these decreased rates of violence, there seems to be more interest in developing interventions that are more rehabilitative. The public generally supports the rehabilitation of juveniles and taxpayers have expressed a willingness to pay for interventions for at-risk children and rehabilitative programs for delinquents (Nagin, Piquero, Scott, & Steinberg, 2006). Yet, this positive attitude toward rehabilitation can change in response to a series of well publicized juvenile crimes, such as the Columbine school murders, and politicians have often felt compelled to enact tough-on-crime legislation for youthful offenders.

Despite the public's support for rehabilitation, many argue that juvenile justice systems have failed to live up to expectations (Feld, 1999; Macallair, 2008). Placement in juvenile facilities is more costly than adult jails or prison and rates of failure (e.g., when youth violate the conditions of their release or reoffend) are generally very high—although some jurisdictions have developed model programs that counter this trend. In most of the chapters in this book, however, the authors address the issue of chronic under-funding of juvenile justice systems and how that impacts programs and services to these troubled youth. If we are truly serious about reducing juvenile crime and increasing public safety, we have to provide the levels of funding that these operations require. In addition, the interventions have to be meaningful and they need to be based on what the research demonstrates about the effectiveness of different programs (see Drake, 2007) rather than misguided perceptions of legislators.

As we started to research the issue of youth justice systems, we quickly found that there was no single work that identified and described the most pressing challenges in juvenile corrections. In response to this gap in the literature, we gathered together a number of juvenile justice experts, practitioners, and academics and put their work together in a single book that would serve as a reference for students, scholars, and practitioners. Our goal was to provide an overview of juvenile corrections, the challenges that staff members in these institutions confront, the interventions that are used to reduce recidivism, and more specialized interventions (such as ensuring security through architectural design, technology, and staff involvement). In the chapters that follow, the authors share their insights into some of the most pressing problems in the field of juvenile corrections and shed some light on strategies to overcome these challenges. The strength of drawing upon such expertise is that this approach enables readers to form their own understandings of the issues based on a number of divergent viewpoints. We hope that after you have finished this book you will have a better appreciation for the challenges confronting juvenile corrections and the possibilities for reform.

Case Cited

Roper v. Simmons 543 U. S. 551 (2005)

References

Chesney-Lind, M., & Shelden, R. G. (2004). *Girls, delinquency, and juvenile justice.* Belmont, CA: Thompson Wadsworth.

Drake, E. (2007). *Evidence-based juvenile offender programs: Program description, quality assurance, and costs.* Olympia, WA: Washington State Institute for Public Policy.

Equal Justice Initiative. (2007). *Cruel and unusual: Sentencing 13- and 14-year old children to die in prison.* Retrieved November 22, 2008, from http://eji.org/eji/files/20071017cruelandunusual.pdf

Fazel, S., Doll, H., & Langstrom, N. (2008). Mental disorders among adolescents in juvenile detention and correctional facilities: A systematic review and metaregression analysis of 25 surveys. *Child & Adolescent Psychiatry, 47,* 1010-1019.

Feld, B. C. (1999). *Bad kids: Race and transformation of the juvenile court.* New York: Oxford University Press.

Macallair, D. (2008). *Time to close the old California Youth Authority.* Retrieved November 24, 2008, from: http://www.cjcj.org/post/juvenile/justice/time/close/old/california/youth/authority

Nagin, D. S., Piquero, A. R., Scott, E. S., & Steinberg, L. (2006). Public preferences for rehabilitation versus incarceration of juvenile offenders: Evidence from a contingent valuation survey. *Criminology & Public Policy, 5,* 627-651.

Redding, R. E. (2008). *Juvenile transfer laws: An effective deterrent to delinquency?* Washington, DC: Office of Juvenile Justice and Delinquency Prevention.

Sabol, W. J., & Couture, H. (2008). *Prison inmates at midyear 2007.* Washington, DC: Bureau of Justice Statistics.

Sabol, W. J., Couture, H., & Harrison, P. M. (2007). *Prisoners in 2006.* Washington, DC: Bureau of Justice Statistics.

Sabol, W. J., & Minton, T. D. (2008). *Jail inmates at midyear 2007.* Washington, DC: Bureau of Justice Statistics.

Singer, S. I. (1996). *Recriminalizing delinquency: Violent juvenile crime and juvenile justice reform.* New York: Cambridge University Press.

Snyder, H. N. (2008a). *Juvenile arrests, 2005.* Washington, DC: Office of Juvenile Justice and Delinquency Prevention.

Snyder, H. N. (2008b). *Juvenile arrests, 2006.* Washington, DC: Office of Juvenile Justice and Delinquency Prevention.

Streib, V. (2005). *The juvenile death penalty today: Death sentences and executions for juvenile crimes, January 1, 1973 – February 28, 2005.* Retrieved February 10, 2008, from http://www.law.onu.edu/faculty_staff/faculty_profiles/coursematerials/streib/juvdeath.pdf

CONTRIBUTORS

Gaylene Armstrong, Ph.D., is an Associate Professor in the College of Criminal Justice at Sam Houston State University. Dr. Armstrong's research focuses on correctional program and policy evaluation within institutional and community corrections settings. She has expertise with both adult and juvenile offender populations and has evaluated programs and policies for specialized populations, such as sex offenders and female offenders. Currently, Armstrong is completing a randomized experiment of a Maricopa County, Arizona, jail based reentry program for sex offenders that includes GPS monitoring of offenders and a randomized experiment of a Texas state jail reentry program.

Cherie Dawson-Edwards is Department Chair in the Division of Social Work and Criminal Justice at Kentucky State University. Dr. Edwards earned a Ph.D. in Public Policy and Administration from Virginia Commonwealth University. In addition, she holds Bachelor's Degrees in Sociology and Journalism from Western Kentucky University and a M.S. in Justice Administration from the University of Louisville where her research concentration was racial profiling. Her research and teaching interests center on the intersection of public policy and criminal justice with a specific focus on the field of corrections. In addition to a career in teaching, Dr. Edwards has held positions in probation and victim services.

Carolyn Eggleston, Ph.D., is currently the Associate Dean for Graduate Programs and Administration for the College of Education at California State University, San Bernardino. She is a Director of the Center for the Study of Correctional Education and a Professor of Special Education. Dr. Eggleston spent 20 years working in corrections as a diagnostician, teacher, school principal, and supervisor. Her doctoral dissertation reviewed the first special education program in an adult reformatory, Elmira, during the late 19th century. She has written about special needs juveniles and adults, historical issues in corrections, and education and reentry issues for inmates. Dr. Eggleston served the Correctional Education Association as Journal Editor, Vice President, and President.

Noelle E. Fearn received her Ph.D. in Criminology and Criminal Justice from the University of Missouri, St. Louis in 2003 and is an Assistant Professor in the Department of Sociology and Criminal Justice at Saint Louis University.

Her work has appeared in *Justice Quarterly*, the *Journal of Criminal Justice*, *Criminal Justice Studies: A Critical Journal of Crime, Law, and Society*, *Social Justice Research*, the *International Journal of Comparative Criminology*, the *International Journal of Offender Therapy and Comparative Criminology*, and the *Californian Journal of Health Promotion*. Her current research focuses on multilevel influences on criminal justice decision making and various issues related to corrections.

Jessica P. Hodge is an Assistant Professor at the University of Missouri – Kansas City. Dr. Hodge teaches undergraduate and graduate courses in the Department of Criminal Justice and Criminology. She received her M.S. in Correctional Administration from Western Oregon University and her Ph.D. in Criminology from the University of Delaware. Her research interests include hate crimes and bias crime legislation, gender issues in crime and criminal justice, and juvenile justice and delinquency. She is the author of *Proving Grounds: The Gender Quandary of Hate Crime Law*, forthcoming from the University Press of New England.

Barry Holman is the Director of Research and Quality Assurance for the Washington, D.C. Department of Youth Rehabilitation Services. He earned his Bachelor's Degree from the University of Wisconsin-Superior and graduate degree from the George Washington University. His research and advocacy has centered on the racism in the justice system and alternatives to incarceration.

Michelle Inderbitzin received her Ph.D. from the University of Washington and is an Associate Professor of Sociology at Oregon State University. Her research interests are primarily in juvenile corrections, juvenile justice, prison culture, and prisoner reentry; her research on these topics has been published in the *Journal of Adolescent Research*, *Journal of Offender Rehabilitation*, *International Journal of Offender Therapy and Comparative Criminology*, and the *Journal of Transformative Education*. Along with her on-campus courses, she currently teaches classes and works with adult male inmates in the Oregon State Penitentiary, and with young women in the state's primary juvenile correctional facility for females.

Erin L. Kelley received her Bachelor's Degree from Eastern Kentucky University with a major in Criminal Justice and a minor in Dispute Resolution. She graduated in July 2008 with her Master's Degree in Criminal Justice.

CONTRIBUTORS

Bitna Kim is an Assistant Professor within the Criminology Department at the Indiana University of Pennsylvania. She received her Ph.D. from the College of Criminal Justice at Sam Houston State University, as well as a Master's Degree in Psychology. Specific areas of interest include statistics, gender issues in the criminal justice system, intimate partner homicide, and hate crimes. Recent publications have appeared in *International Journal of Offender Therapy and Comparative Criminology* and *The Southwest Journal of Criminal Justice.*

Margaret E. Leigey is the Vice Chair in the Department of Political Science at the California State University, Chico. While a Ph.D. candidate at the University of Delaware, she was involved in a research project examining the efficacy of reentry strategies for juvenile offenders. She credits her experience interviewing these juveniles in shaping her research and teaching interests in the area of juvenile justice. Her most recent research focuses on the correctional experiences of special populations of inmates including juveniles incarcerated in adult facilities, older life without parole inmates, and female life-sentenced inmates.

Rebecca Maniglia, Ph.D., is Assistant Professor of Criminology and Criminal Justice at Northern Arizona University. Dr. Maniglia has provided training and technical assistance related to issues of female offenders, juvenile justice, and restorative justice to over 45 states, working with state agencies, private justice programs, and local prevention entities, including schools, to improve services for youth. She has also provided training and/or curricula development for the National Institute of Corrections, American Correctional Association, Office of Juvenile Justice and Delinquency Prevention, National Juvenile Detention Association, American Probation and Parole Association, and the Coalition for Juvenile Justice on topics related to juvenile justice and delinquency prevention.

Karen A. Mason is an Assistant Professor in the Department of Applied Criminology at Western Carolina University. She earned her Ph.D. in Sociology from the University of Tennessee in 1999. She teaches courses in white collar crime, corrections, victimology, and theory. Her current research interests include white collar crime victimization and offending, evaluation outcomes of drug courts, and emergency preparedness in rural areas.

David C. May is a Professor and Kentucky Center for School Safety Research Fellow in the Department of Safety, Security, and Emergency Management at Eastern Kentucky University. He received his Ph.D. in Sociology with emphasis in Criminology from Mississippi State University in 1997. He has published numerous articles in the areas of responses to school violence, perceptions of the severity of correctional punishments, adolescent fear of crime and weapon possession, and two books examining the antecedents of gun ownership and possession among male delinquents.

Richard A. Mendel is an independent writer, editor, and researcher specializing in poverty-related issues in youth development, neighborhood safety, employment and training, and community development. He has authored several national reports on juvenile justice issues for the *American Youth Policy Forum* and The Annie E. Casey Foundation, and a number of articles on juvenile justice for other publications.

Tommy Norris, M.S., has over 30 years experience in corrections including 25 years with the Federal Bureau of Prisons. Mr. Norris retired as the Accreditation Manager in 1999 and joined Eastern Kentucky University as the Director of Correctional Training in the College of Justice and Safety. He also serves as the Executive Director of the Correctional Security Network. Tommy recently developed Eastern Kentucky University's Correctional Officer Safety Program, which provides OSHA certification for Correctional Fire/Safety Officers.

Ryan Patten is an Assistant Professor of Political Science within the Criminal Justice Program at the California State University, Chico. A native of the Puget Sound region, he earned his Bachelor's Degree in Environmental Policy from Western Washington University and both his Master's Degree and Ph.D. in Criminal Justice from Washington State University. His interests include the study of police strength and the duties and roles of wildlife enforcement officers. Prior to his academic career Dr. Patten was an officer for the Bellevue Police Department.

Rick Ruddell is an Associate Professor of Correctional and Juvenile Justice Studies at Eastern Kentucky University. He was a supervisor and manager within the Ministry of Corrections, Public Safety and Policing in Saskatchewan, Canada and served as Director of Operational Research for the Correctional Service of Canada. His research has been published in over 40 scholarly articles, and focuses upon corrections and criminal justice policy. Dr. Ruddell is the co-author of *Making Sense of Criminal Justice* and *Corrections and the Criminal Justice System*, author of *America Behind Bars: Trends in Imprisonment, 1950 to 2000*, and co-editor of *Issues in Correctional Health* and *Understanding Correctional Violence*.

CONTRIBUTORS

Christine A. Saum, Ph.D., is an Assistant Professor in the Department of Law and Justice Studies at Rowan University. She is also a Faculty Associate with the Center for Drug and Alcohol Studies at the University of Delaware. She served as Co-Principal Investigator of a study of drug court offenders and has worked on studies of treatment barriers for drug-using women and juvenile offender reentry strategies and has performed evaluations of corrections-based treatment. She has published in the areas of drug courts, women and substance abuse, juvenile and adult corrections, drug policy, sex in prison, and date rape drugs, and has co-authored a book on cocaine-exposed infants.

Patrick M. Sullivan, FAIA, has been responsible for innovative planning approaches and facility design for 40 years. Since 1975, Patrick Sullivan Associates (PSA) has been recognized as a national design leader in the fields of juvenile shelters. Sullivan is former Chairman of the Department of Architecture, California State Polytechnic University, Pomona. He has presented papers and lectured at ACA and EDRA Conferences, and at college campuses throughout the county. Sullivan is the recipient of numerous awards for excellence in architecture and for applied research. Sullivan holds a Bachelor's Degree in Architecture from the University of Minnesota and a Master's Degree in Architecture from Harvard University, Graduate School of Design.

Matthew O. Thomas is Associate Professor and Coordinator of the Master of Political Science program in the Department of Political Science at the California State University, Chico. His research areas include juvenile justice, policing, and urban politics, and he has published in numerous journals, including *The Journal of Criminal Justice*, *Police Practice and Research*, *The Journal of Ethnicity in Criminal Justice*, *Urban Affairs Review*, and the *Journal of Urban Affairs*. Dr. Thomas previously served as a consultant for the Urban Institute, and is a member of the Butte County Juvenile Justice Commission.

Shelley Zavlek, M.Ed., J.D., is the President of Justice Solutions Group, a New Jersey based juvenile and criminal justice consulting firm. Ms. Zavlek, formerly Assistant Commissioner for Operations and Facility Management for the New York City Department of Juvenile Justice, has over 30 years of experience in justice system and facility administration and planning, law and special education. Ms. Zavlek was a member of the Governing Board of the National Partnership for Juvenile Services, President and a founding member of the Council for Educators of At-Risk and Delinquent Youth, and a member of the Juvenile Corrections Committee of the American Correctional Association.

Jason Ziedenberg is the Policy and Communications Manager for Multnomah County's Department of Community Justice, the county agency for the metro-area covering Portland, Oregon responsible for adult probation and parole supervision, and the juvenile justice system. Prior to his appointment with Multnomah County, Ziedenberg was Executive Director and Research and Policy Director for the Justice Policy Institute, a Washington D.C. based think tank dedicated to reducing society's reliance on incarceration, and promoting effective public safety strategies.

ACKNOWLEDGEMENTS

One of the gratifications of putting together a book with 21 contributors living throughout the United States is that the editors were able to exchange ideas with scholars and practitioners with whom we otherwise would never get the opportunity to meet or interact. Some of the contributors were coaxed into writing a chapter on their areas of expertise. Others were asked to write a chapter based on articles that they had already published in scholarly journals, government reports, or professional magazines. We formally acknowledge the dedication and work that went into each of the chapters that form this volume. Reading, reviewing, and editing these chapters was a great learning experience and both editors finished this project with a much greater understanding of juvenile corrections. Our goal is that our readers have a similar learning experience. We thank our contributors for their patience with the peer review process as well as the time that it takes to review, proofread, edit their work, and then merge these chapters into a finished book—a process that always takes longer than first estimated.

One of the strengths of this book is that we draw upon the expertise of both academicians and practitioners; each group approaches the topic of juvenile corrections from slightly different perspectives. Although their orientations toward the problems addressed in this book are sometimes very different, each can learn from the other and their goals are the same: the safe and humane treatment of juveniles in settings that will contribute to their rehabilitation and ultimately reduce recidivism.

A number of factors inhibit the learning that can occur between practitioners and scholars. For the most part, members of these two groups do not interact with each other and rarely attend the same conferences, hold memberships in the same organizations, or read the same publications. Correctional professionals are often very interested in what academicians have to say—but academics also have to make their research relevant to the field and present it in a manner that practitioners can understand and appreciate. As such, academicians might find it fruitful to disseminate their work in publications such as *Corrections Today* (which publishes special issues on juveniles) and present their research findings at conferences sponsored by the American Correctional Association (ACA), the National Partnership for Juvenile Services, or the North American Association of Wardens & Superintendents.

Finishing this book was a group effort. We would like to extend our formal appreciation to the reviewers: Anne M. Nelsen (President of the National Association of Juvenile Correctional Agencies), Denis J. Shumate (Former

Superintendent with the Kansas Juvenile Justice Authority and current ACA Auditor), Stephen Kmiech (Saskatchewan Ministry of Corrections, Policing, and Public Safety), Martin Guevera Urbina (Howard College), and Jamie Wada (Chadron State College). This manuscript benefited from their critical insights and their observations; their comments enabled us to produce a much stronger book. Furthermore, we thank David W. Roush for agreeing to write the foreword and for his thoughtful comments.

The process of putting together 18 chapters from authors with different writing styles into a more or less consistent format was also a challenge; the editors would like to formally thank Lee Feathers who carefully copyedited the content and whose suggestions and editorial work made the book easier to read. This is the third book that Lee has edited and formatted for Newgate Press and her input has made the editors' task much easier. Kimberly Martin from www.self-pub.net formatted the book and her work is not only top-notch, but she also has the patience of a saint.

Rick Ruddell would specifically like to thank Renu James for her encouragement when the demands of this project outweighed his sense of humor, Alister and Lucie Sutherland for their support, and all his friends still working for the Ministry of Corrections, Public Safety, and Policing in Saskatchewan, Canada and the Correctional Service of Canada — may your time inside the fences pass quickly and without incident. Thanks also to his current and former colleagues and students, from whom he learns every day.

Matthew Thomas would like to thank his parents, John and Jill Thomas, for their lifetime of support. His colleagues at California State University-Chico create the best possible environment for an academic to thrive. His frequent co-authors, Peter Burns and Rick Ruddell, are an endless source of intellectual stimulation and great friends to boot. Finally, but most importantly, his wife Kristen and sons Zachary and Liam bring him joy and happiness every day; for this he is always thankful.

CONTACT INFORMATION

We encourage readers to provide feedback about this book on juvenile corrections; we can be reached at:

rick.ruddell@eku.edu
Department of Correctional and Juvenile Justice Studies
Eastern Kentucky University

mothomas@csuchico.edu
Department of Political Science
California State University-Chico

CHAPTER 1
JUVENILE CORRECTIONS: AN OVERVIEW

Rick Ruddell

The first juvenile correctional facilities in the United States were the Houses of Refuge established in New York in the 1820s. Although reformers had set up these institutions with the best intentions to help dependent and delinquent youth, they were soon embroiled in controversy when they failed to live up to their expectations (Bernard, 1992). Rates of violence in these institutions were high, youth were kept for years in these facilities, and after these adolescents had reached adult status they were often placed out as apprentice domestic workers or farm laborers. Unfortunately, many of these arrangements failed: some youth were exploited and others ran away. Many of these incarcerated youth (also called residents or wards) had not committed criminal acts at all; oftentimes, girls were institutionalized for being unruly or difficult—a pattern that some critical criminologists argue exists today (Chesney-Lind & Shelden, 2004). The House of Refuge movement ended in the late 1800s, with the Illinois Supreme Court finding that the conditions were more consistent with punishment than rehabilitation (Bernard, 1992).

Nearly two centuries later, the treatment of juvenile offenders in some settings is more similar with the failed Houses of Refuge than many realize. Entire juvenile correctional systems—such as the Division of Juvenile Justice in California's Department of Corrections and Rehabilitation or Ohio's Department of Youth Services—are embroiled in litigation (see the *Farrell v. Tilton* and *S.H. v. Stickrath* cases). Plaintiffs in these lawsuits contend that these state correctional systems have created prison-like environments that bring out the worst in the youth placed in the state's care. A second criticism is that juvenile justice leaders have failed to create environments that foster the rehabilitation of these youth. State correctional facilities are not the only juvenile facilities to be criticized for inappropriate care: detention facilities (often called juvenile halls) have come under fire for the poor treatment of youth (Holman & Ziedenberg, 2006) and the U. S. Government Accountability Office (2007) recently released a report critical of private and publically operated juvenile wilderness and boot camp programs.

Yet, working with youthful offenders is not an easy task. Many of the juveniles in the care of local or state authorities have come into contact with law enforcement officials numerous times before their first placement outside the home. Some of these youthful offenders have been charged with serious offenses. Snyder (2008) reported that in 2006, there were 100,700 youth arrested for their involvement in violent offenses, including 1,310 who were arrested for homicide; a quarter million additional youth were arrested for common or simple assaults (p. 3).

To add more complexity to the problems of youth crime, a high percentage of the youth confined in some juvenile facilities have histories of gang involvement, although this varies by jurisdiction. Many of these adolescents also have long histories of abuse, neglect, growing up in poverty and dysfunctional neighborhoods, and have experienced educational failure. Often they suffer from physical or psychological disabilities. Many of these youth have lived at the margins of society and few are optimistic about their futures. All of these factors make working with delinquent youth a challenging task.

One factor that differentiates adult and juvenile corrections is the philosophy of these respective agencies. Most state divisions of juvenile or youth services support the principle of rehabilitation for juvenile offenders and this usually means that juvenile facilities receive a greater amount of resources than their counterparts in adult corrections. These funds are typically invested in a greater number of rehabilitative programs for the youth. Yet, there is also a long history of juvenile correctional systems being operated as divisions of adult correctional systems. In other states, by contrast, juvenile correctional systems are operated by state departments of social services. The parent agency can matter. Interventions may differ depending on whether the juvenile justice system resides in a correctional or social services agency. For example, falling under the auspices of a social service department may result in a more rehabilitative orientation than a division of youth services that reports to the adult correctional system.

The public is generally more optimistic about the reform of juvenile offenders, as they understand that youth are still going through their psychological and physical development. As a result, their behaviors tend to be more impulsive and reckless than adults. Juveniles are more apt than adults to engage in impulsive and risky behaviors; this can result in unintentional injuries, sexually transmitted infections, unwanted pregnancies, and violence. These behaviors are also carried into juvenile residential placements with similar negative consequences. Yet, the public also acknowledges that successfully intervening in the life of a troubled youth during this period can help them work toward a crime free future in the community. This is one of the factors that keep juvenile correctional officers (JCO), youth counselors, teachers, vocational staff, and therapists working in these sometimes chaotic and stressful environments.

CHAPTER 1: JUVENILE CORRECTIONS: AN OVERVIEW

One of the challenges of juvenile corrections is that we know little about what actually occurs in these facilities. While the media is apt to report some scandal, lawsuit, or incident that happens, they are unlikely to report the successes: youth who are released and live responsibly in the community as employees, parents, students, and taxpayers.

Scholars ought to be more critical of the lack of information that is published about these operations. Juvenile justice systems seldom report comprehensive statistics about incidents that have occurred in their facilities, such as suicides, unintentional deaths, assaults, or murders. Some private operators (both corporations and non government organizations) contract with local and state governments to provide youth correctional programs; they may be reluctant to report negative statistics about their operations in fear that their contracts might not be renewed. In addition, there is a range of privately operated residential programs for juveniles (including psychiatric facilities), as well as wilderness programs and boot camps that often operate with no state-level oversight because they do not receive government funding (U. S. Government Accountability Office, 2007). Finally, we have even less understanding of incidents that occur in foster or group home placements.

To be fair, however, academic researchers have also neglected the study of juvenile corrections. In any case, the lack of published information about what occurs in these places is a significant gap in both the correctional and juvenile justice literatures. As a result, one goal of this book is to define the boundaries of juvenile corrections, as well as the challenges and opportunities confronting practitioners, policy makers, the juveniles who reside in these places, and their families. This chapter starts with an overview of public attitudes toward youthful offenders, describes the different types of juvenile facilities, and ends with a short description of the characteristics of residents residing in these facilities. In order to understand some of the challenges of providing effective programs that will reform delinquent youth, we first have to understand who lives within these places. These facts shape the types of interventions that are delivered and, to some extent, the behaviors that occur. Providing supervision and care to a teenage gang-involved homicide offender in a state operated secure facility, for example, poses significantly different challenges than managing unruly middle class youth in a privately operated wilderness program that is funded by a parent's health insurance.

Public Opinion Toward Juvenile Offenders

The type of interventions that a jurisdiction uses to respond to youth crime is often a function of that state's or county's history, legal traditions, economic development, cultural values and beliefs, as well as perceptions about justice. In the United States, public attitudes toward juvenile crime tend to shift— often as a result of the influence of the media. Several decades ago, we perceived juvenile offenders as kids from troubled families who needed our support, help, and guidance. Over time, that perception became more pessimistic and various scholars labeled youth as "the young and the ruthless" (Fox, 1992) or "super-predators" (Bennett, DiIulio, & Walters, 1996). Bernard (1992) suggested that our beliefs about juvenile offenders are a product of several myths about juveniles and juvenile crime. He observed that juveniles, especially males, have always engaged in crime at higher rates than other groups, and that only our perceptions of these youth have changed over time. Yet, our opinions of juveniles and crime are important because they shape the types of juvenile justice systems that we develop. During eras when we consider juvenile crime as out-of-control, policy makers and the public generally support tough-on-crime initiatives such as sentencing youth as adult offenders and sending them to prison rather than trying to reform them in juvenile justice systems.

Beckett and Sasson (2001) argued that both news organizations and politicians are responsible for shaping our ideas about crime and justice. Kappeler and Potter (2005) suggested that the creation of these myths is functional for the objectives of these organizations. During times when rates of violent juvenile crime increase—as they did during the late 1980s and early 1990s— politicians, the media, and law enforcement might benefit from public perceptions that juvenile crime is out of control. Ratings improve for television stations, newspapers increase sales, and police departments can advocate for larger budgets when crime is rising (Ruddell & Decker, 2006). Moreover, politicians can demonstrate to their constituents that they are tough on juvenile crime by advocating for tougher sanctions, such as transfers to adult courts.

Sometimes our perceptions about juvenile crime are based on anecdotal or sensational accounts of rare events. A well publicized school or gang-involved shooting in a community, for instance, increases public attention and outrage to the problem of youth violence. Youth involved in violent crimes and who appear in juvenile court within a few months of those rare events may be more likely to be treated harshly. In essence, these juveniles are being punished for the crimes of the youth who went before them.

Rates of serious juvenile homicide have been decreasing for more than a decade in the U. S. (Snyder, 2008; Stahl, 2008) and this trend may contribute to reductions in the public's fear of crime. In addition, during times of reduced crime, the public may be more supportive of efforts to rehabilitate juveniles rather than punish them. One of the biggest tensions in juvenile justice is the choice between punishing youthful offenders and providing them with educational, psychological, and supportive services that will help them from being involved in further delinquency (in other words, to save children from a life of crime—see Farrington & Welsh, 2007). A number of investigators who have examined public attitudes toward juvenile delinquents have recently found that members of the public support juvenile rehabilitation, even with serious or persistent offenders.

Bishop (2006) reviewed three decades of studies that examined public opinion about juvenile crime and offenders and reported that "despite major fluctuations in crime rates over time, the public has strongly and consistently supported rehabilitation as a response to all but the most violent offenders" (p. 656). But even when members of the public are asked about violent teenaged offenders, such as murderers, this research showed that people generally want to hold these youth accountable—in other words, punishing them—but still providing them with the opportunity to rehabilitate themselves. Bishop (2006) summarized her findings:

> It is clear that the American people would like the vast majority of young offenders to be punished for their offenses, to learn from the experience of being punished, and to receive the sorts of treatment that will help them to move through the troubles of adolescence to become productive and law abiding adults. (p. 657)

Nagin, Piquero, Scott, and Steinberg (2006) reported similar findings: taxpayers expressed a willingness to pay for early intervention for at-risk children and rehabilitative programs for delinquents. Mears, Hay, Gertz, and Mancini (2007) suggested that policy makers believe that the public has punitive feelings toward youthful offenders. Their survey research, however, found that people generally support juvenile rehabilitation, but there were some differences in the ways that respondents thought about young offenders: women and younger respondents, for instance, held less punitive feelings. Overall, our perceptions about juveniles, crime, rehabilitation, and punishment are complex, and shaped by a number of factors (e.g., whether we have ever been victimized by a juvenile, current crime trends, as well as media reports about youth crime). In the end, however, the public is generally supportive of a separate juvenile justice system that provides rehabilitation, support, and guidance to youth in trouble with the law (Mears et al., 2007).

Attitudes toward crime and punishment in the United States are often more punitive than in other wealthy nations. Officials in those nations believe that when juvenile offenders reenter society (as most of them will) with a greater set of skills and fewer mental health or other problems, the public will be safer. Such viewpoints reflect a different set of beliefs, cultural values, and history toward the treatment of youthful offenders. While the studies above show that the public is supportive of juvenile rehabilitation, the United States is the only nation where 13- and 14-year-old youngsters can be sentenced to life in prison without the possibility of parole. In other words, they will die in prison. In fact, it was not until the 2005 U. S. Supreme Court decision of *Roper v. Simmons*, for example, that the United States abolished the death penalty for crimes that 16- and 17-year-olds committed.

While the public generally holds more sympathetic feelings toward juveniles who have been involved in minor offenses, our attitudes are more complex when it comes to murderers. Applegate and King Davis (2006) examined public attitudes toward juvenile murderers and found that the public does not support punitive sentences for all juvenile homicide offenders. Instead, respondents to surveys tended to support dispositions (or sentences) that take into consideration the circumstances of the offense, including factors that would lessen the severity of punishment. In fact, these investigators found that the public generally supported short sentences in rehabilitative settings rather than lengthy terms of imprisonment, except for the most shocking crimes.

A Short Orientation to Juvenile Corrections

The treatment of juvenile offenders rests on a continuum that is bounded by rehabilitation on one side and punishment on the other. No jurisdiction bases their programs entirely on either end of this continuum. But, some counties or states are more rehabilitative or punitive than others; these philosophies will shape the types of juvenile correctional programs that are available. Size matters: the services, supervision, and care that a resident receives at a rural juvenile hall of less than 20 beds may be significantly different than that provided to a minor admitted to a state correctional system with facilities that house hundreds of residents. The following pages outline some of the characteristics of juvenile facilities.

The upper age of juvenile court jurisdiction differs throughout the nation. In 2009, juveniles become adults at 16 (NY and NC), 17 (In ten states: GA, IL, LA, MA, MI, MO, NH, SC, TX, and WI), or 18 years of age (in the remaining states and the District of Columbia), although they can be held in juvenile correctional facilities until their 21st birthday in most states or 25th birthday in California. About 7,000 youth were transferred to adult courts in 2004, which was a significant decrease in the number of transfers (also called waivers) that occurred in 1994-1995 (Benekos & Merlo, 2008). Yet, thousands of youth went directly to adult courts for their involvement in serious crimes, bypassing the juvenile court altogether. Again, one significant gap in our knowledge about juvenile justice is that we do not know how many juveniles are charged, prosecuted, and sentenced as adults each year or what happens to them once they are sentenced.

Youth who are taken into police custody are usually taken to detention facilities (called juvenile halls in many jurisdictions). Livsey, Sickmund, and Sladky (2009) reported that there were 757 detention centers in the United States and most (over 80%) were operated by local or state governments (p. 4). Most of these facilities are fairly small: almost three quarters had 50 beds or less and only 10% housed more than 100 residents (Livsey et al., 2009). Juveniles are typically held in these facilities for a few hours—until their parents or a guardian takes responsibility for them—or their first appearance before the juvenile court. Youth who have committed more serious offenses or repeat offenders will often be confined longer. Even though the average stay in juvenile halls is usually less than two weeks, some youth accused of committing serious offenses may wait months before their court appearances.[1] Holman and Ziedenberg (2006) observed that "often, detained youth are housed in overcrowded, understaffed facilities—an environment that conspires to breed neglect and violence" (p. 2).

Juveniles are admitted directly from the streets into these detention facilities. Many of these youth are under the influence of drugs or alcohol when they are taken into custody. Often, the combination of being taken into custody, their histories of substance abuse, the uncertainty of their legal situation, and fear of the unknown contributes to situations where these juveniles act unpredictably or violently (including a greater risk of self harm or suicide). Part of this aggressive behavior can be attributed to the poor decision making skills that reflect the developmental status of these adolescents; some residents are apt to respond with violence if their behaviors are challenged by the juvenile correctional officers. Last, there are an increasing number of gang-involved youth in juvenile correctional facilities (Thomas & Thomas, 2007) and they have a greater likelihood of acting in a disruptive or aggressive manner than other residents (Colon, 2004).

Community Placements

Most youth who receive a disposition (or sentence) from a juvenile court are supervised in the community on probation (Torbert, 1996). Youth on probation are generally expected to follow a number of conditions, such as participating in alcohol or drug treatment (including attending groups such as Alcoholics Anonymous), to adhere to a curfew, continue their education, and abide by certain restrictions (e.g., reporting to the court when ordered and following the lawful directions of their probation officers). Probation is the most common sanction of the juvenile court, but for the most part, there are few external controls on the youth. Most are required to report to their probation officers on a regular basis (e.g., once per month) and inform them of any major changes.

Probationary sentences can include conditions such as house arrest or electronic monitoring. These sanctions generally require the youth to stay at home (unless attending school or working). Such intermediate sanctions bridge ordinary probation—which is generally considered to be fairly soft on crime—and being placed in a residential facility. Often, the youth is required to wear an electronic monitoring device on his ankle and if he strays too far from a base unit, he is in technical violation of the conditions of his probation. These technical violations can result in the revocation of his probationary sentence and placement in a state training school. In some jurisdictions, the parents must pay the costs of this monitoring (if they have the resources).

Placement in therapeutic foster or group homes, by contrast, provides either a short- or long-term living arrangement for youth. These placements may hold abused or neglected youth, status offenders[2] as well as delinquents. Treatment foster care—covered extensively in Chapter 4—provides a structured homelike environment for one or two youth. Group homes also tend to be relatively small operations. Livsey, Sickmund, and Sladky (2006) reported that of the 868 group homes in 2004, 67% held ten or fewer residents (p. 6). That study showed that only 4% held more than 51 residents and that 81% were operated by private operators. In addition to organizations that run group homes for profit, there is a long history of faith-based, non government, and charitable organizations that operate these facilities.

Group homes are characterized by a rehabilitative orientation and are generally open facilities, meaning that the residents are free to come and go during the day (although there are exceptions). Youth are typically required to attend school during the day, do chores around the facility, and often participate in therapeutic group meetings and other social skill development work. These facilities are often located in regular residential neighborhoods and the intent of these operators is to provide stability, structure, and safety to normalize life as best as possible for the teenagers in their care.

There is also a range of privately and publically operated facilities that provide out-of-home placements for youth. There are two types: outdoor or wilderness experience programs and boot camps. The U. S. Government Accountability Office (2007) reported that "residential treatment programs provide a range of services, including drug and alcohol treatment, confidence building, military style discipline, and psychological counseling for troubled boys and girls with a variety of addiction, behavioral, and emotional problems" (p. 2). Delinquent youth or status offenders are frequently housed in these facilities, but since many are privately operated and funded by parents (or their insurance companies), they fall outside of government scrutiny or oversight. Livsey, Sickmund, and Sladky (2009) reported that there were 118 ranch (wilderness camps) and only 51 boot camps in 2004 (p. 4). Wilderness camps were often run by private and for-profit enterprises (60%), while slightly less than one third of boot camps were privately operated (Livsey et al., 2009).

Boot camp programs were a very popular intervention in the 1980s and 1990s, targeting young first-time, nonviolent offenders. These camps emphasized military style drill and ceremony and kept participants constructively occupied from dusk until dawn. These short-term programs (most were three months or less) were initially very popular with legislators and the public because they were seen as being tough-on-crime, cost effective, and they would reduce overcrowding in regular juvenile and adult institutions (as most of the participants would have served a year or more). Their popularity has waned, in part due to a number of evaluations that showed they never delivered the rehabilitation, cost savings, or reduction in recidivism that they promised (Kurlychek & Kempinen, 2006).

Early boot camps (often called first generation or first wave operations) were innovative departures from traditional corrections, but they failed to respond to the needs of the participants, most of whom had substance abuse problems and poor educational histories. Subsequent generations of boot camps offered enhanced rehabilitative programs that addressed the problems that plagued the participants and supported their return to the community. Lutze (2006) observed that "many third-wave programs maintain highly structured environments, incorporate treatment, and provide aftercare to assist with the transition back to the community" (p. 392). Research by Kurlychek and Kempinen (2006) showed that boot camps that provided better support or aftercare in the community had lower rates of recidivism. This finding, however, came too late to save many boot camps that already closed. Still, a limited number of these programs still existed in 2004 and most were operated by private organizations (Livsey et al., 2009). Chapter 5 presents a history of boot camps and offers insight into the reasons why most have disappeared.

Institutional Placements

The most significant sanction in the juvenile justice system is placement in state juvenile correctional facilities (also called training schools). In 2006, there were about 93,000 youth held in these institutions (Sickmund, Sladky, & Kang, 2008). While these facilities are named training schools, some closely resemble adult prisons. Most are operated by state governments and they are typically large. Livsey and colleagues (2009) reported that of the 236 operations in 2004, 64% had 51 or more beds and 20% housed more than 201 residents. These investigators also found that training schools tended to have higher levels of security and that as the size of the facility increased, so did the security measures.

High levels of security are intended to reduce serious incidents such as assaults, escapes, and disturbances. Many state operated correctional facilities, for instance, are surrounded with wire fences (including razor wire in some jurisdictions) to deter potential escapes. Moreover, most youth reside in living units (also called housing units) or open dormitories that are separated from the other youth by locked doors in order to contain disturbances. Youth with a greater need for security – a topic addressed in Chapter 13 – are often housed in individual rooms, whereas low security youth are often placed in dormitory settings. Youth who are very disruptive are often placed in a hardened cell (e.g., bare concrete walls and a stainless steel sink/toilet) so they cannot harm anybody, escape, or destroy property.

Juvenile correctional facilities tend to offer a range of rehabilitative programs that are intended to keep the youth constructively occupied. Characteristics that differentiate these facilities from their adult counterparts are that juvenile correctional officers (also called counselors in some jurisdictions) work with much smaller groups and the ratio of residents to staff members is much smaller. It is not uncommon, for instance, to have two staff supervise a living unit with 200 adult prisoners, but two or more staff would typically supervise 20 juveniles in a correctional setting (and in some states, these staffing ratios are mandated by legislation). Juveniles require closer supervision because of the characteristics of all adolescent populations: poor decision making and problem-solving skills, immaturity, and a greater likelihood of engaging in risk-taking behaviors. In addition, youth in correctional facilities also tend to have higher than average rates of alcohol and drug dependency, Fetal Alcohol Spectrum Disorders (FASDs), oppositional defiance disorder, anxiety, depression, and learning difficulties. These factors often contribute to higher levels of institutional misconduct.

State operated facilities often house a group of juveniles who have lengthy histories of involvement in crime or were involved in serious offenses. These youth are often difficult to manage and most have had unsuccessful experiences with schools. Furthermore, many juveniles in the care of the state had previously been in foster care and had been placed in group homes or other residential settings as well as detention centers prior to their commitment to the training school. Taylor, Skubic Kemper and Kistner (2007), for example, found that youth in their study of a high security state training school had an average of 11.05 arrests and 5.95 intensive supervision placements (p. 774). Such youth are often drawn to gangs and many express antisocial beliefs (also called criminogenic values or thinking). Irwin (1970) labeled these juveniles as state-raised youth and the prognosis for these juveniles is generally grim as they see the training school, adult jail or prison, or death on the streets as normal outcomes.

Placement of a resident in a facility or housing unit that best matches their needs for security is called classification; this is a very important aspect of juvenile corrections in facilities that have more than one housing unit. For instance, a gang member who is serving a disposition for having committed a violent offense and who has a previous history of running away from group homes or low security residential settings has a different security requirement than a repeat property offender. The first resident would be assigned to a living unit that has a higher degree of security. He or she may, for instance, be placed in a single cell in a living unit and may never leave the unit without an officer's supervision. The second youth, on the other hand, may be placed in a dormitory setting where unsupervised residents regularly leave the living units for recreation or vocational programs (such as working in the facility's kitchen or laundry).

The issue of classification, including the methods that officers use to assess the degree of risk that a youth poses to others, is outlined in Chapter 13. Generally speaking, however, residents are classified based on prior criminal record (e.g., including involvement in violent crimes or escaping custody), their current offense (e.g., whether or not it is violent), as well as prior behaviors while placed outside the home (e.g., such as incidents or disruptive acts), and their involvement in gangs. Some jurisdictions rely upon objective classification (using formal assessment tools), while others rely upon subjective methods (e.g., their "gut feelings"). While classification is based on the notion that the facility staff can place residents on different housing or living units, many smaller operations only have one housing unit.

In order to successfully manage the behavior of youthful offenders, the staff members have to be committed to working with juveniles and receive extensive training, mentoring, and support. Juvenile correctional officers must also be positive role models for the youth in their care. Dowden and Andrews (2004) argued that staff should be guided by core correctional practices where officers are firm but fair and model such practices as effective problem-solving and have positive interpersonal relationships with the youth in their care, including mutual respect (pp. 204-205). Finally, but perhaps most importantly, the staff members working in corrections must have above average levels of optimism and hope.

Sometimes, despite the best of intentions, large prison-like facilities bring out the worst in both the juveniles and the officers who supervise them. Several large juvenile correctional systems, such as California and Ohio, have come under considerable scrutiny because of their treatment of the youth in their care. Cohen (2008) observed that the Ohio Department of Youth Services (DYS) suffers from a "persistent and deeply rooted culture of DYS staff violence [that] either breeds and most certainly reinforces, youth-on-staff and youth-on-youth violence" (p. 5). A culture of violence often is the result of an "us versus them" mentality harbored by both the staff members and the youth; this can sometimes escalate into conflict and violence. One significant problem with such an institutional climate is that when youth are living in fear, the rehabilitative efforts of the staff will have less impact.

However, not all youthful offenders are held in juvenile facilities. Approximately 6,100 persons under the age of 18 years were held in adult jails and another 2,364 resided in state prisons on December 31, 2006 (Sabol, Minton, & Harrison, 2007). Fewer rural jurisdictions, for instance, have juvenile detention facilities, so youth are sometimes held temporarily in local jails. Other juveniles have been charged with a serious offense and their cases were transferred to adult courts. In some states, once they are charged as an adult, they may remain in adult jails until their cases are resolved. There is a long history of scholarship that has outlined the risks of placing juveniles with adult offenders (Schwartz, 1989). Although fewer juveniles are housed with adults today, putting youth in adult jails places them at higher risk of suicide and victimization from adult inmates (Elrod & Brooks, 2003). Leigey, Hodge, and Saum provide a comprehensive examination of the risks of placing adolescents in adult facilities in Chapter 7.

Livsey and colleagues (2009) reported that 57% of juvenile correctional facilities in 2004 were privately operated, although they held less than one third of all juveniles (p. 2). There is a diverse range of private facilities, from community-based group homes to high security detention centers and training schools. Some of these private organizations are run by nonprofit organizations while some youth are held in facilities operated by corporations that contract with local jurisdictions or states to care for juveniles.

There is some controversy about whether correctional interventions should be provided by a profit oriented corporation. While some corporations operate entire juvenile correctional facilities, many local and state operated facilities contract with businesses to deliver a range of correctional programs or services, from rehabilitative interventions to medical care. Many jurisdictions have found that it is cheaper and more efficient, for example, to hire a firm such as Aramark to deliver food and commissary services, rather than hire their own cooks, commissary clerks, and kitchen staff. While these operations might be more efficient, some scholars have questioned whether punishment should be delivered by corporations whose primary motivation is making a profit; some firms have been accused of providing less than adequate care to bolster profits (Price, 2006).

Yet, officials from the corporations who supply correctional services counter this argument by stating that the contracts they sign with a local, state, or federal government dictate the type and amount of interventions provided in these facilities (Seiter, 2005). In order to ensure that these firms deliver the services that were contracted, the government provides staff members who closely monitor the contract; in the event that the vendor does not meet the terms of the agreement, they are subject to fines or cancellation of the contract. As a result, the customer only receives the services that they purchase.

Who Resides in Juvenile Corrections?

In order to appreciate some of the challenges in providing services for incarcerated juveniles, one first has to acknowledge the characteristics of this population. The most recent census of correctional facilities, conducted by the federal government in 2006, shed some light on the issue. First, of the 92,854 youth committed to state training schools or other out-of-home placements (including detention) in 2006, 15% were girls (Sickmund et al., 2008). Of those 13,943 girls, about 29% were being held on violent offenses, with a slightly smaller percentage held on property offenses. Critical criminologists such as Meda Chesney-Lind and Randall Shelden (2004) argued that a large percentage of girls were being held in correctional facilities for status offenses. Yet, the 2006 *Census of Residential Juvenile Placement* revealed that 1,951 young women (or about 14% of all incarcerated girls) were being held for committing acts that would not be crimes if they were older (Sickmund et al., 2008).

Historically, as many as half of the girls held in correctional facilities were status offenders, but recent juvenile arrest data suggests that they are engaging in more serious crimes. Snyder (2008) reported that girls' arrests for violent crimes decreased by 12% between 1997 and 2006, but that males decreased 22% during the same time (p. 8). More serious was the fact that assaults committed by girls increased 19% between 1997 and 2006, while males decreased by four percent. Furthermore, while males had lower rates of drug abuse and liquor law violations, as well as disorderly conduct arrests, the percentage change in girls' arrests increased in all these categories. Last, Snyder (2008) noted that while arrests for male juveniles for driving under the influence (DUI) decreased by 6% from 1997 to 2006, arrests for girls increased by 39% (p. 8).

There is some debate about the reasons for these increases. Some scholars argue that girls in the past were less likely to be arrested because police officers were paternalistic, meaning that they acted in the best interests of the girls. As women achieved more equality, some scholars observed that they were more apt to be treated equally by the justice system as well. In other words, the girls' behavior did not change, but the police are now enforcing the law differently (Steffensmeier, 2008). Chesney-Lind and Shelden (2004) argued that police are less likely to arrest girls for status offenses today, but if girls are involved in family disputes they are more likely to be arrested for assaulting a parent (p. 15). Either explanation is troubling and suggests that we need to increase our understanding of girls' criminality and how the system responds to young women in crisis, including their treatment in juvenile corrections, which is the focus of Chapter 8.

Incarcerated males tend to be more serious offenders and over 35% were committed or detained on violent offenses in 2006 (Sickmund et al., 2008). Otherwise, the offenses tend to be similar to girls, with 29% held on property offenses and 3.4% detained or committed on status offenses—which lends some support to the Chesney-Lind and Shelden (2004) claim that girls are placed outside the home at higher rates than young males for acts that would not be crimes if they were older.

One of the biggest challenges of justice systems is disproportionate minority contact (DMC). From arrests to confinement, minority youth are overrepresented compared to their population in the community. The *Census of Juvenile Residential Placement Data* from 2006 confirms this fact. Although Blacks and Latinos accounted for approximately 12.3% and 12.5% of the national population in 2000, Sickmund and colleagues (2008) reported that Black juveniles represented about 40.2% of the residential population while Latinos accounted for 20.49% of the total in 2006. Thus, both Blacks and Latinos are overrepresented in state correctional systems.

Explaining the overrepresentation of minorities in correctional populations defies a simple or single answer. Mays and Ruddell (2007) listed a number of possible causes, including differential involvement in crime, police responses to calls for services (which tend to be higher in minority neighborhoods), and the fact that there is a greater likelihood that persons from minority groups are poor and that creates a relative disadvantage in justice systems. Other scholars argue, by contrast, that minority youth receive different and harsher treatment in juvenile justice systems (National Council on Crime and Delinquency, 2007). Last, in a comprehensive study of the sources of disproportionate minority confinement, Feld (2003) attributes this overrepresentation to a convergence of social, historical, cultural, economic, and political forces.

Regardless of the causes of minority overrepresentation, state justice systems that receive federal funding for juvenile justice must demonstrate that they are actively trying to reduce DMC. Cabaniss, Frabutt, Kendrick, and Arbuckle (2007) outlined a number of promising practices to reduce minority confinement in juvenile facilities. These investigators observed that promising results were shown through collecting data about minority involvement at different points in the justice system, creating community-based alternatives to detention, providing training to officials in the unique aspects of different cultures, using risk assessments (instead of making subjective decisions about the dangers that youth present), and better involving families in court processes (pp. 395-399). Yet, Cabaniss and colleagues (2007) also warn that unless agency leaders actively work toward reducing DMC, efforts to reform juvenile justice systems will falter.

The last demographic factor that influences the operation of juvenile correctional facilities is age. Younger residents often require more supervision as they tend to be more impulsive and disruptive than older adolescents. Older residents, by contrast, may be less likely to engage in minor misconduct within a facility, but they are also more liable to be involved in aggressive behaviors. As highlighted in Table 1, the juvenile correctional population peaks at the age of 16 years.

Table 1. Age on Census Date – Juveniles in Residential Placement, 2006.

12 and younger	1,207
13	3,424
14	9,127
15	17,574
16	24,646
17	23,761
18 and older	13,115
Total	92,854

Source: Sickmund et al. (2008). Census of Juveniles in Residential Placement Databook.

Younger wards may be more susceptible to being followers than their older counterparts and can sometimes be negatively influenced by older or more sophisticated residents. As a result, most practitioners would probably agree that separating older residents from the youngsters is important to reduce their victimization as well as negative socialization. Yet, this is easier said than accomplished, especially in smaller facilities that have only one living unit.

There are two other characteristics that influence the interventions that juvenile correctional facilities will develop. The first is the percentage of residents with mental health problems. The second is somewhat related: the percentage of youth who have substance abuse problems. Wasserman, Ko, and McReynolds (2004) studied juvenile corrections populations in Illinois and New Jersey; they reported that 18.9% suffered from anxiety disorders (e.g., anxieties, phobias, or panic), 27% had mood disorders such as depression, while almost one third had disruptive disorders (p. 3). Moreover, those investigators also found that almost half (49.3%) reported some type of substance abuse. While alcohol dependence was the highest, many youth also reported using marijuana.

Skowyra and Cocozza (2007) collected information about the prevalence of persons with mental health problems in juvenile corrections and they suggest that as many as 70% of youth have some form of a disorder (p. 1). One significant challenge for juvenile corrections that deserves special attention occurs at the intersection of depression, adolescent impulsiveness, and poor problem-solving skills: suicide ideation and attempts. Wasserman and colleagues (2004) found that 9.1% of respondents in their study of juvenile corrections had thought about suicide in the past month; those who had thought about suicide during their lifetimes was higher (p. 4). As a result, Sickmund (2006) reported that most juvenile facilities (68%) had some form of suicide screening instrument in 2002, although they were more likely to be used in detention centers, reception and diagnostic centers, or training schools (p. 10). The fact that some facilities still do not conduct these assessments is a significant problem given that suicide was the leading cause of death in juvenile corrections between 2002 and 2005 (Mumola & Noonan, 2008).

Last, incarcerated juveniles tend to have lower rates of educational or employment successes and they have histories of abuse and victimization. Each of these factors increases the complexity of providing services for these youth. We often speak of rehabilitation, yet many incarcerated youth have a very poor set of life skills; facility staff must help them develop basic skills such as hygiene, as well as social and interpersonal skills. Furthermore, histories of physical and emotional abuse, as well as victimization, make these tasks more difficult as many of these youth do not trust adults (especially those in positions of authority). Yet, by the end of a youth's stay in a correctional facility, she is often closer to some staff than some of her own family members.

Understanding the demographic and offense related characteristics of the juvenile correctional population is important because these factors shape the types of security and rehabilitative programs that need to be developed. If one half of the residents of a facility are drug or alcohol dependent, for example, a priority of the agency administrators should be the development of substance abuse programs. Having a high percentage of residents who have been convicted of sex offenses, by contrast, will require an expansion in the number of sex offender treatment programs. In addition, a greater number of girls in a population requires a different approach to custody beyond painting the walls pink and removing the urinals from a male housing unit, as girls have a different set of medical, psychological, and social needs and require gender specific programming (see Chapter 8).

The characteristics of the juvenile population are also associated with serious incidents. Adult facilities with a greater number of violent offenders usually have higher levels of violence (Mumola, 2005) and it is likely that this is true in juvenile facilities as well. In Chapter 9, Karen Mason and Noelle Fearn address this topic in their analysis of violence in juvenile facilities.

Conclusions

The Federal Bureau of Investigation (2008) reported that 1,215,839 persons under the age of 18 years were arrested in 2007, which is a decrease of 20.4% from 1998.[3] Many of these arrestees will pass through a juvenile detention center and most will be released within a day or two. Some youth, however, will return: a few will have violated the conditions of their probation (called technical violations), while others have committed further offenses. If these youth keep reappearing before the juvenile court, they will eventually be placed in a residential facility of some sort. If they have wealthy parents, there is a possibility that health insurance will pay for a short stay in a therapeutic setting such as wilderness camp. Less fortunate youth, by contrast, may end up in county or state operated facilities. These facilities are apt to have a high number of youth of color, males, and older adolescents and about a third of them have been arrested or judged delinquent for an act of violence. Many of these residents have mental health disorders and about half have a substance abuse problem.

The 200-year history of juvenile corrections in America is fraught with misadventure, violence, the exploitation of some minors, and a failure to rehabilitate youth. These outcomes are a function of the characteristics of youth placed in these settings and the realities of adolescent development: a time when decision-making abilities, frustration, and poor coping skills result in incidents. In some facilities, high rates of gang involvement inflame these problems. The operations of other institutions are hampered by staff members who are poorly trained and supervised. While many of these staff members are dedicated and professional, their activities are limited by overcrowding and underfunding.

Yet, we cannot forget that there have also been countless successes over the years where the support of the facility staff members have helped youth become employees, taxpayers, and parents once they return to the community. These cases inspire and motivate the staff members who work within these facilities to try harder with the difficult-to-manage cases they confront every day. Ultimately, every youth that the staff members "save" increases public safety.

One significant limitation about juvenile corrections is the lack of meaningful information about these operations. Despite the fact that a census of

17

juvenile facilities is published every few years, we do not know the actual number of locally operated juvenile halls and state training schools on any given day (as some smaller facilities may close). Furthermore, there is no national-level source of information about incidents that occur in these places, the characteristics of the staff (e.g., their education, race, or gender), the daily cost to hold a juvenile, the average length of stay, the likelihood of recidivism for those released, or the rehabilitative programming that occurs — or does not occur — in these institutions. There is even less information about what occurs in the 1,136 group homes across the nation, in privately operated outdoor or wilderness programs, or the remaining boot camps. As a result, all we can do is rely upon results of research conducted in one county or state and apply those findings to the rest of the nation (a strategy that might mislead more than inform).

The contributors to the 17 chapters that follow increase our understanding of the different dimensions of juvenile corrections. In many cases, these chapters were authored or coauthored by practitioners and scholars who have a keen understanding of what occurs behind bars. The first chapters present an overview of different types of residential programs, including boot camps, group homes, and wilderness camps. The second section examines problems that occur in juvenile corrections: placing juveniles in adult jails or prisons, the risks of detention, providing care to girls in correctional facilities, as well as suicide and violence. The last section highlights different programmatic responses that staff members in juvenile correctional facilities have developed and includes an overview of educational programs, security in juvenile corrections, the roles of juvenile correctional officers, and examples of innovative programs that are intended to enhance rehabilitation, such as Missouri's "Small is Beautiful" concept (highlighted in Chapter 15).

If the primarily goal of the juvenile justice system is enhancing public safety through rehabilitation of youthful offenders, then policy makers and their political masters need to ensure that the juvenile justice system does not create conditions that further damage these youth. A necessary first step is to define the boundaries of the problem, by gathering and then publishing the results of studies that shed light on juveniles in residential placements. It is hoped that this book adds to the debate about juvenile corrections and awakens interest in what occurs behind the fences of America's juvenile halls, boot camps, and training schools.

Endnotes

1. The Corrections Standards Authority (2007) reported that the average length of stay in juvenile detention in California during the first quarter of 2007 was 28 days, although this increased to 336 days for youth who

were direct filings to adult court (p. 5). Presumably, these youth would have been charged with more serious offenses.

2. Juvenile and family courts provide care, supervision, and support to abused, neglected, and delinquent youth. Status offenders are youth who have committed an act that would not be a crime if committed by an adult, such as truancy, incorrigibility, being out of parental control, or violating curfew ordinances.

3. These data were drawn from Table 32 of the Uniform Crime Report. During the same era (1998 to 2007), arrests for homicide decreased by 23.4%. It is important to note that the juvenile population rose significantly during that time when arrests decreased.

Cases Cited

Farrell v. Tilton
Roper v. Simmons 543 U. S. 551 (2005)
S.H. v. Stickrath

References

Applegate, B. K., & King Davis, R. (2006). Public views on sentencing juvenile murderers: The impact of offender, offense, and perceived maturity. *Youth Violence and Juvenile Justice, 4*, 55-74.

Beckett, K., & Sasson, T. (2001). *The politics of injustice.* Thousand Oaks, CA: Pine Forge Press.

Benekos, P. J., & Merlo, A. V. (2008). Juvenile justice: The legacy of punitive policy. *Youth Violence and Juvenile Justice, 6*, 28-46.

Bennett, W. J., Dilulio, J., & Walters, J. P. (1996). *Body count: Moral poverty and how to win America's war against crime and drugs.* New York: Simon and Shuster.

Bernard, T. J. (1992). *The cycle of juvenile justice.* New York: Oxford University Press.

Bishop, D. (2006). Public opinion and juvenile justice policy: Myths and misconceptions. *Criminology & Public Policy, 5*, 653-664.

Cabaniss, E. R., Frabutt, J. M., Kendrick, M. H., & Arbuckle, M. B. (2007). Reducing disproportionate minority contact in the juvenile justice system: Promising practices. *Aggression and Violent Behavior, 12*, 393-401.

Chesney-Lind, M., & Shelden, R. G. (2004). *Girls, delinquency, and juvenile justice.* Belmont, CA: Thompson.

Cohen, F. (2008). *Final fact-finding report: S.H. v. Stickrath.* Retrieved January 22, 2008, from http://www.dys.ohio.gov

Colon, T. (2004, April). *Gang members in juvenile detention: A California story.* Presented at the Behavioral and Social Sciences Research Symposium, CSU Chico.

Corrections Standards Authority. (2007). *Juvenile detention profile survey: First quarter, 2007.* Sacramento, CA: Author.

Cullen, F. T., & Gendreau, P. (2000). Assessing correctional rehabilitation: Policy, practice, and prospects. In *Criminal justice 2000: Policies, process, and decisions of the*

CHAPTER 2
A SHORT HISTORY OF JUVENILE CORRECTIONS

Patrick M. Sullivan

Our care for children over the past 2,000 years is a history of neglect, abandonment and desertion. Bernard (1992) observed that, until the 1800s, children were generally treated as though they did not exist at all; this lack of care is attributed to a "combination of high fertility and high infant mortality" and that "people did not become attached to children until they had passed the point at which death was a likely event" (p. 51). Partly as a result of these beliefs, European children were often abandoned (Boswell, 1998). Parents deserted their offspring in desperation when they were unable to support them due to poverty or disaster, when they were unwilling to keep them because of their physical conditions or ancestry, because of religious beliefs, in self interest, or interest in another child (Boswell, 1988).

Most European legal systems either tolerated or regulated the desertion of children. The English Poor Laws, beginning in 1349 and proceeding to 1834, regulated both the working and nonworking poor, including the care of dependent, abandoned, or neglected children. Quigley (1996) noted that "children less than fourteen years of age and above five that live in idleness, and be taken begging may be put to service — to husbandry, or other crafts or labours" (p. 8). By 1601, local authorities were authorized to build housing for the powerless and poor of the parish. If two Justices of the Peace found that children's parents were unable to keep and maintain them, then children could be taken from their parents and made apprentices (Quigley, 1996).

Abandoned and neglected children eventually became the responsibility of the monarch, which was consistent with the principle of *parens patriae* (Quigley, 1996). This doctrine recognized the Commonwealth as the guardian of its ward (the child) and gave courts the right to act in place of the parent, plus the authority to intervene in the family and alter parental rights. Literally meaning "father of the country," the principle of *parens patriae* left children with few personal rights (Schwartz, 1989). *Parens patriae* was not widely recognized until the 17th century, but can be seen in the early English Chancellery Courts which dealt with the protection of dependent and neglected children (Quigley, 1996).

American justice systems and customs were imported from Europe and the English Poor Laws set the groundwork for future social legislation and regulation of the poor in Colonial America.

In England, society's attitude toward delinquent children began to change in the late 1700s. Bernard (1992) noted that "prior to that time children who committed offenses were described as 'black-guard children,' 'stubborn children,' 'poor vagrant children,' or they were simply labeled young criminals" (p. 42). The term "juvenile delinquent" was first used around 1800, and the Philanthropic Society of London—under the influence of John Howard—established an asylum as a place of safety for delinquent boys. Another group, the Society for the Reformation of Juvenile Offenders, established a similar, separate refuge in 1816 and a public institution for juvenile delinquents was opened near Birmingham, England in 1817 (U. S. Bureau of Prisons, 1949).

Early American Juvenile Justice Systems

In America, concerns for the care of delinquent and abandoned children led to the creation of the first juvenile facilities. At that time, officials and reformers were concerned that many urban youth were at risk of becoming paupers. According to Bernard (1992), the conventional view of the era was that:

> Paupers were "undeserving" poor people—those undeserving of charity because of their wicked and dissolute ways. Paupers were deceitful, traitorous, hostile, rude, brutal, rebellious, sullen, wasteful, cowardly, dirty, and blasphemous. Paupers were lazy and refused to work, they got drunk and passed out in the gutters, they stole things and got into fights with each other, and they let their children run around without proper care and supervision. (p. 60)

In 1817, the Society for the Prevention of Pauperism was formed in New York City (U. S. Bureau of Prisons, 1949). The Society argued in an 1822 paper, "*The Penitentiary System in the United States,*" that there was a necessity to provide new and separate prisons for juveniles (Sutton, 1988). However, unlike their adult counterparts, the prisons were to be operated as schools for instruction rather than places for punishment. Vocational training and reformation was emphasized.

The first publicly funded and legally chartered custodial institution for juvenile offenders, the House of Refuge, was established in New York City on New Year's Day in 1825 and admitted 73 youth in the first year (Bernard,

1992). Shortly thereafter, similar institutions were developed in other large cities, such as Boston and Philadelphia, and by 1857 there were 17 of these facilities (Elrod & Ryder, 2005). The first Houses of Refuge were multistory, grim, prison-like institutions. Bernard (1992) noted that "almost all of the children sent to this first House of Refuge were poor, but most of those same children were not criminal" (p. 63). This pattern of placing abused, neglected, and wayward youth in prison-like settings would continue for the next 150 years.

Youth placed in these institutions were subject to hard work and education (Sutton, 1988). It was thought that exposing these youth to intensive work and study would reduce the likelihood of becoming paupers. Yet, these placements were also temporary and the residents had to be discharged by their 21st birthday. One way that these officials used to return these youth to society was the "placing out" system. According to Bernard (1992), approximately 90% of the residents of these Houses of Refuge were sent to live with families (usually farmers) who would provide an apprenticeship. Thus, the House of Refuge served as an early mechanism for dealing with at-risk and delinquent youth and as a model for subsequent juvenile institutions.

The reform school system was introduced in Westborough, Massachusetts at the Lyman Reform School for Boys in 1846 and at the Reform School for Boys in Lancaster, Ohio in 1858. The philosophy of these institutions was based on the belief that juveniles were more likely to be rehabilitated than adults and, therefore, should not be treated within adult institutions (Massachusetts Health and Human Services, 2008). Like many of these rural facilities, the Lyman School was almost self sufficient. Youth raised livestock, grew vegetables, sewed their own clothes, and helped build many of the structures located on the school grounds. These reform schools were the models for Colorado's Mount View Campus in 1881 and Washington's Greenhill School in 1886.

Reform schools were also known as industrial or training schools in some places (Elrod & Ryder, 2005) and these large institutions still exist in some jurisdictions. Many of these facilities were multistory, they were constructed using a linear design where the resident's rooms were arranged in long corridors and the youth would have a common room (or "day room") on each floor where they would congregate. The problem with this arrangement is that it did not allow for very effective staff supervision or interaction, and this design often included many blind spots (places where the staff could not directly observe the residents).

Reform Movements in Juvenile Justice

Despite the increased use of reformatories or training schools, the public's notion of punishment rather than reform was difficult to abolish—a tension that still exists in some contemporary juvenile justice systems. Two early appellate court cases highlighted how attitudes toward the treatment of juveniles changed over time. First, in 1838 the Pennsylvania Supreme Court heard the case of Mary Ann Crouse, who had been placed in a House of Refuge. Her father challenged her placement in the institution on the grounds that she had committed no crime and that she lived in conditions closely akin to punishment. According to Elrod and Ryder (2005):

> The Court ruled that Mary Ann's placement was legal because the purpose of the House of Refuge was to reform youth, not punish them; that formal due process protections afforded to adults in criminal trials were not necessary because Mary Ann was not being punished; and that when parents were unwilling or unable to protect their children, the state had a legal obligation to do so. (p. 126)

A similar case, heard three decades later in the Illinois Supreme Court, however, found that youth in Houses of Refuge did live in conditions of punishment. In the case of *People v. Turner* (1870), the Court found that Daniel O'Conner, who was sent to the Chicago House of Refuge without his parents' consent, was being punished and not reformed. The Court found that O'Conner was being deprived of the care of his parents, that the conditions in the institution were punitive and harsh, and that youth required some due process protections if they were to be placed in such an environment (Bernard, 1992). This decision set the stage for the development of the first juvenile court.

Yet, there were other social forces at work that also pushed toward the creation of a separate youth justice system. In the 1880s, the nation experienced a 50% increase in the number of prison inmates; child offenders constituted one fifth of the prison population (Platt, 1969). Confinement conditions prevalent at the time—such as disease, squalor, and overcrowded living areas—led to public concern (Platt, 1969). Advocates referred to as the child savers opposed the harsh conditions of the reform schools during the 1890s (Krisberg, 1996; Platt, 1969). This group, led by Charles Loring Brace, emphasized the need for prevention. The child savers founded Children's Aid societies to distribute food, clothing, and to provide temporary shelter as well as employment for destitute youth. Urban youngsters were also placed in apprenticeships with farm families in the West and Midwest (Krisberg,

1996). According to Krisberg (1996), Brace declared these families as "God's reformatories" for wayward youth (p. 46).

The child savers movement in Chicago was organized through the efforts of a group of feminist reformers who advocated for special laws for juveniles and the creation of institutions for their care and protection (Becker, 1966). Louise de Koven Bowen and Jane Addams were civic minded philanthropists who transformed child saving from a respectable hobby into a passionate commitment (Richardson, 1894). Bowen's primary interest was the protection and welfare of children. She attributed the rise of youthful crime to the corrupting influences of city life where dirt, crowding, artificiality, and impersonality robbed children of their innocence (Richardson, 1894). Playgrounds, supervised recreation, "morals police," kindergartens, visits to the country, stricter laws, and more efficient law enforcement were her solutions to delinquency.

Addams was the essence of professional philanthropy. Her full time career was centered on youth and family reform interests, and she established Hull House in Chicago. This settlement house provided care and support for the urban poor, including services for at-risk and delinquent youth. In addition to her philanthropic work, Addams also advocated for special judicial and correctional institutions for the identification and management of troubled youth (Luft, 2002). The origins of the definition of the juvenile as a delinquent are found in the programs and ideas put forward by these social reformers (Platt, 1969). This era of public responsibility was an important step in the evolution of social reform and welfare programs in America.

Consistent with the aims of the reformers of progressives such as Addams, Brace, and Bowen, the first juvenile court was established in Cook County (Chicago), Illinois in 1899. This court was supported by the Chicago Bar Association, which advocated for a separate and distinct legal process for mistreated or delinquent juveniles (Shepherd, 2003). This reform used the principle of *parens patriae* to enable the state to act in lieu of the parent and in the best interests of the child. The concept of the juvenile court quickly gained popularity, although the youth who came before the court were unlikely to be serious delinquents. Judge Julian Mack (1909/1995) observed that:

> Most of the children who come before the court are, naturally, the children of the poor. In many cases the parents are foreigners, frequently unable to speak English, and without an understanding of American methods and views. What they need, more than anything else, is kindly assistance. (p. 22)

To provide care and support for these youth, Mack (1909/1995) advocated for residential placements that were wholesome, located in rural areas, and that offered both agricultural and industrial training. Furthermore, Mack (1909/1995) felt that the most effective residential design for these youth was "laid out on the cottage plan, giving opportunity for family life, and in each cottage some good man and woman who will live with and for the children" (p. 20).

The Evolution of 20th Century Juvenile Corrections

Cottage Institutions

An important improvement in institutions that housed and treated juvenile delinquents began when the prison-like barracks were gradually replaced by smaller cottages and operated according to the principles of the family plan by house parents (U. S. Bureau of Prisons, 1949). Living (or housing) units were administered by married resident supervisors who lived with the children. The separate residential cottage plan was first introduced in facilities such as the Lyman Reform School for Boys described above. The physical design of these cottages, and an emphasis on rehabilitation through education and hard work shaped the way that these placements operated.

What differentiated these institutions was the development of a form of self government for the youth (Krisberg, 1996). Self government meant that youth were involved in the definition and enforcement of rules under the close supervision of staff. This concept is still used in treatment methods known as guided group interaction or positive peer culture, although use of those approaches has declined in recent years.

Cottage parents were to provide the parental supervision, understanding, and counsel which were missing in the youth's home life. Feld (1999) argued that these facilities attempted to "create a 'normal' family environment within the institution, and attempted to promote a child's adjustment and development" (p. 71). Early programs stressed the positive aspects of youth care and that a caring surrogate family was better than no family. Today's labor laws, however, restrict these working arrangements in favor of a 40- to 48-hour work week. Therefore, cottage house parents cannot be "at home" except for normal working hours. Their presence has to be supplemented by day counselors and other support staff. Homelike stability, therefore, is confused and relegated to rules and procedures from others, which is the definition of an institution.

Cottage style reformatories still exist. Boys Town in Nebraska, for instance, was established by Father Flanagan in 1917 and still provides care for hundreds of youth. Such nonprofit organizations, often founded by religious or service organizations, were the norm for caring for at-risk children and youth for over a century and some are still operational. Livsey, Sickmund, and Sladky (2009) reported that most large juvenile facilities are operated by state governments, but that there were at least 868 group homes (many of which were operated by nonprofit organizations) in 2004 (p. 4).

Between 1910 and 1940, changes to the architecture of juvenile facilities were minimal. Abandoned correctional facilities, treatment facilities, or state hospital sites were also modified to hold juveniles. There is a long history in juvenile corrections of adapting existing structures to accommodate a population of adolescents. One of the challenges with this approach, however, is that these older or antiquated buildings do not enable the staff members to supervise the residents as effectively as modern architectural designs. As a result, it is likely that there will be higher rates of disorder and misconduct in these older facilities (a topic addressed in the following pages).

A Movement Toward The Professional Treatment Of Juveniles

Following the First World War, there was a movement toward the professionalization of treatment for dependent and delinquent youth. Sutton (1998) reported that there was a growing emphasis on better identifying the causes of delinquent behavior; the professional training of social workers; the development of the social casework method; and the organization of social service agencies (pp. 144-147). Emphasis shifted from the authoritative and even punitive attitudes of earlier reform efforts. Each youth became an individual case. The placement of juveniles in boarding homes and foster care became more widespread (see Chapter 4).

Passage of the Social Security Act of 1935 also encouraged the development of local child welfare services. By the end of the Second World War, the functions of government had increased greatly. Platt (1969) observed that "local agencies provided social services to the public: welfare, health, employment, mental health, education, and services related to the needs of children" (p. 98). The juvenile justice system philosophy expanded to include delinquency prevention and rehabilitation. Juvenile justice systems formalized court procedures, initiated the use of juvenile court referees, and hired probation personnel (Sutton, 1988).

During the post war era, new facilities included camps for the treatment of juvenile delinquents. These early wilderness programs housed and treated youth in a non-secure environment. Removing the juveniles from their existing (usually urban) environments and placing them in nature was seen as treatment oriented and therapeutic. This approach also made it easier to focus on the group or individual treatment plan; the open camp atmosphere eliminated most of the stigma and labeling attached to placement in a juvenile facility. In addition to temporary camp sites, some organizations purchased government facilities and converted them for use as permanent camps. These rural settings supported outdoor work programs (e.g., forestry) and recreational activities such as hiking, canoeing, and camping. These treatment programs usually required a six to nine month placement (see Chapter 3 for a more extensive discussion of wilderness experience programs).

New Generation Ideas

The construction and philosophy of correctional facilities, especially those used to support juvenile rehabilitation programs, radically changed during the 1960s and 1970s. Changes in adult jail and prison management led to the development of direct supervision and the new generation design was the catalyst for creative treatment approaches for incarcerated youth (Beck, 1999; Nelson, 1983). Some of these reforms were the result of a search for new designs and treatment programs and a growing awareness that many of the youth in these facilities were status offenders (Schwartz, 1989).

The Federal Bureau of Prisons promoted a new approach to the architectural design of correctional facilities and accompanying operational philosophy, termed new generation. New generation refers to new or remodeled correctional facilities that are designed with a direct supervision inmate management orientation. A "pod" or "podular design" defines a group or living unit in a correctional facility. The pod contains individual or shared sleeping rooms (including dormitory settings in some units); hygiene facilities; a common dayroom; smaller spaces for education, counseling, or related activities; staff areas; storage; and, in some buildings, dining space. Recreational areas are nearby. The living unit or pod can be any level of security (e.g., maximum, medium, or minimum) (Beck, 1999; Nelson, 1983; Wener, 2006).

The new generation approach is based on common sense principles and the normalization treatment model seeks to manage human behavior positively, consistently, and fairly (Robinson, 1984; Wolfensberger, 1972). If the facility, in its design and management style, expects youth to act uncivilized, it will result in that behavior. If the message is that antisocial behavior is inappropriate, the majority will conform to that standard (Nelson, 1983; Wener, 2006). Most residents want to avoid trouble and will do so if given a chance. The five to ten percent who create problems are separated from the majority (Nelson, 1983).

Direct supervision is undertaken by staff members who work in the living unit with the residents 24 hours a day. The appropriate number of supervisors and counselors has never been definitively decided; however, groups under 10 or 12 are considered small and over 24 are too big in juvenile facilities (Office of Juvenile Justice and Delinquency Prevention, 1980). Along with the new generation architectural design is a philosophy of working with the residents. Kerle (2003) highlighted the goals of a new generation design:

- Effective control
- Effective supervision
- Competent staff
- Safety of staff and inmates
- Manageable and cost-effective operations
- Effective communications
- Classification and orientation
- Justice and fairness
- Staff ownership of operations (p. 240)

Although these goals were established for adult jails and prisons, they are applied to juvenile corrections. The overriding goal is that the new generation design enables staff members to work closely with the youth and helps them develop better social skills (such as interpersonal communication), problem-solving, and behavior management. Using this approach places higher expectations on the residents and helps to reduce disruptive behaviors.

While the new generation design is the primary model for new construction, many older juvenile facilities still exist. There is significant diversity in the types of facilities that are currently used. Local juvenile halls, for instance, tend to be smaller, while training schools are usually larger and they generally have higher levels of security (Livsey et al., 2009). In addition, most county juvenile halls are stand alone facilities, meaning that they are not part of a system.

Larger publicly operated training schools, by contrast, are often part of a system of facilities and many are overcrowded (Livsey et al., 2009). Some state juvenile correctional systems, such as California, hold youth in large prison-like facilities. Newly admitted residents are sent to reception and diagnostic centers, where their physical and mental health needs are assessed. Furthermore, the process of classification is completed to determine the best placement for the youth (see Chapter 13).

Facilities in Missouri and Washington State, by contrast, more closely resemble the cottage style reformatories described earlier. Instead of uniformed security staff, counselors wear street clothes and relationship building is a key goal of the staff (see Chapters 11 and 15). These cottages hold smaller groups of residents and the furnishings more closely resemble homes rather than institutions. While the design and orientation of the California and Missouri facilities differ significantly, the outcomes are also different and Chapter 15 describes how Missouri's recidivism rates are among the lowest in the nation.

Federal Government Involvement in Juvenile Justice

During the 1960s, a number of juvenile justice cases came before the U. S. Supreme Court. These cases resulted in youth being granted more due process protections.[1] One of the foremost challenges of the era was the high numbers of juveniles who were placed in adult jails. Ruddell (2009) observed that this had occurred for centuries, but by the 1940s, there was increasing consensus that impressionable youngsters should be removed from the corrupting influence of adults in local jails. MacCormick (1949) wrote that "thousands of children, some of them as young as eight or nine years of age, are confined every year in county jails in the United States for periods of a few hours to several months, usually under abominable conditions" (p. 150). Larger cities usually had separate detention facilities for juveniles, so jailing juveniles was a more serious problem in smaller or rural jails. It is also likely that these youth might be detained longer, as court is held less frequently in smaller communities (Mendel, 2008). A review of the literature, for example, shows that some youngsters were held in local jails for years (Harding, Hines, Ireland, & Rawlings, 1985).

In addition to the risks of placing a youth in an adult jail, most had not engaged in delinquent or criminal acts. By the 1970s, there was growing concern that as many as one half of all youth placed outside the home were held on status offenses such as truancy, running away from home, curfew violations, or being out of parental control; these acts would not be criminal offenses if they were adults. Schwartz (1989) provided several examples of youth placed in adult jails in the 1980s:

> In 1983, for example, "Kathy Sue Robbins, a 15-year-old, was locked in the Glenn County Jail in California for running away from home. Four days later she committed suicide by hanging herself from a bunk rail."

> There were 1,651 children confined in the Long Beach City Jail between January 1, 1985, and April 30, 1985. Of the juveniles incarcerated, 317 were status offenders and 318 were dependent, neglected, and abused children. (p. 82)

These non-delinquent youth were placed in jeopardy of physical or psychological harm in adult jails. More troubling is the fact that these youngsters were jailed because their parents failed to care for them and the state could not find a more appropriate placement.

Schwartz (1989) outlined how there was increasing political pressure to remove juveniles from adult jails from organizations such as the Boys' and Girls' Club and the National Parent Teachers Association. These lobbying activities led to the enactment of the Juvenile Justice and Delinquency Prevention Act (JJDPA) of 1974 (Brown & McMillen, 1979). The legislation offered grants to states that were willing to remove status offenders from secure custody, separate adult and juvenile inmates, and promote advanced juvenile justice practices (President's Commission, 1967). The enactment of the JJDPA gave tremendous encouragement to child advocates. The Act also supported the development of community-based alternatives to the institutionalization of nonviolent and non-dangerous delinquent youth. Last, the JJDPA authorized the development of the Office of Juvenile Justice and Delinquency Prevention (OJJDP), a federal agency that provides technical assistance to juvenile justice agencies with the goals of preventing delinquency, strengthening juvenile justice systems, protecting children, and enhancing public safety (OJJDP, 2008).

"Get Tough" Juvenile Justice

In the late 1970s, the reform initiative of the JJDPA was opposed by some politicians who were unhappy with the deinstitutionalization of status offenders and the growing emphasis on community-based treatment. Throughout most of the 1980s and 1990s, the public response to juvenile offenders was also decidedly unsympathetic. Part of these feelings might be attributed to the significant increase in the number of juveniles engaged in serious and violent crimes from the mid-1980s to 1993. Snyder (2008) reported that at the peak of the juvenile crime epidemic in 1993, 3,760 juveniles were arrested for murder (p. 1).

Partly in response to increased levels of violent juvenile crime, this period witnessed legislative reforms designed to make it easier to adjudicate youngsters in adult courts (Krisberg, 1996). Furthermore, Krisberg (1996) noted that several states passed laws permitting juvenile correctional officials broad latitude in administratively transferring young people to youthful offender facilities operated by adult corrections departments. In addition, juveniles could still be sentenced to death and Streib (2005) reported that 226 juveniles were sentenced to death from 1973 to 2005, when the juvenile death penalty was found to be unconstitutional (p. 9).

During this "get tough" era, juvenile facilities faced severe conditions of crowding, especially in detention centers. Lengths of stay also increased steadily from 1980 to 1995 (Snyder, 2005). Despite the expanded use of incarceration, public officials did not always invest in new facilities nor were agency budgets increased to accommodate this growth. As a result, during the late 1990s many states and local agencies faced lawsuits that challenged the constitutionality of conditions of confinement in the jurisdictions of juvenile facilities (Krisberg, 1996). This remains a problem today and, as mentioned in Chapter 1, several large state juvenile justice systems are currently engaged in court ordered reforms.

During the 1980s and 1990s, boot camps emerged as a new form of housing youth in military based treatment programs. Delinquents were sometimes confined in adult institutions and overcrowding was so pronounced that lawsuits were brought against jurisdictions to close facilities. However, during these tough times, lessons of the past were not abandoned. States such as Missouri, New Jersey, Ohio, Arizona, Nebraska, and Indiana began positive steps to eliminate large institutions and embrace the ideas of local community-based treatment centers (Krisberg, 1996).[2] Also, the OJJDP's *Comprehensive Strategy on Serious, Violent, and Chronic Juvenile Offenders* focused on blending treatment and public safety concerns (Krisberg, 1996). Professional organizations such as the American Correctional Association, the American Probation and Parole Association, and the National Juvenile Detention Association spoke out against the policies that relegated juveniles to adult jails.

One of the greatest stimuli for architectural change was the Juvenile Crime Enforcement and Accountability Challenge Grant program of 1997, which created matching federal funds for new and remodeled juvenile facilities. The federal program encouraged states to provide direct intervention strategies for youthful offenders and emphasized strategies related to out-of-home placement for low risk juveniles. The Challenge Grant program strongly endorsed the collaboration among the juvenile justice system, community-based programs, and required the development of new rehabilitative approaches for at-risk juveniles.

Summary and Conclusions

Large juvenile facilities have not proven to be effective in the rehabilitation of juvenile offenders (Krisberg & Howell, 1998). The movement toward smaller and more homelike residential placements for juveniles is an outcome of the new generation approach that changed architectural and building designs, and also introduced new philosophies of staffing and treatment. This model also involves a movement away from a "get tough" philosophy to a more rehabilitative model based on self governance and youth learning from positive staff role models who act as counselors rather than correctional officers. States that have introduced these approaches have been rewarded with lower rates of recidivism and higher levels of public safety (Mendel, 2003).

Despite the fact that juvenile correctional placements are less harmful today, there is growing recognition that placement outside the home is a last resort and that youthful offenders be treated in the least restrictive environment. In fact, many youth housed in juvenile correctional facilities pose little threat to the community. Even today, most youth in juvenile corrections are held on nonviolent offenses (Sickmund, Sladky, & Kang, 2008).

The most recent approaches and most effective strategy for treating and rehabilitating juvenile offenders is a comprehensive, community-based model that integrates prevention programming—a continuum of pretrial and sentencing placement options, services, graduated sanctions, and aftercare programs (Howell, 1995; Loeber & Farrington, 1998; Zavlek, 2005). This approach reserves secure placement for only the most violent and serious juvenile offenders; those who pose a threat to public safety or themselves. Even for jurisdictions under pressure to get tough on juvenile crime, planning new facilities within this framework has programmatic, economic, and system wide advantages. Small, community-based, or regional facilities can:

- Engage local communities to provide resources for creating a comprehensive prevention, sanction, and treatment model. Potential community partners include service providers, volunteers and mentors, religious organizations, schools, civic organizations, businesses, and government agencies;
- Help youth forge personal bonds with mentors and other caring adults in the community. A key factor for healthy development is the "capacity, ability, and opportunity to build relationships with caring adults" (Masten & Coatworth, 1998);
- Create ongoing, intensive, family involvement and intervention activities. This approach recognizes the critical role of families in treating young offenders (Thornberry, 1993); and
- Function as a resource for the community such as victim counseling and restitution programs.

Thus, in some jurisdictions, juvenile justice systems have come around full circle, with a return to smaller, more homelike residential placements and abandoning the large training schools and prison-like facilities.

Consistent with the research described above, it is likely that juvenile justice systems will increase investments in community-based interventions that keep at-risk and delinquent youth closer to their families and schools. While future developments within juvenile corrections are still uncertain, it is likely that a greater priority will be placed on prevention and community-based treatment, which is less harmful to youth, more cost effective, and contributes to greater public safety.

Endnotes

1. The main cases were *Kent v. United States, In re Gault, In re Winship, McKeiver v. Pennsylvania, Breed v. Jones,* and *Schall v. Martin.* The rights extended to juveniles included the right to a transfer hearing, assistance of counsel during police interrogations, the ability to review transfer documents, representation by counsel at juvenile court hearings, notices of charges, the ability to confront and cross examine witnesses, and pro-tections against self incrimination. Subsequent cases found that when a youth's freedom was in jeopardy, they were entitled to a standard of proof beyond a reasonable doubt and prohibiting double jeopardy if youngsters were adjudicated delinquent in a juvenile court. Youth may also be subject to preventative detention, but the right to a jury trial was not extended to juveniles.

2. In 1971, Massachusetts sent a definitive message to the rest of the nation by closing all of its state training schools (Miller, 1991). The Lyman School, the first training school in America, was the first to be closed. In a series of events, Massachusetts replaced its large traditional juvenile in-stitutions with a network of small secure facilities and a wide array of community-based services; almost 1,000 youth were removed from out-dated institutions.

Cases Cited

Breed v. Jones, 421 U.S. 519 (1975)
Ex parte Crouse, 4 Whart. 9 (Pa. 1838)
In re Gault, 387 U.S. 1 (1967)
In re Winship, 397 U.S. 358 (1970)
Kent v. United States, 383 U. S. 541 (1966)
McKeiver v. Pennsylvania, 403 U.S. 528 (1971)
People ex rei. O'Connell v. Turner, 55 111. 280, *287* (1870)
Schall v. Martin 467 U. S. 253 (1984)

References

American Correctional Association. (1990). *Standards for adult correctional institutions.* Laurel, MD: Author.

American Correctional Association. (2004). *Standards for juvenile detention facilities.* Laurel, MD: Author.

Beck, A. R. (1999). *New generation jails design - A shift away from 200 years of thinking.* Kansas City, MO: Justice Concepts Incorporated.

Becker, H. S. (1996). *Outsiders: Studies in the sociology of deviance.* New York: Free Press.

Bernard, T. J. (1992). *The cycle of juvenile justice.* New York: Oxford University Press.

Boswell, J. (1988). *The kindness of strangers: The abandonment of children in Western Europe from late antiquity to the renaissance.* Chicago: The University of Chicago Press.

Brown, J. W., & McMillen, M. J. (1979). *Residential environments: A deinstitutionalization perspective.* Washington, DC: Office of Juvenile Justice and Delinquency Prevention.

Center on Juvenile & Criminal Justice. (2004). *Reforming the juvenile justice system.* Retrieved October 12, 2008, from http://www.cjcj.org/jjic/reforming.php

Fabricant, M. (1980). *Deinstitutionalizing delinquent youth, the illusion of reform?* Cambridge, MA: Schenkman Publishing Co. Inc.

Feld, B. C. (1999). *Bad kids: Race and transformation of the juvenile court.* New York: Oxford University Press.

Elrod, P., & Ryder, R. S. (2005). *Juvenile justice: A social, historical, and legal perspective.* Boston: Jones and Bartlett.

Goffman, E. (1961). *Asylums.* Chicago: Aldine Publishing.

Harding, C., Hines, B., Ireland, R., & Rawlings, P. (1985). *Imprisonment in England and Wales: A concise history.* London: Croom Helm.

Howell, J. C. (1995). *Guide for implementing the comprehensive strategy for serious, violent, and chronic juvenile offender.* Washington, DC: Office of Juvenile Justice and Delinquency Prevention.

Hsia, H. H., & Beyer, M. (2000). *System change through state challenge activities: Approaches and products.* Washington, DC: Office of Juvenile Justice and Delinquency Prevention.

Humphrey, M. E. (1937). *Speeches, addresses and letters of Louise de Koven Bowen.* Ann Arbor, MI: Edward Brothers.

Institute of Judicial Administration and American Bar Association. (1977). *Standards relating to architecture facilities.* Cambridge, MA: Ballinger Publishing Co. Author.

Kerle, K. (2003). *Exploring jail operations.* Lanham, MD: American Jail Association.

Krisberg, B. (1996). *The historical legacy of juvenile corrections, correctional trends, juvenile justice programs and trends.* Lanham, MD: American Correctional Association.

Krisberg, B., & Howell, J. C. (1998). The impact of juvenile justice system and prospects for graduated sanctions in a comprehensive strategy. In R. Loeber & D. P. Farington (Eds.), *Serious and violent juvenile offenders: Risk factors and successful intervention,*(pp. 346-366). Thousand Oaks, CA: Sage Publication.

Krisberg, B., Onek, D., Jones, M., & Schwartz, I. (1993). *Juveniles in state custody: Prospects for community-based care of troubled adolescents.* San Francisco, CA: National Council on Crime and Delinquency.

Law Enforcement Assistance Administration. (1974). *Indexed legislative history of the Juvenile Justice and Delinquency Prevention Act of 1974.* Washington, DC: U. S. Government Printing Office.

Livsey, S., Sickmund, M., & Sladky, A. (2009). *Juvenile residential facility census, 2004: Selected findings.* Washington, DC: Office of Juvenile Justice and Delinquency Prevention.

Loeber, R., & Farrington, D. P. (1998). *Serious and violent juvenile offenders: Risk factors and successful intervention.* Thousand Oaks, CA: Sage Publications.

Luft, M. (2002). *About Jane Addams.* Retrieved November 22, 2008, from www.hullhouse.org

MacCormick, A. H. (1949). Children in our jails. *Annals of the American Academy of Political and Social Science, 261,* 150-157.

Mack, J. (1909/1995). The juvenile court. In M. L. Frost (Ed.), *The new juvenile justice,* (pp. 11-26). Chicago: Nelson Hall.

Massachusetts Health and Human Services. (2008). *First in the nation.* Retrieved October 12, 2008, from http://www.mass.gov

Masten, A. S., & Coatsworth, J. D. (1998). The development of competence in favorable and unfavorable environments: A tale of resources, risk and resilience. *American Psychologist, 53,* 205-220.

Mendel, R. A. (2003). *Small is beautiful: The Missouri Division of Youth Services.* Retrieved November 23, 2008, from http://www.aecf.org/upload/publicationfiles/juvenile%20justice%20at%20crossroads.pdf

Mendel, R. A. (2008). *Detention reform in rural jurisdictions: Challenges and opportunities.* Retrieved November 1, 2008, from http://www.aecf.org/~/media/PublicationFiles/15_Rural_Pathways_r20.pdf

Miller, J. M. (1991). *Last one over the wall: The Massachusetts experiment in closing reform schools.* Columbus, OH: Ohio State University Press.

National Advisory Committee for Juvenile Justice and Delinquency Prevention. (1980). *Standards for the administration of juvenile justice.* Washington, DC: Office of Juvenile Justice and Delinquency Prevention.

Nelson, R. (1983). *New generation jails.* Boulder, CO: National Institute of Corrections.

Office of Juvenile Justice and Delinquency Prevention. (1980). *Standards for the administration of juvenile justice.* Washington, DC: Author.

Office of Juvenile Justice and Delinquency Prevention. (2008). *About OJJDP.* Retrieved October 13, 2008, from http://ojjdp.ncjrs.org/about/about.html

Platt, A. M. (1969). *The child savers: The invention of delinquency.* Chicago: The University of Chicago Press.

President's Commission on Law Enforcement and Administration of Justice. (1967). *The challenge of crime in a free society.* Washington, DC: U. S. Government Printing Office.

Quigley, W. P. (1996). Five hundred years of English poor laws, 1349-1834: Regulating the working and nonworking poor. *Akron Law Review, 30,* 73-128.

Richardson, A. B. (1894). The cooperation of woman in philanthropy. In *Proceedings of the National Conference of Charities and Corrections,* (pp. 216-222). Nashville, TN.

Roberts, J. W. (1997). *Reform and retribution: An illustrated history of American prisons.* Lanthan, MD: American Correctional Association.

Robinson, J., Thompson, T., Emmons, P., & Graff, M. (1984). *Towards an architectural definition of normalization: Design principles for housing severely and profoundly retarded adults.* Minneapolis, MN: University of Minnesota.

Ruddell, R. (2009). *American jails: A retrospective examination.* Richmond, KY: Newgate.

Schwartz, I. M. (1989). *(In)Justice for juveniles: Rethinking the best interests of the child.* Lexington, MA: Lexington Books.

Scott, R., & Douglas, J. (1972). *Theoretical perspectives on deviance.* New York: Basic Books.

Sickmund, M., Sladky, T. J., & Kang, W. (2008). *Census of juveniles in residential placement datebook.* Retrieved October 12, 2008, from http://ojjdp.ncjrs.org/ojstatbb/cjrp/

Snyder, H. N. (2005). *Juvenile arrests, 2003.* Washington, DC: Office of Juvenile Justice and Delinquency Prevention.

Snyder, H. N. (2008). *Juvenile arrests, 2005.* Washington, DC: Office of Juvenile Justice and Delinquency Prevention.

Streib, V, (2005). *The juvenile death penalty today: Death sentences and executions for juvenile crimes, January 1, 1973 – February 28, 2005.* Retrieved October 12, 2008, from http://www.law.onu.edu/faculty/streib

Sutton, J. R. (1988). *Stubborn children: Controlling delinquency in the United States, 1640-1981.* Berkeley, CA: University of California Press.

Thornberry, T . P. (1993). *The relationship between childhood maltreatment and adolescent involvement in delinquency and drug use.* Albany, NY: State University of New York at Albany.

U. S. Bureau of Prisons. (1949). *Handbook of correctional institution design and construction.* Washington, DC: Author.

Van Dorn, C. (1992). *A history of knowledge.* New York: Ballantine Publishing Group.

Wener, R. E. (2006). The effectiveness of direct supervision correctional design and management: A review of the literature. *Criminal Justice and Behavior, 33,* 392-410.

Wolfe, M., & Rivlin, L. (1987). The institutions in children's lives. In C. Simon-Weinstein & T. G. David, (Eds.), *Spaces for children: The built environment and child development,* (pp. 89-112). New York: Plenum Press.

Wolfensberger, W. (1972). *The principle of normalization in human services.* Toronto, Canada: National Institute on Mental Retardation.

Zavlek, S. (2005). *Planning community-based facilities for violent juvenile offenders as part of a system of graduated sanctions,* Washington, DC: Office of Juvenile Justice and Delinquency Prevention.

CHAPTER 3
WILDERNESS EXPERIENCE PROGRAMS

Cherie Dawson-Edwards

A number of social, cultural, political, and economic changes have been identified as contributing to the population of at-risk, troubled, and delinquent youth (Feld, 2003). In addition, there are many individual-, family-, and community-level factors that are associated with delinquency (Farrington & Welsh, 2007). While rates of serious and violent crimes committed by juveniles have decreased over the past decade (Federal Bureau of Investigation, 2008), there are still large numbers of at-risk youth who need support, guidance, and direction. These youth sometimes come into contact with the police and juvenile courts, although their offenses are generally not serious, nor do they have histories of persistent delinquency.

There is considerable debate about the best strategies to deal with these youth, as ignoring crimes is not a satisfactory option nor is the placement of these youth in secure residential placements (the second option might actually contribute to their delinquency by exposing them to very antisocial youth) (Dishion, McCord, & Poulin, 1999). As a result, a number of different options have been developed to provide therapeutic interventions for at-risk youth. One such response has been the development of Wilderness Experience Programs (WEPs). An offshoot of outdoor, adventure based programs (such as Outward Bound), these programs vary in nature but ultimately have the same goal—providing short-term outdoor interventions for at-risk and troubled youth. Wilderness Experience Programs can include any of the following: adventure based therapy, wilderness therapy, outdoor behavioral healthcare, experiential learning, or education and wilderness boot camps. Freise, Hendee, and Kinziger (1998) defined these programs as "organizations that conduct outdoor programs in wilderness or comparable lands for purposes of personal growth, therapy, rehabilitation, education or leadership/organizational development" (p. 40).

Livsey, Sickmund, and Sladky (2009) reported that in 2004 there were 118 WEPs operating in the United States and most of these facilities (60%) were privately operated (p. 4). In terms of size, this study showed that 53% held from 21 to 50 residents, although 9% of these facilities held over 100 participants. Livsey and colleagues (2009) noted that few of these facilities were likely to have high security measures (e.g., locked doors or gates).

Despite the fact that the results of this census are the most current available, it is likely that some privately operated facilities were not counted (especially those that receive no government funding), so we do not know the true number of these operations in the United States.

While these programs are very popular, research shows that the effectiveness of these interventions is mixed (MacKenzie, 2006). Some studies report that the positive effect on troubled youth is moderate, while others show that participation in wilderness programs result in increased self esteem and self efficacy as well as decreased recidivism. The downside of wilderness programming is illustrated in media reports where these experiences turned deadly and resulted in the serious injury or death of a participant. This chapter explores the intricacies of WEPs by exploring their history, typologies, effectiveness, and standards of practice.

Wilderness Experience Programs

In North America, wilderness programming can be dated back to the early 1900s when state hospitals used tent therapy as an intervention for adult psychiatric patients (Davis-Berman & Berman, 1994). At the time, no empirical evidence supported the effectiveness of this outdoor therapy and only anecdotal evidence suggested that it benefited the patients. Although the positive effects of these programs were reported in the *American Journal of Insanity*, mental health practitioners had lost interest in this approach by the 1920s.

By the mid-20th century, the emergence of a more progressive outdoor therapy, referred to as therapeutic camps, called attention to using nature as a place where rehabilitative interventions could occur. By the late 1920s, therapeutic camping programs were used as tools for monitoring, diagnosing, and then providing psychotherapy for troubled youth. Camp Ahmek, one of the first outdoor-based programs for children, was created in 1929 to offer recreational and social development. Ultimately, other programs emerged such as the University of Michigan Fresh Air Camp and the Salesmanship Club of Dallas. These outdoor programs are seen as the predecessors to the recent trend of using the wilderness as a setting where interventions with at-risk youth can occur (see Davis-Berman & Berman, 1994; Russell & Hendee, 2000).

In the following decades, the use of outdoor-based interventions continued to evolve and expand. One high point in outdoor-based interventions was the establishment of the Outward Bound program in 1946. Kurt Hahn, often referred to as the moving spirit behind Outward Bound, argued that developing one's character is equally as important as academic success (Kimball & Bacon, 1993). From this European school emerged an international movement that many attribute as the model for contemporary wilderness programs (Russell & Hendee, 2000).

Outward Bound International's (OBI) approach toward experiential education was important in the development of the guiding philosophy behind WEPs. Rather than describing an actual program, the term experiential education actually refers to the approach often used to support wilderness programming, which is defined simply as "learning by doing, with reflection" (Newes, 2001). Kraft and Sakofs, 1985 (cited in Gass, 1993) reported that several factors are commonly associated with experiential education:

- The learner is a participant rather than a spectator in learning.
- The learning activities require personal motivation in the form of energy, involvement, and responsibility.
- The learning activity is real and meaningful in terms of natural consequences for the learner.
- Reflection is a critical element in the learning process.
- Learning must have present as well as future relevance for the learner and the society in which he/she is a member. (p. 4)

In order to understand how these factors may enhance the effectiveness of interventions for at-risk youth, it is necessary to further explore the concept of wilderness programming.

Types of Wilderness Programs

There is no consensus on what constitutes a WEP. Depending on their area of expertise, both researchers and practitioners continue to debate and distinguish between therapy based wilderness, adventure based, and challenge based programs. Therapeutic programs are based on the philosophy of insight oriented therapy and use challenges found naturally in wilderness settings to encourage youth to see themselves from a different perspective. Adventure programs may not always be geared toward changing one's behavior or self concept. They are often designed for recreational purposes though they can also be used therapeutically. Challenge programs may use a wilderness component or include activities involving human created challenges to encourage behavior modification, which may include intimidation tactics, cooperative games, trust activities, and wilderness expeditions. Challenge programs generally focus on behavior modification and can include a boot camp component.

Given this information, perhaps the best way to identify a wilderness program is to determine the significance of its outdoor component. The wilderness component of an intervention program typically follows one of the following formats: (a) base camp expedition programs; (b) contained expedition programs; (c) continuous flow expedition programs; and (d) residential expedition programs.

Base camp expedition programs (BE) consist of the youth and their wilderness leaders or treatment team setting up a base camping area. These camps are often held in remote and natural settings. The entire program generally lasts from three to eight weeks with wilderness expeditions that last for one to two weeks. During these expeditions, the participants are taken away from the base camp in small groups and backpack, canoe, or raft (Crisp, 1998; Russell, 2001). Contained expedition (CE) programs, by contrast, take participants on a wilderness expedition for the duration of the program. The treatment team and participants remain as an intact unit for three to four weeks. Continuous flow expedition programs (CFE) generally last up to eight weeks. They are called "continuous flow" because of the rotation of expedition leaders that takes place throughout the program. For example, in a two week interval, wilderness leaders might work eight days and then take six days off. Moreover, the clientele may also include new participants joining existing groups in the field.

In addition to the categories mentioned above, WEPs can be further classified by whether they are considered an adjudicated or private placement program. Both of these program types can be used officially by juvenile justice officials or unofficially by parents or guardians seeking an intervention for a troubled teen to offer an alternative to commitment, traditional therapy, residential treatment centers, or psychiatric treatment.

Adjudicated programs, also called court programs, often utilize a base camp supplemented by overnight wilderness excursions. Participants might be placed in these programs as part of an informal or formal probationary order. As an alternative to incarceration, they typically require a one year commitment from a participant and are often operated by private agencies that contract their services with state agencies. The typical participant has previously been involved with juvenile justice systems and is usually from a single parent, lower income background. Their behavioral problems are characterized by substance abuse, school failure or dropout, sexual promiscuity, running away, and resistance to authority (Cooley, 1998; Russell & Hendee, 2000).

Private placement programs are the most common type of contemporary WEP (Livsey et al., 2009). These experiences are often presented as options for parents or custodians of troubled teens. Private placement participants are typically White, male, and aged from 13 to 17 years who are from middle to upper class backgrounds. These young people are less likely to have involvement with the justice system and generally do not have serious emotional problems. However, they have often failed to benefit from outpatient or community mental health programs. Their behavior problems are often similar to adjudicated program participants.

For adjudicated youth, these programs may serve as an intervention or a type of conditional release ordered by juvenile justice officials. For example, in South Carolina once a juvenile has been adjudicated and committed, they may be conditionally released to a wilderness program while under aftercare supervision. State contracted wilderness programs in South Carolina may also be used as an alternative to commitment for less serious juvenile offenders. Another example of an adjudicated program is the Sante Fe Mountain Center, which was introduced in 1979 as a component of New Mexico's juvenile justice system. It can be categorized as an outdoor behavioral healthcare program that uses wilderness experiences to supplement other forms of treatment.

Privately operated wilderness programs are widely advertised to the parents of at-risk youth. Programs, such as the Aspen Achievement Academy, which offer a "clinical insight oriented philosophy" provide at-risk or troubled youth an avenue for developing self awareness through a number of interventions, including traditional therapy, experiential education, and hands-on outdoor education.

Conner (2006) found that WEPs usually include "experiential activities in outdoor settings that offer natural and technical challenges and result in learning through a combined use of training, action methods, processing and debriefing" (p. 1). However, this is the same description also used for adventure programming, which is a broader term encompassing therapeutic or recreational purposes that may serve adults or youth who may or may not be offenders. As such, it is important to examine the types of wilderness terminology and programming currently in use.

Adventure Based Therapy

The terms adventure therapy and adventure programming are often used interchangeably. Adventure based therapy (AT) refers to programs that are offered by the operators of residential placements and the outdoor intervention occurs in close proximity to the facility (Gass, 1993). In general, adventure programming includes outdoor activities that are said to be therapeutic regardless of whether that was the original intent of the program. For instance, some adventure programs are designed for recreational purposes; however, they may advertise as having a therapeutic effect on an individual because recreation is a healthy activity. Some adventure therapists define a program as therapeutic only if its activities include supervision by qualified healthcare providers who have developed specific treatment goals for the program participants. Others use a more general view of AT and suggest that it encompasses programs that emphasize change occurring through group based experiential learning under the supervision of professional therapists. They also argue that a wilderness setting is not a requirement. Though the outdoor element is often present, it may actually take place in a non wilderness setting and include group-based activities and outdoor intervention methods such as:

- outdoor education
- outdoor leadership training
- mountaineering
- rock climbing
- whitewater rafting
- kayaking
- backpacking
- expeditions

These methods create the perception of risk and place the participant in unfamiliar surroundings, which helps therapists create eustress, or positive stress. Eustress is an important tool utilized to unbalance the participant, which makes them depend less on their familiar behavioral patterns and forces them to develop new ways to solve problems, as well as their communication and social skills. As such, camps have a similar impact upon delinquent or non-delinquent youth. Herbert (1996) observed that "stressful experiences that are likely to occur throughout an adventure based program serve as impetus for individual change" (p. 5).

Outdoor Behavioral Healthcare

A newer approach to outdoor intervention is the concept of outdoor behavioral healthcare (OBH). It is similar in nature to other wilderness experience programs and can be categorized as such. It is nearly synonymous with WEPs, but OBHs are required to have clinically-licensed staff members and are available to youth who have been adjudicated delinquent or youth with special needs (e.g., mental health). OBHs also must have a treatment team present, which typically consists of a clinical supervisor, medical supervisor, field therapist, and wilderness guides. As a more specific concept, Russell and Hendee (2000) observed that OBHs are specifically "aimed at changing destructive, dysfunctional or problem behaviors in clients through clinically supervised therapy, therapeutic activities and educational programs in an outdoor setting" (p. 9).

Wilderness Therapy

A great deal of the research related to WEPs has been conducted on Wilderness Therapy (WT). Hill (2007) defined this type of program as "using traditional counseling techniques in an outdoor setting that incorporates adventure based activities" (p. 339). WT programs typically operate using a base camp format and participants staying in an isolated area for periods as short as one week to as long as one month. The leader of the WT program is referred to as a wilderness therapist. These individuals are not necessarily required to have any formal education or certification related to experiential activities. In fact, some suggest that the only requirement should be a wilderness leader who has good judgment and survival skills. These wilderness leaders support the activities of the staff members who counsel the youth. Some of the leading experts in WT suggest that counseling teams should be supervised by a licensed mental health practitioner (Davis-Berman & Berman, 1994; Russell, 2001).

Long-term Residential Camping

Long-term residential camping places participants in travel units. These units encourage the group based component of wilderness treatment and force the participants to provide for their own survival needs while considering that of others. According to Gass (1993), "the client change is seen to be associated with the development of a positive peer culture, confronting the problems associated with day-to-day living, and dealing with existing natural consequences" (p. 10). Although there is little available information on this type of WEP and its impact upon troubled youth, it is important to acknowledge the existence of these programs. Unlike the other WEPs described above, the wilderness component lasts throughout the entire program, which generally ranges from several months to over a year. This type of wilderness programming is also available to both at-risk and adjudicated youth.

Wilderness Boot Camps

Juvenile boot camps were created to offer an alternative to incarceration and originally consisted of a military style training program to shock offenders out of delinquency or criminal behavior. They eventually grew in popularity and evolved into an intervention method for troubled youth (see Chapter 5). Primarily sponsored by state and local governments and housed in facilities resembling military training compounds, Benda (2005) noted that boot camps can be generally characterized as follows:

(a) programs designed with military regimens and routines,
(b) discipline and rules adopted from the armed services' model, and
(c) secured facility intended to be a community alternative to traditional prison. (p. 2)

As boot camps became more popular in the 1990s, operators from the private sector began to offer these programs. Some of these boot camps moved outdoors after these entrepreneurs found that they could decrease operating costs by eliminating fixed housing structures. Some boot camps became wilderness boot camps and enjoyed a broad appeal. Wilderness boot camps retain the militaristic philosophy of quickly obtaining control, compliance, and obedience to authority.

As shown in the information above, the history of juvenile boot camps does not parallel that of WEPs. The underlying philosophies for each are vastly different and are seemingly disconnected and contradictory to treatment models. However, they seem to come together with the concept of Wilderness Boot Camps.

Effectiveness of Wilderness Programs

There is a long history of parents sending their children to camp settings to temporarily escape the city, expose these youth to new environments, forge new friendships, and enable them to build new skills. In the past few decades, WEPs have become a popular intervention and alternative to commitment for troubled adolescents; there have been several attempts to assess their effectiveness. However, the variations in WEPs (e.g., intervention formats, program types, and target populations) make it difficult to make any general statements about their effectiveness. This challenge increases when one considers that these camps often operate with different goals, provide services to different groups of participants (e.g., at-risk youth compared to delinquents), and camp staff have varying degrees of competence. This section provides an overview of the evaluation research on WEPs.

One of the first studies to examine the effectiveness of WEPs was conducted by Carson and Gillis (1994), who used a meta-analysis (when the statistical effects of a number of studies are combined to produce a single result) that drew upon a total of 43 published studies. Carson and Gillis found that participants in WEPs improved their behaviors. More specifically, they reported that adolescents, ranging in age from 11 to 16 years, had better grades and higher levels of positive self concept than youth who had not participated in WEPs. They also found, however, that WEPs were no more effective for adjudicated youth than with other adolescent participants.

Though these findings showed support for WEPs, this study is often criticized because it included a wide variety of WEPs, which consisted of college courses with an outdoor component as well as Outward Bound programs. While the Cason and Gillis (1994) meta-analysis is worth discussing as the first attempt at consolidating the available research at that time, subsequent studies have produced more sound results. These studies tend to focus on three main categories: increasing self concept and social skills and lowering both substance abuse and recidivism.

Research has suggested that there is a relationship between poor self concept and juvenile delinquency (Brownfield & Thompson, 2005). Self concept is the way a person perceives his/herself and is developed through his/her experiences and shaped by environmental factors and feedback from significant others. Several studies have shown that WEPs have a positive impact on the self concept of troubled adolescents (Russell & Hendee, 2000). Others have found that WEPs improve self image as well. Deficient social skills have also been associated with disruptive and antisocial behavior, which inhibits the formation of close interpersonal relationships. In addition, delinquency can be exacerbated by a lack of social skills and positive attachments. WEPs, with their group based activities and challenges, emphasize the development of social skills. As such, much of the evaluation research has focused on the ability of WEPs as they relate to improving social skills. An important concept that derives from the evaluation literature on the relationship between WEPs and social skills is the idea of deterioration effects (Moos, 2008). Deterioration occurs when the positive influences of an intervention program erode over time. This effect was found in a sample of students who initially had positive results that faded in the long term. This idea was earlier conceptualized as fading effects and was found to occur once the program was completed. The deterioration or erosion of the positive effects, however, does not negate the apparent positive influence of WEPs.

Adolescent substance abuse negatively effects youth, their families, and the communities in which they reside. These effects can be called collateral consequences of substance abuse and can include delinquent behaviors such as declining grades, absenteeism, and a higher likelihood of dropping out of school. However, more serious consequences can also occur. For instance, a youth who abuses drugs is more likely to die because of suicide, homicide, an accident, or illness (Office of Juvenile Justice and Delinquency Prevention, 1998). There is also an inextricable association between substance abuse and delinquency; an adolescent substance abuser is also more likely to encounter the juvenile justice system. Even with these apparent connections, there has not been a lot of research that relates the impact of WEPs on substance abuse. Russell and Hendee (2000), for example, only found three such studies, all of

49

which reported WEPs to have a positive impact on participants with drug abuse problems.

As noted above, substance abuse is directly related to juvenile delinquency and crime. Furthermore, the issues leading to substance abuse are often the same that push adolescents down the path to other delinquent and criminal behaviors. Similarly, since emotional disorders have also been linked to delinquency and juvenile crime, reducing recidivism is an important issue in juvenile justice. WEPs are believed to be effective in reducing recidivism as well, though there are only a few studies that support this association. One example is the VisionQuest program. VisionQuest is touted as one of the first outdoor programs designed for youth adjudicated as delinquent. It was founded in the 1970s by a group of correctional officers who were unhappy with the lack of options for juvenile offenders. It used a graduated approach by which participants entered at one level and worked their way through a series of steps toward successful completion. Two studies evaluated VisionQuest's impact on recidivism, both of which found that program graduates were less likely to recidivate than comparison groups (Greenwood & Turner, 1987).

Overall, previous research appears to support the effectiveness of WEPs for some offenders. Unfortunately, these positive effects are overshadowed by some reports that find WEP placement to be the worst decision made by parents or juvenile justice officials. In the last two decades, a series of deaths have been attributed to a lack of care provided in some WEPs. A report recently published by the U. S. Government Accountability Office (GAO) examined problems in residential treatment programs for adolescents. The report described programs that ranged from having a minimal (e.g., boarding schools) to a primary wilderness component (e.g., wilderness therapy). The review found thousands of allegations of abuse and highlighted ten fatalities that occurred to illustrate the problems that have happened in some of these settings. Below is a summary of one of the cases reported by the GAO (2007):

> In May 1990, a 15-year-old female was enrolled in a 9-week wilderness program. Although the program brochure claimed that counselors were "highly trained survival experts," they did not recognize the signs of dehydration when she began complaining of blurred vision, stumbling, and vomiting water 3 days into a hike. According to police documents, on the fifth day and after nearly 2 days of serious symptoms, the dying teen finally collapsed and became unresponsive, at which point counselors attempted to signal for help using a fire because they were not equipped with ra-

dios. Police documents state that the victim lay dead in a dirt road for 18 hours before rescuers arrived. (pp. 3-4)

Upon review of the fatalities at WEPs, the GAO (2007) concluded that the following factors contributed to these deaths:

- Untrained staff;
- Lack of adequate nourishment; and
- Reckless or negligent operating practices. (p. 14)

If WEPs continue to be a viable intervention option for at-risk youth, then reporting standards must be determined and required, definitions for what constitutes a legitimate WEP must be clarified, and an oversight system must be put into place to ensure the safety and treatment for their participants.

In addition to serious injury or death, there are other problems associated with these programs. Behar (2007) and associates listed the following:

- substandard psychotherapeutic interventions and education by unqualified staff;
- failure to assess individual needs of residents;
- denial of full access by parents to their children in residence;
- financial opportunism and misrepresentations to parents by program operators; and
- financial incentives to educational consultants who serve as case finders and recruiters of families. (p. 401)

Given these findings, it is important that some level of oversight be provided to ensure that the youth in these programs receive appropriate levels of care.

There is a growing acknowledgement that different accrediting or governing bodies should monitor or oversee these operations. For example, the Alliance for the Safe, Therapeutic, and Appropriate Use of Residential Treatment (A START) was established to develop solutions to problems that occur in these types of facilities. A START specifically addresses the issues of unlicensed programs that are neither operated nor funded by governments. Many of the private placement programs could fall under this category. In addition to A START, the American Bar Association (ABA) has issued a resolution that "urges state, territorial, and tribal legislatures to pass laws that require the licensing, regulation, and monitoring of residential treatment facilities that are not funded by public or government systems, but are otherwise privately operated overnight facilities for troubled and at-risk youth under the age of 18 years" (Behar, Friedman, Pinto, Kazt-Leavy, & Jones, 2007, p. 403).

The Future of WEPs in the Juvenile Justice System

Wilderness experience programs will continue to be one option available to families of at-risk youth in search of an intervention that helps their sons or daughters develop their skills and decrease their involvement in delinquent or destructive behaviors. Furthermore, some publically funded agencies rely upon these types of programs for youth in their care. According to the National Center for Mental Health and Juvenile Justice (NCMHJJ), the juvenile justice field is desperately in need of interventions that are responsive to the mental health and emotional needs of adolescents. As a result, in 2000, the NCMHJJ initiated one of the largest research efforts on mental health and the juvenile justice system to date. One of the important outcomes of their efforts was the presentation of a number of core principles. Skowyra and Cocozza (2006) observed that the following should guide juvenile justice practice with youth who have mental health problems:

- Youth should not have to enter the juvenile justice system solely in order to access mental health services or because of their mental illness[es].
- Whenever possible and when matters of public safety allow, youth with mental health needs should be diverted into evidence-based treatment in a community setting.
- If diversion out of the juvenile justice system is not possible, youth should be placed in the least restrictive setting possible, with access to evidence-based treatment.
- Information collected as part of a pre-adjudicatory mental health screen should not be used in any way that might jeopardize the legal interests of youth as defendants.
- All mental health services provided to youth in contact with the juvenile justice system should respond to issues of gender, ethnicity, race, age, sexual orientation, socio-economic status, and faith.
- Mental health services should meet the developmental realities of youth. Children and adolescents are not simply little adults.
- Whenever possible, families and/or caregivers should be partners in the development of treatment decisions and plans made for their children.
- Multiple systems bear responsibility for these youth. While at different times, a single agency may have primary responsibility, these

youth are the community's responsibility and all responses developed for these youth should be collaborative in nature, reflecting the input and involvement of the mental health, juvenile justice, and other systems.

- Services and strategies aimed at improving the identification and treatment of youth with mental health needs in the juvenile justice system should be routinely evaluated to determine their effectiveness in meeting desired goals and outcomes. (p. 5)

WEPs work well with these principles on many levels. First, they are becoming more accessible as they increase in popularity and gain acceptance with insurance companies. In addition, they are no longer merely alternatives for the worst adjudicated offender or the wealthy troubled teen. Some programs, for example, offer scholarships and development endowments to support youth who would otherwise be unable to participate.

Second, research has been conducted to examine the effect that WEPs have on different demographic groups. For example, a recent study found that White participants responded more positively than minority participants in a WT program (Orren & Werner, 2007). Yet, the findings from different studies are sometimes contradictory. MacKenzie (2006) reported that these differences can be attributed to "(1) the programs included in the analysis, (2) the samples, and (3) the outcomes" (p. 186). Thus, researchers who include at-risk youth with actual delinquents and have different measures of recidivism will produce different results.

Third, the movement away from adventure and challenge oriented programs toward an OBH model for troubled youth acknowledges the important relationship between mental health and delinquency. The linkage between delinquency and mental health problems is well documented and WEPs may play a significant role in improving wellness for some youth. For those at-risk youth who are privately placed in WEPs, their treatment could prevent them from becoming delinquent. Yet, despite this need for mental health services, there is some evidence to show that wilderness programs do not provide the range of services that troubled youth require. Sickmund (2006) reported that 25% of these programs did not screen youth for suicide risk (p. 10) and that only 45% of these operations provided a mental health screening for each resident completed by an in-house professional (p. 12).

While the research has not conclusively demonstrated that wilderness experience programs successfully reduce delinquency, there is optimism that these programs can prevent some at-risk youth from engaging in delinquent behavior and reduce recidivism rates of youth who have been adjudicated delinquent. As such, these WEPs may continue to be a promising component in juvenile justice systems. Yet, this optimism must also be matched by studies that conclusively determine the effectiveness of these interventions.

References

Behar, L., Friedman, R., Pinto, A., Kazt-Leavy, J., & Jones, W. G. (2007). Protecting youth placed in unlicensed, unregulated residential "treatment" facilities. *Family Court Review, 45,* 399-413.

Benda, B. (2005). Introduction: Boot camps revisited. *Journal of Offender Rehabilitation, 40,* 1-25.

Berman, D. S., & Davis-Berman, J. (1995). *Outdoor education and troubled youth.* Retrieved June 29, 2008, from www.ericdigests.org/1996-1/outdoor.htm

Brownfield, D., & Thompson, K. (2005). Self-concept and delinquency: The effects of reflected appraisals by parent and peers. *Western Criminology Review, 6,* 22-29.

Buie, A. (1996). *National Association for Therapeutic Wilderness Counseling: History.* Retrieved June 29, 2008 from www.natwc.org/history.html

Carson, D., & Gillis, H. L. (1994). A meta-analysis of outdoor adventure programming with adolescents. *Journal of Experiential Education, 17,* 40-47.

Cocozza, J., & Schufett, J. (2006). *Youth with mental disorders in the juvenile justice system: Results from a multi-state prevalence study.* Retrieved August 15, 2008, from http://www.ncmhjj.com/pdfs/publications/PrevalenceRPB.pdf

Cocozza, J., & Skowyra, K. (2000). Youth with mental health disorders: Issues and emerging responses. *Juvenile Justice, 7,* 3-13.

Conner, M. G. (2006). *What is adventure therapy?* Retrieved November 22, 2008, from www.adventureprograms.org/Articles/WhatIsAdventureTherapy.htm

Cooley, R. (1998). Wilderness therapy can help troubled teens. *International Journal of Wilderness, 4,* 18-20.

Crisp, S. (1998, July). *International models of best practice in wilderness and adventure therapy.* Presented at the International Adventure Therapy Conference, Perth, Australia.

Davis-Berman, J., & Berman, D. S. (1994). *Wilderness therapy: Foundations, theories and research.* Dubuque, IA: Kendall/Hunt.

Dishion, T. J., McCord, J., & Poulin, F. (1999). When interventions harm: Peer groups and problem behavior. *American Psychologist, 54,* 755-764.

Farrington, D. P., & Welsh, B. C. (2007). *Saving children from a life of crime.* New York: Cambridge University Press.

Federal Bureau of Investigation. (2008). *Crime in the United States, 2007.* Washington, DC: Author.

Feld, B. (2003). The politics of race and juvenile justice: The "due process revolution" and the conservative reaction. *Justice Quarterly, 20,* 765-799.

Friese, G., Hendee, J. C., & Kinziger, M. (1998). The wilderness experience program industry in the United States: Characteristics and dynamics. *Journal of Experiential Education, 21,* 40-45.

Gass, M. A. (1993). *Adventure therapy: Therapeutic applications of adventure programming.* Dubuque, IA: Kendall/Hunt.

Greenwood, P. W., & Turner, S. (1987). *The VisionQuest program: An evaluation.* Santa Monica, CA: Rand.

Herbert, J. T. (1996). Use of adventure based counseling programs for persons with disabilities. *Journal of Rehabilitation, 62,* 3-9.

Hirschfield, P., Maschi, T., White, H. R., Traub, L. G., & Loeber, R. (2006). Mental health and juvenile arrests: Criminality, criminalization or compassion. *Criminology, 44,* 593-630.

Ireys, H. T., Achman, L., & Takyi, A. (2006). *State regulation of residential facilities for children with mental illness.* Rockville, MD: Center for Mental Health Services, Substance Abuse and Mental Health Services Administration.

Kimball, R. O., & Bacon, S. B. (1993). The wilderness challenge model. In M. A. Gass (Ed.), *Adventure therapy: Therapeutic applications of adventure programming,* (pp. 11-41). Dubuque, IA: Kendall/Hunt.

Kraft, R., & Sakofs, M. (1985). *The theory of experiential education.* Boulder, CO: Association of Experiential Education.

Livsey, S., Sickmund, M., & Sladky, A. (2009). *Juvenile residential facility census, 2004: Selected findings.* Washington, DC: Office of Juvenile Justice and Delinquency Prevention.

MacKenzie, D. L. (2006). *What works in corrections: Reducing the criminal activities of offenders and delinquents.* New York: Cambridge University Press.

Moos, R. H. (2008). Iatrogenic effects of psychosocial interventions for substance use disorders: Prevalence, predictors, prevention. *Addiction, 100,* 595-604.

Newes, S. L. (2001). *Predicting recidivism among juvenile offenders participating in adventure based therapy intervention.* Unpublished doctoral dissertation. The Pennsylvania State University.

Office of Juvenile Justice and Delinquency Prevention. (1998). *Drug identification and testing in the juvenile justice system.* Washington, DC: Author.

Orren, P. M., & Werner, P. D. (2007). Effects of brief wilderness programs in relation to adolescents' race. *Journal of Experiential Education, 30,* 117-133.

Russell, K. C. (2001). What is wilderness therapy? *Journal of Experiential Education, 24,* 70-79.

Russell, K. C., & Hendee, J. C. (2000). *Outdoor behavioral healthcare: Definitions, common practice, expected outcomes, and a nationwide survey.* Moscow, ID: Idaho Forest Wildlife and Range Experiment Station.

Sickmund, M. (2006). *Juvenile residential facility census, 2002: Selected findings.* Washington, DC: Office of Juvenile Justice and Delinquency Prevention.

Skowyra, K. R., & Cocozza, J. (2007). *Blueprint for change: A comprehensive model for the identification and treatment of youth with mental health needs in contact with the juvenile justice system.* Delmar, NY: National Center for Mental Health and Juvenile Justice.

CHAPTER 4
TREATMENT FOSTER CARE
AS A CORRECTIONAL STRATEGY

David C. May and Erin L. Kelley

T reatment/therapeutic foster care (TFC) is an important component of juvenile correctional systems and tens of thousands of troubled youth each year are placed in these therapeutic settings. Despite this fact, the caregivers who provide these important services are often overlooked and their efforts are under appreciated. Foster parents are a valuable resource. Nevertheless, we do not always acknowledge how their roles as substitute parents, who provide supervision and treatment in a residential setting, are far less intrusive and stigmatizing than placing a youth in a high security juvenile facility with uniformed officers. This chapter introduces readers to the concept of therapeutic or treatment foster care, provides a short historical overview of these services, highlights some of the characteristics of these placements, and explores both the challenges and opportunities of operating these homes.

To fully understand therapeutic/treatment foster care (TFC) in the 21st century, it is important to understand both the origins of TFC and the foster care system. As such, we begin our discussion of TFC with a short review of how the current foster care system evolved. In the mid-19th century, abandoned, neglected, or dependent children were often placed in orphanages. These placements, however, were often less than desirable: some youth were turned away when these facilities were overcrowded or if the youth were considered inappropriate for admission. Orphanage operators were criticized for their selective admission policies, which were often made on the basis of race, ethnicity, or religion. Furthermore, they often relied upon harsh discipline systems and were able to discharge children arbitrarily. Children's advocates of the era were critical of the facts that this type of institutional care did not prepare children for life in the community and that most children did not want to live in an orphanage. These factors lead to the creation of the placing out program (Cook, 1995).

In the placing out program, youth and young adults were provided the opportunity to live with rural families in hopes of assisting them to become productive citizens. Between 1854 and 1930, approximately 150,000 youth were moved from New York City and placed in homes throughout the Midwest. These youth were selected for the program in various ways: some were referred from the courts, while others came from juvenile facilities or other institutions. In addition, some parents brought their children to the agency for placement. Youth selected to be placed out were usually home-less, abandoned, dependent, or neglected. In reality, only a few were or-phans and parents were required to give their permission for the youths' participation in the placement program.

Youth selected to be placed out were often put on trains destined for the Midwest and were accompanied by the Children's Aid Society (CAS) and care giving staff. Along the way, they met with families who wanted to provide a home for these children (Bernard, 1992). Some families made arrangements to receive a particular child, but most often the youth were lined up for interested adults to view and select. Children who were not chosen during this process would be transported to the next town for consideration. The CAS required that a child go with a family willingly and that the agent make a home visit before settling the placement. Families had to provide an education and proper care. The CAS also required follow-up personal visits and correspondence with the children until they reached adulthood and were living on their own (Cook, 1995).

Placing out programs peaked in 1875 and then began a steady decline that ended in 1930. The demise of the program was attributed to the intro-duction of new ways of coping with industrialization, the recognition of environmental factors as causes for some social problems, and the reforms of the Progressive Era, including compulsory school attendance and child labor laws. Another relevant development was the emergence of social work as a profession, which focused on new methods for working with impoverished children and families. Social workers and children's advocates sponsored strategies such as: (a) publicly funded aid to mother headed families to prevent the need for out-of-home care; (b) the development of family foster home programs; (c) the promotion of temporary rather than permanent out-of-home care whenever possible; (d) a more comprehensive approach to regulating agencies and monitoring out-of-home care resources; and, (e) the redesign of orphanages, using homelike cottages rather than large dormito-ries (Cook, 1995; Holt, 1992; Patrick, Sheets, & Trickel, 1990).

In the 1920s, as placing out was losing its momentum, boarding out be-came more popular among child welfare agencies. In boarding out, a child was sent to live with a family, but the family was paid to care for the child. Payment for care helped to prevent child labor and allowed the children to receive an education rather than working to provide for the host family. By the 1930s, it was becoming clear that boarding out was outpacing both institutional care and placing out. By 1950, more children were in foster homes than in institutions and by 1968, more than three times as many children were in foster care as institutions (Hacsi, 1995).

Foster care has been shaped by two important federal Acts. The creation of Title IV of the Social Security Act of 1935 (Aid to Dependent Children) allowed states to become financially involved in care for children and later amendments to this Act created federal matching funds for children placed in foster care. In 1980, the federal Adoption Assistance and Child Welfare Act provided money to states for preventative programs and family reunification efforts. Both of these acts allowed for the payment of parents to supervise foster care children (Rosen, 1998).

Recent Developments in Therapeutic/Treatment Foster Care

Bryant (1981) argued that the development of TFC could be described in two stages. During the first stage, which began in the early 1950s and lasted into the 1960s, TFC programs were used as supplements to existing institutional treatment facilities. In this era, TFCs were used as halfway houses to provide supervised transitions for youth from residential treatment facilities to community life. The second stage in the development of TFC began with the focus on removing youth from large institutions in the late 1960s. In this stage, TFC programs began to be used as alternatives to institutionalization. As such, an important difference between first and second phase TFC was the shift in the primary source of treatment in the TFC and increasing responsibility of TFC caregivers as treatment agents.

Founders of these early programs made several modifications to existing foster care placements to house children with serious behavior problems. These changes included: (a) reduced caseload size for the foster care case worker; (b) a small additional payment beyond the standard rate at the time because of the added demands placed on TFC parents by the severe behavior disorders of the children; and, eventually, (c) placement decisions made in consultation between the foster care caseworker, a psychiatric consultant, and the foster care supervisor (Bryant, 1981). All three components of that program—founded over 50 years ago—are still present in today's TFC programs.

According to Chamberlain (1998), the goals of TFC programs are as follows:

- Reinforce youth's appropriate and positive behaviors.
- Closely supervise youth at all times.
- Carefully monitor peer associations.
- Specify clear, consistent rules and limits.
- Consistently follow through with consequences.

- Encourage youth to develop academic skills and positive work habits.
- Encourage family members to improve communication skills.
- Decrease conflict between family members. (p. 2)

Each of the aforementioned goals are important in their own right, but the key goals for most TFC programs revolve around support for positive behaviors and positive peers, close supervision, and proper modeling of how a family should operate. Because many children who are placed in TFC have natural families that are dysfunctional, perhaps the greatest benefit of a TFC program is that youth can see how a "normal" family operates and model that behavior in their own lives.

Welkowitz (1987) identified three major elements of the treatment philosophy of TFC programs:

- Behavior/Learning Based Approaches. Parents are trained to use a behavioral approach and learning-based therapy. This method uses programs aimed at specific behaviors, is easily communicated to both TFC parents and children, and the effectiveness of these programs is easy to measure.
- Supportive Family Setting. In these programs, the family setting is a vital part of the intervention, as the child benefits from a stable, supportive family environment. This healthy family is seen as the most important ingredient of TFC.
- Family Systems Approach. One of the key factors in some children with behavior problems is their biological family encourages deviant behavior. By removing children from that environment, TFC reduces the negative influences of the natural family with the hope that the child will learn the skills needed to manage negative family environment while in TFC.

TFC programs use intensive supervision strategies. Children placed in TFC homes are generally closely supervised by TFC parents and program staff and they are not allowed unsupervised free time in the community. As they successfully advance in the program, levels of structure and supervision are reduced (Chamberlain, 1998).

Children in 21st Century Foster Care

It is difficult to determine the true number of children currently in foster care. Nevertheless, Hacsi (1995) stated that the number of children in foster care grew rapidly in the 1990s, due to a greater number of children entering care and longer stays after entry. He further suggested that an important reason for the increase in foster care caseloads has been the growing popularity of foster placement with relatives (called kinship care).

By 1990, formal kinship foster care had become an important part of foster care services. Informal care by relatives, however, has always been used for large numbers of children with parents who are unwilling or unable to properly care for their children. Between 1980 and 2004, for example, the number of children being reared by their grandparents rose from two to 5.6 million—a number that dwarfs the foster care population (Dye, 2006) and this number continues to grow (U. S. Census Bureau, 2008). Despite the increase in the number of fostered children throughout the 1990s, more recent estimates suggest that the number of children in foster care has steadily declined since 2000, when 552,000 were in foster care. By 2006, this number had declined to approximately 510,000 children (Trends in Foster Care and Adoption, 2008).

Therapeutic/Treatment Foster Care

Reddy and Pfeiffer (1997) defined therapeutic/treatment foster care as an:

> Approach that uses treatment parents in an explicitly defined treatment program, views treatment parents as change agents that provide treatment services to children with emotional, behavioral, and/or medical problems, and perceives treatment parents as members of the treatment team. (p. 582)

TFC is distinguished from regular foster care because its primary function is to provide a treatment environment for a troubled child, whereas the primary function of regular foster care is to provide a substitute family environment for dependent children (Stroul, 1989).

TFC is considered the least restrictive form of out-of-home therapeutic placement for children committed to the juvenile justice system. In TFC, children are placed in private homes supervised by foster parents trained to provide specific services and interventions. These programs are often funded by state juvenile justice, child welfare, and/or mental health agencies that are responsible for arranging for foster parent training and oversight (Substance Abuse and Mental Health Services Administration [SAMHSA], 2008). TFC programs are also delivered by voluntary, nonprofit agencies. One reason private agencies are so involved in TFC is the difficulties public agencies may face in delivering TFC. The primary challenges include: small caseloads required of caseworkers and turf problems between regular foster care and

TFC staff. As a result, it is often easier for private foster care providers to navigate these difficulties to effectively deliver TFC programs (Stroul, 1989).

TFC programs originated because of dissatisfaction with the institutional care for children. These problems included: the fact that young people distrust and dislike large institutional settings; the climate of institutions is socially depriving and inadequate for educational and social skills; the negative peer influences (which may reduce the likelihood of success upon release); and the difficulty for youth to learn acceptable behaviors in institutions compared to TFC (Bryant, 1981).

TFC homes are able to offer intensive therapeutic services for children who have been committed to the custody of the state. These youth typically are placed in TFC instead of a juvenile correctional facility. As such, TFC can be viewed as a less expensive and restrictive environment. In fact, one reason for the growing popularity of TFC is the escalating costs of institutional care and TFC provides cost effective care compared to institutional placement (Reddy & Pfeiffer, 1997).

Table 1. Names of TFC Programs.

- Enriched foster care
- Family treatment homes
- Foster family-based treatment
- Individualized residential treatment
- Intensive foster care
- Multidimensional treatment foster care
- Professional foster care

- Professional parenting
- Professional treatment homes
- Special foster care
- Specialized foster care
- Therapeutic family care
- Treatment family care
- Treatment foster care

Source: Adapted from Stroul (1989).

TFC programs have a number of different titles (see Table 1) and vary considerably from one jurisdiction to the next. This wide variety of names and delivery strategies makes it difficult to collect basic data about the numbers and types of TFC programs available, children served by TFC programs, and parents delivering those programs. As Hussey and Guo (2005) observed:

> youth[s] in treatment care are hard to identify and investigate as a distinct subgroup, given the varieties of samples and methods used in the published research and the lack of

> clarity regarding the meaning of long-term, treatment, spe-
> cialized, and therapeutic foster care. (p. 486)

Although TFC programs have a number of different titles and often vary considerably from one jurisdiction to another, they do have some common features that distinguish them from regular foster care programs. According to Stroul (1989), these features included:

- TFC homes provide a nurturing family environment for children with special needs or behavioral issues.
- TFC parents are treated as professional staff members who are the primary treatment agents for the child.
- TFC program staff provides supervision, consultation, and support to treatment parents.
- TFC program staff members have small caseloads (generally averaging less than 15 children under their supervision).
- TFC provides services in the context of the treatment home. These interventions are based on the individual needs of the child. Many programs use an initial assessment, a goal oriented treatment plan, daily tracking of progress on treatment goals, and periodic review of the treatment plan.
- TFC staff members provide 24-hour crisis intervention services to TFC families and children. Most programs also have back up placement options for instances when a child needs to be removed from a home in an emergency situation.
- TFC programs carefully select and train parents.
- TFC programs provide support to parents to help them avoid burnout. One of the most important supports is respite (where TFC parents may temporarily leave their children with another set of parents). Many programs also encourage and support the creation of support networks of TFC homes.
- TFC programs involve the natural parents in the treatment process. Programs vary widely in how they accomplish this, but most encourage communication between natural and TFC parents, particularly as the [children] get closer to the day when they are ready to return to the natural parents.
- TFC programs maintain active interaction with a variety of community agencies including: educational, vocational, mental health, health care, substance abuse treatment, sexual abuse interventions, job training, and recreational services. Program staff must have good working relationships with personnel from all [of] these

agencies, but the most important interaction is with the school system. (pp. 22-26)

Because children spend nearly as much time in school as they do with the TFC parents—and a substantial percentage of TFC children experience problems in school—a strong link between the TFC parents and the local school system is an essential element of a successful placement. TFC programs may encourage school systems to become involved in pre-placement decisions and planning or to provide aides, tutors, and other supports necessary to assist TFC children. At the very least, TFC parents must maintain close communication with teachers and other school personnel and they must respond quickly when schools make requests for support or interventions with these youth. Because of these difficulties, in some cases where programs are available, TFC children attend schools operated by the juvenile justice system to ensure that the educational needs of that child are met promptly and efficiently (Stroud, 1989).

TFC differs from traditional foster care in at least five different ways. First, TFC parents are selected based on their skills and willingness to handle children with severe emotional and behavioral disturbances. Regular foster care parents, by contrast, are selected based on their willingness and ability to provide a supportive, nurturing environment for children. Second, the number of children placed in a TFC is generally very small (often one child at a time) and the caseloads of the social service personnel who supervise the TFC families remain small, allowing the case managers to work closely with the parents and the child. There is frequent contact between case managers and the TFC family; the case manager has more access to additional resources and mental health services than with traditional foster care families. Third, TFC parents receive a higher stipend than that given to traditional foster parents. Fourth, children are placed with foster parents who are trained to work with children with special emotional and behavioral needs. These parents receive extensive pre-service and in-service training while they are serving as TFC parents (SAMHSA, 2008). Finally, TFC parents receive far more support and supervision from mental health professionals and caseworkers than do traditional foster parents, who get fewer home visits from caseworkers. Altogether, TFC children receive far more support and services than their counterparts in regular foster care.

TFC Program Delivery

Phase 1. Pre-placement

Most referrals to TFC programs in juvenile justice originate from juvenile justice agencies. When a youth is referred to TFC, documentation is required: the reason for referral; the social history of the youth; and a description of the youth's placements, the family history of the youth, a history of emotional and mental health problems, medical and psychiatric history, and school records. Generally, a committee reviews the child's information to determine if he is well suited for TFC (some children may be excluded if they are viewed as dangerous). If the youth is determined to be a good fit, a matching process is used to select a TFC family with the most appropriate characteristics and skills to assist them. Factors considered in this process include: parenting style, the ability to manage problem behaviors, the ages and gender of other children in the TFC house, socioeconomic status, cultural differences, the type and amount of religious involvement, preferred leisure activities, type of home and neighborhood, location in an urban or rural environment, proximity to natural family, and the availability of an appropriate educational setting. In addition, the preferences of the TFC family and the child entering TFC are also considered (Stroul, 1989).

Youth considered for placement in TFC programs are interviewed by program staff members who identify a potential TFC family in whose home the child may be placed. When a family is identified, they are provided with information about the child. Some programs use videotaped interviews with the youth while others have the potential parents come into the office and watch an interview through a one way mirror. Many programs also use trial or pre-placement visits that may last for one or two nights. If both parties agree to the placement, then a placement date is set. The placement process may range in length from two weeks to several months. In some cases, natural parents may be resistant to placement; in the event that this happens, staff efforts are needed to reduce the discomfort of both children and parents (Stroul, 1989)

Phase 2. Intervention

Most programs develop an initial treatment plan based upon the referral information gathered by the caseworker(s). Generally, these plans have both short- and long-term goals. Categories of services provided by TFC programs include:

- Treatment within the treatment home. The family plays a major role in the therapeutic process. Treatment parents are seen as the primary source of intervention. These parents teach and role model appropriate behavior and community living skills.
- Support services to the treatment home. In most TFC programs, support and consultation is provided to TFC parents by program staff. Telephone and face-to-face contacts occur frequently, sometimes daily. Most programs have crisis intervention services available 24 hours a day, seven days a week. Many programs also have a network where parents communicate with one another regarding effective TFC program delivery. The overriding goal in most TFC programs is to keep the youth in the TFC homes where they were placed.
- Ancillary services. TFC parents and children receive mental health and special education services, substance abuse counseling, after school and weekend programs, tutoring, extracurricular lessons in music, athletics, crafts, and independent living skills.

Phase 3. Discharge and Follow-up

The goal of TFC programs is to eventually return all children to their natural families; this is considered a favorable discharge. In order to return home, the child has usually achieved or made significant progress toward treatment goals or an appropriate placement is identified and prepared for the child. The average length of stay in a TFC program varies widely between programs (e.g., from one month to five years). Unfortunately, after most youth are discharged, limited or nonexistent follow-up or aftercare services are provided.

In some cases, youth may be terminated from TFC programs prior to a favorable discharge. Reasons for premature termination include an unsuccessful placement (when the youth does not advance toward the goals of the treatment plan), court decisions (where the juvenile is charged with new crimes or has violated the conditions of his/her probation), or a change in the natural family (where a problematic parent or sibling is removed from the natural family due to death, abandonment, or imprisonment), among others (Stroul, 1989).

Characteristics of TFC Parents

TFC parents undergo an extensive application process prior to being hired. In addition to the items included on most employment applications, applicants must also submit to a criminal background check and must provide their arrest history, information about their housing arrangements (e.g., whether they own or rent, the number of bathrooms and bedrooms, whether the child they are considering fostering would share a bedroom), and an extensive list of personal references.

This specialized training that TFC parents receive allows them to offer a safe, supportive, therapeutic environment. Below, we have included the training required by the Idaho Department of Health and Welfare (IDHW) for the TFC parents employed in that state. The following courses, required by the IDHW (2003), are representative of the training received by TFC parents:

- Crisis management
- Observation and documentation
- Implementation of positive behavior modification techniques
- Parenting techniques
- Treatment plan implementation
- Involving the child's family in the delivery of treatment
- CPR, First Aid, and HIV/AIDS awareness
- Medication management

Within the TFC home, parents deliver specialized interventions that are designed (sometimes in conjunction with mental health professionals, but often by the parents themselves) to be specific to each child's needs. TFC parents are also responsible for insuring that their children have access to community resources that will help facilitate their development.

Effectiveness of TFC

Because of the wide variety of titles given to TFC programs, it is difficult to find research that establishes the effectiveness of TFC programs in reducing delinquency and encouraging positive behavior. The most ambitious attempt at doing so was done by Reddy and Pfeiffer (1997). Drawing upon 40 studies done in the United States, Canada, England, and Finland, Reddy and Pfeiffer (1997) found that TFC was associated with a number of positive social psychological changes in children. The strongest positive outcomes were reported in improvements of children's social skills and the permanency of placement (e.g., youth remaining in the same placement). As such, the research suggests that TFC placement increases family stability for youth in those programs and improves their social skills. Additionally, the research revealed that TFC reduces behavioral problems and increases the psychological adjustment of participants in those programs. Finally, the research also indicated that — at least for some TFC programs — children were likely to be discharged to an adoptive home or an independent living facility, rather than a more restrictive setting. Nevertheless, Reddy and Pfeiffer (1997) observed that the outcomes were "neither uniformly positive nor persuasively strong as one might expect in light of the enormous growth in program development and professional and political support for treatment foster care" (p. 585).

Recent research has also supported the claim that TFC is an effective placement for troubled youth. Chamberlain, Leve, and DeGarmo (2007) found that TFC girls spent more than 100 fewer days in locked settings than their counterparts in group care; TFC girls were less likely to engage in delinquency than their counterparts in group care as well. Leve and Chamberlain (2007) also determined that girls who participated in TFC were more likely to attend school and complete homework than girls incarcerated in group homes (see Leve, Chamberlain, & Reid, 2005) and have fewer referrals for criminal offenses than youth in group homes (Leve et al., 2005). Hahn et al. (2005) also found that TFC was more effective than placement in group homes in reducing both general and serious delinquency. Altogether, the research suggests that TFC provides a more stable home environment and increases the social and psychological skills of its participants and is somewhat effective in reducing delinquency and school related problems.

Advantages and Challenges of TFC

Stroul (1989) listed a number of advantages and challenges of TFC programs; although it is almost two decades old, this list is still timely. The advantages and challenges of TFC are listed below:

Advantages

- TFC provides a minimally restrictive, natural environment for the treatment of youth in a community setting. This is the most normalized type of residential treatment environment and provides the closest alternative to the child's natural family environment.
- Because youth are not exposed to the negative peers they would find in a residential facility and are provided programming from positive role models in an environment closely akin to the one to which they

will return, both the programming and the durability of the positive ideas learned are more likely to be permanent.

- TFC is highly flexible and can thus be used to meet the needs of a wide range of youth. Because treatment in TFC is highly individualized, treatment plans can be developed for youngsters and older adolescents and delivered effectively in the same environment.
- TFC programs provide the participants with a sense of family connectedness. Because this bond is so strong, children often stay in touch with TFC parents for years after their discharge.
- The amount of negative community reaction is less for TFC programs than for residential treatment centers. This helps decrease the stigma for the youth involved in these programs.
- Start up costs for TFC are much less expensive than residential treatment programs and they are cheaper to operate than other residential options. Furthermore, the design of TFC programs allows a greater percentage of the actual costs to be spent on program delivery compared to other residential placements. (pp. 82-87)

Challenges

- Recruiting qualified parents. Finding parents both capable and willing to work with children with behavioral challenges is often difficult. Additionally, the stress associated with these positions creates high burnout rates and TFC parents must be replaced at regular intervals.
- Developing and maintaining a reliable referral system. Because TFC programs are relatively unknown and many agencies are unaware of the distinctions between TFC and regular foster care, children are sometimes placed in residential centers when they would be better served in TFC homes. As such, additional outreach and educational efforts are necessary to increase the viability of TFC programs.
- Maintaining a collaborative relationship with the schools. TFC program partners suggest that a great deal of time is spent with the school system in an attempt to ensure the best educational options for TFC children. Unfortunately, many school districts have obstacles that are difficult for TFC parents to bypass.
- Engaging natural families. TFC parents often find it difficult to work with natural families in the treatment portion of the program. Some natural families have a number of long standing problems that are not easily solved and may be resistant to working with TFC parents and staff. Additionally, obstacles such as transportation costs, geographic distance, and lack of reimbursement to natural families for

travel creates difficulty in insuring that the natural family parents are involved with the TFC program in the most effective manner.

- Handling allegations against treatment parents. An inevitable problem of programs such as TFC is allegations of abuse against TFC parents. Although these allegations are rarely substantiated, programs must ensure they have an efficient, effective policy in place to deal with the investigation of these allegations without bringing harm to the child, the alleged offender, or the bond between the two parties. Programs that maintain a stance of "innocent until proven guilty" and actually use that philosophy provide the most support for TFC parents during these difficult times. If the allegations are substantiated, TFC staff must remove the child from the home immediately (and follow protocols to deal with the TFC parents).

- Dealing with disturbing behaviors of children. TFC parents are often faced with incidents of acting out, committing crime, or destroying property. TFC programs and parents must be aware of these risks and develop steps to reduce the impact of these acts.

- Providing follow-up services. One of the limitations of most TFC programs is an inconsistent (or nonexistent) mechanism through which children released from TFC homes are provided aftercare upon their return to their natural families.

- Obtaining independent living services. In some cases, youth remain in TFC until they reach the age of maturity or move to independent living situations. These youth need services designed to help them meet the needs of daily adult life, yet these services are not widely available.

- Preventing burnout among TFC parents and staff. Given the volatile nature of the clients whom they supervise and the stressful environment in which these programs operate, rates of burnout among TFC parents and staff are high. As a result, program managers need to develop strategies (including better benefit packages, small caseloads, extensive training, and consultation) in an effort to prevent burnout.

- Returning children to troubled natural families. Some TFC parents suggest that returning all children to natural families after they have met their treatment goals may undermine the effectiveness of the TFC programming, particularly when these homes are dysfunctional and have undergone no substantive changes since the time the child was removed. (pp. 82-87)

Conclusions

This chapter provided an overview of TFC programs, including the definition, history, characteristics, and current state of the research. Additionally, a number of strengths of TFC programs were identified that make them a desirable treatment option for youth within the juvenile justice system. Along with those advantages, a number of challenges were identified that are faced by TFC programs. As we close this chapter, we use those challenges to frame a discussion of TFC in the future.

The first and most important recommendation regarding TFC is that better data are needed regarding TFC programming, particularly in services delivered to clients in juvenile justice settings. While the limited evidence available suggests that TFC programs reduce problem behaviors among their clients, future examinations of their effectiveness should compare TFC youth to those in other out-of-home placements to study whether the positive outcomes discovered so far can be replicated and generalized to all TFC programs. Until data regarding the types and program delivery strategies of those programs are readily available, it will be difficult to say without a doubt that TFC programming is effective. In fact, we cannot even reliably offer an estimate of either (a) the number of TFC programs available in the United States, or (b) the number of children placed in TFC programs each year. Until better data are available, the knowledge regarding TFC will continue to grow slowly at best.

Despite the limited evidence available about TFC programs that cater specifically to youth in the juvenile justice system, some of the limitations identified above will almost certainly remain as challenges for TFC in the 21st century. The most important challenge faced by these programs centers on the difficulty of recruiting qualified parents to effectively deliver TFC services. Given the high burnout rates among these parents and the limited financial resources available to support TFC programming, states must increase payments and benefits for these individuals. One method of making TFC parenting more attractive is to make TFC programming an entity delivered by the state and then make TFC parenting a hazardous duty profession, where TFC parents can receive enhanced retirement benefits. This benefit, coupled with comprehensive respite strategies and support networks, should make TFC parenting attractive to a larger group of people, thus making it easier to recruit parents when the inevitable turnover occurs.

Another challenge that will continue to test TFC programs in the 21st century concerns the relationships between TFC providers and local educational systems. TFC programs catering primarily to juvenile offenders will continue to find it difficult to navigate the obstacles they must face in providing education for the children in their households, particularly those children with greater special education needs and behavioral challenges (see Chapter 14). As a result, it is essential that juvenile justice leaders in each jurisdiction work closely with school systems to ensure that TFC children are given every opportunity to succeed. While there is no solution to make this relationship work every time in every jurisdiction, effective communication between the two groups is probably the most important aspect of these programs and all efforts to facilitate this communication by all partners will increase the chances that these groups can work together for the good of the youth in these placements.

Last, the aftercare services provided by TFC programs to children who return to their natural families after the completion of their TFC placement is often nonexistent. In fact, if there is one finding that is consistent for practically all juvenile justice programs, it is that without aftercare, the positive behaviors and strategies learned by juveniles who have been under the care of the juvenile justice system will erode (whether the youth was involved in a mentoring program, a boot camp, or a residential facility). As such, TFC programs need to foster relationships with both the school and the juvenile probation systems to develop strategies to ensure that youth who leave TFC programs have an effective support system to help them remain successful when they return to their natural families.

Overall, these challenges are neither overwhelming nor insurmountable. Furthermore, the limited evidence available suggests that TFC programs are at least as effective as residential treatment and group homes in reducing delinquency and increasing positive behaviors and psychosocial skills among juveniles — although this could be due to that fact that these youth were at relatively low risk to commit further crimes in the first place (which was why they were placed in a community rather than institutional setting). Although there are currently not enough studies examining the effectiveness of TFC to come to any definitive conclusion, we feel safe in agreeing with Reddy and Pfeiffer (1997) that "clinicians and policy makers alike may be guardedly optimistic about the potential role of treatment foster care in the 'system of care' for children and adolescents" (p. 587).

References

Bernard, T. J. (1992). *The cycle of juvenile justice*. New York: Oxford University Press.

Bryant, B. (1981). Special foster care: A history and rationale. *Journal of Clinical Child Psychology, 10*, 8-20.

Chamberlain, P. (1998). *Treatment foster care*. Washington, DC: Office of Juvenile Justice and Delinquency Prevention, Retrieved October 24, 2008, from http://www.ncjrs.gov/pdffiles1/ojjdp/173421.pdf

CHAPTER 4: TREATMENT FOSTER CARE AS A CORRECTIONAL STRATEGY

Chamberlain, P., Leve, L., & DeGarmo, D. S. (2007). Multidimensional treatment foster care for girls in the juvenile justice system: 2-year follow-up of randomized clinical trial. *Journal of Consulting and Child Psychology, 75*, 187-193.

Cook, J. F. (1995). The history of placing-out: The orphan trains. *Child Welfare, 74*, 181-197.

Dye, J. (2006, August). *Co-resident grandparents and grandchildren with no parent present in the household: 2000 to 2004.* Presented at the American Sociological Association, Montreal, Quebec.

Hacsi, T. (1995). From indenture to family foster care: A brief history of child placing. *Child Welfare, 74*, 162-180.

Hahn, R. A., Lowy, J., Bilukha, O., Snyder, S., Briss, P., Crosby, A., Fullilove, M. T., et al. (2004). *Therapeutic foster care for the prevention of violence.* Retrieved October 24, 2008, from http://www.cdc.gov/mmwr/preview/mmwrhtml/rr5310a1.htm

Hussey, D. L., & Guo, S. (2005). Characteristics and trajectories of treatment foster care. *Child Welfare League of America, 84*, 485-506.

Idaho Department of Health and Welfare. (2003). *Therapeutic foster care standards.* Boise, ID: Author. Retrieved October 24, 2008, from http://www.healthandwelfare.idaho.gov/_Rainbow/Documents/health/therapeutic_foster_care.pdf.

Leve, L., & Chamberlain, P. (2007). A randomized evaluation of multidimensional treatment foster care: Effects on school attendance and homework completion in juvenile justice girls. *Research on Social Work and Practice, 17*, 657-663.

Leve, L., Chamberlain, P., & Reid, J. (2005). Intervention outcomes for girls referred from juvenile justice: Effects on delinquency. *Journal of Consulting and Clinical Psychology, 73*, 1181-1185.

Reddy, L. A., & Pfeiffer, S. I. (1997). Effectiveness of treatment foster care with children and adolescents: A review of outcome studies. *Journal of the American Academy of Child Adolescent Psychiatry, 36*, 581-588.

Rosen, M. (1998). *Treating children in out-of-home placements.* New York: The Haworth Press.

Stroul, B. A. (1989). *Therapeutic foster care, volume III. Series on community-based services for children and adolescents who are severely emotionally disturbed.* Washington, DC: Child and Adolescent Service System Program, Georgetown University Child Development Center.

Substance Abuse and Mental Health Services Administration. (2008). *Therapeutic foster care.* Rockville, MD: Author.

Thurston, H. W. (1930). *The dependent child.* New York: Columbia University Press.

Trends in Foster Care and Adoption. (2008). *The AFCARS Report.* Retrieved October 24, 2008, from http://www.acf.hhs.gov/programs/cb/stats_research/afcars/tar/report14.htm

U. S. Census Bureau. (2008). *Grandparents day 2008.* Retrieved June 26, 2009, from http://www.census.gov/Press-Release/www/releases/archives/cb08ff-14.pdf

Welkowitz, J. (1987). *A report on therapeutic foster care.* Waterbury, VT: Department of Mental Health, Child, and Adolescent Service System Program.

CHAPTER 5
THE RISE AND FALL OF JUVENILE
BOOT CAMPS IN THE UNITED STATES

Gaylene Armstrong and Bitna Kim

S ome might call boot camps one of the most innovative approaches to managing a correctional population since the early ideas of Alexander Maconochie, who pioneered parole in the mid-1800s, and Zebulon Brockway, who was instrumental in introducing rehabilitation in early U. S. prisons. Others may call boot camps a failed experiment. The notion of overlaying a military regimen within a correctional facility reemerged in the United States during the 1980s as a means to instill the necessary structure and motivation to affect behavioral change; this was not unique, but it had been more than a century since it was implemented for the first time with a correctional population. The concept fit well politically during a perceived period of crisis with rising crime rates and a get-tough perspective on crime. Boot camps allowed jurisdictions to obtain additional federal and state funding for treatment by using a popular correctional approach. It is important to remember, as time passes, that these programs were initially used as a means to obtain resources to provide offenders with additional treatment. This approach, described in detail by MacKenzie and Souryal (1995), allowed for a new program that was accepted with open arms by both the government and, arguably more importantly, the voters. Boot camps experienced substantial growth during the 1990s only to come to a screeching halt and virtually disappear as quickly, if not more quickly, than they initially appeared. A few programs still exist around the country and, as we discuss at the end of the chapter, may even experience some renewed interest.

Few correctional programs have experienced the same tumultuous history as boot camps. Some researchers and public interest groups were more outspoken against these programs than others during the height of their popularity, but the support for boot camps by the media, public, and politicians was almost unprecedented. Relying on minimal evidence that boot camps were effective in leading to change, a large number of jurisdictions across America implemented these programs for men, women, and youth. Not far behind the state and federal implementation of the programs was the development of boot camps by the private sector for both correctional populations and non-system involved youth who were perceived by their parents as in need of discipline and structure. These private operators allowed parents to pay for a boot camp stay for their children in an attempt to set their children on the prosocial pathway and avoid juvenile or justice system involvement.

The unprecedented decline in popularity of the boot camp programs was fueled by reports of staff abuses of youth and a number of deaths while the youth were in the custody of these programs (some of these incidents are discussed later in this chapter). It is important to disentangle the studies and effects discussed in the research literature as it applies to boot camps. The results of research reported in this chapter pertain to government operated boot camps and not the boot camps operated for youth who are not involved in the criminal justice system. We suspect that if these same studies were replicated in these private, non-criminal justice boot camps, the results would be even more dismal.

In this chapter, we provide an overview and development of boot camp programs with a focus on juvenile boot camps, describe a typical experience, and summarize the research on recidivism. We also highlight some of the cases that contributed to the decline of boot camp programs and end with a description of a new generation boot camp that was introduced in Maryland.

Overview of Juvenile Boot Camps

As boot camp programs moved from adult to juvenile corrections, new challenges arose (Austin, Jones, & Bolyard, 1993; Cronin, 1994). For example, while adult programs could target nonviolent offenders in prison, nonviolent juveniles are much less likely to be incarcerated. Thus, net widening and the associated costs have become critical issues in the development of juvenile programs. Net widening occurs when a juvenile, who would normally remain in the community on a lesser sanction such as probation, is instead scooped up into a more punitive program (e.g., boot camp) merely because the program exists. Had this program not been available, the youth would not receive this more serious punishment. Thus, the net that captures youth in more severe punishment is widened when we have a greater number of programs available. This is particularly relevant given the history of placing nonviolent juveniles or status offenders in detention—which can be harmful to youth (see Chapter 6).

The idea of providing discipline and structure for disruptive juveniles means there was a real threat that increasingly large numbers of juveniles would be placed in boot camps, regardless of whether it was a suitable alternative sanction. Furthermore, in contrast to adult boot camps, academic and therapeutic programming—as well as aftercare (programs that support a youth's reentry into the community)—are viewed as necessary components in juvenile programs. In fact, besides the military atmosphere, there are questions about how much the boot camp programs actually differ from other residential facilities for juveniles.

The emergence of juvenile boot camps was an explosive trend that occurred after the development and rise of adult boot camps in the mid-1980s. In June 1995, MacKenzie and Rosay (2004) surveyed state and local juvenile correctional administrators and identified a total of 37 programs operating at that time. Only one of these programs opened prior to 1990 with nearly all of them opening during or after 1993. The passage of the 1994 Crime Act permitted the Department of Justice to allocate funding for juvenile boot camps; 12 jurisdictions were awarded grants to develop programs for juveniles and another 12 jurisdictions received funds for the renovation of existing facilities or the construction of new ones.

Juvenile boot camp programs tend to be fairly similar. Unlike adult boot camps, juvenile programs are rarely limited to individuals convicted of their first serious offense and are not necessarily voluntary. The typical juvenile boot camp participant was a nonviolent male between the ages of 14 to 18 years who was placed in the program by a juvenile court judge. However, only about half of the boot camps were solely limited to nonviolent offenders while the other half accepted youth convicted of violent crimes. Differences among programs can be found in population capacities and program length. The capacities of juvenile boot camps ranged from 12 to 396 participants and the lengths of the programs varied from one day to one year.

Almost all boot camps for juveniles emphasized a military atmosphere with drill and ceremony, platoon grouping, and strict discipline. About half used military titles and uniforms for both staff and juveniles. In addition to the military atmosphere, the majority of programs included physical labor in the daily activities. Youth also engaged in physical fitness, sports activities, and some types of challenge or adventure programming. Overall, juveniles spent between one and ten hours per day in physical training, military drill, and work. In comparison, on average they spent about six-and-a-half hours in educational classes or counseling. Because of this emphasis on education and counseling, it comes as no surprise that juvenile boot camp administrators rated rehabilitation and reducing recidivism as very important goals of their programs.

Traditional Boot Camp Experience

Upon arrival at the boot camp, males typically have their heads shaved (females are permitted short haircuts) and they are informed of the strict rules. At all times, they are required to address staff members as "Sir" or

"Ma'am," to request permission to speak, and to refer to themselves as "this inmate." Punishments for minor rule violations are swift and certain, frequently involving physical exercise such as pushups or running: major rule violations may result in dismissal from the program.

In a typical boot camp, the 10- to 16-hour day begins with a predawn wake up. Inmates dress quickly and march to an exercise yard where they participate in an hour or two of physical training followed by drill and ceremony. Then, they march to breakfast where they are ordered to stand at parade rest while waiting in line and to exercise military movements when the line moves. Inmates are required to stand in front of the tables until commanded to sit and are not permitted to make conversation while eating. Meal consumption is also timed to military precision, such as allowing ten minutes for breakfast. After breakfast, inmates march to school to attend academic classes. When the 6- to 8-hour school day is over, youth return to the compound where they participate in more exercise and drill. A quick dinner is followed by evening programs consisting of counseling, life skills training, additional academic education and study time, or drug education and treatment.

Participants gradually earn more privileges and responsibilities as their performances and time in the program warrants. A different color hat or uniform may be the outward display of their higher statuses. Depending upon the facility, somewhere between 8% and 50% will fail to complete the program. For those who successfully complete the program, an elaborate graduation ceremony occurs with visitors and family members invited to attend. Awards are often given for achievements made during the program. In addition, the inmates often perform the drill and ceremony they have practiced throughout their time in the boot camp. Graduation is oftentimes an emotional ceremony as some youth become close with their instructors and fellow platoon members. Youth who succeed are proud of their accomplishments and new identities as they return to their home communities.

The question remains at this point whether the skills they have learned during boot camp will translate to success on the outside. Programs vary on whether this is the final stage for youth or whether they will continue under some form of supervision and aftercare. We will first discuss research on juvenile boot camps as it pertains to participation in the program alone and then we will address the aftercare component (see also Chapter 16).

Juvenile Boot Camps and Recidivism

The boot camp was met with much optimism for juvenile offenders during the early 1990s (Bottcher & Ezell, 2005). Despite the program's popularity with the public and political leaders, recidivism rates for juvenile boot camp graduates were disappointingly high (Tyler, Darville, & Stalnaker, 2001). Over 60% of the boot camp participants reoffended after release, as seen in the Office of Juvenile Justice and Delinquency Prevention pilot programs, in some Florida boot camps (Kaczor, 1997), in some Texas camps (Tyler, Stalnaker & Darville, 1999), as well as in programs in Oklahoma, Texas, Georgia, Florida, and South Carolina (Tyler et al., 2001). With rare exceptions, correctional boot camps for juvenile offenders appear to be unable to reduce recidivism at a rate greater than that of traditional youth correctional programs or probation (Lutze & Bell, 2005; MacKenzie, Wilson, Armstrong, & Gover, 2001).

A number of studies have tested the effectiveness of juvenile boot camps in terms of recidivism rates (Lutze & Bell, 2005) by comparing youth who participate in boot camps with those who participate in some other correctional alternative such as probation. In a multi-site study of boot camps for juvenile offenders, Peter, Thomas, and Zamberlan (1997) found that boot camps had not reduced recidivism rates. Based on an extensive search of the literature and a subsequent meta-analysis (when the statistical effects of a number of studies are combined to produce a single result), MacKenzie, Wilson, and Kider (2001) found no overall differences in recidivism between boot camp participants and comparison samples. In general, research that compares boot camp graduates to participants who served other sentences (or who had been confined in another type of traditional correctional facility for juveniles) has not demonstrated any differences in recidivism rates (Clawson, Coolbaugh, & Zamberlan, 1998; MacKenzie, Wilson, Armstrong, & Gover, 2001).

Juvenile boot camp programs vary in numerous aspects, including the lengths of the camps, how rigorously they adhere to the original military model, the amount and type of treatment and aftercare, and effectiveness (Tyler et al., 2001). The failure of juvenile boot camp programs to reduce recidivism has been primarily ascribed to low dosage effects, a hypermasculine environment, a shortage of cognitive based treatment programs, and the absence of aftercare programs (Parent, 2003).

Low Dosage Effects

Correctional boot camps are short-term incarceration programs (MacKenzie, Wilson, & Kider, 2001). However, the length of programs varied from a weekend to 300 days at the original program in Orleans Parish, Louisiana (Tyler et al., 2001; Zaehringer, 1998). Although more research is required to determine an optimal amount of time spent in a boot camp program (Tyler et al., 2001), the literature suggests that programs of too short a duration are less likely to reduce recidivism (Lutze & Bell, 2005).

A Hypermasculine Environment

In contrast to traditional correctional programs, boot camps use the masculine military model that incorporates aggressive interaction, physical exercise, physical labor, and corporal punishment in the daily schedule (Styve, MacKenzie, Gover, & Mitchell, 2000). It is quite evident that boot camps depend upon a masculine structure that strengthens masculine values and stereotypically masculine ideologies (Lutze & Bell, 2005).

Some correctional experts and researchers have expressed concerns about the potential stressfulness of the hypermasculine environment, the possibility that the paramilitary structure will be detrimental to the juveniles, and its potential effects on offender success (MacKenzie, Wilson, Armstrong, & Gover, 2001). They argued that boot camp programs reinforce hypermasculine behaviors that have been found to be the strongest predictors of criminal offending and high risk behaviors directly related to offending (Benda, Toombs, & Peacock, 2002; Kilmartin, 2000).

A number of government officials have asserted that boot camp programs are both ineffective and could be harmful to juveniles (Tyler et al., 2001). MacKenzie, Wilson, and Kider (2001) found that a military atmosphere in a correctional setting is not effective in reducing recidivism. According to Lutze and Bell (2005), the interaction between the masculinity in boot camps and the hypermasculine beliefs and behaviors of the juvenile offenders helps to explain the failure of boot camps to reduce recidivism. Prior research strongly suggests that, rather than focusing on discipline and rigorous physical training in correctional settings, juvenile boot camps should place more importance on the therapeutic programming in order to reduce recidivism (Lutze & Bell, 2005; MacKenzie, Wilson, & Kider, 2001).

Shortage of Cognitive Based Treatment Programs

There is sufficient research demonstrating that proper correctional treatment and therapy are central to reducing recidivism (MacKenzie et al., 2001a). Given the research findings that boot camps are not any more or less effective than other correctional alternatives, MacKenzie, Wilson, and Kider (2001) suggested that boot camps might only differ from the alternatives in the military aspects and not in therapy and treatment levels. MacKenzie and Souryal's (1994) multisite study showed that correctional boot camp programs with more hours committed to treatment and therapy resulted in lower rates of recidivism (Lutze & Bell, 2005).

The boot camps differ greatly not only in the amount of focus given to therapeutic programming, but also in the type of the therapy and treatment such as academic education, drug treatment, or enhancing cognitive skills.

Styve, MacKenzie, Gover, and Mitchell (2000) suggested that boot camps for juveniles should devote more time to cognitive based treatment programs that have been found to be effective in reducing recidivism. Although some juvenile boot camps incorporate this type of treatment and therapy into the regime of the camps (Clark & Aziz, 1996; MacKenzie et al., 2001a), treatment programs in boot camps have generally been criticized for failing to use cognitive based approaches (Lutze & Bell, 2005).[1] For example, some boot camp programs provide drug and alcohol education, but not treatment that attempts to replace negative thought processes and behaviors with positive ones (Lutze & Bell, 2005).

Bottcher and Ezell (2005) investigated recidivism from the LEAD boot camp (a California Youth Authority program that emphasized leadership, esteem, ability, and discipline). This program was developed for low-risk offenders and incorporated a shorter period of incarceration—averaging 4.6 months and an intensive aftercare program—but the results showed that it failed to reduce recidivism. Bottcher and Ezell suggested that the cause of this failure may be in the lack of the effective treatment methods focusing on individual needs and professionally trained treatment staff to develop the program.

The Decline of Juvenile Boot Camps: Deaths in Correctional Custody

Some people believe that boot camps should be eliminated because the military atmosphere of the camp poses an inherent danger to residents. From this perspective, the strict discipline and harsh standards imposed by boot camp staff are some of the primary goals of boot camps. They believe the boot camps focus on punishment and they find this especially problematic for juvenile delinquents. However, research has found the opposite to be true. Based on their survey of all existing juvenile boot camp programs, MacKenzie and Rosay (2004) found that rehabilitation and lowering recidivism were important goals and punishment was not. Furthermore, juvenile perceptions of danger in the camps are not significantly different from the levels perceived by juveniles in traditional correctional facilities (Styve et al., 2000).

Although punishment is not an important goal of boot camps—on average, inmates do not believe the camps pose an elevated risk to them—some of the traditional activities, such as the exercise components that include lengthy runs, have been hazardous, resulting in a number of deaths. These fatalities have occurred despite the medical checkups inmates receive during the intake and assessment process. These deaths led Riak (2003) to write:

81

My reading of the evidence suggests that the camps' clientele are nothing more than grist for a very profitable mill. The old-style reform school, but with "training" substituted for flogging, and phony "tough love" jargon substituted for the blunt (but more honest) cruelties of the original model, is enjoying a heady revival these days. It's a seller's market and business is booming. There's just one minor nuisance: the deaths. (p. 1)

When a sociologist was asked to comment on the death of a boot camp inmate, he stated, "It's a situation that lends itself to abusive conditions. Any time you have someone use lock and key, the person who has the lock and key has the power to abuse, and they often do" (Blackwood, 2001).

Several incidents that resulted in the deaths of juvenile boot camp participants led to questions about the application of the military model to juvenile corrections. Two of these deaths occurred while the youth were exercising. One incident involved Gina Score, a young girl who was placed into a South Dakota boot camp program. According to a report in the *New York Times*, "Gina Score was placed in the camp in July 1999 after stealing a bike, skipping school and shoplifting. Two days into the program, the 226-pound, 5' 4" girl joined other girls on a 2.7 mile required run" (Blackwood, 2001). According to the state investigator's report, Score collapsed during the run, frothing at the mouth; lost control of her bladder; progressively lost her ability to communicate; and eventually became unresponsive. The staff at the boot camp did not allow other residents to assist her, commenting that they should not make things easy or comfortable for her. Boot camp staff left Score where she fell for over three hours before transporting her to the hospital. Upon her arrival at the hospital, Score's body temperature registered 108 degrees (the upper limit of the thermometer). Doctors were not able to revive her and pronounced her dead an hour after she was admitted into the hospital.

Shortly after Gina Score's death, Human Rights Watch (2000) submitted a letter to South Dakota Governor William Janklow detailing the events reported above and requesting immediate action be taken to alter South Dakota's juvenile sentencing guidelines and discipline practices. In the letter, Human Rights Watch charged that:

guards shackle youth in spread eagled fashion after cutting their clothes off (a practice known as four pointing), chain youth inside their cells (bumpering), and place children in isolation twenty three hours a day for extended periods of time. (p. 1)

Human Rights Watch (2000) described physical abuses of authority, including other inappropriate actions such as male guards supervising the strip searches of female juveniles, as well as "grossly inadequate mental health care, glaring deficiencies in education and other substandard conditions of confinement" (p. 1). According to the *New York Times*, Governor Janklow, who himself was a product of the Marines and thus very familiar with the boot camp regimen, "blamed 'rogue' employees for Score's death and other problems" (Blackwood, 2001). Because of the incident, two staff members were charged, but later acquitted, on child abuse charges in the death and other alleged problems at the camp, including making girls run in shackles until their ankles bled.

In a 1998 incident, 16-year-old Nicholas Contreraz died at the privately operated Arizona Boys Ranch boot camp. In their report of the incident, the Pinal County Sheriff's Office noted that (1998):

> Nick Contreraz was performing physical training (pushups) in the amphitheatre. Mr. Lewis indicated due to Nick's lack of effort and aggressive behavior, he was being physically assisted. Mr. Lewis stated it had been forty minutes since the last hydration. So the staff took Nick to get water from his canteen. Mr. Lewis stated when staff was giving Nicholas water he did not respond. Mr. Lewis stated he had been playing like he was passing out several times during the day. Mr. Lewis stated the staff checked Nicholas' pulse and breathing and found nothing. Mr. Lewis and staff immediately administered CPR and called for assistance. Mr. Lewis stated CPR continued until Nicholas was taken with medical assistance team. (p. 1)

According to the same report:

> The charge nurse Sue, from Northwest hospital, contacted me to let me know that Mr. Contreraz had died and there were signs of abuse on the body. I asked what these were and she said he had abrasions from head to toe. He had bruising on his flanks, he had a rigid stomach and he had blood in his stomach. (p. 1)

An autopsy revealed that the youth died of complications from a lung infection that were made worse by physical activities. Another autopsy by a forensic pathologist showed that the boy had been handled roughly, causing bruising, abrasions, scratches, and minor puncture wounds to the head and body.

The Pinal County, Arizona Sheriff's report of the incident stated that some staff members thought that Contreraz was faking his breathing problems, even though he repeatedly coughed and vomited in the days before he died. As a result of the 1998 incident, two staff members were fired, four were suspended, and the program director was replaced. All 17 staff members employed at the Boys Ranch at the time were placed on Arizona's Child Abuser Directory, which is a list used to screen people for foster care and other children's services. Prosecutors eventually dropped all charges filed against six boot camp staff members.

Critical incidents in boot camps, such as the Gina Score and Nicholas Contreraz cases, are not specific to programs designed for juvenile delinquents. Similar events have occurred in privately operated boot camps in which parents are able to voluntarily send their disruptive teen for a few weeks of boot camp training. These camps fall outside of the juvenile justice system. The programs are designed with the same military emphasis as the juvenile correctional boot camps, but they tend to focus more on the militaristic components than therapeutic treatment, reflective of Scared Straight programs.[2] Often, these privately operated boot camps are not accredited and are subject to little or no regulation or oversight (U. S. Government Accountability Office, 2007).

These privately operated boot camp programs have also experienced tragic deaths of their residents. In 2001, fourteen-year-old Anthony Haynes died in an Arizona desert boot camp after collapsing in the 110 degree heat. Haynes was sent to the camp by his mother after he slashed her vehicle's tires and was caught shoplifting. Newspaper reports about the camp after Haynes' death reported that the daily regimen included forced marches; wearing black uniforms in triple-digit temperatures; in-your-face discipline; and a daily diet limited to an apple, a carrot, and a bowl of beans. Markham (2002) reported that:

> On the day Haynes died, he reportedly was hallucinating and refusing water before camp supervisors took him to a nearby motel and left him in a tub with the shower running. They returned to find the boy face down in the water and that he had vomited mud, which boot camp staff had forced him to eat earlier in the day. (p. 14)

Charles Long, the head of the boot camp program, was subsequently arrested on charges of second degree murder, aggravated assault, and eight counts of child abuse. A second staff member was also arrested on child abuse charges for allegedly spanking, stomping, beating, and whipping more than 14 children. In January 2005, Long was found guilty of manslaughter and aggravated assault; he was sentenced to six years in prison (Kiefer, 2005). The staff member was sentenced to six months in jail and three years probation.

When disasters such as these cases occur in boot camps, opponents of the programs point to the risks, including the structure and the potential for abuse of authority by untrained or undertrained staff. Regarding Gina Score's death in South Dakota, Jerry Wells (Director of the Koch Crime Institute) pointed to the staff as the cause of the death, suggesting the camp had "untrained staff." Wells stated, "The surprise to me was that it was a surprise, because it was a recipe for disaster" (Blackwood, 2001, p. 1).

Deaths in residential placements can have a significant impact upon the operations of a juvenile justice system. The case of Martin Lee Anderson, a 14-year-old Florida youth who died in a Bay County boot camp, drew international attention to boot camps as the youth's treatment by staff members was recorded on video and widely distributed on the Internet (Loney, 2007). Although seven officers and a nurse were acquitted of manslaughter charges, this case led to the closure of all of Florida's juvenile boot camps in 2006. In addition, Anderson's family received several million dollars in compensation from both the State of Florida and Bay County (who operated the boot camp).

Because of these types of incidents, it is often no surprise that when people learn about boot camp programs, they experience a type of negative gut reaction that forms the basis of their opinions about the programs. Media presentations of these incidents have helped to develop emotional responses to programs, so that it would seem boot camps are a dangerous alternative sanction.

However, before final judgments are made, fatal incidents such as the ones reported above must be placed into the context of all injuries and deaths, including suicides, that occur in other juvenile correctional facilities across the country. What are the actual rates of deaths and/or severe injuries in boot camps as compared to other facilities? To truly determine the extent of the dangerousness of boot camps, we need to consider injuries and deaths in all types of correctional facilities, including traditional residential programs. One of the limitations of our knowledge is that statistics about deaths in juvenile training schools are now being published (see Bureau of Justice Statistics, 2008), but we still do not know how many youth die in boot camps—in part because some of these camps are privately operated and there is little oversight in these operations (U. S. Government Accountability Office, 2007).

The Importance of Aftercare in Boot Camp Programs

Supporters of boot camps argue that the programs have the potential to reduce overcrowding in correctional facilities and provide therapy while acting as a cost effective approach if net widening is avoided (Anderson, Dyson, & Burns, 1999). As boot camp programs have matured, many shifted away from the pure military style training to incorporate the enhanced treatment component. Despite arguments that support boot camp programs, prior research has found little evidence that juvenile boot camps alone have long-term impacts on reducing recidivism (Benda & Pallone, 2005; Lutze, 2006). Experts point out that research that fails to support boot camps may not be an indication of a flaw of the boot camp programs. Rather, it is because of a lack of an effort to assist boot camp graduates to successfully incorporate the skills and behaviors learned in the boot camps (Kurlychek & Kempinin, 2006; Lutze, 2006; MacKenzie, 2006; Wells, Minor, Angel, & Stearman, 2006).

One of the biggest criticisms of all residential programs is that persons released from a structured or therapeutic environment are returned to the same communities where they were arrested, and most find it difficult to avoid the criminogenic factors that contributed to their arrest (Anderson et al., 1999). The communities to which the juvenile offenders return are frequently characterized by family dysfunction (including parental incarceration), poverty, limited employment opportunities, poor school adjustment, and harmful peer relationships (Baltodano, Platt, & Roberts, 2005).

Aftercare addresses this criticism made about boot camps (Anderson et al., 1999). Aftercare programs are designed to maintain the behavioral, social, and attitudinal changes that boot camps have instilled in participants (Anderson et al., 1999; Austin et al., 1993). These programs may represent a community-based extension of a boot camp program by emphasizing intervention and community adjustment rather than basic supervision (Wells et al., 2006). In discussing adult boot camps, MacKenzie and Piquero (1994) make a similar argument contending that "only boot camps that are carefully designed, target the right offenders, and provide them [with] rehabilitative services and aftercare are likely to…reduce recidivism" (p. 222).

While participating in aftercare programs, boot camp graduates are provided with rigorous programming that may include surveillance and monitoring, but they are also supplemented with education, counseling, treatment, meaningful job skills, and the opportunity to work upon release (Anderson et al., 1999; MacKenzie & Rosay, 2004). Beyond these basic components, aftercare programs stress a wide array of other elements such as anti-gang programs, community service projects, mentorships, independent living training, recreation programs, and financial resources and assistance (MacKenzie & Rosay, 2004). A more comprehensive discussion on aftercare in juvenile corrections is presented in Chapter 16.

New Generation Boot Camps: The Maryland Experiment

Despite the dismantling of boot camp programs throughout the country, a few programs remain; more frequently encountered are adult, rather than juvenile operations. While acknowledging the differences between juvenile and adult programs (including the different needs of the juvenile population) — a model adult interventions is presented in the following paragraphs that might prove to be instructive for the development of juvenile boot camps. As previous trends have demonstrated, if successful, this same type of programming may be replicated with juveniles.

As discussed earlier, a substantial body of prior literature indicates that offenders who are sentenced to boot camp programs do not have significantly different rates of recidivism when compared to offenders serving other types of sentences (e.g., traditional probation supervision). However, boot camps have recently experienced a significant transformation from their original design. These new generation boot camps devote more time in the daily schedule to treatment and education. Initial evidence suggests that these new generation boot camps may be more effective in reducing rates of recidivism as compared to traditional boot camp and correctional programs.

MacKenzie and Armstrong (2004) argued that early evaluations that did assess the impact of boot camps are not very reliable due to the implementation difficulties within the camps studied. Furthermore, researchers have not thoroughly addressed whether combining treatment with the structured, military style environment of boot camps yields lower recidivism rates than alternatives that also emphasize treatment (e.g., prison treatment program) within a traditional correctional environment. In response to this gap in the literature, researchers began a study in 2002 that randomly assigned adult inmates to either an adult boot camp in Maryland with a strong treatment emphasis or to an alternative correctional facility that also emphasized therapeutic programming but without a military component.

Maryland's Toulson Boot Camp program, established in 1990, was the boot camp involved in the study. Toulson Boot Camp uses a military model with the typical components described earlier in this chapter, but also incorporates drug education, life skills training, and academic education. The program lasts six months and is divided into three different phases, each of which spans a two month period. The daily schedule and activities of the boot camp participants vary depending upon their seniority in the program. Participants are in Phase One when they enter the camp. This phase emphasizes discipline and self control in a highly structured daily schedule that focuses on military drill, physical training, academic education, and other therapeutic education programs. During the following two phases, the daily activities have less emphasis on drill and physical training and more emphasis on work projects.

Analysis of the 234 adult males who participated in the experiment demonstrated some benefits to the boot camp participants. As MacKenzie, Bierie, & Mitchell (2007) noted:

> Boot camp releasees had marginally lower recidivism compared to those released from the traditional prison. A pretest, post-test self report survey indicated the boot camp program had little impact on criminogenic characteristics except for a lowering of self control. In contrast, inmates in prison became more antisocial, lower in self control, worse in anger management, and reported more criminal tendencies by the end of their time in prison. Criminogenic attitudes and impulses were significantly associated with recidivism. The impact of the boot camp diminished to nonsignificance when antisocial attitudes or anger management problems were added to the models predicting recidivism. (p. 22)

A secondary analysis conducted by Bierie (2007) focused on the costs and benefits of the Toulson boot camp versus the prison program. The intriguing result here was that the boot camp was actually cheaper to run than traditional prisons on a per inmate cost basis, largely because the boot camp atmosphere and style of management are able to operate more efficiently. The reduction in recidivism from the boot camp was more pronounced when using valuation (cost of crime) methods to quantify the difference in the types of recidivism—again showing an even larger benefit to the boot camp.

Whether these promising results with respect to recidivism and cost efficiency sparks a renewed interest and revival of boot camps remains to be seen. What is clear is that if boot camps do once again become popular as an alternative sanction option, we must be careful to learn from our past experiences. We must carefully monitor staff employed within these institutions. We must also be careful to balance the military structure with treatment components so that a hypermasculine environment is avoided. Finally, to be a promising alternative, we must allow for ample time to implement a comprehensive continuum of care that includes cognitive behavioral treatment programs and an evidence-based aftercare component for every residential program, including boot camps.

Endnotes

1. Cognitive behavioral interventions target the participant's counterproductive thoughts and interpretation of events; they attempt to restructure these cognitions to more productive and useful ways of interpreting events and managing their attitudes and behaviors.
2. Scared Straight programs take at-risk youth to visit prisons, where they would be lectured, scolded, and berated by the prisoners who attempted to "scare them straight."

References

Anderson, J. F., Dyson, L., & Burns, J. (1999). *Boot camps: An intermediate sanction.* New York: University Press of America.

Austin, J., Jones, M., & Bolyard, M. (1993). A survey of jail-operated boot camps and guidelines for their interpretation. In D. L. MacKenzie & E. E. Herbert (Eds.), *Correctional boot camps: A tough intermediate sanction,* (pp. 119-134). Washington, DC: National Institute of Justice.

Baltodano, H. M., Platt, D., & Roberts, C. W. (2005). Transition from secure care to the community: Significant issues for youth in detention. *Journal of Correctional Education, 56,* 372-388.

Benda, B., & Pallone, N. (2005). *Rehabilitation issues, problems, and prospects in boot camp.* Binghamton, NY: The Hawthorne Press.

Benda, B., Toombs, N., & Peacock, M. (2002). Ecological factors in recidivism: A survival analysis of boot camp graduates after three years. *Journal of Offender Rehabilitation, 35,* 63-85.

Bierie, D. M. (2007). *Cost matters: Application and advancement of economic methods to inform policy choice in criminology.* Unpublished dissertation.

Blackwood, A. (2001, July 6). *Death spotlights youth boot camps.* Retrieved November 22, 2008, from http://www.nospank.net/n-i06.htm

Bottcher, J., & Ezel, M. E. (2005). Examining the effectiveness of boot camps: A randomized experiment with a long-term follow up. *Journal of Research in Crime and Delinquency, 42,* 309-332.

Bureau of Justice Statistics. (2008). *State juvenile correctional facility deaths, 2002-2005.* Retrieved September 19, 2008, from http://www.ojp.usdoj.gov/bjs/dcrp/juvenileindex.htm

Clark, C., & Aziz, D. (1996). Shock incarceration in New York state: Philosophy, results, and limitations. In D. L. MacKenzie & E. Herbert (Eds.), *Correctional boot camps: A tough intermediate sanction,* (pp. 39-68). Washington, DC: National Institute of Justice.

Clawson, H., Coolbaugh, K., & Zamberlan, C. (1998, November). *Further evaluation of Cleveland's juvenile boot camp: A summary report.* Presented at the American Society of Criminology, Washington, DC.

Cronin, R. C. (1994). *Boot camps for adult and juvenile offenders: Overview and update.* Washington, DC: National Institute of Justice.

Human Rights Watch. (2000). *South Dakota: Stop abuses of detained kids*. Retrieved November 1, 2008, from http://www.hrw.org/press/2000/03/sdakota.htm

Kaczor, B. (1997). Studies find boot camps have high re-arrest rates. *Bradenton Herald*. Retrieved March 21, 2001, from http://www.bradenton.com/

Kiefer, M. (2005, January 3). Boot camp director found guilty in teen's death. *East Valley Tribune*. Retrieved September 19, 2008, from http://www.eastvalleytribune.com/story/34164

Kilmartin, C. (2000). *The masculine self*. Boston: McGraw-Hill.

Kurlychek, M. C., & Kempinen, C. (2006). Beyond boot camp: The impact of aftercare on offender reentry. *Criminology & Public Policy, 5*, 363-388.

Loney, J. (2007, October 13). Florida boot camp staff cleared in teen's death. *Reuters*. Retrieved November 22, 2008, from http://in.reuters.com/article/worldNews/idINIndia-29975620071012

Lutze, F. E. (2006). Boot camp prisons and corrections policy: Moving from militarism to an ethic of care. *Criminology & Public Policy, 5*, 389-400.

Lutze, F. E., & Bell, C. A. (2005). Boot camp prisons as masculine organizations: Rethinking recidivism and program design. *Journal of Offender Rehabilitation, 40*, 133-152.

MacKenzie, D. L. (2006). Aftercare following a correctional bootcamp may reduce recidivism. *Criminology & Public Policy, 5*, 359-362.

MacKenzie, D. L., & Armstrong, G. S. (2004). *Correctional boot camps: Military basic training or a model for corrections?* Thousand Oaks, CA: Sage Publishers.

MacKenzie, D. L., Bierie, D., & Mitchell, O. (2007). An experimental study of a therapeutic boot camp: Impact on impulses, attitudes and recidivism. *Journal of Experimental Criminology, 3*, 221-246.

MacKenzie, D. L., & Piquero, A. (1994). The impact of shock incarceration programs on prison crowding. *Crime & Delinquency, 40*, 222-249.

MacKenzie, D. L., & Rosay, A. B. (2004). Correctional boot camps for juveniles. In D.L. MacKenzie & G. S. Armstrong (Eds.), *Correctional boot camps, military basic training or a model for corrections?* (pp. 26-45). Thousand Oaks, CA: Sage.

MacKenzie, D. L., & Souryal, C. (1994). *Multi-site evaluation of shock incarceration: Executive summary*. Washington, DC: National Institution of Justice.

MacKenzie, D. L., & Souryal, C. (1995). Inmates' attitude change during incarceration: A comparison of boot camp with traditional prison, *Justice Quarterly, 12*, 325-354.

MacKenzie, D. L., Wilson, D. B., & Kider, S. (2001). Effects of correctional boot camps on offending. *Annals of the American Academy of Political and Social Sciences, 578*, 126-143.

MacKenzie, D. L., Wilson, D. B., Armstrong, G. S., & Gover, A. R. (2001). The impact of boot camps and traditional institutions on juvenile residents: Perceptions, adjustment, and change. *Journal of Research in Crime and Delinquency, 38*, 279-313.

Markham, C. (2002, February 20). Charges filed against boot camp leaders. *West Valley View* (Arizona), p. 14.

Parent, D. (2003). *Correctional boot camps: Lessons for a decade of research*. Washington, DC: National Institute of Justice.

Peter, M., Thomas, D., & Zamberlan, C. (1997). *Boot camps for juvenile offenders program summary*. Washington, DC: Office of Juvenile Justice and Delinquency Prevention.

Pinal County Sheriff's Office. (1998). *Offense report.* Retrieved November 1, 2008, from http://www.nospank.net/azranch.htm

Riak, J. (2003). *Deadly restraint.* Retrieved September 19, 2008, from www.nospank.net/camps.htm

Styve, G. J., MacKenzie, D. L., Gover, A. R., & Mitchell, O. (2000). Perceived conditions of confinement: A national evaluation of juvenile boot camps and traditional facilities. *Law and Human Behavior, 24,* 297-308.

Tyler, J., Darville, R., & Stalnaker, K. (2001). Juvenile boot camps: A descriptive analysis of program diversity and effectiveness. *Social Science Journal, 38,* 455-471.

Tyler, J., Stalnaker, K., & Darville, R. (1999). Juvenile boot camps: Are they worth the cost? *Texas Probation, XIV,* 15-18.

U. S. Government Accountability Office. (2007). *Residential treatment programs: Concerns regarding abuse and death in certain programs for troubled youth.* Washington, DC: Author.

Wells, J. B., Minor, K. I., Angel, E., & Stearman, K. D. (2006). A quasi-experimental evaluation of a shock incarceration and aftercare program for juvenile offenders. *Youth Violence and Juvenile Justice, 4,* 219-233.

Zaehringer, B. (1998). *Juvenile boot camps: Cost and effectiveness vs. residential facilities.* Koch Crime Institute White Paper Report.

CHAPTER 6
THE DANGERS OF DETENTION

Barry Holman and Jason Ziedenberg

D espite the lowest youth crime rates in 20 years, hundreds of thousands of young people are admitted to and discharged from the nation's 757 secure detention centers each year.[1] Detention centers are intended to temporarily house youth who pose a high risk of reoffending or who are deemed likely not to appear for their court appearances.[2] In most cases, youth who are detained spend a day or two in these placements and are then released to their families. While juvenile detention is intended to be a short-term placement, some youth can spend months in these facilities, especially those accused of being involved in serious offenses.

In 2006, there were about 26,000 youth in detention on any given day and this number is down slightly from 1997 (Sickmund, Sladky, & Kang, 2008). One concern of many advocates for youth is that about two-thirds of these youth are detained for nonviolent offenses (Sickmund et al., 2008). The unnecessary use of secure detention exposes troubled youth to an environment that more closely resembles adult prisons and jails than the kinds of community- and family-based interventions proven to be most effective. Detention centers, said a former Deputy Mayor of New York of that city's infamous Spofford facility, are indistinguishable from a prison (Stertz, 1984). Commenting on New York's detention centers, Supreme Court Justice Marshall said that "fairly viewed, pretrial detention of a juvenile gives rise to injuries comparable to those associated with the imprisonment of an adult" (see Justice Marshall's dissent in *Schall v. Martin*).

Detained youth are frequently held pre-adjudication and awaiting their court dates, or sometimes waiting for a transfer to another facility or community-based program. These youth can spend anywhere from a few days to a few months in locked custody. Very few jurisdictions publish information about average stay in detention, but the Corrections Standards Authority (2007) in California reported that in the first quarter of 2007, youth served an average of 28 days in juvenile halls (p. 5). At best, detained youth are physically and emotionally separated from the families and communities who are the most invested in their recovery and success. Often, detained youth are housed in overcrowded, understaffed facilities—an environment that conspires to breed neglect and violence.

Detention centers do serve a role by temporarily supervising the most at-risk youth. However, with almost 70% held for nonviolent offenses, it is not clear whether the mass detention of youth is necessary, or being borne equally. While youth of color represent about a third of the youth population, the latest figures show that they represent 69% of detained youth (Sickmund et al., 2008). Youth of color are disproportionately detained at higher rates than Whites, even when they engage in delinquent behavior at similar rates as White youth.

The following pages highlight a number of consequences of placing youth in detention. Admitting youth into these facilities may, in some cases, be iatrogenic—meaning that their placement actually leads to harmful effects—especially in terms of the juvenile being at higher risk of injury or self-harm. Moreover, there may be significant long-term legal, educational, and employment-related consequences to incarcerating a youth. The chapter ends with a discussion of some promising alternatives to detention that may save money, reduce crime, and save youth from a life of crime.

The Dangers of Detention

Detention Can Increase Recidivism

Instead of reducing crime, the act of detaining a youth may in fact facilitate increased crime by increasing the likelihood of recidivism. An evaluation of secure detention in Wisconsin, conducted by the state's Joint Legislative Audit Committee, reported that in the four counties studied, 70% of youth held in secure detention were arrested or returned to secure detention within one year of release (Bezruki, Varana, & Hill, 1999). The researchers found that "placement in secure detention may deter a small proportion of juveniles from future criminal activity, although they do not deter most juveniles" (p. 30). Yet, this is not surprising because the risk factors that contributed to the youth's involvement in delinquency and led to the placement in detention will not change unless there is some form of meaningful intervention.

Studies on Arkansas' incarcerated youth found not only a high recidivism rate for incarcerated young people, but that the experience of incarceration is the most significant factor in increasing the odds of recidivism (Benda & Tollet, 1999). Sixty percent of the youth studied were returned to the Department of Youth Services (DYS) within three years. The most significant predictor of recidivism was prior commitment and the odds of returning to DYS increased 13.5 times for youth with a prior commitment. Among the youth incarcerated in Arkansas, two-thirds were confined for nonviolent offenses. Similarly, the crimes that landed the serious offenders under the

94

supervision of adult corrections were overwhelmingly nonviolent, and less than 20% were crimes against persons.

Congregating Delinquents Negatively Affects Youth

Behavioral scientists are finding that bringing youth together for treatment or services may make it more likely that they will engage in delinquent behavior, especially when low-risk youth are mixed with juveniles with higher levels of risk and longer histories of delinquency. Nowhere are deviant youth brought together in greater numbers and density than in detention centers, training schools, and other confined institutions.

While some believe that placing juveniles in detention achieves a "short-sharp-shock" that will deter future delinquency, the opposite might occur. Dishion, McCord, and Poulin (1999) found that congregating youth together for treatment in a group setting causes them to have a higher recidivism rate and poorer outcomes than youth who receive individual treatment. The researchers call this process peer deviancy training and reported statistically significant higher levels of substance abuse, school difficulties, delinquency, violence, and adjustment difficulties in adulthood for those youth treated in a peer group setting. Dishion and colleagues (1999) found that "unintended consequences of grouping children at-risk for externalizing disorders may include negative changes in attitudes toward antisocial behavior, affiliation with antisocial peers, and identification with deviancy"(p. 756). Affiliation with antisocial peers, for instance, may result in recruitment into gangs, which increases the risk of future delinquency.

Studies have shown that once young people are detained, even when controlling for their prior offenses, they are more likely than non-detained youth to end up going deeper into the system (Frazier & Cochran, 1986). Detained youth are more likely to be referred to courts, see their cases progress through the system to adjudication and disposition, have formal dispositions filed against them, and receive more punitive dispositions.

Alternatives to Detention Can Curb Crime and Recidivism

Several studies have shown that youth who are incarcerated are more likely to recidivate than youth who are supervised in a community-based setting or not detained at all. Young people in San Francisco's Detention Diversion Advocacy Program, for example, have about half the recidivism rate of young people who remained in detention or in the juvenile justice system (Shelden, 1999). Research from Texas suggested that young people in community-based placements are 14% less likely to commit future crimes than youth who have been incarcerated (Fendrich & Archer, 1998).

Most young people will engage in some delinquent behavior, but despite high incarceration rates, a relatively small percentage of youth are detained for delinquency. Elliott (1994) has shown that as many as a third of young people will engage in delinquent behavior before they grow up but will naturally "age out" of the delinquent behavior. While this rate of delinquency among young males may seem high, the rate at which they end their criminal behavior (called the desistance rate) is equally high (Sampson & Laub, 1993). Most youth will desist from delinquency by themselves. For those who have more trouble, Elliott has shown that establishing a relationship with a significant other (a partner or mentor) as well as employment usually results in youthful offenders of all races aging out of delinquent behavior as they reach young adulthood.

Whether a youth is detained or not for minor delinquency has lasting ramifications for that youth's future behavior and opportunities. Carnegie Mellon researchers, for example, have shown that incarcerating juveniles may actually interrupt and delay the normal pattern of aging out because detention disrupts their natural engagement with families, school, and work (Golub, 1990).

The Relationship Between Detention and Community Crime

While there is a need to incarcerate some high risk youth, the detention of half a million youth each year is not necessarily reducing crime. During the first part of the 1990s, as juvenile arrests increased, the use of detention rose far faster. By the middle of the 1990s, as juvenile arrests began to plummet (and the number of youth aged 10-17 years in the population leveled off), the use of detention continued to rise. In other words, while there may be some youth who need to be detained to protect themselves (or the public), there is little observed in the relationship between the increased use of detention and crime.

To the contrary, several communities have found ways to reduce both detention and crime, better serving the interests of youth development and public safety. According to the Annie E. Casey Foundation (2008), the following jurisdictions decreased their detention populations between the late 1990s and 2005: Bernalillo County, New Mexico (58%); Cook County, Illinois (37%); Multnomah County, Oregon (65%); and Santa Cruz, California (65%) (p. 1). Yet, community safety was not compromised and the same report shows that arrests for violent offenses dropped between 37% and 54% in these counties. In addition, racial disparities were also reduced at the same time and youth of color were less likely to be incarcerated after alternatives to detention programs were developed (Annie E. Casey Foundation, 2008).

The Impact of Detention on Youths' Mental Health

Of all the various health needs that detention administrators identify among the youth they see, unmet mental and behavioral health needs rise to the top. While researchers estimate that upward of two-thirds of young people in detention centers could meet the criteria for having a mental disorder, a little more than a third need ongoing clinical care—a figure twice the rate of the general adolescent population (Grisso, 2004).

Why is the prevalence of mental illness among detained youth so high? First, detention has become a new dumping ground for young people with mental health issues. In other words, there are few alternative residential placements for youth with mental illness in some jurisdictions. As a result, juvenile detention may be used for youth with emotional troubles who have been involved in some delinquent acts. Whereas the youth's real problem is his or her mental health, the juvenile justice system is used because there is no other place that can provide services to him or her. This problem may be more pronounced in smaller or rural communities that might not have very extensive community-based mental health services (Mendel, 2008).

Current research, for instance, shows that there is a high percentage of youth with psychiatric problems in detention (Teplin, Abram, McClelland, Mericle, Dulcan, & Washburn, 2006). Fazel, Doll, and Langstrom (2008) reported that:

> adolescents in detention and correctional facilities were about 10 times more likely to suffer from psychosis than the general adolescent population. Girls were more often diagnosed with major depression than were boys, contrary to findings from adult prisoners and general population surveys. (p. 1010)

In some places, the juvenile justice system might parallel the adult system. Lamb, Weinberger, and DeCuir (2002), for instance, called adult jails the "place that just can't say no." In other words, people are placed in detention because no alternative exists and the jail or juvenile hall is obliged to take these arrestees. An indicator of the shift was spelled out by a 2004 Special Investigations Division Report of the U. S. House of Representatives, which found that two-thirds of juvenile detention facilities were holding youth who were waiting for community mental health treatment; on any given night, seven percent of all the youth held in detention were waiting for community mental health services (Committee on Government Reform, 2004).

The trauma associated with the rising violence in the late 1980s and early 1990s in some urban centers had a deep and sustained impact on young people (Voisin et al., 2008). At the same time, new laws were enacted that reduced judicial discretion to decide if youth would be detained, decreasing the system's ability to screen out and divert youth with disorders. All the while, community youth mental health systems deteriorated during this decade, leaving detention as the dumping ground for youth with mental health problems. Given the challenges that these youth pose, the operators of juvenile detention facilities would rather have these youth placed in community programs, but what are the alternatives?

Another reason for the rise in the prevalence of youth with mental illnesses in detention is that the kind of environment generated in the nation's detention centers and the conditions of that confinement conspire to create an unhealthy environment. Livsey, Sickmund, and Sladky (2009) found that about 14% of publicly and 4% of privately operated detention centers were overcrowded, which contributes to violence and chaos (see Chapter 9). Far from receiving effective treatment, young people with behavioral health problems simply get worse in detention, not better. Research showed that for one-third of incarcerated youth diagnosed with depression, the onset of the depression occurred after they began their incarceration (Kashani et al., 1980). Forrest, Tambor, Riley, Ensminger, and Starfield (2000) commented that "the transition into incarceration itself may be responsible for some of the observed effect [increased mental illness in detention]" (p. 289).

Research conducted in Oregon shows that 24% of detained youth were found to have suicidal ideation (thinking about suicide) over a seven-day period, with 34% of the youth suffering from a significant level of depression (Mace, Rohde, & Gnau, 1997). As a result, it is possible that poor mental health and the conditions of detention conspire together to generate higher rates of depression and suicide idealization. Yet, it is often difficult to disentangle the impact of placement in detention. Abram and colleagues (2008) conducted a study of youth in detention and reported that over one-third of all detainees (and almost one-half of female residents) had thought about death in the six months prior to being incarcerated (p. 291). In addition, about ten percent of those detainees had actually attempted suicide while living in the community.

Some researchers have found that the rate of suicide in juvenile institutions is about the same as the community (Hayes, 2004, but also see Gallagher & Dobrin, 2007). Others have found that incarcerated youth experience from double to four times the suicide rate of youth in community (Parent, Leiter, Kennedy, Livens, Wentworth, & Wilcox, 1994). Parent and colleagues (1994) reported that 11,000 youth engaged in more than 17,000 acts of suicidal behavior in the juvenile justice system annually. Another monograph published by Office of Juvenile Justice and Delinquency Prevention (OJJDP) found that juvenile correctional facilities sometimes incorporate responses to suicidal threats and behavior in ways that endanger the youth further, such as placing them in isolation (Hayes, 1999).

Suicide in juvenile facilities is the leading cause of death. The Bureau of Justice Statistics (2008) reported that suicide was the cause of almost one-half of all deaths in state operated juvenile correctional facilities. Yet, there are no national-level statistics for deaths in detention facilities, so we do not know the scope of the problem. We do know that a youth's initial placement in detention is a period of very high risk for self-harm; also, suicide reduction programs are more sophisticated today and this subject is examined in Chapter 10.

The Impact of Detention on School and Employment

It has long been recognized that many delinquent youth have histories of school failure (Centers for Disease Control and Prevention, 2007). Juvenile detention can interrupt a young person's education and, once incarcerated, some youth have a hard time returning to school—although this depends on the length of time that a youth is placed in detention, the youth's educational history, parental support, and the willingness of the community school to accept the youth. For some youth who are placed in detention, educators at the facility are able to help them with their studies and help them minimize the harms from having their education interrupted, but this is not always the case (MacDonald, Mitchell, & Moeser, 2007). Yet, a significant problem is that many community schools are reluctant to readmit these troubled youth once they are returned to the community.

An early Department of Education study showed that 43% of incarcerated youth receiving remedial education services in detention did not return to school after release; another 16% enrolled in school but dropped out within five months (LeBlanc, 1991). Another study found that most incarcerated 9th graders return to school after incarceration; but, within a year of re-enrolling, two-thirds to three-fourths withdraw or drop out of school: after four years, less than 15% of these incarcerated 9th graders had completed their secondary education (Balfanz, Spiridakis, Neild, & Legters, 2003).

Young people who leave detention and who do not reattach to schools face collateral risks. High school dropouts face higher unemployment, poorer health (and a shorter life), and earn substantially less than youth who do successfully return and complete school. The failure of detained youth to return to school also affects public safety. The U. S. Department of Education (1994) reported that dropouts are 3.5 times more likely than high school graduates to be arrested. The National Longitudinal Transition Study revealed that approximately 20% of all adolescents with disabilities had been arrested after being out of school for two years (Wagner, D'Amico, Marder, Newman, & Blackorby, 1992).

If detention disrupts educational attainment, it logically follows that detention will also impact the employment opportunities for youth as they spiral down a different direction from their non-detained peers. A growing number of studies show that incarcerating young people has significant immediate and long-term negative employment and economic outcomes.

A study done by the National Bureau of Economic Research found that jailing youth and young adults (aged 16-25 years) reduced work time over the next decade by 25-30% (Freeman, 1991). Looking at individuals aged 14 to 24 years, Western and Beckett (1999) found that youth who spent some time incarcerated in youth facilities experienced three weeks less work a year (for African-American youth, five weeks less work a year) as compared to youth who had no history of incarceration. Due to the disruptions in their education and the natural life processes that allow young people to age out of crime, Bushway (1998) argued that the process of incarceration could actually change an individual into a less stable employee (p. 477).

A monograph published by the National Bureau of Economic Research has shown that incarcerating large numbers of young people seems to have a negative effect on the economic well being of their communities. Places that rely most heavily on incarceration reduce the employment opportunities in their communities compared to places that deal with crime by means other than incarceration. Freeman and Rodgers (1999) observed that "areas with the most rapidly rising rates of incarceration are areas in which youth, particularly African-American youth, have had the worst earnings and employment experience" (p. 14). The loss of potentially stable employees and workers—and of course, county, state, and federal taxpayers—is one of numerous invisible costs that the overuse of detention imposes on the country and on individual communities.

Detention is More Expensive than Alternatives to Detention

The fiscal costs of incarcerating youth are a cause for concern in these budget-strained times. According to Earl Dunlap, head of the National Juvenile Detention Association (now part of the National Partnership for Juvenile Services), the annual average cost per year of a detention bed—depending on geography and cost of living—could range from $32,000 ($87 per day) to as high as $65,000 a year ($178 per day), with some big cities paying far more. Dunlap (2005) said that the cost of building, financing, and operating a single detention bed costs the public between $1.25 and $1.5 million over a 20-year period of time.

By contrast, a number of communities that have invested in alternatives to detention have documented the fiscal savings they achieved in contrast to what they would spend on detaining a youth. The New York City Department of Juvenile Justice (2001) reported that one day in detention ($385) costs 15 times what it does to send a youth to a detention alternative ($25). The Tarrant County, Texas Juvenile Services Department (2004) found that it costs a community 3.5 times as much to detain a youth per day ($121) versus a detention alternative ($35), and even less for electronic monitoring ($3.75).

There will always be a need for juvenile detention: some youth are dangerous to the community and others require a period of assessment and stabilization prior to returning home. Given those facts, detention must be used sparingly and only for the youth who most require such a setting. Risk assessments and other objective tools might be able to help guide these decisions (Gebo, Stracuzzi, & Hurst, 2006). If juveniles are placed in these facilities, they must be professionally operated, appropriately staffed and funded, and have a high degree of oversight—factors discussed in Chapter 17.

Detention is Not Cost Effective

Whether compared to alternatives in the here and now—or put to rigorous economic efficiency models that account for the long-term costs of crime and incarceration over time—juvenile detention is not always a cost-effective way of promoting public safety or meeting the needs of the youth who are detained.

The Washington State Institute for Public Policy (WSIPP), a non-partisan research institution that, at legislative direction, studies issues of importance to Washington State, was directed to study the cost effectiveness of the state's juvenile justice system. WSIPP found that there had been a 43% increase in juvenile justice spending during the 1990s and that the main factor driving those expenditures was the confinement of juvenile offenders. While this increase in spending and juvenile incarceration was associated with a decrease in juvenile crime, Aos (2002) found "the effect of detention on lower crime rates has decreased in recent years as the system expanded. The lesson: confinement works, but it is an expensive way to lower crime rates" (p.3). Aos (2002) noted that the legislature directed them to take the next step and answer the question, "Are there less expensive ways to reduce juvenile crime?" (p. 3).

WSIPP found that for every dollar spent on county juvenile detention systems, $1.98 of benefits in terms of reduced crime and costs of crime to taxpayers was achieved. By sharp contrast, diversion and mentoring programs produced $3.36 of benefits for every dollar spent, aggression replacement training produced $10.00 of benefits for every dollar spent, and multi-systemic therapy produced $13.00 of benefits for every dollar spent. A juvenile justice system that concentrates juvenile justice spending on detention or confinement drains available funds away from interventions that may be more effective at reducing recidivism and promoting public safety. Follow-up studies have recently reported similar benefits from delinquency reduction interventions based on diverting youth from the court system and traditional out-of-home placements (Drake, 2007).

Given the finding by Cohen and Piquero (2009) that the cost of a youth offender's crimes and incarceration over his or her lifetime (including adult) can cost as much as $2.6 to 5.3 million (p. 25), a front-end investment in interventions proven to help young people would seem to be more effective public safety spending.

The Rise of Youth Detention: Policy or Politics?

With falling youth crime rates and a growing body of research that shows that alternatives are less expensive and more effective than detention, why do juvenile justice systems continue to spend valuable resources building more locked facilities to detain low-risk youth? Similar to the fate of the adult criminal justice system, the traditional mission of the juvenile justice system has been altered by the politicization of crime policy in this country.

At the turn of the century, when reformers developed the nation's first juvenile court in Chicago, Illinois, they set up a separate system for youth to meet the needs of adolescents, acknowledging that youth have different levels of culpability and capacity than adults. They also believed that youth deserved a second chance at rehabilitation. Within 30 years, every state in the nation had a juvenile court system based on the premise that young people were developmentally different than adults.

But the tough-on-crime concerns of the 1980s and 1990s changed the priorities and orientation of the juvenile justice system. Rising warnings of youth super-predators, school shootings, and the excessive media reporting of serious episodes of juvenile crime in the biggest cities fueled political momentum to make the system tougher on kids (Feld, 2003). By the end of the 1990s, every state in the nation had changed their laws in some way to make it easier to incarcerate youth in the adult system. As many states made their juvenile justice systems more punitive, the courts placed more youth in detention.

CHAPTER 6: THE DANGERS OF DETENTION

The Rise of Youth Detention Borne by Youth of Color

The rapid expansion of the use of juvenile detention has hit some communities harder than others. From 1985 to 1995, the number of youth held in secure detention nationwide increased by 72%. But during this time, the proportion of White youth in detention actually dropped, while youth of color came to represent a majority of the young people detained. The detained White youth population increased by 21%, while the detained minority youth population grew by 76%. By 1997, in 30 out of 50 states (which contain 83% of the U. S. population) minority youth represented the majority of youth in detention (Sickmund & Snyder, 1997). Even in states with tiny ethnic and racial minority populations (like Minnesota, where the general population is 90% White, and Pennsylvania, where the general population is 85% White), more than half of the detention population are youth of color. In 1997, the OJJDP found that in every state in the country (with the exception of Vermont), the minority population of detained youth exceeded their proportion in the general population (Snyder & Sickmund, 1999).

The latest figures show that the shift in the demographics of detention that occurred during the 1980s and 1990s continues today. In 2003, African-American youth were detained at a rate 4.5 times higher than Whites and Latino youth were detained at twice the rate of Whites. Minority youth represented 69% of all youth detained in 2006 (Sickmund et al., 2008).

The greatest levels of racial disparity in the use of detention are found in the least serious offense categories. For example, surveys from the late 1990s found that Whites used and sold drugs at rates similar to other races and ethnicities, but that African-Americans were detained for drug offenses at more than one and a half times the rate of Whites (Sickmund, 2004). White youth self reported using heroin and cocaine at six times the rate of African-American youth, but African-American youth are almost three times as likely to be detained for a drug crime (Sickmund et al., 2008). On any given day, African-Americans comprise nearly half of all youth in the United States detained for drug offenses (Sickmund et al., 2008).

The causes of the disproportionate detention of youth of color are rooted in some of the nation's deepest social problems, many of which may play out in key decision-making points in the juvenile justice system—from taking a youth into custody, deciding whether to detain him or her, whether a prosecutor will proceed with the case (or rely on an alternative to formal court processing), and the decisions of the court (Leiber & Fox, 2005). Furthermore, the problem of disproportionate minority contact (DMC) seems almost intractable in juvenile justice systems (Kempf-Leonard, 2007).

In many jurisdictions, juvenile officers make the decision about whether a youth will be detained or released to his or her parents or guardians. These officials may allow stereotypes to influence their decision. One study shows that juvenile officers charged with the decision of holding youth prior to adjudication are more likely to say a White youth's crimes are a product of his or her environment (e.g., a broken home), while an African-American youth's delinquency is caused by personal failings—even when youth of different races are arrested for similar offenses and have similar offense histories (Bridges & Steen, 1998). One of the key issues in juvenile justice is DMC and, in the chapters that follow, a number of strategies are outlined for reducing this problem.

Juvenile Detention Reforms Taking Hold Across the Nation

The way to reduce the impact of detention on young people is to lower the number of youth needlessly or inappropriately detained. The Juvenile Detention Alternatives Initiative (JDAI)—an initiative of the Annie E. Casey Foundation—is a response to the inappropriate and unnecessary detention of youth in the nation's juvenile justice systems. JDAI is a public-private partnership being implemented nationwide and pioneering jurisdictions, which include: Santa Cruz County, California; Multnomah County (Portland), Oregon; Bernalillo County (Albuquerque), New Mexico; and Cook County (Chicago), Illinois.

JDAI is a process, not a conventional program, whose goal is to make sure that locked detention is used only when necessary. In pursuing that goal, JDAI restructures the surrounding systems to create improvements that reach far beyond detention alone. To achieve reductions in detention populations, the JDAI model developed a series of core strategies, which include:

- Inter-governmental collaboration: bringing together the key actors in the juvenile justice system—especially courts, probation, and the police—as well as actors outside the justice system, such as schools and mental health.
- Reliance on data: beginning with data collection and leading to continuous analysis of data as well as the cultural expectation that decisions will be based on information and results.
- Objective admissions screening: developing risk-assessment instruments and changing procedures so they are always used to guide detention decisions.

- Alternatives to secure confinement: creating programs and services in the community to ensure appearance and good behavior pending disposition and to be available as an option at sentencing.
- Expedited case processing: to move cases along so youth don't languish in detention for unnecessarily long time periods.
- Improved handling of "special cases": youth who are detained for technical probation violations, outstanding warrants, and pending services or placement create special management problems and need special approaches.
- Express strategies to reduce racial disparities: "good government" reforms alone do not eliminate disparities; specific attention is needed to achieve this goal.
- Improving conditions of confinement: to ensure that the smaller number of youth who still require secure detention are treated safely, legally, and humanely.

The fundamental measure of JDAI's success is straightforward: a reduction in the number of youth confined on any day and admitted to detention over the course of a year and a reduction in the number of young people exposed to the dangers inherent in detention.

Decreasing the use of detention has not jeopardized public safety. In the counties implementing JDAI, juvenile crime rates fell as much as, or more than, national decreases in juvenile crime (Annie E. Casey Foundation, 2008). These communities have also experienced an improvement in the number of young people who appear in court after they have been released from detention, further reducing the need for detention. In some cases, the cost savings from JDAI have local governments questioning whether their detention facilities should remain open. An April 2008 newspaper article highlighted how the Monmouth County, New Jersey Sheriff is considering closing the Youth Detention Center because average daily populations dropped (Jordan, 2008).

Like the impact of detention, which can extend beyond the walls of the locked facility, reducing detention populations influences the entire juvenile justice system. Cities and counties engaged in detention reform also note their progress by their acceptance in the community. Cook County officials engaged youth in the system and their parents for advice about how to improve the system—they persevered (and supported the staff) through some daunting complaints. In the aftermath, the probation department adjusted its office hours and locations and changed the way it communicated with clients and their families. Now, community members are genuinely engaged in decisions including policy formulation, program development, and hiring. It is not a formal measure, but it leads to improved services and priceless levels of respect and engagement in the community.

Rural Detention Reform

There is increasing interest in the operations of justice systems in rural areas. Historically, criminologists paid little attention to what occurred in rural areas, but the fact is that at least 59 million Americans live in rural areas (Tarmann, 2003). Justice systems in these communities often have fewer community-based resources and facilities are often underfunded. Mendel (2008) outlined a number of reasons why detention reform is necessary in rural communities and they are summarized as follows:

- A substantial share of America's youth and America's delinquency problem resides in rural America.
- Rural areas face different and often more difficult challenges than urban communities in operating detention programs and in implementing detention reform.
- Rural jurisdictions have identified a number of innovative strategies and promising practices for addressing the special challenges of rural detention reform.
- Bringing detention reform only to urban and suburban communities and not to rural areas would allow an unacceptable double standard in the treatment of court-involved youths. (pp. 14-15)

There are numerous challenges to providing services to youth from rural areas that are not consistent with juvenile courts in urban areas. Fewer juveniles are arrested and a youth might be detained for a longer period of time before his or her court date. In addition, there might not be detention facilities in many rural counties and youth might be held in adult jails.

Mendel (2008) provided several examples of jurisdictions that have implemented alternatives to detention programs. He reported that smaller counties have entered into partnerships between juvenile justice agencies, have introduced risk-assessment instruments (to increase consistency in detention decisions), and have developed community-based alternatives to detention. Such changes, however, are not always easy to implement and juvenile justice systems have long histories of resisting reform (Feld, 1999). Furthermore, reform in rural areas can be frustrated by the small tax base, long travel distances, and small caseloads. Ultimately, however, Mendel (2008) argued that what is needed is "determined leadership to drive the detention reform process and to develop a consensus among local officials in support of detention reform's underlying principles" (p. 57).

A Better Future: Invest Juvenile Justice Funds in Programs Proven to Work

If detention reform is successful, communities should be able to reinvest the funds that are spent on detention beds and new detention centers in other youth-serving systems or other interventions proven to reduce recidivism. The Center for the Study and Prevention of Violence, the Office of Juvenile Justice and Delinquency Prevention, the Washington State Institute for Public Policy, and other research institutes have shown that several programs and initiatives are proven to reduce recidivism and crime in a cost effective matter. Some common elements in proven programs include:

- Treatment occurs with their families or in a family-like setting.
- Treatment occurs at home or close to home.
- Services are delivered in a culturally respectful and competent manner.
- Treatment is built around the youth and family strengths.
- A wide range of services and resources are delivered to the youth, as well as their families.

Most of these successful programs are designed to serve the needs of youth in family-like settings, situated as close to home as possible with services delivered in a culturally sensitive and competent manner.

These proven programs identify the various aspects of youth — their strengths and weaknesses as well as the strengths and resources of their families and communities. Progress is based on realistic outcomes and carefully matches the particular needs of the youth and family to the appropriate intervention strategy.

Endnotes

1. This chapter was initially published as a report by the Justice Policy Institute (JPI), who received funding from the Annie E. Casey Foundation to conduct the research. In addition to changes in formatting, this chapter was updated and includes citations from recent research.
2. Schiraldi and Ziedenberg (2003) defined detention as a form of locked custody of youth pre-trial who are arrested. Juvenile detention centers are the juvenile justice system's version of "jail," in which most young people are being held before the court has judged them delinquent. Some

youth in detention are there because they fail the conditions of their probation or parole or they may be waiting in detention before their final disposition (e.g., sentence to a community program or juvenile correctional facility).

Case Cited

Schall v. Martin 467 U. S. 253 (1984)

References

Abram, K. M., Choe, J. Y., Washburn, J. J., Teplin, L. A., King, D. C., & Dulcan, M. K. (2008). Suicidal ideation and behaviors among youths in juvenile detention. *Child & Adolescent Psychiatry, 47*, 291-300.

Annie E. Casey Foundation. (2008). *Results from the Juvenile Detention Alternatives Initiative.* Retrieved October 24, 2008, from http://www.aecf.org/MajorInitiatives/JuvenileDetentionAlternativesInitiative/JDAIResults.aspx

Aos, S. (2002). *The juvenile justice system in Washington State: Recommendations to improve cost-effectiveness.* Olympia, WA: Washington State Institute for Public Policy.

Balfanz, R., Spiridakis, K., Neild, R., & Legters, N. (2003, May). *Neighborhood schools and the juvenile justice system: How neither helps the other and how that could change.* Presented at the School to Prison Pipeline Conference, Boston, MA.

Benda, B. B., & Tollet, C. L. (1999). A study of recidivism of serious and persistent offenders among adolescents. *Journal of Criminal Justice, 27*, 111-126.

Bezruki, D., Varana, D., & Hill, C. (1999). *An evaluation of secure juvenile detention.* Madison WI: Legislative Audit Bureau.

Bridges, G., & Steen, S. (1998). Racial disparities in official assessments of juvenile offenders: Attributional stereotypes as mediating mechanisms. *American Sociological Review, 63*, 554-570.

Bureau of Justice Statistics. (2008). *State juvenile correctional facility deaths, 2002-2005.* Retrieved September 20, 2008, from http://www.ojp.usdoj.gov/bjs/dcrp/tables/juvtab1.htm

Bushway, S. D. (1998). The impact of an arrest on the job stability of young white American men. *Journal of Research in Crime and Delinquency, 34*, 454-479.

Centers for Disease Control and Prevention. (2007). *Youth violence prevention.* Retrieved September 20, 2008, from http://www.cdc.gov/ncipc/dvp/YVP/YVP-risk-p-factors.htm

Cohen, M. A., & Piquero, A. R. (2009). New evidence on the monetary value of saving a high risk youth. *Journal of Quantitative Criminology, 25*, 25-49.

Committee on Government Reform, Special Investigations Division, Minority Staff. (2004). *Incarceration of youth who are waiting for community mental health services in the United States.* Retrieved September 20, 2008, from www.house.gov/reform/min

Committee on Government Reform, Special Investigations Division, Minority Staff. (2004). *Incarceration of youth with mental health disorders in New Mexico.* Retrieved September 20, 2008, from www.house.gov/reform/min

Corrections Standards Authority. (2007). *Juvenile detention profile survey.* Retrieved October 25, 2008, from http://www.cdcr.ca.gov/Divisions_Boards/CSA/FSO/Docs/1Q07_JDS_full_report.pdf

Dishion, T. J., McCord, J., & Poulin, F. (1999). When interventions harm: Peer groups and problem behavior. *American Psychologist, 54,* 755-764.

Drake, E. (2007). *Evidence-based juvenile offender programs: Program description, quality assurance, and costs.* Olympia, WA: Washington State Institute for Public Policy.

Dunlap, E. (2005, July 29). Personal correspondence.

Elliot, D. S. (1994). Serious violent offenders: Onset, developmental course, and termination. *Criminology, 32,* 1-21.

Fazel, S., Doll, H. M., & Langstrom, N. (2008). Mental disorders among adolescents in juvenile detention and correctional facilities: A systematic review and metaregression analysis of 25 surveys. *Child & Adolescent Psychiatry, 47,* 1010-1019.

Federal Bureau of Investigation. (1997). *Crime in the United States, 1996.* Washington, DC: Author.

Federal Bureau of Investigation. (2003). *Crime in the United States, 2002.* Washington, DC: Author.

Feld, B. (1999). *Bad kids: Race and the transformation of the juvenile court.* New York: Oxford University Press.

Feld, B. (2003). The politics of race and juvenile justice: The "due process revolution" and the conservative reaction. *Justice Quarterly, 20,* 765-800.

Fendrich, M., & Archer, M. (1998). Long-term re-arrest rates in a sample of adjudicated delinquents: Evaluating the impact of alternative programs. *The Prison Journal, 78,* 360-389.

Forrest, C. B., Tambor, E., Riley, A. W., Ensminger, M. E., & Starfield, B. (2000). The health profile of incarcerated male youths. *Pediatrics, 105,* 286-292.

Frazier, C. E., & Cochran, J. C. (1999). Detention of juveniles: Its effects on subsequent juvenile court processing decisions. *Youth and Society, 17,* 286-305.

Freeman, R. B. (1991). *Crime and the employment disadvantage of youth.* Cambridge, MA: National Bureau of Economic Research.

Freeman, R. B., & Rogers, W. M. (1999). *Area economic conditions and the labor market outcomes of young men in the 1990s expansion.* Cambridge, MA: National Bureau of Economic Research.

Gallagher, C. A., & Dobrin, A. (2007). Risk of suicide in juvenile justice facilities. *Criminal Justice & Behavior, 34,* 1362-1376.

Gebo, E., Stracuzzi, N. F., & Hurst, V. (2006). Juvenile justice reform and the courtroom workgroup: Issues of perception and workload. *Journal of Criminal Justice, 34,* 425-433.

Golub, A. (1990). *The termination rate of adult criminal careers.* Pittsburgh: Carnegie Mellon.

Grisso, T. (2004). *Double jeopardy: Adolescent offenders with mental disorders.* Chicago: University of Chicago Press.

Hayes, L. (1999). *Suicide prevention in juvenile correction and detention facilities.* Washington, DC: Office of Juvenile Justice and Delinquency Prevention.

Hayes, L. (2004). *Juvenile suicide in confinement: A national perspective.* Retrieved November 23, 2008, from http://www.ncjrs.org/pdffiles1/ojjdp/grants/206354.pdf

Jordan, B. (2008). Juvenile lockup could be closed: Detainee total down; costs up. *Asbury Park Press.* Retrieved May 6, 2008, from www.app.com

Lamb, H. R., Weinberger, L. E., & DeCuir, W. J. (2002). The police and mental health. *Psychiatric Services, 53,* 1266-1271.

Kashani, J. H., Manning, G. W., McKnew, D. H., Cytryn, L., Simonds, J. F., & Wooderson, P. C. (1980). Depression among incarcerated delinquents. *Psychiatry Resources, 3,* 185-191.

Kempf-Leonard, K. (2007). Minority youths and juvenile justice. *Youth Violence and Juvenile Justice, 5,* 71-87.

LeBlanc, L. A. (1991). *Unlocking learning: Chapter 1 in correctional facilities.* Washington, DC: U. S. Department of Education.

Leiber, M. J., & Fox, K. C. (2005). Race and the impact of detention on juvenile justice decision making. *Crime & Delinquency, 51,* 470-497.

Livsey, S., Sickmund, M., & Sladky, A. (2009). *Juvenile residential facility census, 2004: Selected findings.* Washington, DC: Office of Juvenile Justice and Delinquency Prevention.

Mace, D., Rohde, P., & Gnau, V. (1997). Psychological patterns of depression and suicidal behavior of adolescents in a juvenile detention facility. *Journal of Juvenile Justice and Detention Services, 12,* 18-23.

Mendel, R. A. (2008). *Detention reform in rural jurisdictions: Challenges and opportunities.* Retrieved November 1, 2008, from http://www.aecf.org/~/media/PublicationFiles/15_Rural_Pathways_r20.pdf

MacDonald, S., Mitchell, D. E., & Moeser, J. (2007). Defining reentry for short-term stays. In C. Rapp Zimmerman, G. Hendrix, J. Moeser, & D. W. Roush (Eds.), *Desktop guide to reentry for juvenile confinement facilities,* (pp. 65-77). Annapolis, MD: American Correctional Association.

Parent, D. G., Leiter, V., Kennedy, S., Livens, L., Wentworth, D., & Wilcox, S. (1994). *Conditions of confinement: Juvenile detention and corrections facilities.* Washington, DC: Office of Juvenile Justice and Delinquency Prevention.

Sampson, R., & Laub, J. (1993). *Crime in the making: Pathways and turning points through life.* Cambridge, MA: Harvard University Press.

Schiraldi, V., & Ziedenberg, J. (2003). *The Multnomah experiment: Reducing disproportionate minority confinement.* Washington, DC: The Justice Policy Institute.

Shelden, R. G. (1999). *Detention diversion advocacy: An Evaluation.* Washington, DC: Office of Juvenile Justice and Delinquency Prevention.

Sickmund, M. (2004). *Juveniles in corrections.* Washington, DC: Office of Juvenile Justice and Delinquency Prevention.

Sickmund, M., Sladky, T. J., & Wang, W. (2008). *Census of juveniles in residential placement databook.* Retrieved May 31, 2008, from www.ojjdp.ncjrs.org/ojstabb/cjrp/

Sickmund, M., & Snyder, H. (1997). *Juvenile offenders and victims: 1997 update on violence, statistical summary.* Washington, DC: Office of Juvenile Justice and Delinquency Prevention.

Snyder, H., & Sickmund, M. (1999). *Juvenile offenders and victims: 1999 national report.* Washington, DC: Office of Juvenile Justice and Delinquency Prevention.

Snyder, H. (2005). Is suicide more common inside or outside of juvenile facilities? *Corrections Today, 67,* 84-85.

Tarmann, A. (2003). *Fifty years of demographic change in rural America.* Retrieved July 22, 2006, from http://www.prb.org/rfdcenter/50yearsofchange.htm

Teplin, L. A., Abram, K. M., McClelland, G. M., Mericle, A. A., Dulcan, M. K., & Washburn, J. J. (2006). *Psychiatric disorders of youth in detention.* Washington, DC: Office of Juvenile Justice and Delinquency Prevention.

U. S. Department of Education. (1994). *Mini-digest of education statistics.* Washington, DC: National Center for Education Statistics.

Voisin, D. R., Salazar, L. F., Crosby, R., DiClemente, R. J., Yarber, W. L., & Staples-Horne, M. (2008). Witnessing community violence and health-related risk behaviors among detained juveniles. *American Journal of Orthopsychiatry, 77,* 506-513.

Wagner, M., D'Amico, R., Marder, C., Newman, L., & Blackorby, J. (1992). *What happens next? Trends in postschool outcomes of youth with disabilities.* The second comprehensive report from the national longitudinal transition study of special education students. Menlo Park, CA: SRT International.

Western, B., & Beckett, K. (1999). How unregulated is the U. S. Labor market? The penal system as a labor market institution. *The American Journal of Sociology, 104,* 1030-1060.

CHAPTER 7
KIDS IN THE BIG HOUSE: JUVENILES INCARCERATED IN ADULT FACILITIES

Margaret E. Leigey, Jessica P. Hodge and Christine A. Saum

Writing for the majority of the United States Supreme Court in *Kent v. United States* (1966), Justice Fortas wrote of the "tremendous consequences" associated with trying juveniles as adults (p. 554). However, it is not clear what specific ramifications he was referencing. Was he referring to incarceration with adult inmates, one potential outcome of an adult conviction for juvenile offenders,[1] and the subsequent increased risk of physical and sexual abuse (Bishop & Frazier, 2000; Glick & Sturgeon, 2001) or the increased risk of suicide for juveniles held in adult facilities (Memory, 1989; Mumola, 2005)? Or was Justice Fortas considering the collateral consequences of an adult felony conviction, such as the loss of the right to vote or diminished employment opportunities (Allard & Young, 2002; Redding, 1999)? This chapter examines the characteristics of juvenile offenders who are incarcerated in adult institutions, highlights various aspects of daily life as experienced by juveniles in such facilities, and presents issues associated with not only waiving juveniles to adult court but also incarcerating juvenile offenders with adults.

While avenues have always existed by which juveniles could be transferred into adult court, there has been an increase in the past two decades of the different types of mechanisms available for juvenile offenders to be waived into adult criminal court (Myers, 2003). The juvenile justice system has been criticized for failing to rehabilitate offenders—which is the guiding principle behind the establishment of a separate system for juveniles (Fagan, 1990; Jensen & Metsger, 1994)—or deterring juvenile offending, as evidenced by high rates of juvenile violence that started in the 1980s and peaked in 1993 (Centers for Disease Control and Prevention, 2007; Steiner & Wright, 2006). Other criticisms are related to the lenient treatment of juvenile offenders (Fritsch, Caeti, & Hemmens, 1996a; Myers, 2003). Some critics believe that the system has risked public safety by failing to incapacitate violent juvenile offenders (Fagan, 1996; Myers, 2003) or failed to properly address the serious offenses committed by some juvenile offenders (Myers, 2003). Consequently, one expression of the "get tough" attitude necessary to manage or deter

113

serious juvenile offending is the transfer into the adult system, where juvenile offenders would receive a more severe punishment and deterrence has a greater likelihood of being achieved (Austin, Johnson, & Gregoriou, 2000; Centers for Disease Control and Prevention, 2007; Myers, 2003).

Juvenile offenders are transferred[2] into the adult system by one of three types of waivers: (a) judicial waiver; (b) prosecutorial waiver, also referred to as direct file; or (c) legislative waiver, also known as statutory exclusion (Steiner & Wright, 2006). As part of a blended sentence, a judge can also impose a mix of juvenile and adult penalties, such as transfer to an adult facility when the offender reaches a specified age (Wolfson, 2005). In states with "once an adult, always an adult" legislation, juvenile offenders are subject to prosecution in adult court in future cases (Griffin et al., 1998). Juveniles legally emancipated from parental authority, would also be under the jurisdiction of the adult criminal court (Martin, 2005).

If transferred into the adult system, juveniles are generally eligible for the same types of criminal sanctions as any adult defendant, such as confinement, which could include life without the possibility of parole (Hartney, 2006; Leighton & de la Vega, 2007). Currently, the only sentence juveniles are ineligible to receive in the adult court, as decided in the case of *Roper v. Simmons* (2005), is the death penalty. However, between 1973 and 2005, death sentences were handed down to 226 offenders who were under 18 years of age at the time of their offenses (Streib, 2005).

Juveniles in Adult Correctional Facilities

Research indicates that a sizeable number of juveniles who are convicted in adult court receive a sentence of incarceration and, depending upon the length of the sentence, serve their sentences in either jails or prisons (Fagan, 1996; Kupchik, 2006). However, there is wide variability in the estimates of how many juveniles receive sentences of confinement. For example, in a sample of 40 urban counties, Rainville & Smith (2003) found that approximately 64% of juveniles who were convicted in adult criminal court were incarcerated in either prison or jail, with a prison sentence being the more likely option.[3] Alternatively, in his study comparing juvenile defendants adjudicated in the New Jersey juvenile justice system to juvenile defendants who were processed in the adult criminal court in New York, Kupchik (2006) found that approximately 35% of juveniles convicted in adult court received a sentence of incarceration. The Bureau of Justice Statistics estimates that there were approximately 7,400 persons under the age of 18 years admitted to state prisons and another 9,100 juveniles held in jails in 1997 (Strom, 2000) either awaiting trial or sentencing, serving sentences of less than one year, or awaiting transfer to another institution.[4] While it appears that pre-adjudication detention is more common for juvenile defendants in the adult system as compared to in the juvenile justice system (Kupchik, 2006), it is uncommon for juveniles who are convicted as adults to be incarcerated in private facilities (Stephan & Karberg, 2003).[5]

Strom (2000) provided the most recent profile of juveniles who have been convicted and incarcerated in state prisons during 1985-1997.[6] The number of individuals under the age of 18 years who were admitted to state prisons more than doubled from 3,400 in 1985 to 7,400 in 1997 (Strom, 2000). The percentage of juvenile offenders admitted to adult state facilities has, however, remained consistent, as they comprised approximately two percent of new inmate admissions for each year in the period 1985-1997 (Strom, 2000). In other words, juveniles who are incarcerated in adult prisons encompass a small fraction of inmates who enter the state prisons each year. While the population is small, it appears to be relatively common for jurisdictions to confine juvenile offenders in adult institutions. For example, in a survey of 54 jurisdictions, including jails and prisons, Austin et al. (2000) found that 87% of the surveyed jurisdictions reported housing juveniles in adult facilities.

Of the juveniles who were admitted to state facilities in 1997, the vast majority were males (97%) and a disproportionate number were minorities (Strom, 2000). About one-quarter were White non-Hispanic, 58% were Black non-Hispanic, 15% were Hispanic, and two percent were identified as Other (Strom, 2000). The disproportionate number of minority juveniles who are incarcerated in adult prisons raises concerns over fairness in the administration of both the juvenile and criminal justice systems (Campaign for Youth Justice, 2007; Hartney & Silva, 2007).[7]

About 95% of juvenile offenders admitted to adult facilities in 1997 were 16 or 17 years of age (Strom, 2000). It appears that educational deficiencies are common in this population, as only five percent of the juveniles who were admitted were 15 years or under; however, 28% had a level of education of eighth grade or less (Strom, 2000). Strom (2000) also reported that 61% of the juveniles had been convicted of violent offenses, followed by property crimes (21%), drug offenses (11%), and crimes against the public order (5%).

Three trends influence the number of youth in adult prisons: the likelihood of receiving a prison sentence, the length of the prison sentence received, and the actual time served while incarcerated. The likelihood of receiving a prison sentence had increased in the period from 1985 to 1997 (Strom, 2000). To put it another way, there was an increase in the likelihood that juveniles would receive a sentence of incarceration as opposed to community-based sanctions, such as probation, house arrest, or electronic monitoring (Strom, 2000). Additionally, while the average length of sentences in 1997 had decreased slightly to 82 months from the average length of sentences imposed in 1985 of 86 months, the average time served had increased from 35 months in 1985 to 44 months in 1997. Although juvenile offenders were receiving shorter sentences, they were serving longer portions of them. This was especially true for violent offenders, as the average length of actual time served for violent offenses increased from 47 to 59 months (Strom, 2000).

Differences Between Juvenile and Adult Facilities

The Juvenile Justice Delinquency and Prevention Act of 1974 (JJDPA) required that juvenile offenders who are being processed in the juvenile justice system must be separated (in sight and sound) from adult offenders, but this protective measure is not always applied to juveniles being prosecuted in adult criminal court (Austin et al., 2000). In fact, jurisdictions utilize a variety of housing options for juvenile offenders convicted and sentenced to confinement by an adult court. The federal system, for instance, maintains a policy of separating juvenile offenders from adult inmates, as federal law requires that juvenile offenders who are convicted in federal adult court be sent to juvenile facilities (Hartney, 2006).

States vary in their placement of juveniles in adult correctional facilities. Austin et al. (2000) found that 43 states and the District of Columbia incarcerated juvenile offenders in adult jails and prisons. Of these 44 jurisdictions, 17 states and the District of Columbia had separate housing units for juvenile offenders (Austin et al., 2000). However, according to Austin and colleagues (2000), two cautions must be mentioned that may influence these estimates. First, juveniles might be held with adult inmates if the segregated housing area is overcrowded (Austin et al., 2000). Second, of the jurisdictions surveyed, some employed a broader definition of youthful offenders that included young adults, such as inmates under the age of 25 years (Austin et al., 2000). In addition, even if juveniles are housed in separate units, they may still be exposed to adult inmates when receiving services in the institution (e.g., when receiving treatment in a prison's medical unit).

Like incarcerated adults, juveniles experience the same pains of imprisonment, such as the deprivations of liberty, autonomy, security, heterosexual relationships, and goods and services (Sykes, 1958). Adult prisons, however, tend to be larger and more formidable than juvenile facilities (Bishop & Frazier, 2000). Moreover, a higher proportion of staff members in adult facilities, such as correctional officers, are focused on custody and security rather than treatment (Bishop & Frazier, 2000). When combined, these factors can create a disorienting and stressful experience for juveniles. For example, one 16-year-old juvenile offender characterized his placement in prison as similar to visiting a foreign land: "Coming up here for a kid is like emigrating to another country. You have to learn the language, the customs, the people, the ropes" (Eisikovits & Baizerman, 1982, p. 9).

To further compound the challenges imprisoned juveniles face, they must also negotiate a variety of critical developmental transitions while incarcerated, including biological, psychological, cognitive, and social changes (Owens, 1999; Woolard, Odgers, Lanza-Kaduce, & Daglis, 2005). The long-term impacts on their self identity, social relations, and coping skills are unknown for juveniles who have experienced these milestones in adolescent development while confined. It is likely, however, that the normally difficult transition to adulthood is sufficiently complicated by the challenges for youth incarcerated in adult facilities (Saum, Gray, & Walters, 2006).

Daily Life

Despite the increase in the number of juveniles serving time in adult facilities, relatively little is known about their experiences (Woolard et al., 2005). There have only been a few in-depth studies conducted with male juvenile offenders who were tried as adults and are serving sentences in adult prisons. All of these studies compared the experiences, attitudes, and perceptions of juvenile offenders in adult facilities with those of juvenile offenders held in juvenile facilities.[8]

While there is little known about male juvenile offenders, there is even less research about the correctional experiences of female juvenile offenders in adult jails or prisons (Campaign for Youth Justice, 2007). In fact, only one study has focused on this population.[9] Past research, however, has attempted to document the consequences of detaining girls in adult jails. As Chesney-Lind and Shelden (1992) explained, adult jails are "woefully ill-equipped to house juvenile females," which often results in young girls being held in solitary confinement (p. 155). Due to the isolation, lack of supervision, and the fact that a significant number of these girls have histories of physical and sexual abuse, solitary confinement can often lead to tragic results such as suicide (Chesney-Lind & Shelden, 1992).

Victimization

Daily survival is a major concern for youth serving time in adult institutions (Abramsky, 2001; Eisikovits & Baizerman, 1982; Lane et al., 2002). Specifically, they are fearful of victimization (Eisikovits & Baizerman, 1982). There are several explanations for the vulnerability of juvenile offenders in adult facilities. While residents interviewed in juvenile facilities reported being powerful and having high statuses (because of their size, strength, or previous experience with confinement), juveniles in adult facilities reported that they were continually reminded of their low statuses (Eisikovits & Baizerman, 1982; Forst et al., 1989). Prison status is synonymous with toughness. Like adult prisoners, juvenile inmates may be forced to demonstrate their toughness by engaging in verbal or physical displays of aggression (Bishop & Frazier, 2000). However, because of their smaller statures, they are unlikely to be successful in these physical confrontations with adult inmates (Beyer, 1997). Juvenile offenders, because of their immaturity, may also be more susceptible to peer pressure and use violence after being bullied or manipulated by other inmates (Beyer, 1997; Bishop & Frazier, 2000).

Previous research suggests that juveniles are at a higher risk of physical, sexual, and economic victimization in adult prisons compared to residents in juvenile institutions (Beyer, 1997; Bishop & Frazier, 2000; LaFree, 2002). Forst and colleagues (1989) found that a higher percentage of juvenile offenders in adult prisons were victimized compared with their counterparts in juvenile facilities. About nine percent of the juveniles in adult prisons reported being physically assaulted by an inmate compared with 6.8% of those in juvenile placements. Use of a weapon was also more common in prisons and 32.1% of juveniles in these facilities reported the use of a weapon in an attack, compared to 23.7% of the youth confined in juvenile facilities. In regard to economic victimization, a higher percentage of juveniles in adult facilities reported theft of property compared to respondents in juvenile facilities (48.1% vs. 44.1%), destruction of personal property (18.5% vs. 16.9%), and the surrender of property by force or threat of injury (18.5% vs. 15.3%) (Forst et al., 1989). One limitation of these data, however, is that they are two decades old and much has changed to increase the safety and security in both juvenile and adult facilities (see Chapter 13).

As is the case with physical and economic victimization, sexual victimization is also more likely to be reported in adult facilities compared with juvenile facilities (Forst et al., 1989). About nine percent of juveniles in adult facilities reported being a victim of an attempted sexual assault or rape compared with 1.7% of the residents confined in juvenile placements (Forst et al., 1989). It is important, however, to remember that estimates of victimization are susceptible to underreporting by study participants, especially in cases of sexual victimization (Beyer, 1997).

Official data also indicate an increased risk of sexual victimization for inmates under the age of 18 years, especially in jails. Of the substantiated cases of sexual violence involving an inmate victim and an inmate perpetrator in jails, about 21% in 2005 and 13% of cases in 2006 involved a victim who was below the age of 18 years (Beck & Harrison, 2006, 2007). Of substantiated prison cases of sexual victimization in 2005 and 2006, about one percent involved an inmate perpetrator and victims who were below the age of 18 years (Beck & Harrison, 2006, 2007).

Victimization can have a profound effect on an individual, contributing to the loss of property, perceptions of masculinity, and status (Dumond, 1992). Physical consequences of victimization can include injury or the transmission of life-threatening diseases (Franklin & Franklin, 2008), while emotional consequences could include "anxiety, fear, depression, shame, anger, mood swings, phobic reactions," difficulty concentrating, or flash-backs (Cotton & Groth, 1982, p. 51). Indeed, fear of victimization may become a self fulfilling prophecy as fear is interpreted in the prison community as an indicator of weakness. Consequently, being fearful might lead to future victimization (Bishop & Frazier, 2000). Fear also contributes to other negative emotional states such as anxiety and depression (Hochstetler, Murphy, & Simmons, 2004). Taking action to avoid victimization may come at the expense of quality of life as juveniles may be transferred to protective custody. However, inmates who are in protective custody are typically not permitted to engage in programming, such as recreational and educational programs (Minor, Hutchinson Wallace, & Parson, 2008).

Eisikovits & Baizerman (1982) provided insight into the adaptations juvenile offenders use in adult facilities to survive a prison term. They found that one strategy is to conform to the inmate culture. For example, respondents reported that they learned the customs, the prison slang, and adopted the personalities and behaviors of adult inmates (Eisikovits & Baizerman, 1982). Juvenile inmates experimented with different roles as they adjusted to the inmate subculture. Eisikovits and Baizerman (1982), reported the case of an 18-year-old inmate:

> I had to stop being scared stiff. I knew I was going to be here for a while. The first 4 or 5 weeks I didn't say anything to anybody hardly except hello. Then you start playing. You wear the masks. I wore 3 or 4 different ones when I first wanted to know where I was sitting at. (p. 12)

In order to avoid victimization and increase their statuses in the prison community, juveniles employed several techniques. To compensate for their smaller physical size, inmates reported that they learned to rely on their "street smarts" or shrewdness to obtain power and respect. Others relied on inmates of the same race or ethnicity to provide protection (Eisikovits & Baizerman, 1982). Another strategy that inmates reported using was maintaining a low profile (Eisikovits & Baizerman, 1982). However, this was problematic because blending in was made difficult because of their ages—as state prisoners tend to be much older (Sabol & Couture, 2008). Ultimately, juvenile offenders became accustomed to living under the constant threat of victimization. One 17-year-old inmate in Eisikovits and Baizerman's (1982) study stated that:

> Everybody has that fear of getting stabbed. Everyone tells you: Get off my back or I'll stab you. After a while you just don't worry. You live with it like you know you'll die of lung cancer if you smoke but you still do. You think it'll never happen to you. (p. 14)

Based on the comment above, it appears that some juveniles may deny the possibility of being victimized as a coping mechanism in order to protect their mental health and ability to function within the prison on a daily basis.

Female juvenile offenders also reported a fear of being physically or sexually assaulted by adult inmates (Gaarder & Belknap, 2004). Although housed separately to protect them from potential adult harassment, abuse, or manipulation, they interacted with the adult women during meals, work, and programs. Respondents commented on the conflicting attitudes of being convicted as an adult, yet housed separately to be protected from older inmates. For example, one female juvenile prisoner in the Gaarder and Belknap (2004) study reported that:

> The separation is a problem. We were bound over as adults. If protecting us from adults is that big of a concern, they should have sent us to [name of the largest delinquent girl institution in this state]. (pp. 62-63)

Most of the respondents in the sample reported that they experienced negative interactions with adult women, including name-calling or sexual innuendos (Gaarder & Belknap, 2004). But, unlike the studies that focused on male juvenile offenders, none of the girls reported any physical or sexual victimization. While the respondents were fearful of victimization by adult women, they were also concerned with potential violence from other female juveniles. Respondents were concerned that they had no escape if they were involved in an altercation with an offender who resided in the same housing unit (Gaarder & Belknap, 2004).

Relationships with Older Inmates

Not all adult inmates present a threat to juvenile offenders. Some jurisdictions place juvenile offenders with older inmates because it is believed that they will exert a calming influence on them (Austin et al., 2000). In addition, interactions between younger and older inmates could produce positive effects on the juveniles' behavior and mental well being. For example, prison staff members at a female institution believed that the older women could mentor the younger inmates, teach them necessary life skills, such as hygiene, and ease their adjustment to incarceration (Gaarder & Belknap, 2004).

One danger, however, related to the interaction of juvenile and adult inmates is the negative influence that the adult inmates may have on them. Youth reported that their interactions with adult offenders afforded them new knowledge about committing crimes or avoiding detection (Abramsky, 2001; Bishop & Frazier, 2000; Lane et al., 2002; Wolfson, 2005). Staff members also expressed concern that female juvenile offenders may adopt as mentors the adult inmates who are troublemakers, which could negatively impact their behavior (Gaarder & Belknap, 2004).

Relationships with Staff Members

Staff members have different functions in adult facilities compared with those working in juvenile institutions. Correctional officers manage and control inmates, while juvenile facility staff members help guide youth toward law-abiding behavior (Inderbitzin, 2006). In addition, there is variation in the level and nature of interaction between officers and inmates. Compared with juvenile institutions, Bishop and Frazier (2000) observed that there was less interaction between inmates and officers, except when officers were giving orders. It seems that officers were focused on their responsibilities of maintaining the security of the facilities through surveillance and the enforcement of rules (Bishop & Frazier, 2000).

These differences help to shed light on the inmate perceptions of staff members in adult and juvenile facilities reported in the study conducted by Forst and colleagues (1989) and Kupchik (2007). Both studies reported that compared with youth confined in juvenile facilities, juveniles in adult state prisons rated staff members lower in several dimensions, including staff mentoring and institutional fairness compared to those confined in juvenile facilities (Kupchik, 2007).

Overall, inmates in juvenile facilities were more likely to describe staff members in positive terms, while juveniles in adult facilities viewed correctional officers negatively (Forst et al., 1989). For example, juvenile offenders characterized staff members as "mean or apathetic" (Lane et al., 2002, p. 448) and "hostile and derisive" (Bishop & Frazier, 2000, p. 256), claiming that the staff members viewed them as criminals who were incapable of change (Bishop & Frazier, 2000). In addition, juvenile offenders felt that correctional officers humiliated them and would provoke them into acting out just to punish them (Bishop & Frazier, 2000). Like their male peers, female juvenile offenders also felt that staff members treated them with disregard (Gaarder & Belknap, 2004). They commented on the impersonal nature of their interactions with correctional officers; because the correctional officers did not refer to the girls by name, it made them feel as though they had lost their individuality (Gaarder & Belknap, 2004).

One issue related to staff and juvenile inmate interaction is that few jurisdictions provide special training to staff members who work with young offenders, including juveniles in adult facilities (Gaarder & Belknap, 2004; LIS, Inc., 1995). While juvenile offenders expressed dissatisfaction with prison staff, it seems the feeling is mutual. In a survey administered to prison officials, respondents claimed that juveniles were more difficult to deal with than adult offenders (Reddington & Sapp, 1997). Furthermore, in interviews with staff members who interacted with female juvenile offenders, staff members revealed that they preferred not to be assigned to juvenile housing units (Gaarder & Belknap, 2004). Staff members described the juvenile housing unit as chaotic, disorderly, difficult to manage, and they felt that the female juveniles treated them in a disrespectful manner (Gaarder & Belknap, 2004). In addition, there was also a concern among staff that correctional officers who wanted to work with the juveniles were seen as motivated by ulterior or illegitimate reasons, such as sexual interest (Gaarder & Belknap, 2004).

Programming and Services

As there is variation in the housing of juvenile offenders who are incarcerated in adult institutions, specialized programming and services for juvenile offenders also vary. Some jurisdictions do not provide programming specifically designed for young offenders (Austin et al., 2000; Reddington & Sapp, 1997). As a result, they are treated the same as adults in regard to "housing, health care services, education, vocation and work programs, and recreational activities" (U. S. General Accounting Office, 1995, pp. 29-30).

Other jurisdictions provide special programs to juvenile offenders including diet and nutrition, family counseling, career training, prison survival training, special education programs, alternatives to violence programs, and drug and alcohol counseling (General Accounting Office, 1995; Reddington & Sapp, 1997). Specialized programs for juveniles are usually held in the separate housing units of juvenile offenders. Strom (2000) observed that:

> In Florida persons under 18 convicted in criminal court can be sentenced to the youthful offender program that separates ages 14-18 from ages 19-24. These programs offer youthful offenders specialized educational, vocational, and

life skills training, as well as substance abuse treatment. (p. 10)

The study of female juvenile offenders by Gaarder and Belknap (2004) provided a detailed account of the perceptions of rehabilitative programming. Female juvenile offenders were required to participate in education programs such as general educational development (GED) classes or college courses. These prisoners, however, were often dissatisfied with the poor quality of instruction by the teachers and the limited nature of the classes available (Gaarder & Belknap, 2004). There were exceptions to this general pattern, though, as some respondents credited their participation in education programs as a factor in improving their behavior (Gaarder & Belknap, 2004).

According to the female respondents, there were only a few available programs at the institution specifically designed and offered for the female juvenile population: anger management, substance abuse, Girl Scouts, and gang awareness (Gaarder & Belknap, 2004). In general, the juvenile offenders had a low participation rate for both the programs specially designed for them and those programs that were created for adult prisoners. When female juveniles did participate, there was a high attrition rate and most did not complete the programs (Gaarder & Belknap, 2004).

While special programming was not commonly offered, staff members in both male and female facilities reported that juvenile offenders should receive special programs. Prison administrators recommended prison survival training, career training, and family counseling (Reddington & Sapp, 1997). Staff members in female institutions believed that programs focusing on issues such as self esteem, domestic violence, dysfunctional families, and sexual abuse would be beneficial for juvenile prisoners (Gaarder & Belknap, 2004).

According to male and female samples of juvenile offenders, two other areas that needed improvements were work assignments and recreation. Male respondents reported that there were not enough work assignments to accommodate all inmates who desired one (Bishop & Frazier, 2000). Female offenders reported a need for recreational equipment that was suitable for young people, such as volleyball, and to have more physically demanding recreational activities (Gaarder & Belknap, 2004).

The lack of programming and services in jails appears to be especially dire. According to the Campaign for Youth Justice (2007), "many youth in adult jails sleep in excess of 15 hours a day, do not receive adequate nutrition or exercise, and do not have access to educational programming. In addition, they have little to no access to a counselor" (p. 7). Other anecdotal evidence describes the lack of programming and services available in jails as similarly sparse (Mlyniec, 2001).

There is considerable variance in program participation for juveniles depending on the type of facility (e.g., juvenile, juvenile unit within an adult facility, or an adult prison) and the state in which the facility is located. Both LaFree (2002) and Kupchik (2007) found that juveniles in the adult system were less likely to be involved in an educational program. Other variations exist in the availability of drug treatment and participation in substance abuse counseling. Juveniles in adult facilities reported greater access to drug treatment programs than in juvenile facilities (Kupchik, 2007). However, LaFree (2002) found that juveniles in adult facilities were less likely to report participation in substance abuse programming. These findings suggest that although juveniles in adult facilities may have greater access to substance abuse counseling, they might not participate in these programs.

Correctional Health

There is also a need for specialized programs for juvenile offenders, especially in the area of correctional health (Ruddell & Tomita, 2008). The need for mental health programming is bolstered by the increased risk of suicide among juveniles in adult institutions compared with juvenile placements. Memory (1998) reported that the rate of suicide for juveniles confined in adult jails was 2,041 per 100,000 as compared to the suicide rate of 57 per 100,000 for residents in juvenile detention facilities. Not only is the suicide rate higher for juveniles in adult facilities compared to those in juvenile facilities, but more recent research also indicates that juvenile jail detainees are at an increased risk of suicide compared to adult detainees. Across all age groups, jailed individuals under 18 years of age had the highest suicide rate at 101 suicides per 100,000 inmates (Mumola, 2005). In an analysis of suicides in juvenile facilities, Hayes (2004) noted that one possible precipitating factor is fear of transfer to the adult system (see Chapter 10).

Previous research indicated that juveniles who are involved in the juvenile justice system have a higher prevalence of mental health problems than the general youth population (Teplin et al., 2006). While this estimate focused on the mental health problems of offenders in the juvenile detention, there is no reason to believe that juveniles who are transferred to the adult system would not have similar rates or types of conditions. In fact, one potential contributing factor to high rates of depression is especially relevant to juveniles confined in adult facilities. Prolonged periods of isolation that can occur in order to increase the safety of juvenile offenders may have the undesirable consequence of increasing the risks of depression, suicide, or worsening mental health conditions (Campaign for Youth Justice, 2007).

Male and female respondents in adult facilities also expressed dissatisfaction with their access to health care and the quality of the care received (Cohen, 2008; Gaarder & Belknap, 2004). As a result, they reported treating their medical problems themselves or relying on the advice of their parents to remedy the condition (Gaarder & Belknap, 2004). The failure to seek medical attention raises concerns that minor medical conditions if left untreated or treated improperly could lead to serious health issues (Ruddell & Tomita, 2008). Along the same lines, while female juvenile offenders reported receiving a physical exam upon prison entry, they claimed there were no preventative health care services offered, such as teeth cleaning (Gaarder & Belknap, 2004).

Respondents were also reluctant to talk about sensitive issues, such as molestation, with male mental health staff members; however, a small number of girls did report that counseling was helpful (Gaarder & Belknap, 2004). Some female juvenile offenders reported that they were hesitant to disclose any mental health issues because they were fearful of being treated with prescription medications (Gaarder & Belknap, 2004). They claimed that it was relatively easy to obtain a prescription for these psychotropic medications and some admitted to having used this medication for recreational purposes (Gaarder & Belknap, 2004).

Disciplinary Misconduct

The conduct of inmates is one indicator of their adjustment to confinement (DeRosia, 1998). There have been several studies that have addressed the conduct of juveniles in adult facilities. Eisikovits & Baizerman (1982) contended that juveniles were more likely to engage in institutional misconduct, such as moving around the prison without permission. Other research has compared the disciplinary misconduct of juvenile offenders in adult facilities to youth in juvenile facilities or young adults incarcerated in adult facilities.

LaFree (2002) reported that juveniles who were confined in adult facilities had an average number of disciplinary violations that was approximately double the average for juveniles incarcerated in juvenile facilities: 14.4 disciplinary reports compared to 7.8. LaFree (2002) suggested that variations in monitoring and length of time incarcerated might explain part of the difference. Another possible explanation is that juveniles who are transferred to the adult system might have a higher likelihood to engage in disruptive or illegal conduct—either on the streets or in prison—than youth whose cases stayed in the juvenile justice system.

Using several measures of disciplinary misconduct, McShane and Williams (1989) found that juvenile offenders—who were incarcerated for an offense committed prior to the age of 17 years—were more of a disciplinary problem than young adult offenders who were 17 to 21 years of age when they committed their offenses. In a recent comparison of the disciplinary records of juveniles confined in adult prisons to youthful adult inmates (18-20 years of age) and older adults, Kuanliang, Sorensen, and Cunningham (2008) found that juvenile offenders had higher rates of violent or potentially violent misconduct than comparison groups of adult offenders. Furthermore, younger juveniles (13-15 years of age) were more violent and disruptive than older youth (16-17 years of age). Research also suggests that a small group of juvenile offenders were responsible for a disproportionate number of major disciplinary offenses, such as assault (Fanning, Jaskulske, & Zimmel, 2001).

Community Reentry

In general, juvenile offenders offer a pessimistic account of their correctional experiences in adult facilities (Lane et al., 2002). When reflecting on the impact of punishment, juveniles in the adult system were more likely to perceive that there was little or a negative change in their attitudes or behaviors compared with juveniles who were adjudicated in juvenile courts (Lane et al., 2002). Juvenile offenders in the adult system felt that prison provided them with the opportunity to reflect on the future, brought about an increased maturity, and deterred them from future crimes because of the "horrible" experience of prison (Lane et al., 2002, p. 444).

In describing the experiences of juveniles in adult facilities, Bishop and Frazier (2000) concluded that:

> The vast majority perceived little that was positive in their experience in the adult corrections system. For most, it was at best a test of will and endurance from which they hoped to emerge intact. At worst, it was a painful and denigrating experience that they pointed to as reason or justification for becoming more angry, embittered, cynical, and defeated, and/or skilled at committing crime. (p. 259)

Juveniles in adult facilities also expressed little confidence in their abilities to be law-abiding in the future (Bishop & Frazier, 2000). Based on evidence from the research discussed below, it appears their concerns are accurate because transferred juveniles have a greater risk of recidivating.

One area that has received a great deal of attention is whether juveniles sentenced in adult courts are more likely to recidivate than juveniles adjudicated in the juvenile justice system. Regardless of how recidivism is measured (e.g., re-arrest, re-conviction, or re-incarceration), research has consistently demonstrated that juveniles who are sentenced as adults have an increased likelihood of recidivism compared with juveniles whose cases stayed in the juvenile justice system.[10] For example, Podkopacz & Feld (1996) found that 58% of juveniles who were tried as adults reoffended in the two years following their releases compared to 42% of juveniles whose cases remained in the juvenile justice system.

Not only were juvenile offenders who were tried as adults more likely to reoffend, other research indicates that juveniles whose cases were processed in adult criminal courts were more likely to recidivate in a shorter period of time following release, to commit serious or violent offenses, and to recidivate—on average—more often compared with youth who stayed in the juvenile justice system (Fagan et al., 2003; Myers, 2003; Winner et al., 1997). Furthermore, juvenile offenders who are incarcerated in adult prisons are more likely to recidivate than their adult counterparts. For example, Langan and Levin (2002) found that inmates who were between the ages of 14 and 17 years, when released from state prisons, had higher percentages of re-arrest, re-conviction, and re-incarceration than inmates of all other age groups.

There are several explanations for the increased recidivism of transferred juveniles. Because the transferred juveniles are considered to be less amenable to treatment or pose a higher risk to public safety (Centers for Disease Control and Prevention, 2007; Forst et al., 1989), it makes intuitive sense that they would be more likely to reoffend than youth who were adjudicated in the juvenile justice system (Myers, 2003; Woolard et al., 2005). Alternatively, the juvenile justice system could provide more effective treatment because there is a greater focus on rehabilitation in juvenile corrections compared with the punishment orientation in adult corrections (Myers, 2003; Wolfson, 2005).

Another explanation may be that adult incarceration has a crime-causing or criminogenic effect (Myers, 2003; Podkopacz & Feld, 1996). As mentioned previously, juveniles in adult prisons reported that adult inmates taught them new methods in which to engage in crime or escape detection (Bishop & Frazier, 2000; Lane et al., 2002). Another factor that might increase recidivism is the perception of fairness of criminal justice processing. Youth who believe that they were treated unfairly may experience anger or frustration and they may reoffend out of defiance (Bishop et al., 1996). In addition, the role of criminal justice officials, such as "police preferences for arrest and the closer supervision of adolescents on juvenile probation caseloads," may account for some of the differences in recidivism (Fagan et al., 2003, p. 66).

The consequences of conviction and incarceration as an adult are much more severe than adjudication in the juvenile court. For example, a felony conviction in adult court carries with it the loss of the right to vote, to enlist in the military, to own a firearm, to be on a jury, to serve in public office, and disqualification from receiving certain sources of federal financial aid for educational advancement (Allard & Young, 2002; Bishop & Frazier, 2000). Depending on the jurisdiction, offenders convicted of felony drug offenses may also lose their eligibility to secure public housing or to receive welfare benefits (Mauer, 2003). Because of these collateral consequences, juveniles may re-offend as a result of being disengaged from and stigmatized by conventional society (Bishop & Frazier, 2000).

Adult felony convictions can also have negative employment consequences because the conviction is a matter of public record and must be reported on employment applications (Allard & Young, 2002; Wolfson, 2005). Difficulties associated with obtaining employment are an issue of concern for this population (Campaign for Youth Justice, 2007). Bishop and Frazier (2000) noted "transferred youth expressed worry about finding a good job. Several anticipated that they would be turned down by prospective employers for jobs for which they were qualified" (pp. 260-261). It seems that their apprehension is warranted because research indicates that men who were incarcerated when they were young had a greater difficulty obtaining lawful employment compared to those who had not been incarcerated (Freeman, 1992). Difficulty in obtaining employment may lead to recidivism because it limits lawful employment opportunities (Redding, 1999). In addition, an adult conviction may mean that the offender will be treated as an adult in any future offenses committed as a minor (e.g., once an adult, always an adult statutes) and the offense may be considered in habitual sentencing statutes, such as Three Strikes legislation (Allard & Young, 2002).

If legislators and criminal justice officials are trying juveniles as adults in the hopes of deterring future crimes, then based on these research findings, it does not seem as if they are successfully achieving this objective (Bishop et al., 1996; Centers for Disease Control and Prevention, 2007; Kupchik, 2006; Myers, 2003). For example, juvenile offenders may be unaware that they can be tried as adults and therefore, do not take this into account when deciding whether to commit an offense (Jensen & Metsger, 1994; Singer & McDowall, 1988). Moreover, the increased length of time it takes for case resolution in the adult criminal court compared with the juvenile justice system may erode any specific deterrent effect (Rudman et al., 1986).[11]

Conclusion

Even though a small percentage of offenders who were convicted in adult court while under the age of 18 years receive sentences of life or life without the possibility of parole[12] (Rainville & Smith, 2003) most of these offenders will be released from prison. Furthermore, a majority will be released within several years: of those sentenced when under the age of 18 years, 78% are expected to be released prior to their 21st birthday (Strom, 2000). In other words, the majority of juvenile offenders sentenced and incarcerated as an adult will reenter society at a young age. Consequently, it is important to consider the degree to which the adult incarceration experience will impact the social and psychological functioning of youth and whether the incarceration experience influences future offending.

As discussed throughout this chapter, it appears the effects of incarcerating juveniles in adult correctional facilities are largely negative and counterproductive to rehabilitation. The incidences of physical, sexual, and emotional victimization and the rates of suicide are higher for juveniles in adult facilities as compared with residents of juvenile facilities. In addition, adult inmates often teach these younger inmates new techniques to offend or techniques to escape detection. Juveniles in adult facilities also are generally more critical of the programs and staff involvement. Therefore, it appears that there is the potential for greater harm than good by incarcerating juveniles with adults.

This position is bolstered by research that overwhelmingly indicates that juvenile transfer into the adult system has not served as a deterrent, that recidivism rates are high, and that successful reentry is difficult for individuals who were incarcerated with adults at a young age. Altogether, it is necessary to consider the value of continuing to incarcerate juveniles in adult facilities.

Endnotes

1. Not all transferred juveniles who receive a jail or prison sentence serve their time in adult facilities. For example, juvenile defendants convicted in federal criminal courts are incarcerated in juvenile facilities, not adult institutions (Hartney, 2006).

2. The terminology for the transfer of juvenile cases into the adult system varies and includes waiver, certification, bind-over, and remand (Griffin, Torbet, & Szymanski, 1998).

3. In fact, empirical evidence indicates that juveniles convicted in adult criminal court may receive harsher sentences than young adult offenders, even after taking into account variables such as the type of offense, offender characteristics (e.g., prior record, gender, and race/ethnicity), and arbiter of the case—for example, judge or jury (Kurlychek & Johnson, 2004).

4. Depending on the measure, estimates of the number of juveniles incarcerated in adult facilities vary. Strom (2000) estimated that there were 5,400 individuals under the age of 18 years in state prisons on December 31,

1997; however, as stated above, the number of juveniles admitted to state prisons at any point during 1997 was 7,400.

5. Using census data of inmates incarcerated in state, federal, and private facilities on June 30, 2000, Stephan and Karberg (2003) estimated that only 168 of the 4,095 total inmates who were below the age of 18 were held in private correctional facilities.

6. A similar profile of the demographics of juveniles admitted or held in jails was not included in the report.

7. One question that arises when considering this disparity is whether the race of the offender has a direct effect on the decision to prosecute a case in the adult system. Fagan, Forst, and Vivona (1987) found that race did not exhibit a direct influence on the decision to transfer a case in three of the four sites they examined: Boston, Newark, and Phoenix. However, race did exert a direct effect on the transfer decision in Detroit.

8. First, Eisikovits and Baizerman (1982) interviewed 43 youth who were incarcerated for violent offenses, such as homicide, armed robbery, assault, or criminal sexual conduct. Sixteen of the youth had been convicted in adult court and were serving time in an adult facility, while the remainder of the sample was confined in juvenile facilities. Next, Forst et al. (1989) interviewed male youth who were incarcerated for violent offenses in juvenile and correctional facilities in Boston, Newark, Memphis, and Detroit.

9. Gaarder and Belknap (2004) interviewed 22 young women who were convicted when they were below the age of 18 and serving time in an adult female prison. Most of the girls were housed in a separate unit for inmates who were under the age of 21.

10. There are, however, several exceptions to this overall pattern. First, Winner and colleagues (1997) found that juveniles whose cases were adjudicated in the juvenile justice system were more likely to be rearrested in the future than juveniles whose cases involving property offenses were transferred into adult criminal court. Second, Fagan (1996) found no difference in the re-arrest prevalence for offenders convicted of burglary whose cases were tried in adult court as opposed to being adjudicated in juvenile court. Third, Fagan and associates (2003) found an increased probability of re-arrest for drug offenders adjudicated in the juvenile court compared to adult criminal court.

11. Other research indicates that case-processing time is slightly greater in the juvenile justice system than adult system (Fagan et al., 2003).

12. There are approximately 2,400 inmates in the United States serving sentences of life without parole (LWOP) for crimes they committed when they were age 18 or below (Leighton & de la Vega, 2007).

CHAPTER 7: KIDS IN THE BIG HOUSE: JUVENILES INCARCERATED IN ADULT FACILITIES

Cases Cited

Kent v. United States, 383 U. S. 541 (1966)
Roper v. Simmons, 543 U. S. 551 (2005)

References

Abramsky, S. (2001). Hard-time kids. *The American Prospect, 12*, 16-21.

Allard, P., & Young, M. (2002). *Prosecuting juveniles in adult court: Perspectives for policy makers and practitioners.* Washington, DC: The Sentencing Project.

Austin, J., Johnson, K. D., & Gregoriou, M. (2000). *Juveniles in adult prisons and jails: A national assessment.* Washington, DC: U. S. Department of Justice.

Barnes, C. W., & Franz, R. S. (1989). Questionably adult: Determinates and effects of the juvenile waiver decision. *Justice Quarterly, 6*, 117-135.

Beck, A. J., & Harrison, P. M. (2006). *Sexual violence reported by correctional authorities, 2005.* Washington, DC: Bureau of Justice Statistics.

Beck, A. J., & Harrison, P. M. (2007). *Sexual violence reported by correctional authorities, 2006.* Washington, DC: Bureau of Justice Statistics.

Belknap, J. (2001). *The invisible woman: Gender, crime, and justice.* Belmont, CA: Wadsworth.

Beyer, M. (1997). Experts for juveniles at risk of adult sentences. In P. Puritz, A. Capozello, & W. Shang (Eds.), *More than meets the eye: Rethinking assessment, competency and sentencing for a harsher era of juvenile justice,* (pp. 1-21). Washington, DC: American Bar Association Juvenile Justice Center.

Bishop, D., & Frazier, C. (2000). Consequences of transfer. In J. Fagan & F. Zimring (Eds.), *The changing borders of juvenile justice: Transfer of adolescents to the criminal court,* (pp. 227-276). Chicago: University of Chicago Press.

Bishop, D. M., Frazier, C. E., Lanza-Kaduce, L., & Winner, L. (1996). The transfer of juveniles to criminal court: Does it make a difference? *Crime & Delinquency, 42*, 171-191.

Campaign for Youth Justice. (2007). *The consequences aren't minor: The impact of trying youth as adults and strategies for reform.* Campaign for Youth Justice. Retrieved December 18, 2007, from http://www.campaignforyouthjustice.org

Centers for Disease Control and Prevention. (2007). *Effects on violence of laws and policies facilitating the transfer of youth from the juvenile to the adult justice system.* Atlanta, GA: Author.

Chesney-Lind, M., & Shelden, R. (1992). *Girls: Delinquency and juvenile justice.* Pacific Grove, CA: Brooks Cole Publishing Company.

Cohen, F. (2008). *Final fact-finding report: S.H. v. Stickrath.* Retrieved May 24, 2008, from: www.dys.ohio.gov

Cotton, D. J., & Groth, A. N. (1982). Inmate rape: Prevention and intervention. *Journal of Prison & Jail Health, 2*, 47-57.

DeRosia, V. R. (1998). *Living inside prison walls: Adjustment behavior.* Westport, CT: Praeger.

Dumond, R. W. (1992). The sexual assault of male inmates in incarcerated settings. *International Journal of the Sociology of Law, 20*, 135-157.

Eisikovits, Z., & Baizerman, M. (1982). "Doin' time": Violent youth in a juvenile facility and in an adult prison. *Journal of Offender Counseling, Services, & Rehabiliation, 6,* 5-20.

Fagan, J. (1990). Social and legal policy dimensions of violent juvenile crime. *Criminal Justice and Behavior, 17,* 93-133.

Fagan, J. (1996). The comparative advantage of juvenile versus criminal court sanctions on recidivism among adolescent felony offenders. *Law & Policy, 18,* 77-113.

Fagan, J., Forst, M., & Vivona, T. S. (1987). Racial determinants of the judicial transfer decision: Prosecuting violent youth in criminal court. *Crime & Delinquency, 33,* 259-286.

Fagan, J., Kupchik, A., & Liberman, A. (2003). Be careful what you wish for: The comparative impacts of juvenile versus criminal court sanctions on recidivism among adolescent felony offenders. *Columbia Law School Public Law & Theory Working Paper Group.* Retrieved January 23, 2008, from http://papers.ssrn.com/sol3/papers.cfm?abstract_id=491202#PaperDownload

Fanning, T. R., Jaskulske, D. C., & Zimmel, T. L. (2001). Institutional adjustment for youthful offenders in adult facilities. In B. Glick & E. E. Rhine (Eds.), *Journal of correctional best practices: Juveniles in adult correctional systems,* (pp. 141-148). Lanham, MD: American Correctional Association.

Flanagan, T. J. (1980). Time served and institutional misconduct: Patterns of involvement in disciplinary infractions among long-term and short-term inmates. *Journal of Criminal Justice, 8,* 357-367.

Forst, M., Fagan, J., & Vivona, T. S. (1989). Youth in prisons and training schools: Perceptions and consequences of the treatment-custody dichotomy. *Juvenile & Family Court Journal, 40,* 1-14.

Franklin, T. W., & Franklin, C. A. (2008). Violence reduction: Incarceration shouldn't be a death sentence. In R. Ruddell & M. Tomita (Eds.), *Issues in correctional health,* (pp. 103-121). Richmond, KY: Newgate.

Freeman, R. B. (1992). Crime and the employment of disadvantaged youth. In G. Peterson & W. Vroman (Eds.), *Urban labor markets and job opportunity,* (pp. 201-237). Washington, DC: Urban Institute Press.

Fritsch, E. J., Caeti, T. J., & Hemmens, C. (1996a). Spare the needle but not the punishment: The incarceration of waived youth in Texas prisons. *Crime & Delinquency, 42,* 593-609.

Fritsch, E. J., Hemmens, C., & Caeti, T. J. (1996b). Violent youth in juvenile and adult court: An assessment of sentencing strategies in Texas. *Law & Policy, 18,* 115-136.

Gaarder, E., & Belknap, J. (2004). Little women: Girls in adult prison. *Women & Criminal Justice, 15,* 51-80.

Glick, B., & Sturgeon, W. (1998). *No time to play: Youthful offenders in adult correctional systems.* Lanham, MD: American Correctional Association.

Glick, B., & Sturgeon, W. (2001). *Recess is over: A handbook for managing youthful offenders in adult systems.* Lanham, MD: American Correctional Association.

Griffin, P., Torbet, P., & Szymanski, L. (1998). *Trying juveniles as adults in criminal court: An analysis of state transfer provisions.* Washington, DC: Office of Juvenile Justice and Delinquency Prevention.

Hartney, C. (2006). *Youth under age 18 in the adult criminal justice system*. The National Council on Crime and Delinquency. Retrieved December 7, 2007, from http://www.nccd-crc.org/nccd/pubs/2006may_factsheet_youthadult.pdf

Hartney, C., & Silva, F. (2007). *And justice for some*. The National Council on Crime and Delinquency. Retrieved December 7, 2007, from http://www.nccdcrc.org/nccd/pubs/2007jan_justice_for_some.pdf

Hayes, L. (2004). *Juvenile suicide in confinement: A national survey*. Washington, DC: Officer of Juvenile Justice and Delinquency Programs.

Hochstetler, A., Murphy, D. S., & Simmons, R. L. (2004). Damaged goods: Exploring predictors of stress in prison inmates. *Crime & Delinquency, 50*, 436-457.

Human Rights Watch and Amnesty International. (2005). *The rest of their lives: Life without parole for child offenders in the United States*. New York: Human Rights Watch.

Inderbitzin, M. (2006). Lessons from a juvenile training school. *Journal of Adolescent Research, 21*, 7-26.

Jensen, E. L., & Metsger, L. K. (1994). A test of the deterrent effect of legislative waiver on violent juvenile crime. *Crime & Delinquency, 40*, 96-104.

Kinder, K., Veneziano, C., Fichter, M., & Azuma, H. (1995). A comparison of the dispositions of juvenile offenders certified as adults with juvenile offenders not certified. *Juvenile and Family Court Journal, 46*, 37-42.

Kuanliang, A., Sorensen, J. R., & Cunningham, M. D. (2008). Juvenile inmates in an adult prison system: Rates of disciplinary misconduct and violence. *Criminal Justice and Behavior, 35*, 1186-1201.

Kupchik, A. (2006). *Judging juveniles: Prosecuting adolescents in adult and juvenile courts*. New York: New York University Press.

Kupchik, A. (2007). The correctional experiences of youth in adult and juvenile prisons. *Justice Quarterly, 24*, 247-270.

Kupchik, A., Fagan, J., & Liberman, A. (2002). *Punishment, proportionality and jurisdictional transfer of adolescent offenders: A test of the leniency gap hypothesis*. Columbia Law School Public Law & Theory Working Paper Group. Retrieved December 18, 2007, from http://papers.ssrn.com/sol3/papers.cfm?abstract_id=334061

Kurlychek, M. C., & Johnson, B. D. (2004). The juvenile penalty: A comparison of juvenile and young adult sentencing outcomes in criminal court. *Criminology, 42*, 485-517.

LaFree, G. (2002). *New Mexico – Mixing juveniles with adults*. Retrieved December 7, 2007, from http://www.jrsa.org/pubs/reports/sjsreport/new_mexico.html

Lane, J., Lanza-Kaduce, L., Frazier, C. E., & Bishop, D. M. (2002). Adult versus juvenile sanctions: Voices of incarcerated youth. *Crime & Delinquency, 48*, 431-455.

Langan, P. A., & Levin, D. J. (2002). *Recidivism of prisoners released in 1994*. Washington, DC: Bureau of Justice Statistics.

Lanza-Kaduce, L., Bishop, D. M., Frazier, C. E., & Winner, L. (1996). Changes in juvenile waiver and transfer provisions: Projecting the impact in Florida. *Law & Policy, 18*, 137-150.

Leighton, M., & de la Vega, C. (2007). *Sentencing our children to die in prison: Global law and practice*. San Francisco: Center for Law and Global Justice.

LIS, Inc. (1995). *Offenders under age 18 in state adult correctional systems: A national picture.* Longmont, CO: National Institute of Justice.

Martin, G. (2005). *Juvenile justice: Process and systems.* Thousand Oaks, CA: Sage Publications.

Mauer, M. (2003). Introduction: The collateral consequences of imprisonment. *Fordham Urban Law Journal, 30,* 1491-1499.

McShane, M. D., & Williams, III, F. P. (1989). The prison adjustment of juvenile offenders. *Crime & Delinquency, 35,* 254-269.

Memory, J. M. (1989). Juvenile suicides in secure detention facilities: Correction of published rates. *Death Studies, 13,* 455-463.

Mlyniec, W. J. (2001). The hidden evil of children living in jail. *Children's Legal Rights Journal, 21,* 2-11.

Mumola, C. J. (2005). *Suicide and homicide in state prisons and local jails.* Washington, DC: Bureau of Justice Statistics.

Myers, D. L. (2003). The recidivism of violent youths in juvenile and adult courts: A consideration of selection bias. *Youth Violence and Juvenile Justice, 1,* 79-101.

Office of National Drug Control Policy. (2001). *Drug treatment in the criminal justice system.* Washington, DC: Author.

Orenstein, B., & Levinson, R. (1996). Juveniles waived into adult institutions. *Corrections Today, 58,* 148-151.

Owens, T. (1999). Dual track management of the youthful offender. *Corrections Today, 61,* 102-105.

Podkopacz, M. R., & Feld, B. C. (1996). The end of the line: An empirical study of judicial waiver. *The Journal of Criminal Law & Criminology, 86,* 449-492.

Pollock, J. M. (2002). *Women, prison, & crime.* Belmont, CA: Wadsworth.

Rainville, G. A., & Smith, S. K. (2003). *Juvenile felony defendants in criminal courts.* Washington, DC: Bureau of Justice Statistics.

Redding, R. E. (1999). Juvenile offenders in criminal court and adult prison: Legal, psychological, and behavioral outcomes. *Juvenile and Family Court Journal, 50,* 1-20.

Reddington, F. P., & Sapp, A. D. (1997). Juveniles in adult prisons: Problems and prospects. *Journal of Crime and Justice, 20,* 139-152.

Ruddell, R., & Tomita, M. (2008). *Issues in correctional health.* Richmond, KY: Newgate.

Rudman, C., Hartstone, E., Fagan, J., & Moore, M. (1986). Violent youth in adult court: Process and punishment. *Crime & Delinquency, 32,* 75-96.

Sabol, W. J., & Couture, H. (2008). *Prison and jail inmates at midyear 2007.* Washington, DC: Bureau of Justice Statistics.

Saum, C. A., Gray, A. R., & Walters, J. A. (2006). Therapeutic community treatment for juveniles sentenced as adults: Findings from Delaware's Young Criminal Offender Program. *Offender Substance Abuse Report, 6,* 67-78.

Sickmund, M. (2004). *Juveniles in corrections.* Washington, DC: Office of Juvenile Justice and Delinquency Prevention.

Singer, S. I., & McDowall, D. (1988). Criminalizing delinquency: The deterrent effects of the New York Juvenile Offender Law. *Law & Society Review, 22,* 521-536.

Steiner, B., & Wright, E. (2006). Assessing the relative effects of state direct file waiver laws on violent juvenile crime: Deterrence or irrelevance? *The Journal of Criminal Law & Criminology, 96,* 1451-1477.

Stephan, J. J., & Karberg, J. C. (2003). *Census of state and federal correctional facilities, 2000*. Washington, DC: Bureau of Justice Statistics.

Streib, V. (2005). *The juvenile death penalty today: Death sentences and executions for juvenile crimes, January 1, 1973 – February 28, 2005*. Retrieved November 1, 2008, from http://www.law.onu.edu

Strom, K. J. (2000). *Profile of state prisoners under age 18, 1985-97*. Washington, DC: Bureau of Justice Statistics.

Sykes, G. M. (1958). *The society of captives: A study of a maximum security prison*. Princeton, NJ: Princeton University Press.

Teplin, L. A., Abram, K. M., McClelland, G. M., Mericle, A. A., Dulcan, M. K., & Washburn, J. J. (2006). *Psychiatric disorders of youth in detention*. Washington, DC: Office of Juvenile Justice and Delinquency Prevention.

U. S. General Accounting Office. (1995). *Juvenile justice: Juveniles processed in criminal courts and case dispositions*. Washington, DC: Author.

Winner, L., Lanza-Kaduce, L., Bishop, D. M., & Frazier, C. E. (1997). The transfer of juveniles to criminal court: Reexamining recidivism over the long term. *Crime & Delinquency, 43*, 548-563.

Wolfson, J. (2005). *Childhood on trial: The failure of trying & sentencing youth in adult criminal court*. Washington, DC: Coalition for Juvenile Justice.

Woolard, J. L., Odgers, C., Lanza-Kaduce, L., & Daglis, H. (2005). Juveniles within adult correctional settings. Legal pathways and developmental considerations. *International Journal of Forensic Mental Health, 14*, 1-18.

CHAPTER 8
DEVELOPING CORRECTIONAL FACILITIES FOR FEMALE JUVENILE OFFENDERS: PROGRAMMATIC AND DESIGN CONSIDERATIONS

Shelley Zavlek and Rebecca Maniglia

G irls are a challenge for the juvenile justice system. Their unique needs have to be considered in all aspects of facility design and operations. While much work has been done to explain what female responsive programming looks like in a variety of settings, little has been done to explain how that programming might affect the design of juvenile residential facilities. This chapter on female juvenile offenders is an effort to show how the programmatic needs of girls can translate into design concepts for more effective and responsive facilities for girls; it is based on a review of research as well as the authors' first-hand experience and interviews with both staff and residents of juvenile correctional facilities.

Girls in the Juvenile Justice System

From the mid-1980s to the mid-1990s there was a precipitous increase in the overall number of juvenile arrests. However, the 10-year trend in rising juvenile crime appeared to have reached a plateau by the mid-1990s and the number of arrests began to decline. According to Federal Bureau of Investigation (FBI) data, there was a 25% decrease in the overall number of juvenile arrests each year from 1996 to 2000. During that period, while the total number of juveniles arrested each year decreased by 25%, the number of females arrested decreased by only 11%. Although overall juvenile arrests have remained fairly constant since 2000, the number of female juveniles arrested has steadily increased. Whereas females under the age of 18 years made up 25% of all juveniles arrested in 1996, they made up 30% of juveniles arrested in 2004—and that percentage has been increasing every year since 1996 (FBI, 2005). There is also a growing concern that arrests of girls for aggravated assault and other more aggressive offenses are not decreasing at the same rate as those of boys (Schaffner, 2006).

A Comparison: Female and Male Juvenile Offenses

Arrest numbers alone do not tell the whole story. They do not reflect the tremendous disparity between the nature of offenses for which female and male juveniles are arrested and institutionalized. Girls are not only being arrested for less serious offenses than boys, but there is also an increase in the use of detention for girls for these less serious offenses (Chesney-Lind & Shelden, 2004). In November 2005, the Annie E. Casey Foundation released a report by Francine Sherman entitled *Detention Reform and Girls: Challenges and Solutions*, which examined data on the detention of girls from 1990 through 2001. According to Sherman (2005), the number of girls entering juvenile detention nationwide rose 50% between 1990 and 1999, compared with only a four percent increase for boys.

Girls are far more likely than boys to be detained for misdemeanors, technical violations of probation and parole, and status offenses such as underage drinking or curfew violations that would not be crimes if committed by an adult, the report notes. Nationwide, girls represented 19% of the young people detained in 2001, but they account for 24% of those detained specifically for technical violations and 43% of those detained for status offenses. Sherman (2005) suggested that, contrary to the statutory purposes of detention, many jurisdictions are detaining girls not simply to maintain public safety, but to protect and arrange services for girls who have not committed serious crimes—including many who have run away from chaotic or abusive homes (Sherman, 2005).

A report issued jointly by the American Bar Association (ABA) and the National Bar Association (NBA)—*Justice by Gender, The Lack of Appropriate Prevention, Diversion and Treatment Alternatives for Girls in the Justice System*—documented a 65% increase in the use of detention for girls between 1988 and 1997, as compared with a 30% increase for boys. Research demonstrates that many of these girls, specifically adolescent females of color, have a much greater chance of being placed away from their homes and in a detention center for status offenses or "those offenses that have not historically been 'criminal' in nature or are specific to youth because of their age" (ABA, 2001, p. 26). When a male juvenile commits these same offenses, however, it usually does not result in similar treatment.

The increase in the use of detention for girls is "consistent with the documented use of detention as a means of social control of girls' behavior considered dangerous to themselves" (ABA, 2001). For example, girls who are victims of sexual abuse are more likely to run away and girls are more likely than boys to be arrested and ultimately placed outside the home for this behavior (ABA, 2001). Therefore, instead of dealing with the larger issues of what is happening to the girls, we punish the victim and use detention as a means to protect them. This situation is exacerbated by the fact that youth coming to court from detention are more likely to be incarcerated following adjudication than youth coming to court from home. Thus, an increase of girls in detention results in increased female incarceration rates.

The rising number of females entering the juvenile justice system has generated an increased concern over the perceived emergence of the violent juvenile female offender. The *Justice by Gender* report examined the rise in the number of females in the juvenile justice system. It questioned whether that rise correlates with an increase in violent and aggressive behavior. Although further research is necessary, preliminary studies suggest that what appears to be changing is not the behaviors of girls, but rather our response to those behaviors (Steffensmeier, 2008).

Regardless of the final answer to girls' violence, it remains true that far too many juvenile girls are being arrested for acts that have more to do with their age and the potential danger to themselves than the threat they pose to society. In addition, some experts attribute the rise in the number of violent offenses among female juveniles to the re-labeling of girls' family conflicts as violent offenses, along with changing police practices regarding domestic violence and aggressive behavior (Steffensmeier, 2008). Another explanation offered by experts is gender bias in the processing of misdemeanor cases, which results in more severe treatment of girls than boys for similar offenses (Chesney-Lind & Shelden, 2004). Perhaps the most distressing explanation offered for the burgeoning number of girls in the juvenile justice system is a fundamental systemic failure to understand the life circumstances, needs, and unique developmental issues facing girls today (ABA, 2001; Sherman, 2005).

These facts underscore the need for jurisdictions to develop a greater spectrum of responses to address crimes and delinquency among girls. Community-based facilities that are part of a comprehensive continuum of services and sanctions are well situated to address the complex array of issues confronting females who come in contact with the juvenile justice system. Such facilities would accomplish this through a coordinated approach to services and sanctions that engages the female juvenile and her family and support network. It would involve the cooperative efforts of the local police and prosecutor's office, the courts, probation, community corrections, detention and placement agencies, as well as aftercare and community-based service providers.

While the current situation requires a number of solutions, the remainder of this chapter focuses on the secure facilities designed to house female juveniles—specifically on how the programmatic needs of girls can translate into design concepts for more effective and responsive girls' facilities.

Commonalities of Female Juvenile Offenders

While there are many standard considerations (including safety, security, and cost) that impact the design of secure juvenile facilities, programming and space should also shape facility design. Therefore, in order to consider the design implications of the female juvenile population, one must first understand the characteristics of this population as well as the key elements of a female responsive program. The past ten years have seen research that has expanded and confirmed early academic work articulating the needs of girls and young women. Whether using national, state, or local populations, a reliable list of needs and key issues arise again and again for this population. The fact that these issues vary by location, age, socio-economic class, and race/ethnicity has resulted in the creation of standard recommendations for female responsive services.

Sexual, physical, and/or emotional victimization are among the most important commonalities found in populations of girls and young women involved in juvenile justice (Zahn, 2007). For instance, in a 1998 study of girls in California, the National Council on Crime and Delinquency (NCCD) identified victimization, primarily sexual abuse, as the most critical pathway to female delinquency for young girls (Accoca & Dedel, 1998). The report indicated that 92% of the girls interviewed reported a history of physical, sexual, and/or emotional abuse. Citing other studies that found girls were three times more likely than boys to have been sexually abused, the Office of Juvenile Justice and Delinquency Prevention's (OJJDP) Guiding Principles for Promising Female Programming (1998) identified victimization as a key issue for juvenile female offenders. In fact, victimization is now commonly seen as a key pathway to delinquency for girls (Belknap & Holsinger, 2006; Zahn, 2007). State studies have identified similar concerns (Maniglia, 1998).

Studies also show a connection between depression and involvement in criminal activity. In a report entitled *Adolescent Girls: The Role of Depression in the Development of Delinquency,* Earls and Obeidallah (1999) asserted that "57% of mildly to moderately depressed girls engaged in higher levels of aggressive behavior, compared with only 13% of those who were not depressed" (p. 3). Recent studies have shown that girls are more likely to have mental health problems than their male counterparts. Teplin and colleagues (2006) reported that in juvenile detention populations "nearly two-thirds of males and three-quarters of females met diagnostic criteria for one or more psychiatric disorders" (p. 1).

Research conducted by NCCD also identified family fragmentation, academic failure, and health and mental health issues as the greatest concerns for girls and young at-risk women (Acoca, 1999). The American Bar Association's (2001) report affirmed the work of earlier research in identifying critical concerns that programmatic solutions must address: family problems, victimization both inside and outside of the formal juvenile justice system, health and mental health issues, and school failure. OJJDP publications since the mid-1990s have made similar claims, citing substance abuse, teen pregnancy, academic failure, mental health needs, gang membership, and societal pressure as issues of concern for this population (Budnick & Shields-Fletcher, 1998) and academic studies have confirmed this standard list (Bloom & Covington, 2001).

Female Responsive Programming

Generally, it can be said that in a female responsive program all aspects of the specific service delivery system (and the larger system in which it operates) are designed through a female responsive lens (sometimes called gender responsive by scholars). Practitioners, therefore, make an intentional effort to understand the shifting literature on female identity and development and to use this information when designing specific program elements and general service delivery systems. In essence, all policy and program development is examined to ensure that it meets the specific and varied gender and cultural needs of girls and young women.

The five female responsive values, developed for the National Institute of Corrections as part of its training efforts for juvenile female offenders, represent one theoretical framework in which female responsive services exist (Maniglia, 2003). There are similar frameworks that exist for adult female offenders (Bloom & Covington, 2001). It is the belief that if these conditions are not present, a program or service delivery system cannot, in good conscience, call itself female responsive. The following five female responsive values, therefore, set a high standard by which services delivered to girls and young women ought to be evaluated.

Inclusive

Movements of gender equality have historically focused on gender as the primary social category to be addressed. This has resulted in criticisms that the conceptions of gender around which advocacy takes place are those of the majority population. Thus, women's movements have become defined around the needs and desires of White, middle class, heterosexual women and have ignored the unique circumstances of women of color, women living in poverty, and bisexual or lesbian women. Likewise, the female responsive services movement has been envisioned as focusing exclusively on the issues emerging from gender. However, in their intended form, female responsive services allow girls and young women to understand gender, race, sexual orientation, class, religion, and other social categories and individual life experiences as interconnecting to shape their self identity. Therefore, female responsive services seek to integrate treatment approaches in ways that allow for multiple perspectives and that encourage advocacy concerning all forms of oppression.

Relational

It has been said that relationships are the glue that hold girls' lives together (Brown & Gilligan, 1992). It is often in the context of relationships that girls define their self identities—looking to others' perceptions when shaping their own ideas about the world. The relational aspects of female delinquency and crime are well known and documented. Girls often experience delinquency and crime collectively (by shoplifting as a group or engaging in violent physical encounters with one another). Therefore, female responsive programming acknowledges the role that relationships play in the development of healthy life skills. Typically, girls are better than boys at accepting accountability for their harmful actions to others and confronting the emotional and physical difficulties they have experienced in their own interpersonal relationships when they are given the opportunity to connect relationally with service providers.

Restorative

In recent years, many states have adopted new practices for handling crime and punishment based on restorative justice practices, which have become increasingly popular in state juvenile justice systems (Pranis, Stuart, & Wedge, 2003). The roots of restorative justice theory can be found in the practices of indigenous peoples throughout the world, as well as in the early forms of criminal justice practiced in Europe (Braithwaite, 1989). In contemporary justice understandings, however, restorative justice focuses on a philosophical belief that crime should be redefined as harm done to specific victims (including a community) rather than as a violation of arbitrary state laws that identify particular behavior as criminal. Therefore, the proper response to crime is restoration of the damage done. Victims receive compensation and offenders are restored through the process of making amends—often emotionally, through the expression of remorse, and materially, through restitution or community service (Zehr, 2000).

For girls and young women, adopting a female responsive philosophy means allowing them the opportunity to experience meaningful accountability to their victims and restoring their broken relationships. Therefore, programmatically responding to the high rates of victimization among girls is as critical as helping them to develop empathy skills and opportunities for restitution. While a program may choose not to use all of the formal mechanisms of restorative justice, it should be operating under the basic philosophy that crime and treatment are, in essence, about broken relationships that need restoration.

Aware of the Social Context

All girls and young women receive social pressure based on the societal expectations related to their gender. This social pressure can be further complicated by a young woman's membership in an additional social category of individuals who experience oppression, such as those based on race or ethnicity, sexual orientation, religion, or class. While female responsive services do not believe that society is the sole cause of the individual behaviors of girls, there is an assumption that the social pressure girls experience does influence their own self perception. Therefore, female responsive services attempt to assist girls in becoming critical consumers of media and other forms of social influence, while at the same time creating environments that offer alternatives.

Multileveled

Juvenile justice systems exist within a specific historical context that shapes the choices and quality of the services delivered. For instance, the juvenile justice system has historically created programs designed to serve the needs of its majority (and most violent) population: boys and young men. This has resulted in girls having access only to programming that has been designed for this separate and distinct population. Thus, those involved in the development and delivery of female responsive services must confront systemic environments and system policies that hinder the ability to assist girls and young women in the work that they need to accomplish.

One of the challenges of female responsive programming is that while it is relatively easy to articulate the need for gender responsive programs, many initiatives fail to be implemented correctly. Consequently, Bloom, Owen, and Covington (2003) developed six principles for successfully implementing female responsive programs: (a) gender does make a difference; (b) correctional staff should create an environment where women feel safe and where they are treated with dignity and respect; (c) officials should acknowledge the role that relationships play in women's lives and make relationships a core in programming; (d) comprehensive services and supervision should address the issues of the interaction of substance abuse, trauma, and mental health; (e) economic self sufficiency should be encouraged through traditional and non-traditional academic and vocational programs; and (f) comprehensive, individualized, and collaborative services should be provided to females to ensure their successful community reintegration.

Female Responsive Facility Design

An important aspect of designing a facility for girls is acknowledging the specific requirements of female responsive programming. The past experiences and current needs of girls and how these are addressed by residential programming have critical facility design implications. While it may be true that there are certain design features that are appropriate and useful for all juvenile facilities, there are hidden issues specific to the gender of the population housed. For instance, both male and female juvenile offenders need "structure, education, training and support to succeed" (Marler & Scoble, 2001, p. 89), yet how each of these is manifested in the structural design and atmosphere of a facility can vary with the population served. The information provided below aims to address the ways in which aspects of facility design might be affected by gender. The remainder of this section discusses how secure juvenile residential facilities can be designed to be more responsive to and effective for girls.

Safety, Security and Safe Places

Security and safety are of paramount importance in a correctional system. Efforts should be directed toward preventing any breach of security that might endanger staff, juveniles, visitors, or members of the surrounding community. Safety is maintained in accordance with modern standards and in compliance with guidelines established by state and local agencies responsible for such planning. Furthermore, architectural elements including; grilles, registers, fittings, and all fixtures in areas accessible to residents, particularly bedrooms and bathrooms should be suicide-resistant. Most suicides and suicide attempts take place in bedrooms and bathrooms where youth may be alone without direct supervision for intervals of time (Hayes, 2004).

For girls, the efforts to create physical safety are paramount. However, efforts must also extend to ensuring emotional and cultural safety. In a female responsive program, one of the most important safety and security tools any facility has is the quality of relationships—relationships among staff, between girls and staff, and among the girls. Therefore, meeting girls' relational needs through policies and physical space that allow for healthy and safe connections is a first step in making a facility safe for girls.

Also, physical and emotional safety are affected by the high rates of victimization found in the juvenile female population (Hennessey, Ford, Ko, & Siegfried, 2004). Many, if not most, girls in a correctional facility will have suffered sexual and/or physical abuse prior to entering the facility, creating an environment where feeling safe is an important prerequisite to being able to work on treatment issues. Louise Bill (1998) recognizes that "childhood and adult victimization of girls and women frequently is a precursor to female criminality;" she argues that "the prison system often contributes to the re-victimization of these women by perpetuating feelings of powerlessness and vulnerability" (p. 106). Procedures such as restraints, strip searches, and intrusive explorations of body parts further exacerbate these feelings of vulnerability by presenting a threat of further sexual assaults (OJJDP, 1998). Policies and procedures that reflect this knowledge should be adopted. For example, the manner in which security procedures are conducted should be modified so that they are not disempowering. The physical space in which security procedures are conducted should be calming and respectful and should provide the maximum degree of privacy without compromising safety.

Privacy

Ensuring privacy and confidentiality are important considerations for facility design. Whenever possible, private interview rooms should be available for intake questioning, which typically includes questions about sexual behavior and abuse, as well as health information such as sexually transmitted infections. Since this medical information is confidential, facility administrators must ensure that they do not violate the Health Insurance Portability and Accountability Act (HIPAA) regulations about health records. Moreover, close attention should be paid to the placement of windows and vision panels in the area where body searches are performed.

Opaque shower curtains in front of multiple single shower units and saloon doors on bathrooms satisfy privacy needs without compromising institutional security. Girls can be made to feel that there is something giving them privacy from the watchful eyes of staff, while giving staff the ability to observe what they must for security reasons (DeBell, 2001).

Although providing natural lighting is critical, it must be achieved while being sensitive to privacy needs when designing facilities for girls. Providing appropriate covering for bedroom windows allows for privacy and yet does not eliminate natural light or prohibit staff monitoring of girls while in their rooms. For example, bedroom windows that face courtyards or other areas that are accessible to youth or to the public may have diffused or obscured glazing that allows light into the room but blocks visual access from the outside. This is especially important if the facility is one of a number of buildings located on a coed campus.

Sightlines and Visibility

The internal layout of a juvenile facility should provide for maximum visibility and supervision, with minimal reliance on electronic surveillance or security escort. Blind spots must be avoided as much as possible throughout the facility. Although closed circuit TV could be used to monitor certain areas, it is important that staff have a direct line of sight to as much of the facility as possible to allow ease of movement and visual supervision. Furthermore, the design of any office and/or program spaces in or adjacent to the housing pods (also known as housing or living units) should have vision panels that allow for indirect visual supervision of youth by office staff.

Issues of visibility are of particular importance to girls and young women because they are often at risk of self-harming behaviors, such as self mutilation. Girls may also be at risk of exploitation by staff members. Recent information from the Prison Rape Elimination Act (PREA) suggested that staff sexual misconduct is a significant issue in adult facilities (Beck & Harrison, 2007) and researchers from the Bureau of Justice Statistics are currently studying this issue in juvenile facilities. As a result, enhanced visibility reduces staff opportunities for inappropriate contact and reduces the risk of having false charges filed against them. For these reasons, it may also be undesirable to rely on the use of isolation rooms or small segregation units, which are often supervised by a single staff member.

Electronic Technology

Electronic technology may be used in a facility to enhance security and surveillance, but must not be substituted for direct staff supervision. Dependence on electronic systems, monitors, and closed circuit TV within the facility should be minimized. Some areas, such as sleeping and recreation spaces, cannot be adequately supervised without the presence of a staff member.

Given the relational nature of girls and their particular issues of safety and security, technology can never replace the importance of staff on the floor interacting and participating in the program model. For instance, if a staff-duty office is created, it should not be used as a break room for staff or a place to watch girls from a distance, nor should it be positioned so as to encourage such activity. Whenever possible, there should be no staff-duty office on the housing unit for direct-care staff. In order to know what is going on in any population of girls and to ensure effective supervision in high risk situations, it is important that staff members are with the girls in the day room during activities. The use of isolation for security or safety issues is not necessarily effective, given girls' needs for connection. It is far better in situations of suicide risk, self-harm risk, and aggressive acting-out risk to have a staff member stay close by a girl whether or not she chooses to interact with that staff person.

Relationships

Honoring the relationships a juvenile brings into a facility and allowing her to create healthy and meaningful relationships with facility staff is a key element of any program. Whether it is family, friends, or the community, young women thrive in an environment where they are able to tend to the relationships in their lives and even form new ones. For this reason, whenever possible, states should build smaller, locally-based facilities that allow juveniles to be kept close to their families and community support systems (Marler & Scoble, 2001; Zavlek, 2005). Community-based programming allows for the facility to bring in outside resources both for staff training, program development, and direct service delivery. Agencies such as sexual assault centers and domestic violence shelters can be vital resources to a female responsive residential program; this kind of networking is enhanced when facilities are not geographically isolated.

Placing female juveniles in a facility that is in close proximity to their homes, families, and community support networks also helps to ease subsequent reintegration to the outside community. Removing girls from their communities for placement in a remote facility not only breaks the ties these girls need with their families and support networks, it disrupts the chain of services and relationships that they have with counselors, therapists, and other staff members with whom they are involved in the local community. Although this is important for all juveniles, many of the risk factors for girls and young women originate in the home; involving the family and a girl's community as part of the recovery is an important element of treatment and rehabilitation.

This respect for relationship in a gendered context has many important implications for facility design. The design of the housing pods should encourage interaction between staff and juveniles, ensuring that the day room is an integral part of the housing pod. Movable furniture can help encourage relationship-building by providing a setting conducive to small groups and intimate interactions between staff and girls and by creating a dayroom where people feel comfortable having personal conversations.

Many juvenile female offenders are also teen mothers. They are, in essence, raising the next generation—even while they are being held in facilities. Therefore, designing family visiting rooms with child-sized chairs and toys and supplying spaces where mothers and their children can interact in a positive and healthy environment will strengthen these vital relationships. The room should be large enough to accommodate visitors and ensure privacy for families who wish to talk about difficult issues with facility staff. Such spaces need to have access to restroom facilities with baby changing tables for families. However, it should be noted that many families are suspicious of juvenile justice efforts to include them because these efforts often have ulterior motives associated with blame, issue identification, or abuse disclosure. This needs to be taken into consideration when using spaces intended to encourage familial interaction.

The need to honor relationships also has implications for the design of facility living spaces for girls. Anecdotal information suggests that double occupancy rooms can be beneficial to girls by allowing them to cultivate a new and important relationship and by giving the occupants a better sense of community. However, double rooms can also create unsafe environments for girls, so any decisions about room occupancy must take place within the context of other efforts to ensure safety and security.

Normative Environments

All juveniles should be provided the opportunity to be in the least restrictive, appropriate environment. Since the majority of juveniles in the system are nonviolent, creating an environment that is as close as possible to a real world setting is important. Furthermore, housing youth in a facility they must care for and respect keeps them from lapsing into the bad habits anticipated by a more institutional and high security environment. The normative characteristics of the residential and programmatic environment cue the expected behavior of the residents and staff. Selective use of commercial grade carpets and furnishings, as well as a residential color palette resembling a college dorm, allows the building to be used as a tool for teaching responsibility and provides a positive environment for treatment. Carpeting can also be used to achieve noise reduction, which creates a calmer environment that tends to limit the amount of tension and stress experienced by staff and youth.

The furnishings and fixtures must be durable, easy to maintain, and appropriate for a secure residential facility. Dayrooms should contain movable tables and chairs with sufficient mass/weight to avoid their use as a weapon—or light enough to be harmless if used in such a manner. Natural light is also important in maintaining a rehabilitative environment and should be provided in each bedroom and program space, while still maintaining safety and security. Some jurisdictions have determined that for the majority of the population in their care, security hardware (which is very expensive) is unnecessary. In many facilities, recreation yards are located in central courtyards surrounded by buildings; there are no barb wire or razor wire fences, no traditional security locks, and no traditional cells. Housing units may contain a combination of single-occupancy, double-occupancy, and/or dormitory-style sleeping areas. These areas may have features such as freestanding beds and desks (which, depending on the population, may be fixed in place), high security marker boards for personal notes or pictures, a mirror, and space for personal effects. Private or shared bathrooms should, where possible, be placed in the common area of the housing unit.

Creating a female friendly environment means, when possible, achieving all of the recommended elements, while adding little touches that make the living environment feel more like a home. This can be accomplished by adding design features such as curtains. The design of girls' housing units might also include attention to details such as additional sinks, toilets, mirrors, outlets for equipment (such as blow dryers or curling irons), and adjusting the height of equipment or door handles. Creating larger grooming areas with amenities such as bathtubs can also be important.

Another way to make the environment more comforting is by providing dayrooms with bookcases and reading materials that include a wide array of books on female issues and women's fiction (particularly including those written by African-American and Latino women). Also, including high security bulletin boards in bedrooms can be an outlet for self expression. Furthermore, since many of the girls have suffered feelings of powerlessness due to their victimization, granting them some control over their environment—such as being able to turn the light switches on and off (with appropriate overrides)—can provide a good tool for empowerment and rehabilitation.

Programming Spaces and Learning Environments

Residential facility design usually requires that spaces serve multiple purposes. Classrooms, multipurpose rooms, and program spaces should be flexible to accommodate a variety of activities and teaching methods. Classroom design should accommodate individualized programming to meet the needs of students at varying academic levels. Educational programming spaces should offer a stimulating learning environment for academic learning and vocational training. They should include high security display cabinets and bulletin boards to display students' work. Noise reduction and natural light are also very important, with calming colors used whenever possible. In a coed facility, it is not unusual for facility classrooms to contain only one or two girls per class. Therefore, providing teachers with direct visual access to all areas of the classroom, as well as space for girls to sit separately or near adult staff, will ensure that girls are safe in the school environment.

It is also important to include space where females can talk and learn about female development and health issues with a level of confidentiality and where they can gather written information on issues such as pregnancy, sexually transmitted infections, contraception, and overall female health. The design of medical exam rooms is also critical because gynecological exams can cause many girls to relive issues of victimization. These rooms should be private and should not contain cameras. They should have appropriate medical exam tables and equipment used exclusively by a female nurse practitioner whenever possible.

A specific facility feature that needs to be adjusted for female offenders is the type of food served. It is important to develop a menu specifically for girls. DeBell (2001) noted that "Female offenders are fed the same meals as their male counterparts—equal in calorie count, carbohydrates and sugars" (p. 57). Such a diet often contributes to weight gain and may have negative health impacts, including development or exacerbation of eating disorders. As a result, adding a salad bar to the cafeteria can have a significant positive impact. Last, facility staff developing female-specific programming should consider health promotion activities that include a focus on diet and healthy lifestyles (Ruddell & Tomita, 2008).

Single-Sex Versus Coed Facilities

There is no dispute that most females in the juvenile justice system are victims of abuse and require a safe environment for effective treatment and recovery. However, there is still much debate over whether eliminating young males from juvenile facilities is a necessary prerequisite to creating effective treatment environments. The importance of single-sex programming is reflected in the debate among juvenile justice experts and practitioners concerning the advantages and disadvantages of coed verses single-sexed juvenile correctional facilities. While there are many issues that must be taken into consideration when designing a juvenile facility, we would assert that (whenever possible) single-sex environments should be considered best practice, including living arrangements, dayrooms, and educational spaces. To this end, we have addressed below the most common arguments made in defense of coed environments.

It is argued that single-sex environments do not provide a realistic model of a world in which males and females are in contact with one another on a daily basis. This argument suggests that learning how to successfully interact with boys and men is a critical prerequisite for girls to succeed in the outside world. However, research asserts that girls benefit when given their own safe space in which to explore their identities apart from their relationships with men and boys (Greene, Peters, & Associates, 1998; Valentine Foundation, 1990). This opportunity allows them to enter the community at some later time with greater skill and confidence in their own gendered identity.

Furthermore, much of the structure and programming historically provided in juvenile justice facilities is not designed to be a model of the world outside the facility. Instead, it is intentionally designed to give juveniles a respite from the pressures of the outside world and to provide an opportunity to learn to be accountable for their actions, deal with life stressors, and develop new personal and corporate skills. A female responsive environment includes consideration of gender, recognizing that in a male dominated society, girls need respite from being forced to incorporate male attention into their personal development.

Because there are fewer girls than boys in the juvenile justice system, jurisdictions often do not have enough female juveniles in confinement to justify the investment in an all-girls facility. In order to develop an all-girls facility, it is often necessary to move away from the small, community-based model toward a larger, centralized facility. This must be weighed against the benefits of operating a larger, coed facility that keeps both girls and boys close to their home environments. Both of these approaches have advantages and disadvantages.

Larger facilities are usually designed to provide a full range of physical and programmatic resources. These may include a full sized gym, full service medical and mental health units, an educational center, library, chapel, and vocational programs. Furthermore, larger facilities can afford greater staffing resources and potentially allow for a more extensive range of academic and programming opportunities. Despite the benefits of an all-female environment for girls, economic realities will almost always prevent the inclusion of these types of resources in an 8- or 16-bed facility. Consequently, most jurisdictions will elect to develop a larger full service coed facility rather than a small all-girls facility.

It is critical to understand, however, that girls are significantly outnumbered by boys in most coed facilities. This disparity in numbers may result in a physical plant that requires girls to sleep in units on male dominated wings, attend school in classrooms where they may be the only girls, shower and receive medical attention in isolation, and pass through male dominated areas to reach centralized program spaces. As such, girls' access to available services is often gained at the cost of their sense of safety and security or limited to a restricted schedule of use around the schedules of the predominant male populations. Furthermore, it is virtually impossible to provide specialized female responsive services without a critical mass. This has very real, and often detrimental, consequences for the female population.

Due to the relatively small number of girls in many coed facilities, it is also difficult to provide for separate housing units for the female population based on classification systems that take into account relevant risk factors (e.g., offense, age, acting-out behavior) and the girls' needs (e.g., history of trauma). Often, the girls become a single classification, despite the fact that many fall into as many classifications as the males based on the risk that they pose or their special needs.

Creative design solutions in coed facilities can address some of the girls' safety and security concerns. For example, shared program spaces including a school, a gym, and dining and medical services may be placed strategically (e.g., between male and female units) so that girls do not have to pass by boys' units to get to those spaces. Services that are most commonly used by the girls should be easily accessible to their housing unit. For example, a large programming space designed for multiple, gender specific uses (e.g., education, dance, exercise, arts and crafts, sports and recreation) could be designed adjacent to and accessible from the girls housing (see Figures 1-3 below).

Creative design solutions can also provide different housing options for purposes of classification, even where there is only a small population of girls. This is equally important in both a large coed facility with a small population of girls and in a small, community-based, all-girls facility. Provision for different classifications can be made through the inclusion of features such as segregation rooms adjacent to or within a housing unit; flexible subdivisions within a single housing unit; or adjoining units with bedrooms that can be shifted based on need. In order to achieve staffing efficiency, these spaces can be designed to be supervised by a common staff person. Figures 1 through 3 present several creative housing layouts that afford a high level of flexibility.

Figure 1 illustrates two 8-bed housing units adjoined by a 3-bed flexible housing unit (sometimes referred to as a "swing" or "flex" unit). Each of the units feeds into a multipurpose programming space that provides easy access to dining and an outdoor courtyard. This configuration provides a great deal of flexibility to respond to changing populations and classification needs. For example, operated as three separate housing units, the 3-bed flex unit can be reserved for girls requiring a high level of security or segregation from other residents.

Figure 1. Flexible Housing Units.

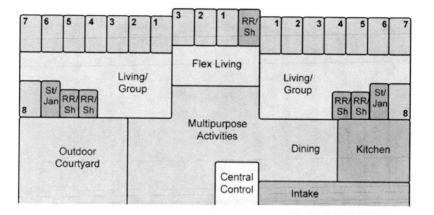

The two 8-bed units can provide space for girls in two different classifications based on an assessment of risk and/or needs. An 8-bed unit can be expanded into an 11-bed unit by opening the door to the adjacent flex unit. The 11-bed unit can be expanded into a 19-bed unit by opening both doors between the flex unit and the adjoining units. Furniture, fixtures, finishes, and room design can vary between the units in response to the programmatic and security needs presented. For example, segregation rooms may have fixed security-grade furniture, fixtures, and toilets, while other bedrooms are designed in a more normative fashion with access to shared private bathrooms.

The housing configuration shown in Figure 2 also provides flexibility. Each 9-bed unit (including two double-occupancy rooms) can be operated separately. Each can offer design features and programming that meets the particular needs of the girls assigned to them. The multipurpose space can be used by the girls from each unit based on a schedule of use or can be used by the girls from both units for shared programming. This may also be operated as one 18-bed unit by opening doors between the two housing units and the multipurpose space. When spaces are designed creatively, the possibilities for creative programming and resident and staff interaction and use are limited only by the imagination of the facility staff.

Figure 2. Flexible Housing Units.

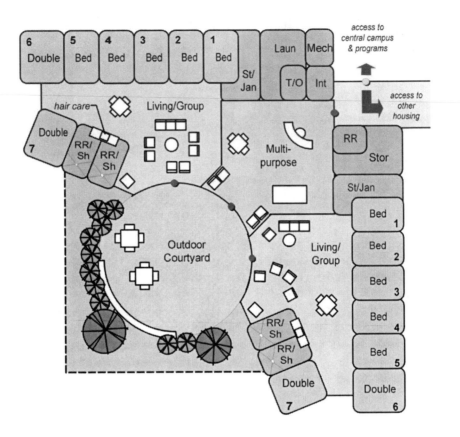

Figure 3 shows two adjoining housing units that can operate as one 8-bed unit (or up to a 16-bed unit if double-occupancy bedrooms are used throughout). If the door adjoining the two units is locked, staff can operate housing as one 3-bed unit and one 5-bed unit. Each unit has its own toilet and shower so that girls can be completely segregated if necessary for security reasons or merely for more effective programming. The education space, located adjacent to both housing units, is easily accessible to all residents on a controlled basis, with residents mixing at staff discretion. Immediate access to dayrooms supports expanded educational opportunities and a number of small and large groups.

Figure 3. Flexible Housing Units.

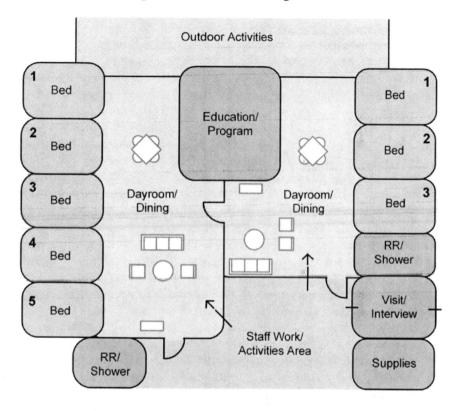

The challenges of coed facilities described above can be addressed by developing larger regional facilities exclusively for girls. The economies of scale would allow for all of the expanded physical space and programming resources of a larger facility—all of which can be designed to meet the gender specific programming requirements of the female population. These benefits must be weighed against the downside of regionalization, which is the need to move girls further away from their homes and communities. This potentially makes it difficult to maintain critical connections to family, children, and support networks within their communities. It should be recognized, however, that technology allows for new opportunities to include family members in the treatment program despite the obstacles of distance or geography.

Advantages of Single-Sex Facilities

In female responsive programming, it is easier to provide this critical sense of safety in a single-sex environment that allows for separate housing units, courtyards, and program space. Given the rates of victimization, primarily by male offenders, a single-sex environment may even enhance the recovery process by eliminating concerns over the threat of young males, whether real or perceived. Designing a "space that is physically and emotionally safe, and removed from the demands for attention of adolescent males" (Valentine Foundation, 1980) may help to foster an atmosphere where a girl feels safe enough to focus on other aspects of her personal development.

Anecdotal information suggests that girls in a single-sex facility relate to each other in a better way than they are able to in a coed facility. Juvenile justice staff and female residents, who are initially resistant to being in an all-female environment, often discover that it allows girls to form positive relationships with other girls and staff that would not have been possible otherwise. In a heterosexual, male dominated culture, girls are trained to focus their attentions on relationships with boys and men. They are trained to perceive one another as competition for male attention and, as such, do not have opportunities to work together collaboratively.

In an all-girl facility, competition for boys' attention is eliminated, which can lead to a decrease in fighting among the girls. As one facility director who had run both single-sex and coed facilities noted, the females had an easier time building relationships with one another within the all-girls' facility. The housing units were designed with double occupancy bedrooms and, although they feared that two girls to a room might create tension or adversarial relationships, they found the opposite to be true. In fact, frequently, the roommates formed a close bond with one another, helping to create a sense of cohesion and camaraderie within the facility. It is noted, however, that facility design should always provide the option of single occupancy housing for girls who pose a threat or otherwise demonstrate behaviors that make double occupancy housing unsuitable.

Regionalized single-sex facilities allow for the critical mass of girls necessary to provide the basic elements of female responsive programming. It is well established that girls and boys have different treatment needs, learning modalities, and pathways to the juvenile justice system. It is easier to address the specific needs of girls within a single-sex facility because the facility programming and physical plant can be designed with female responsive values and elements of female responsive programming in mind. For instance, all-girls' educational programs may apply tools and methods that focus on traditionally female strengths and styles of learning and eliminate competing demands for attention by boys in the classroom, creating a positive academic impact on girls.

Specialized Programming Within a Coed Facility

Although we believe that single sex facilities offer best practice for juvenile female offenders in residential care, we do understand that the financial realities of some jurisdictions may require coed facilities. The following are some suggestions on how to create the best possible environment for girls within a coed facility. While it is often assumed that coed programming means simply putting boys and girls together into a physical plant, it can mean any number of numerical realities, each creating completely different circumstances. For instance, sometimes coed means equal numbers of girls and boys, thus structuring the environment to allow for separate programming and equity in resources and access. Unfortunately, it is more likely that a coed facility will result in small numbers of girls housed with large numbers of boys, creating unsafe and potentially harmful situations for the female residents. Therefore, the first consideration when designing a coed program is to create a balance in gender whenever possible.

It may be possible to create a hybrid facility where all services and units within the physical plant are neither exclusively coed nor exclusively single-sexed. This can be achieved through sensitive, female responsive programming and thoughtful, female responsive design within a coed facility. The hybrid facility provides gender separation, with opportunities for limited and controlled interaction, within a coed facility. This does not mean simply accepting the practice of placing girls in male oriented facilities and painting the walls pink. Instead it means addressing the distinct needs of the girls in confinement, creating female responsive programming, and designing female controlled and programmed spaces.

Even in environments where it is not financially feasible to provide a completely separate gymnasium or program space, the use of wall partitions are important, as well as separate entrances and equity in access. Within a coed facility, it is important to recognize that there are two distinct genders with unique pathways that lead them to the correctional environment. These unique needs must be addressed, regardless of the physical plant, through specialized and separate programming that honors the female responsive values as a treatment modality.

A coed facility that provides separate housing with specialized design considerations for females and that includes gender specific programs could have a number of benefits. It would be large enough to afford a broad range of physical space and staffing amenities for both males and females; also, it would present a realistic model of the world, with controlled opportunities for interaction between boys and girls. This creates opportunities to teach youth to interact appropriately and safely. At the same time, it could (through scheduling or design) create separate space for females in housing, programming, and recreation; as such, it could embrace the benefits of single-sexed facilities as well. The needs of both males and females could, as a result, be addressed by the design and programming of the facility.

Conclusion

The issues surrounding female offenders in the justice system are complex. The research is clear on certain matters. Most young females entering the juvenile justice system are victims of abuse and require a healing and safe environment. Most enter the system for nonviolent offenses and up to a one-third are held for status-type offenses. Relationships are critical to young females. Therefore, whenever possible, it is essential to include family and other significant relationships in the development of treatment plans and as part of the treatment process. Program elements—such as mentors (who can relate to the girls' experiences) and opportunities for girls to develop relationships of trust and interdependence with other women already present in their lives (such as friends, relatives, neighbors, and/or church members)— are essential for effective gender specific programming for adolescent females. Each of these programmatic needs of girls can translate into design concepts for more effective and responsive girls' facilities. It is evident that jurisdictions should make careful choices when designing or converting facilities for female juveniles.

References

Acoca, L., & Dedel, K. (1998). *No place to hide: Understanding and meeting the needs of girls in the justice system.* San Francisco: National Council on Crime and Delinquency.

American Bar Association. (2001). *Justice by gender: The lack of appropriate prevention, diversion, and treatment alternatives for girls in the justice system.* Retrieved May 24, 2008 from http://www.abanet.org/crimjust/juvjus/justicebygenderweb.pdf

Beck, A. J., & Harrison, P. M. (2007). *Sexual victimization in state and federal prisons reported by inmates, 2007.* Washington, DC: Bureau of Justice Statistics.

Belknap, J., & Holsinger, K. (2006). The gendered nature of risk factors for delinquency. *Feminist Criminology, 1,* 1-24.

Bill, L. (1998). The victimization and revictimization of female offenders. *Corrections Today, 60,* 106-111.

Bloom, B., & Covington, S. (2001, November). *Effective gender-responsive interventions in juvenile justice: Addressing the lives of delinquent girls.* Presented at the American Society of Criminology, Atlanta, GA.

Braithwaite, J. (1989). *Crime, shame, and reintegration.* New York: Cambridge University Press.

Brown, L., & Gilligan, C. (1992). *Meeting at the crossroads: Women's psychology and girls' development.* Cambridge, MA: Harvard University Press.

Budnick, K., & Shields-Fletcher, E. (1998). *What about girls?* Washington, DC: Office of Juvenile Justice and Delinquency Prevention.

Chesney-Lind, M., & Shelden, R. G. (2004). *Girls, delinquency, and juvenile justice.* Belmont,CA: Thompson Wadsworth.

DeBell, J. (2001). The female offender: Different...not difficult. *Corrections Today, 63,* 56-61.

Earls, F., & Obeidallah, D. (1999). *Adolescent girls: The role of depression in the development of delinquency.* Washington, DC: National Institute of Justice.

Federal Bureau of Investigation. (2004). *Crime in the United States.* Washington, DC: Author.

Greene, Peters, and Associates. (1998). *Guiding principles for promising female programming.* Washington, DC: Office of Juvenile Justice and Delinquency Prevention.

Hayes, L. (2004). *Juvenile suicide in confinement: A national survey.* Washington, DC: Office of Juvenile Justice and Delinquency Programs.

Maniglia, R. (1998). *Juvenile female offenders: A status of the states report.* Washington, DC: Office of Juvenile Justice and Delinquency Prevention.

Marler, B., & Scoble, M. (2001). Building a juvenile system to serve the majority of offenders. *Corrections Today, 63,* 89-91.

Pranis, K., Stuart, B., & Wedge, M. (2003). *Peacemaking circles: From crime to community.* St. Paul, MN: Living Justice Press.

Ruddell, R., & Tomita, M. (2008). *Issues in correctional health.* Richmond, KY: Newgate.

Schaffner, L. (2006). *Girls in trouble with the law.* Piscataway, NJ: Rutgers University Press.

Sherman, F. T. (2005). *Pathways to juvenile detention reform: Detention reform and girls.* Baltimore, MD: Annie E. Casey Foundation.

Steffensmeier, D. (2008, March). *Trends in girls' violence and the gender gap: Analysis of diverse longitudinal sources.* Presented at the Blueprints Conference, Denver, CO.

Teplin, L. A., Abram, K. M., McClelland, G. M., Mericle, A. A., Dulcan, M. K., & Washburn, J. J. (2006). *Psychiatric disorders of youth in detention.* Washington, DC: Office of Juvenile Justice and Delinquency Prevention.

Valentine Foundation. (1990). *A conversation about girls.* Bryn Mawr, PA: Author.

Zahn, M. (2007). The causes of girls' delinquency and their program implications. *Family Court Review, 45,* 456-465.

Zavlek, S. (2005). *Planning community-based facilities for violent juvenile offenders as part of a system of graduated sanctions.* Washington, DC: Office of Juvenile Justice and Delinquency Prevention.

Zehr, H. (2000). *Victims, judges, and juvenile court reform through restorative justice.* Washington, DC: Office for Victims of Crime Bulletin.

CHAPTER 9
VIOLENCE: PREVALENCE AND CAUSES

Karen A. Mason and Noelle E. Fearn

J uveniles who end up confined in correctional facilities are oftentimes serious or chronic offenders who have continued to commit delinquent and/or criminal offenses while involved in community-based programs such as probation. The supervision, management, and rehabilitation of a population of chronic delinquents in a secure environment often fosters tense emotional situations that sometimes escalate to assaults and other acts of violence among juveniles and between juveniles and staff. While considerable scholarly attention has examined violence in adult jails and prisons, there has been comparatively little attention paid to violence in juvenile corrections. This is a significant limitation in our knowledge because the aftermath of a violent act may have long-term repercussions for the youth and the staff.

In addition to the potentially serious physical effects of a fight between residents, these incidents can have long-term psychological effects for the participants and observers, including the staff members. Moreover, such acts disrupt the functioning of a facility and contribute to a climate of fear, insecurity, and distrust. Such feelings undermine the rehabilitative efforts of the correctional staff. It is difficult, for example, for residents to focus on their schoolwork if they are fearful of being assaulted.

Along with the residents of a facility, the staff members are also adversely affected by violent incidents. Although Gordon, Moriarty, and Grant (2003) found that juvenile correctional officers generally have low levels of self reported fear of victimization, the long-term exposure to violence may increase stress, officer burnout, and employee turnover. Thus, it is in everybody's interest that we better understand the scope of the problem of violence in juvenile corrections, factors that contribute to violence, and strategies to reduce these incidents.

To help fill this gap in the literature, this chapter explores what is known about violence in youth corrections. We begin with a description of the prevalence of violence in these facilities. Next, findings from recent research on factors contributing to violence are discussed, including issues such as gang-involved youth and the factors that contribute to a culture of violence. Last, the chapter concludes with suggestions for future research examining violence in juvenile corrections.

Prevalence of Violence in Juvenile Corrections

Sexual Misconduct

One of the limitations of studying violence within juvenile facilities is that there is no national-level data that reports on the prevalence of these acts. As a result, it is difficult to define the boundaries of this problem. The U. S. Department of Justice, by contrast, provides estimates of rates of assaults in adult corrections in their *Census of Jails and Prisons*. One exception is the recent data collection effort conducted by the Bureau of Justice Statistics (BJS) to study sexual violence in corrections that was authorized in the Prison Rape Elimination Act of 2003 (PREA). In 2004, BJS researchers found that rates of sexual violence in juvenile correctional facilities were almost ten times greater than sexual assaults in adult state prisons (Beck & Hughes, 2005). The more recent 2005/2006 data also suggest that rates of substantiated incidents of sexual violence are higher in juvenile correctional facilities (3.0 per 1,000 juveniles) than in adult facilities (.52 per 1,000 adult jail inmates and .46 per 1,000 adult state prison inmates) (Beck, Adams, & Guerino, 2008).

Beck and colleagues (2008, p. 2) estimated that there were 2,821 acts of sexual misconduct in 2004; 2,047 incidents in 2005; and 2,025 acts in 2006. The corresponding rates of allegations of sexual misconduct for 2005 and 2006 were 16.7 and 16.8 per 1,000 residents, respectively. Allegations were roughly 4-5% higher in state operated juvenile facilities as compared to local or privately operated institutions for this two-year period (Beck et al., 2008, p. 2). Beck and colleagues (2008) also reported that 36% of the sexual violence allegations involved youth-on-youth nonconsensual sexual acts (such as genital contact or penetration) while 21% of these allegations involved youth-on-youth abusive sexual contacts (such as unwanted intentional touching). Approximately 21% of all youth-on-youth allegations of sexual violence were substantiated (e.g., investigated and determined to have occurred).

One of the most troubling aspects of these recent BJS reports is staff sexual misconduct and harassment directed toward residents (Roush, 2008). It is important to acknowledge that definitions for staff sexual misconduct and harassment are broader than for youth-on-youth sexual violence as incidents of voyeurism and invasion of privacy are reported as misconduct. Consensual contact between a staff member and a youth is illegal because the staff member is in a position of power over the youth and the residents cannot legally give consent to engage in sexual activities. Allegations of staff sexual misconduct accounted for 32% of all allegations of sexual violence reported in juvenile state, local, and privately operated facilities during 2005 and 2006 (Beck et al., 2008, p. 2). Allegations of staff sexual harassment (e.g., inappropriate verbal statements, comments of a sexual nature, demeaning or derogatory statements about body or clothing) accounted for approximately 11% of all allegations within the 2005/2006 data collection period (Beck et al., 2008, p. 2). Furthermore, almost one in five allegations (18%) of staff-on-youth sexual violence was substantiated through correctional investigations.

More specifically, in state operated juvenile facilities, there were 99 substantiated allegations of staff-on-youth sexually violent incidents (out of 795 total allegations). In local or privately operated facilities, by contrast, 196 of these allegations were substantiated (out of 979 total allegations). At the time this report was released, however, over 150 of these allegations of sexual violence toward youth by staff were still under investigation by correctional authorities (50 in state-run facilities and 105 in local/privately operated institutions) (Beck et al., 2008, p. 3). While the definition of correctional staff in these studies was quite broad (e.g., including employees, volunteers, or agency representatives), such findings underscore the need for further research.

It is important to note that both of these BJS data collection efforts were based on administrative or correctional authority records, rather than surveys of the youth. Thus, it is very likely that the information presented in these reports is influenced by inconsistent reporting practices and a lack of accurate data. As a result, the information reported above should be used with some caution because there may be a critical difference between the acts that occur and those that are actually reported to correctional authorities. BJS has recently developed and tested an approach to account for these limitations and to obtain this sensitive information directly from confined youth using an anonymous, self administered survey—the National Survey of Youth in Custody (NSYC)—expected to be completed sometime by the end of 2008 (Beck et al., 2008). It is likely that this effort will shed additional light on sexual violence within juvenile correctional facilities.

Assaults and Homicides

The Arizona Department of Juvenile Corrections (ADJC) is one of the few state agencies that has published data about violent incidents in juvenile corrections. Vasquez, Vivian, Chengalath, and Grimes (2004) reported that rates of assaults ranged from 13.5 per 100 incarcerated juveniles in August 2002 to 15.5 assaults per 100 youth in November 2003 (p. 6). Fearn and Ruddell (2009) reported that assault rates for adults in California's prison system ranged from 4.28 to 4.43 per 100 prisoners during 2002 and 2003 (p. 3). This finding suggests that assaults in juvenile corrections are approximately three times more frequent than assaults in adult prisons. However, one has to interpret these findings with some caution. It is possible, for instance, that incidents in juvenile facilities are more likely to be discovered because the ratio of staff to residents is higher. Moreover, definitions of assault and the types of incidents that are reported might vary greatly between states and correctional institutions. Still, these results, along with the information about sexual assaults in adult and juvenile facilities reported above, suggest that juvenile correctional facilities are more dangerous places than their adult counterparts — at least for assaults.

Mumola and Noonan (2008) recently published information about deaths of juveniles in state correctional facilities. Between 2002 and 2005, 43 youth died in these facilities. Of the 43 deaths that occurred, five were classified as homicides (although the causes of another five were unknown). Since there were approximately 32,000 juveniles residing in state training schools in 2003 (see Sickmund, Sladky, & Kang, 2005), this suggests that the homicide rate was approximately 3.9 per 100,000 juveniles. By contrast, Mumola (2005) reported that the homicide rate in adult jails was 3 per 100,000 adults and 4 per 100,000 inmates in state prisons. Thus, the homicide rate in juvenile correctional facilities appears to be very similar to the homicide rate in adult institutions.

However, this similarity between homicides in juvenile and adult corrections warrants further clarification. First, since homicides are rare events and the state juvenile population is relatively small, even one murder can dramatically increase the rate. For example, there were no murders in juvenile facilities in 2004 (although the cause of death for some residents was unknown). Moreover, we do not know the number of murders that occurred in juvenile detention facilities or in wilderness and boot camps. Thus, the lack of information makes it very difficult to make any general statements about murders in juvenile corrections, other than the rate appears to be very consistent with homicides in adult facilities. This finding, however, suggests that researchers investigate these incidents more closely.

One possible source of information about violence in juvenile corrections is through the Performance-based Standards (PbS) program, which is an initiative of the Council of Juvenile Correctional Administrators (CJCA). PbS (which is discussed at length in Chapter 17) collects information about different dimensions of safety in juvenile detention and long-term facilities, including rates of assaults (resident-on-resident and resident-on-staff members). According to Loughran (2007) there are a growing number of facilities participating in PbS and over ten percent of all incarcerated youth are held in participating institutions. This information may be important to establish national-level benchmarks regarding institutional violence and may contribute to our understanding of the boundaries of this problem.

Juvenile Correctional Institutions

Violence in correctional facilities is shaped, in part, by the characteristics of the persons incarcerated and the settings in which they live. All other factors being equal, for instance, research suggests that a higher population of violent adult offenders will be associated with higher rates of violence (e.g., Fearn & Ruddell, 2009). It is likely that youth corrections follows a similar pattern; a recent national study reported that of the juveniles in custody in 2003, the highest percentage (38%) were youth who were involved in crimes against persons (Snyder & Sickmund, 2006). Twenty-eight percent of these youth were held on property offenses, while public order offenders (e.g., youth taken into custody for offenses such as driving while intoxicated, prostitution, or disorderly conduct) represented only one-tenth of the population. Technical violations of probation orders accounted for 15% of the total residential population and five percent of all residents in these facilities were status offenders (Snyder & Sickmund, 2006).

Although most juveniles in custody were held in facilities operated by county or state governments, the number of delinquents in privately operated facilities remains significant. Public facilities held seven of ten delinquents in custody and three of ten status offenders. Most large, high security institutions are public while a large share of ranches and camps are private (Snyder & Sickmund, 2006). Whether public or private, juvenile correctional institutions vary by security level and their orientation toward either custody (security) or rehabilitation. In adult correctional systems, there is generally a greater likelihood of violence in higher security facilities and this pattern seems to hold true for violence that occurs in juvenile corrections.

There are several different types of juvenile correctional institutions. Some facilities resemble adult prisons, while others have less security and offer a more relaxed or therapeutic environment. As previously mentioned, a growing number of juvenile facilities are privately operated. Private facilities tend to be smaller than their public counterparts and hold fewer residents. Private facilities also tend to hold more status offenders, while public facilities hold more juveniles committed as delinquents (Snyder & Sickmund, 2006). Whether publicly or privately owned and operated, the main types of juvenile correctional institutions are ranches, forestry camps, boot camps, juvenile detention centers (commonly called juvenile halls), reception and diagnostic centers, and training schools.[1]

As highlighted in Chapter 3, ranches and forestry camps are minimum security facilities, which typically house first-time offenders and youth who have committed less serious crimes. Because these community-based facilities are minimum security placements, residents tend to have committed non-violent offenses or status offenses. In addition to pursuing their education, many residents are engaged in physical work on the ranches or conservation work in state parks. Many also participate in some form of group therapy, supported by individual treatment sessions and other forms of vocational or rehabilitative programming. In general, juveniles are more positive about completing their sentences in these environments than in more secure settings. Considering the more relaxed atmosphere it is not surprising that violence among juveniles and between juveniles and staff members in these facilities is lower than that which occurs in high security facilities (Parent, Leiter, Kennedy, Livens, Wentworth, & Wilcox, 1994).

Boot camps, by contrast, are medium security correctional operations that were developed to deter juveniles from committing crimes. First-generation boot camps (also called shock incarceration) emphasized military and physical training along with regimented activity. Staff members dressed in military style uniforms and acted as drill instructors. Individual and group punishments were often delivered for failure to comply with the rules. Typically, the sentence to a shock incarceration program ranges between 90 and 120 days, which is followed by a period of community supervision. Boot camps serve middle-range offenders who are not suitable for lesser sanctions like community supervision but who have not been designated as serious or chronic delinquents. Most programs prohibit serious offenders such as sex offenders and violent offenders from participating.

Later-generation boot camps provide more opportunities for education, as well as social and life skills development. They typically also offer better community-based support or aftercare upon the youth's release. Despite the fact that these camps are popular with legislators, the public, and some youth, they are gradually disappearing. One study comparing the experiences of juveniles in boot camps and those in more traditional facilities reported that, overall, residents found the boot camp to be more positive than traditional correctional facilities (MacKenzie, Wilson, Armstrong, & Gover, 2000). Yet, the same research has criticized these camps for failing to lower recidivism.

Research on the likelihood of violence in boot camps and wilderness and ranch programs has produced mixed results. MacKenzie and colleagues (2000), for example, found boot camps to be more therapeutic and less hostile and dangerous than training schools. Yet, a recent report published by the U.S. Government Accountability Office (GAO) found that many of these programs operated without any form of formal oversight and that between 1994 and 2004 at least ten youth died in these facilities. Furthermore, the GAO (2007) reported that "during 2005 alone, 33 states reported 1,619 staff members involved in incidents of abuse in residential programs" (p. 2). Such findings suggest that youth-on-youth violence in these settings might be less serious, but that staff members may become overzealous in their role (especially those in military style camps) and engage in abusive behaviors. Moreover, since many of these facilities are privately operated, there is very little oversight of their activities, including whether the staff working in them have received any training prior to working with youth.

Many youth who are taken into custody by the police are placed in juvenile halls (also called youth detention facilities). There are 757 of these high security facilities in the United States (Livsey, Sickmund, & Sladky, 2009) and they are often run by county or city agencies. These detention facilities typically house youth until their juvenile court appearances, including youth who have violated the conditions of their probation or parole. Other youth are held temporarily until they can be released to their parents or guardians. As a result, the average stay in these types of facilities tends to be relatively short. Because of the characteristics of the population, however, these facilities are thought to have higher than average rates of violence than long-term correctional facilities.

Youth admitted to detention for the first time are often fearful about their upcoming court dates and uncertain about the future and their legal troubles. In addition, these juveniles are sometimes under the influence of alcohol or drugs at the time of their arrests and they may be suffering from withdrawal. Furthermore, much like adult jails, conditions in these facilities tend to be noisy, crowded, and chaotic — youth are continually being admitted, discharged, and shifted between living units to reduce conflict (especially between gang members). Crowding and high resident-to-staff ratios (e.g., when there are few staff members to oversee the youth) also contribute to higher levels of violence (Mendel, 2007). These factors, combined with the immaturity, risky behaviors, and poor decision-making abilities of adolescence contribute to high rates of self-harm and violence in detention facilities (Holman & Ziedenberg, 2006).

Juveniles adjudicated (sentenced) to lengthy terms of incarceration are often sent to state operated facilities. As outlined in Chapter 2, in larger youth correctional systems, juveniles are first sent to reception and diagnostic centers to assess their needs and develop treatment plans. After the assessments are completed in these high security institutions, youth are transferred to other facilities. Assessments typically take between four and six weeks (Parent et al., 1994). The assessment includes an evaluation of youths' mental and physical health status, educational achievement, social functioning, and the dangers that they might pose. Evaluations are completed by a combination of educational staff, social workers, psychologists, and physicians. Very little is known about the specific rates of violent acts in these reception centers. Given the level of instability created by the constant turnover of residents and staff, acts of aggression and violence may be higher than in other facilities (Parent et al., 1994).

Facilities that house the greatest number of serious or persistent juvenile offenders are training schools, also known as juvenile correctional facilities. Training schools generally hold youth serving longer dispositions and are often state-run (although some private corporations contract with state agencies to provide care for these juveniles). Large states may have a diverse range of facilities, while smaller states might only have a few of these operations. They range in size from small cottages with a "home-like" feel to large concrete institutions that resemble adult prisons and are surrounded by razor wire fences with the perimeters patrolled by uniformed juvenile correctional officers.

Training schools hold a variety of offenders including the most serious and chronically delinquent youth. Administrators of these facilities often focus on keeping youth occupied with educational or rehabilitative and recreation programs during most of their waking hours. The quality of services and staff training, however, varies greatly among institutions. Historically, these facilities were built large to benefit from economies of scale (e.g., to reduce cost and maximize efficiency). Recent research, however, suggests that smaller cottages that have a more home-like environment may be safer for youth and reduce recidivism (see Chapter 15).

While not technically juvenile correctional facilities, local jails in some jurisdictions hold juveniles. Often, these jails are in small counties that do not have separate detention facilities for youth. Other juveniles have been charged as adults and these youth will be held in local jails until their cases have gone through the courts (in some states). Although these youth are supposed to have sight and sound separation from adults, this is not always the case. One of the cornerstones of the Juvenile Justice and Delinquency Prevention Act of 1974 (JJDPA) was the removal of juveniles from adult jails and, although there has been substantial progress, this problem still exists over three decades after the legislation was enacted.

Whether youth are confined to the more extreme and harsh environments of adult jails or juvenile training schools or the more relaxed atmosphere of wilderness ranches, they face particular challenges that may increase their vulnerability to acts of violence as either victim or aggressor. The next section of this chapter presents the special challenges of adjustment for juveniles detained in correctional facilities that may impact the occurrence of violence.

Adjustment to Incarceration

Despite the fact that research on the effects of adult incarceration has a long tradition (e.g., Clemmer, 1958; Sykes, 1958), we still know very little about the impact it has on juveniles. Most studies focus on the imported characteristics brought into the institution by the adult prisoner or the impact of deprivations and other characteristics of the institutional environment (Poole & Regoli, 1983; Sykes, 1958). Research using a developmental perspective on adjustment to institutional confinement is scarce. Furthermore, the research that does employ a developmental perspective focuses mainly on the origins of aggression and delinquency and seldom on the impact of the correctional environment on institutional misconduct or future violence (Greve, 2001).

What is known about the adjustment of juveniles to confinement is that they react to the pains of imprisonment in ways similar to adults (Bartollas, 1982). Specifically, juveniles develop and adhere to an inmate code of conduct while also utilizing several coping strategies to adjust (Bartollas, Miller, & Dintz, 1976). Comparable to incarcerated adults, juveniles develop a set of norms, or inmate code, that all residents are expected to follow. Some of the principles of this code, as reported in a study of a maximum security training school include: "Don't rat on your peers," "Be cool," and "Don't get involved in another inmates' affairs" (Bartollas et al., 1976, pp. 63-64). By far, the most accepted informal norm is the one prohibiting informing on another resident (McEwen, 1978). Not surprisingly, offenders in maximum security facilities with longer sentences are the most likely of all juveniles to accept and adhere to this code (Bartollas, 1982).

In addition, juvenile adjustment to incarceration is similar to their adult counterparts and these residents employ various means to cope with their incarceration. Confinement produces intense emotions among juveniles including hopelessness, shame, fear, and anger (Bartollas et al., 1976). To deal with these strong emotions, juveniles tend to develop different coping strategies. In a study of a maximum security training school for males, Bartollas and colleagues (1976) found five distinct adjustment strategies. The most frequently used adjustment mechanism was for youth to capitalize on opportunities to gain access to privileges and amenities to make life easier. Using this strategy, youth attempt to gain as many institutional privileges as possible. While this strategy is less likely to promote violence, manipulation of other residents and staff to "get one up" could conceivably create situations where violence erupts.

A second adjustment strategy found in juvenile corrections is youth who conform to institutional rules and staff directives, which foster prosocial attitudes. Youth adopting this approach were more likely to avoid violent situations and instead focus on gaining skills for the future. The third mode of adaptation is to avoid adherence to either the inmate code or institutional rules. This strategy is typified by phrases such as "playing it cool" or "doing my own time." Juveniles using this strategy have learned to keep their emotions under control and try to remain more private and independent (Bartollas et al., 1976). The avoidance of violent situations is a primary goal of this coping strategy. The fourth adjustment mechanism is withdrawal. This adaptation was accompanied by feelings of shame, fear, anxiety, and humiliation. Violence promoted by this coping mechanism is more likely to be directed inward by attempts of suicide or by attempts to escape. The last adaptation tactic is rebellion. Residents who rebelled confronted staff in every way possible, including attacking them. Not only are these residents prone to violence, but they also attempt to instigate violence among other juveniles and with staff.

The development of different modes of adaptation and the acceptance of an inmate code offer some insight into violence in juvenile corrections. Like adults, juveniles who adhere strictly to tenets of the inmate code and those who rely on manipulation and rebellion to cope with confinement are more likely to be involved in acts of violence, either as the victim or the aggressor. While research has not addressed how adolescent development influences adjustment in correctional settings, a few studies have examined the internal and external factors that contribute to juvenile correctional violence. The following section discusses two primary approaches to the study of juvenile violence in correctional environments and recent research in these areas.

Explaining Violence: Deprivation and Importation Models

The deprivation and importation models of (adult) prison adjustment have guided most research on the causes of juvenile correctional violence (Gover, MacKenzie, & Armstrong, 2000; MacDonald, 1999; Trulson, 2007; Vivian, Grimes, & Vasquez, 2007). The major assumption of the deprivation model is that prison behavior, including violence, is the product of prisoner responses to the abnormal and extreme environment of the prison (Goodstein & Wright, 1991). According to Poole and Regoli (1983), inmate misconduct is a "normal reaction of normal people to abnormal conditions. Coercive, brutal, and dehumanizing prison conditions may force inmates into predator behavior in order to cope with the pains of imprisonment" (p. 215).

According to the deprivation model, there are several features of the correctional institution itself that affect the occurrence of violence, including arbitrary rule enforcement by staff and correctional officers, orientation of the institution (e.g., custody vs. treatment), staff-to-inmate ratio, overcrowding, and the length of juveniles' sentences (MacDonald, 1999; Trulson, 2007). With respect to rule enforcement, if youth perceive juvenile correctional staff and officers' actions as unjust, there is the threat of violence at the group level, including disturbances (such as riots). At the individual level, residents who believe they are being treated unfairly are more likely to violate rules (McCorkle, Miethe, & Drass, 1995).

In addition to rule enforcement, the orientation of the facility might also contribute to the deprivations experienced by incarcerated youth. Institutions with greater emphasis on custody and security as compared to treatment are thought to produce greater resistance among juvenile residents and thereby increase the amount of institutional violence (MacDonald, 1999; McCorkle et al., 1995). A caution to this argument is the finding that some institutions with lower levels of security have higher levels of role conflict among staff that promote alienation and violence among incarcerated populations (Hepburn & Albonetti, 1980).

Another component of the deprivation model is that the structure of a facility may facilitate violence. Researchers have emphasized the impact of crowding and the staff-to-inmate ratio on adjustment in juvenile corrections (Holman & Ziedenberg, 2006). The lack of space and privacy makes residents more irritable and increases the probability of violence. Overcrowding has also been associated with acts of violence by individuals and with group disturbances. Other indicators of deprivation can include poor food services, environmental conditions (e.g., excessively hot or cold), inadequate rehabilitative programming, and access to outdoor recreation.

In contrast to the deprivation argument, the importation model challenges the view that inmate behavior is a reflection of the hardships imposed by the prison environment. Rather, the importation model asserts that prison behavior is largely determined by past experiences and characteristics that prisoners bring into a correctional setting.

According to this view, the correctional environment has little to do with an inmate's behavior—rather, an inmate's characteristics, experiences, and lifestyle are imported into the prison. As stated by Poole and Regoli (1983), "Violence in prison is the logical and predictable result of the commitment of a collection of individuals whose life histories have been characterized by disregard for law, order and social convention" (p. 215). Thus, those factors that lead to crime and violence on the streets also lead to violence inside the prison. These variables include education level, prior gang membership, race, arrest history, personality, parental and sibling criminality, history of drug use, history of violence, and age (Hochstetler & DeLisi, 2005).

In terms of violence in juvenile placements, two of the above listed factors are particularly relevant. First, research has shown that a history of drug use and a history of violence are related to institutional violence among adults and juveniles (Harer & Steffensmeier, 1996; MacDonald, 1999). These studies support the argument that tendencies in lifestyle, adjustment, and coping skills are brought into the facility by the individual. Second, there is support for the association between the age of the individual and the increased probability of violence (Trulson, 2007). The relationship between age and institutional violence may be explained by the fact that younger offenders are more likely to react violently to facility conditions while older, more "institutionalized" offenders cope with these conditions by bonding with other inmates for support or in an effort of collective resistance. The relationship between youth and institutional violence may also be explained by levels of low self control and, like other (antisocial) behaviors, the likelihood of violence by individuals in an institutional setting diminishes with age (see Gottfredson & Hirschi, 1990).

The brief review presented above suggests that both the deprivation and importation models may be helpful in understanding and subsequently alleviating violence in juvenile corrections. However, neither model, by itself, adequately explains juvenile correctional violence. In an effort to address the shortcomings of each perspective, some researchers have sought to combine or integrate these theories (Camp, Gaes, Langan, & Saylor, 2003; Hochstetler & DeLisi, 2005). Integrated approaches view offenders as arriving at correctional facilities with deep-seated attitudes reflective of close social associations drawn from their particular outside culture. Once entering the institution, these same offenders are exposed to conditions of confinement that affect their already aggressive and volatile attitudes.

Understanding Juvenile Correctional Violence: An Integrated Approach

Integrated approaches appear prominently in recent studies of violence in juvenile corrections; however, only four studies have addressed violence in U. S. juvenile institutions in the last 25 years (see MacDonald, 1999; Poole & Regoli, 1983; Trulson, 2007; Vivian et al., 2007). Poole and Regoli (1983) conducted one of the earliest studies of violence in juvenile institutions. Observational, interview, and official data for males from four juvenile correctional institutions in four states were collected. The analysis included four importation variables — race, age, attitudes toward aggression, and pre-institutional violence — and three deprivation variables — assimilation to the inmate code, type of institution, and length of time served. The results of this study indicated that pre-institutional violence (from the importation model) was the most significant predictor of institutional violence. Additionally, two variables drawn from the deprivation model, institutional type (custody vs. treatment) and adherence to the inmate code, were strongly related to the amount of violence in a facility. These investigators found that confinement in a more custody oriented environment and acceptance of the inmate code increased the likelihood of violence.

In a study of incarcerated and paroled youth from the California Youth Authority (CYA) during the mid-1980s, MacDonald (1999) examined the impact of importation and deprivation factors on institutional violence and drug use. Importation variables included time between first arrest and most

recent confinement, number of previous arrests, parental and sibling criminality, prior gang involvement, violent criminal history, drug criminal
history, and race. Deprivation variables included the level of institutional
security and the staff-to-inmate ratio. MacDonald (1999) found that youth
with a history of violence and gang involvement were significantly more
likely to be involved in violence, thus partially supporting the importation
model. However, he also found that juveniles in high security settings were
significantly more likely to be involved in violence than residents in institutions with lower levels of security, thus providing some support for the
deprivation model. These findings, however, should be accepted with some
caution, as youth placed in higher security facilities tend to be more violent
or have longer histories of delinquency.

Vivian and colleagues (2007) analyzed over 10,000 incidents in the Arizona Department of Juvenile Corrections (ADJC) involving actual or potential injury assaults among juvenile residents and between juvenile residents
and staff. The individual and contextual variables used in the analysis are
those typically used in tests of the importation and deprivation models,
although they were not identified as such by the researchers. The individu-
al/importation variables included in the study were violent history, separation commitments, delinquent peer relationships, and history of drug use.
The contextual or deprivation model variables included identification of
specific housing units (characterized in the top quartile for juvenile self
referral to separation [segregation from the general juvenile population]); the
separation rate; the presence of youth with prior assaults while adjudicated;
youth with previous violent convictions; emotional/mental stability; and
delinquent peers. The findings revealed that population density or a limited
deprivation model alone does not explain juvenile correctional violence.

These investigators also examined the likelihood of the escalation of a
violent incident into a more serious incident involving injury and found
support for a combined importation and deprivation model. Individual or
importation factors that predicted the escalation of an incident into violence
with injury included: (a) youth with high numbers of referrals to segregation;
(b) youth involved had two or more prior assault offenses; and (c) mentally
unstable youth. The contextual/deprivation factors that predicted escalation
of an incident to one of violence with injury included: (a) housing units with
high separation/segregation rates and (b) housing units with high assault
rates. The findings from this study indicate that violence is more likely to
result from the placement of mentally unstable juveniles with extensive
assault histories into housing units that were already unstable.

Another recent study of juvenile corrections examined violence among
nearly 5,000 youth released from a large Southern juvenile correctional
system. Trulson (2007) examined factors that affect both occurrences of

institutional violence (e.g., danger) and institutional disruption. The discussion here addresses only those findings related to institutional violence and danger. Institutional violence was defined as assaults on staff, assaults on another resident, and possession of a weapon while confined. Unlike the studies previously discussed, only importation factors were considered. The variables included were: demographic characteristics, age at first referral, age at state commitment, age at release from incarceration, length of incarceration, number of felony adjudications, gang membership at time of commitment, previous family violence, educational achievement, history of abuse/neglect, emotional abuse, mental challenges, and mental illnesses. The findings revealed that male, non-White youth with gang influences and those with earlier and more extensive serious delinquent histories were significantly more likely to commit acts of institutional violence than were their counterparts.

Based on the results of these recent studies there are two factors that appear to have the most impact on violence in juvenile institutions. From the importation model, the prior history of the juvenile has a significant effect on behavior while confined. All of the recent studies found that violent acts and relationships with delinquent peers (e.g., gang involvement) prior to incarceration significantly increase the likelihood of violence. From the deprivation model, research findings reveal that being housed in highly secure custodial environments or in units with higher levels of instability significantly increased the likelihood of assaults.

In reality, these two factors may interact to create and escalate situations of violence. The more coercive the institutional conditions, the fewer resources available to alleviate the pains of confinement, which may then push those juveniles over the edge into victimizing fellow residents and staff. In addition to the various importation- and deprivation-related factors that have been found to influence violence in juvenile correctional facilities, the presence of gangs, gang-affiliated youth, and what some have termed a "culture of violence" certainly also contribute to violence within these institutions.

Gangs and Violence in Juvenile Corrections

Gangs are one of the biggest challenges facing the security and safety of residents in youth corrections. A national-level study of gangs, conducted by Curry, Howell, and Roush (2000), found that "nearly 9 out of 10 detention centers have gang members among their residents. Almost half of the detention centers said that about a third or more of their inmates belong to a gang" (p. 15). Gangs are disruptive in any correctional facility, but the problem may be more serious in juvenile facilities because gang members undermine the rehabilitative philosophy and staff authority. This can result in violence and Curry and colleagues (2000) reported that:

> Slightly over half of the detention centers reported gang-related assaults, almost half reported problems with gangs recruiting members, nearly one-third reported threats/intimidation of staff, and one-fourth reported threats/intimidation of non-gang members. These high levels of gang-related violence and disruption in detention centers is not surprising, given the proportion of inmates that belong to gangs, the presence of multiple gangs in most detention centers, the lack of risk assessment and security classification, and the lack of effective programs geared toward them. (p. 15)

The problem of gangs in juvenile corrections is more serious in some states than others. There is, for example, a long history of gang involvement in California facilities (see Lerner, 1986). The presence of gangs is so severe that many youth feel they have to join a gang in order to gain protection and respect from other residents. As a result, the incarceration of youth gang members imports the violent subculture of the streets (MacDonald, 1999).

The presence of members from rival gangs will often lead to conflict, which may erupt into violence. Thus, the level of violence will be higher than normally expected when institutions are filled with gang-affiliated youth. A recent publication by the California Standards Authority (CSA) provides further support for this argument by reporting that in the first quarter of 2007, there were 183 assaults by juveniles on correctional staff in California juvenile halls (CSA, 2007, p. 4). Additionally, CSA reports that there were 15 escapes and 71 suicide attempts in these facilities. Californian camps or ranch facilities appear to be somewhat less dangerous — and less secure (as compared to the juvenile halls) — with 22 juvenile assaults on staff members, 167 escapes, and 6 suicide attempts reported for the first quarter of 2007 (CSA, 2007, p. 4).

During the 2004 calendar year, in one California juvenile institution — Preston Youth Correctional Facility — 54 incidents of battery (and attempted battery) by youth targeted toward correctional staff were reported (CSA, 2005). The CSA publication further reported that 82% of the juveniles confined in this particular facility "have documented gang affiliations" — thus lending support for the link between gang presence in juvenile correctional facilities and violence within these institutions (CSA, 2005, p. 4).

Culture of Violence

A number of recent investigations of state operated juvenile correctional systems have identified what some youth advocates have called a "culture of violence." Although the specific definition of a culture of violence differs somewhat between investigators, this term refers generally to the development of an aggressive staff culture that ultimately supports or advances interpersonal violence among juvenile residents as well as between juvenile residents and correctional staff. Anderson, Norris, and Zulpo-Dane (2005) attributed this culture in the California Department of Corrections and Rehabilitation's (CDCR) Chaderjian (Chad) facility to "Chad's prison design, confrontational environment and staff antagonism," stating that these factors "create a culture saturated with manipulation and violence. Youth are forced to fight for their survival. Excessive force by guards often leaves youth seriously injured" (p. iii). It is possible that such a culture forms when youth are placed in prison-like environments, although to be fair, the CDCR holds youth who committed crimes as juveniles until their 25th birthday and few would agree that a 24-year-old is still a juvenile.

Anderson and colleagues (2005) also reported that "Over the course of just four months in 2003, staff maced or used force 482 times in incidents involving over 800 youth," and that "the prison environment and staff foster fear, mandate segregation, and encourage physical violence among the youth" (p. 13). An environment that is steeped in violence is apt to increase levels of stress as youth cope with the possibility that an attack might occur at any time. Again, one factor that might increase this stress and fear is the high level of gang involvement and gang-affiliated youth in California's Division of Juvenile Justice. Researchers also claim, however, that staff members create situations or circumstances that might escalate aggressive behavior, such as placing youth from rival gangs in the same area. While juvenile correctional officers are typically trained in methods of verbal de-escalation of conflict, Anderson and colleagues (2005) have observed that "instead of practicing de-escalation, tolerance, intensive therapy, or helping youth cope, staff often use excessive force and instigate violence, hatred, and gang enmity" (p. 16).

Such problems are not unique to California. Abrams (2006) has also written about a "culture of violence" that exists (or existed) in the following state juvenile correctional systems: Arizona (prior to 1993), Georgia, Maryland, and South Dakota. He attributed this culture to underfunding, apathy toward juvenile offenders (especially in terms of the tension between warehousing youth and providing them with meaningful treatment or rehabilitation), and the fact that many youth in the juvenile justice system are from minority groups and there is little political willingness to help them.

Cohen (2008) recently released the results of an investigation into violence in correctional facilities operated by Ohio's Department of Youth Services (DYS). Ohio's correctional system came under scrutiny of the U. S. Department of Justice in response to complaints that the civil rights of youth were being violated. Cohen (2008) reported that a code of silence (where correctional officers provide tacit approval to violence by not reporting the inappropriate use of force by fellow officers) supports a culture of staff violence in some facilities. Similar to the California example discussed above, Cohen (2008) described the culture of violence in Ohio's juvenile correctional facilities:

> The system avoids information and concepts from the child-care and adolescent perspectives. The heavy emphasis on the correctional aspects (security, staff safety, and control) seems to preclude information about adolescence and the legal rights of juveniles that could be helpful in altering behavior. This preoccupation creates a condition where the absence of a broad-based training experience and the lack of openness to the uniqueness of adolescence, combine to enforce the culture of violence we have observed. (pp. 131-132)

Cohen suggested that the staff members in Ohio youth facilities have created a negative environment for the youth and that these juvenile residents model what they observe. If the correctional staff members are preoccupied with confrontation or use physical force or threats in an unfair, illegitimate, unnecessary, or unjust manner, youth may imitate the same attitudes and behaviors.

It is important to note, however, that working in a juvenile correctional facility is a very stressful occupation and this stress may be exacerbated by overcrowding, a lack of funding for rehabilitative or recreational programs, forced overtime, rotating shifts, and a fear of some residents. Many of the youth who are placed in state correctional facilities, for instance, are long-term offenders, have significant mental health problems, and are aggressive. In addition, many of these juveniles are gang-involved and have little attachment to prosocial values. Last, youth frequently test the staff's boundaries and this can set up situations where the staff members act aggressively. While these factors do not excuse any unnecessary use of force or abuse by authority, one must understand the complex institutional context in which these violent incidents occur.

Conclusion

Based on the information from the studies presented here, it is obvious that much more research on violence in juvenile corrections is needed. A first step is to obtain accurate information about the prevalence of violence in these facilities so that patterns and trends can be identified and tracked. In addition, it is likely that qualitative studies may reveal factors specific to the development of adolescents that might influence the occurrence and escalation of violence. As reported above, the few studies that we currently have on juvenile correctional violence rely heavily upon the study of adult correctional institutions. Research designed to more closely examine and understand the specific developmental challenges of incarcerated youth would offer new insights into the adjustment of juveniles to institutional confinement.

Another area for future research concerns the managerial styles that directly affect the quality of life in juvenile institutions (Bartollas, Miller, & Dintz, 2007). Identifying and examining the administrative rules, policies, and mandates that regulate staff control of violent and disruptive youth may further explain — and subsequently help to reduce — acts of violence in juvenile corrections. Additionally, research should focus on how interpersonal relationships between the residents and staff and comprehensive rehabilitative programs (including case management) counter violence.

Unfortunately, the most striking revelation from this chapter is the lack of research focused on violence in juvenile correctional institutions. The study of violence in juvenile corrections is important for a great many reasons, but especially because violence directly undermines the rehabilitative philosophy that underlies juvenile justice. It is surprising — and disappointing — that more attention has not been paid to juvenile correctional violence given the current focus among academics (and others) about "what works" in corrections (Cullen, 2005). By ignoring violence in juvenile correctional facilities, researchers and juvenile justice officials commit a huge disservice to juveniles confined in all types of custodial settings.

Endnote

1. Foster and group homes are eliminated from this analysis. See Mutchnick and Fawcett (1990) for a study of variables predicting violence in juvenile group homes.

References

Abrams, D. E. (2006). Reforming juvenile delinquency treatment to enhance rehabilitation, personal accountability, and public safety. *Oregon Law Review, 84*, 1001-1092.

Anderson, L., Norris, Z., & Zulpo-Dane, M. (2005). *Voices from inside: The case for closing California's "Chad" youth prison.* Oakland, CA: Books Not Bars.

Bartollas, C. (1982). Survival problems of adolescent prisoners. In R. Johnson & H. Toch (Eds.), *The pains of imprisonment,* (pp. 165-179). Beverly Hills, CA: Sage Publications.

Bartollas, C., Miller S. J., & Dintz, S. (1976). *Juvenile victimization: The institutional paradox.* New York: Halsted.

Bartollas, C., Miller S. J., & Dintz, S. (2007). Managerial styles and institutional control. *Youth Violence and Juvenile Justice, 5*, 57-70.

Beck, A. J., Adams, D. B., & Guerino, P. (2008). *Sexual violence reported by juvenile correctional authorities, 2005-06.* Washington, DC: Bureau of Justice Statistics.

Beck, A. J., & Hughes, T. A. (2005). *Sexual violence reported by correctional authorities, 2004.* Washington, DC: Bureau of Justice Statistics.

Camp, S., Gaes, G., Langan, N., & Saylor, W. (2003). The influence of prisons on inmate misconduct: A multilevel investigation. *Justice Quarterly, 20*, 501-533.

Clemmer, D. (1958). *The prison community.* Boston, MA: Christopher.

Cohen, F. (2008). *Final fact-finding report: S.H. v. Stickrath.* Retrieved May 28, 2008, from http://www.dys.ohio.gov

Corrections Standards Authority. (2005). *Preston Youth Correctional Facility: Staff safety evaluation.* Sacramento, CA: Author.

Corrections Standards Authority. (2007). *Juvenile detention profile survey, first quarter 2007.* Sacramento, CA: Author.

Cullen, F. T. (2005). The twelve people who saved rehabilitation: How the science of criminology made a difference. *Criminology, 43*, 1-42.

Curry, G. D., Howell, J. C., & Roush, D. W. (2000). *Youth gangs in juvenile detention and corrections facilities: A national survey of juvenile detention centers.* Washington, DC: Office of Juvenile Justice and Delinquency Prevention.

Fearn, N. E., & Ruddell, R. (2009). *Understanding correctional violence.* Richmond, KY: Newgate.

Goodstein, L., & Wright, K. N. (1991). Inmate adjustment to prison. In L. Goodstein & D. L. MacKenzie (Eds.), *The American prison,* (pp. 229-251). New York: Plenum Press.

Gordon, J. A., Moriarty, L. J., & Grant, P. H. (2003). Juvenile correctional officers' perceived fear and risk of victimization. *Criminal Justice and Behavior, 30*, 62-84.

Gottfredson, M. R., & Hirschi, T. (1990). *A general theory of crime.* Stanford, CA: Stanford University Press.

Gover A., MacKenzie, D. L., & Armstrong, G. (2000). Importation and deprivation explanations of juveniles' adjustment to correctional facilities. *International Journal of Offender Therapy and Comparative Criminology, 44*, 450-467.

Greve, W. (2001). Imprisonment of juveniles and adolescents: Deficits and demands for developmental research. *Applied Developmental Science, 5*, 21-36.

Harer, M., & Steffensmeier, D. (1996). Race and prison violence. *Criminology, 34*, 323-355.

Hepburn, J. R., & Albonetti, C. (1980). Role conflict in correctional institutions. *Criminology, 17*, 445-459.

Hochstetler, A., & DeLisi, M. (2005). Importation, deprivation and varieties of serving time: An integrated lifestyle-exposure model of prison offending. *Journal of Criminal Justice, 33*, 257-266.

Holman, B., & Ziedenberg, J. (2006). *The dangers of detention: The impact of incarcerating youth in detention and other secure facilities.* Washington, DC: Justice Policy Institute.

Lerner, S. (1986). *Bodily harm: The pattern of fear and violence at the California Youth Authority.* Bolinas, CA: Common Knowledge Press.

Light, S. C. (1990). The severity of assaults on prison officers: A contextual study. *Social Science Quarterly, 71*, 267-284.

Livsey, S., Sickmund, M., & Sladky, A. (2009). *Juvenile residential facility census, 2004: Selected findings.* Washington, DC: Office of Juvenile Justice and Delinquency Prevention.

Loughran, N. (2007, October). *Performance-based standards (PbS) for youth correction and detention facilities.* Presented at the Correctional Security Network Conference, Cincinnati, OH.

MacDonald, J. M. (1999). Violence and drug use in juvenile institutions. *Journal of Criminal Justice, 27*, 33-44.

MacKenzie, D. L., Wilson, D. L., Armstrong, G. S., & Gover, A. R. (2000). The impact of boot camps and traditional institutions on juvenile residents: Perceptions, adjustment, and change. *Journal of Research in Crime and Delinquency, 38*, 279-313.

McCorkle, R. C., Miethe T. D., & Drass, K. A. (1995). The roots of prison violence: A test of the deprivation, management, and "not-so-total" institution models. *Crime & Delinquency, 41*, 317-331.

McEwen, C. A. (1978). *Designing correctional organizations for youths: Dilemmas of subcultural development.* Cambridge, MA: Ballinger.

Mendel, R. A. (2003). *Small is beautiful: The Missouri Division of Youth Services.* Retrieved January 29, 2008, from http://www.ctjja.org/media/resources/resource_9.pdf

Mendel, R. A. (2007). *Beyond detention: System transformation through juvenile detention reform.* Baltimore, MD: Annie E. Casey Foundation.

Mumola, C. J. (2005). *Suicide and homicide in state prisons and local jails.* Washington, DC: Bureau of Justice Statistics.

Mumola, C. J., & Noonan, M. E. (2008). *Deaths in custody statistical tables.* Retrieved January 30, 2008, from http://www.ojp.usdoj.gov/bjs/dcrp/dictabs.htm

Mutchnick, R. J., & Fawcett, M. R. (1990). Violence in juvenile corrections: Correlates of victimization in group homes. *International Journal of Offender Therapy and Comparative Criminology, 34*, 43-56.

Parent, D. G., Leiter, V., Kennedy, S., Livens, L., Wentworth, D., & Wilcox, S. (1994). *Conditions of confinement: Juvenile detention and correctional facilities.* Washington, DC: Office of Juvenile Justice and Delinquency Prevention.

Poole, E. D., & Regoli, R. M. (1983). Violence in juvenile institutions: A comparative study. *Criminology, 21*, 213-232.

Roush, D. W. (2008). Staff sexual misconduct in juvenile justice facilities: Implications for work force training. *Corrections Today, 70*, 32-34, 70.

Sickmund, M., Sladky, T. J., & Kang, W. (2005). *Census of juveniles in residential placement databook.* Retrieved January 30, 2008, from http://www.ojjdp.ncjrs.org/ojstatbb/cjrp

Snyder, H. N., & Sickmund, M. (2006). *Juvenile offenders and victims: 2006 national report.* Washington, DC: Office of Juvenile Justice and Delinquency Prevention.

Sykes, G. (1958). *The society of captives: A study of a maximum security prison.* Princeton, NJ: Princeton University Press.

Trulson, C. R. (2007). Determinants of disruption: Institutional misconduct among state-committed delinquents. *Youth Violence and Juvenile Justice, 5*, 7-34.

U. S. Government Accountability Office. (2007). *Residential treatment programs: Concerns regarding abuse and death in certain programs for troubled youth.* Washington, DC: Author.

Vasquez, S., Vivian, J. P., Chengalath, G., & Grimes, J. (2004). *Assaults within ADJC secure care facilities.* Phoenix, AZ: Arizona Department of Juvenile Corrections.

Vivian, J. P., Grimes, J. N., & Vasquez, S. (2007). Assaults in juvenile correctional facilities: An exploratory study. *Journal of Crime and Justice, 30*, 17-34.

CHAPTER 10
PREVENTING SUICIDE AND SELF-HARM

Ryan Patten

W hile adolescent suicide has long been a serious concern in the United States, administrators in some facilities that hold youth seem to be disregarding some of the interventions that have been used to prevent these tragedies. While there is not an overarching, all encompassing cause or reason for suicides, motivations for youth suicides (both inside and outside correctional facilities) are strikingly similar. Common factors in most successful juvenile suicides are mental illness or other disabilities; histories of emotional, physical, sexual, and substance abuse; and a predisposition for self-harm.

Some facilities fail to employ adequate intake screening to detect suicidal juveniles, provide insufficient or inadequate staff training, and few written policies to reduce these tragedies. These shortcomings promote opportunities for suicide attempts, self-harm, and suicides. Unfortunately, some of these failures have yet to be systematically addressed in some facilities, and the slow pace at establishing suicide prevention remedies is cause for concern. Until these deficiencies are identified, improved, and normalized within these institutions, lives will continue to be lost. This chapter examines the prevalence of adolescent suicide in the general population, within juvenile facilities, the predictors of these events, as well as some of the efforts undertaken to prevent suicide.

Adolescent Suicide

Although suicide is rare in youngsters under ten years of age, incidents of suicide begin to increase in the early teen years through the early twenties (Gould, Greenberg, Velting, & Shaffer, 2003). While girls are more likely to have suicidal ideation and attempt suicide (Garrison, McKeown, Valois, & Vincent, 1993), young men aged 15 to 19 years are five times more likely to complete suicide (Anderson, 2002). Juvenile suicide rates are the highest among American Indians and lowest among Asian/Pacific Islanders; however, adolescent Whites are the most common victims (Anderson, 1992).

In the past, concern over youth suicide, especially regarding children detained in adult facilities, was so strong that one of the main goals of the

1974 Juvenile Justice and Delinquency Prevention Act (JJDPA) was to remove juveniles from adult jails and prisons (Flaherty, 1980; Schwartz, 1989). Adolescent suicide rates in secure, adult detention facilities from the 1970s illustrate the severity of the problem at that time. Memory (1989) estimated the suicide rate of juveniles in adult jails at 2,041 per 100,000 residents and the suicide rate of adolescents in youth detention centers at 57 per 100,000 residents. The latter figure was 4.6 times higher than the suicide rate of persons in the community aged 12 through 24 years.

Studies have consistently shown that incarcerated juveniles have higher levels of suicide risk and completed suicides compared to the general youth population. A Centers for Disease Control and Prevention (CDC) study, for instance, revealed that suicide attempts for incarcerated teens was eight percent higher and the injury rate after the suicide attempt was six percent higher than the national average (CDC, 1991). Abram and colleagues (2008) reported that:

> More than one third of juvenile detainees and nearly half of females had felt hopeless or thought about death in the six months before detention. Approximately one in ten juvenile detainees had thought about committing suicide in the past six months, and one in ten had ever attempted suicide. (p. 291)

Although suicide among juveniles has been on a downward trend over the past 20 years, in 2002 suicide was still the second leading cause of death among 14- to 17-year-olds (Thompson, Kingree, & Ho, 2006). By 2004, the risk of suicide among incarcerated youth was five times higher than the national average (Farand, Chagnon, Renaud, & Rivard, 2004). A recent study by the Bureau of Justice Statistics (BJS) revealed that suicide was still the leading cause of death for adolescents detained in juvenile correctional facilities from 2002 to 2005 (Mumola & Noonan, 2008). It is clear that the rates of suicide, especially for incarcerated youth, are exceedingly high. Suicide, however, is also a problem for juveniles in the general population because early diagnosis and treatment of these problems is difficult. Moreover, juveniles often act in a rash and impulsive manner—which is a function of their development—and this also contributes to high levels of harmful behaviors in correctional facilities, including suicide.

Predictors for Juvenile Suicides in the General Population

There is a known set of predictors regarding suicidal ideation, attempts, and completed suicide among youth: mental health problems (such as depression, but also including suicidal ideation); substance abuse; histories of emotional, physical, and sexual abuse; prior delinquency; and previous self injurious behavior and suicide attempts.

Psychiatric disorders are found in over 90% of completed juvenile suicides (Gould et al., 2003). Disorders such as depression also increase the likelihood of attempts and suicides (Brent et al., 1988; Brent et al., 1993). Some of the difficulty with diagnosing adolescents as having a mental health problem may stem from the dismissive attitudes of the adults who are supposed to care for them. Instead of identifying a potentially serious mental condition in the youth, adults may be quick to label the troubled behavior as acting out or malingering (which is a term for an individual who is fabricating or exaggerating symptoms). Schizophrenia, while linked to an increase in suicides later in life, is less of a concern with juveniles because the symptoms of the disease do not typically appear until late adolescence (Drake, Gates, Cotton, & Whittaker, 1984).

Substance Abuse

Abuse of both drugs and alcohol significantly increases the likelihood of suicide. Previous research indicated that substance abuse led to a greater chance of suicide for juveniles when compared to adults (Holland & Griffin, 1984). The risk of suicide is also greatly enhanced for juveniles suffering from both mental illness and substance abuse, a problem that mental health professionals define as co-occurring disorders (Brent, 1995; Cavaiola & Lavender, 1999). These findings are understandable because a youth with a mental health problem might turn to alcohol or illicit drug use in order to cope with his problems (Feldman, 1984), what many practitioners call self medicating.

Histories of Abuse

Personal trauma in terms of physical and sexual abuse is also associated with juvenile suicide. Specifically, having a history of childhood physical abuse has been consistently associated with adolescent suicide (Brent, Baugher, Bridge, Chen, & Chiappetta, 1999). Physical abuse in early childhood can lead to poor social skills (Johnson et al., 2002) and an inability to interact with peers can create a sense of social isolation. It is this isolation that can lead to an increase in attempts and completed suicides. Perhaps somewhat surprisingly, the literature has indicated the link between sexual abuse and juvenile suicides to be less significant than physical abuse (Fergusson, Horwood, & Lynskey, 1996). One potential reason for this finding could revolve around the fact that sexual abuse is more difficult to identify because children are less inclined to disclose their abuse due to fear and shame.

Self-Harm and Delinquency

Studies have generally shown that the greatest predictor of a youth suicide is a past attempt (Marttunen, Aro, & Lonnqvist, 1992). These attempts can be viewed as a cry for help. According to a Norwegian study, for example, almost one-quarter of juvenile suicides had engaged in prior attempts (Groholt, Ekeberg, Wichstrom, & Haldorsen, 1997). A previous suicide attempt represents a 30-fold elevated risk for completed suicide in boys and a threefold increased risk for girls (Shaffer et al., 1996). Without proper treatment, and sometimes in spite of adequate help, these adolescents still commit suicide.

One the other hand, one of the weakest predictors of suicidal conduct in juveniles is delinquent behavior. Thompson and colleagues (2006) reported that boys and girls aged 14 to 17 years with histories of delinquency were more likely to have suicidal ideation, had created a suicide plan, and attempted suicide than their non-delinquent peers. Researchers, however, have been unable to find a strong relationship between delinquency and completed suicides, although studies have demonstrated that juveniles who have had contact with the justice system have higher rates of suicide attempts (Fergusson & Lynskey, 1995). As a result, relying solely on a delinquent past is not an effective method to identify a potential victim.

With the exception of youth suffering from severe depression, it is clear that there is no one common factor between juveniles and completed suicides. There are, however, several other predictors of suicides in the youth population. Perhaps the most troubling aspect of these predictors is the fact that rates of mental health problems, substance abuse, suicidal ideation, and delinquency are more pronounced with juveniles in detention centers and correctional facilities than their non-detained peers. A concentrated population of adolescents saddled with mental health, physical, or substance abuse problems—or a combination of similar personal demons—would result in an increased rate of attempts and suicides. Stopping or limiting these suicides, however, has proven to be an extremely challenging task.

Predictors of Suicides in Juvenile Correctional Facilities

Once admitted into a facility, a youth may struggle with physical, emotional, or psychological difficulties, which may be exacerbated by his legal troubles as well as feelings of shame. A recent study, for example, showed that in juvenile detention populations "nearly two-thirds of males and three-quarters of females met diagnostic criteria for one or more psychiatric disorders" (Teplin et al., 2006, p. 1).

Some of the factors associated with suicide in juvenile correctional facilities may be related to uncertainty, fear, and shame. Juveniles brought into custody on relatively minor offenses have killed themselves due to feelings of shame and a fear of disappointing their families. Other youth might resort to self-harm behavior because of fear of the unknown (including the possibility of long-term incarceration) or an inability to cope with serious charges. Altogether, suicide may occur at the intersection of adolescent risk-taking and impulsive behavior, fear of the unknown, shame, and the fear of disappointing others.

Mental Health Problems

Although studies have found that between 14% and 20% of youth in the general population have mental health disorders, the rate of mental illness is twice as high for juveniles inside the justice system (Robertson & Husain, 2001). Because delinquent youth are more likely to be incarcerated or detained, it is understandable that these individuals might be more prone to suicide. Hayes (2004) discovered that 74% of those completing suicide inside a youth facility had a history of mental illness. Additionally, 53% of the suicide victims had been taking psychotropic medications—such as antidepressants or other mood modifying drugs—at the time of their deaths. Anxiety and depression appear to be particularly prevalent among incarcerated youth who committed suicide.

A large percentage of incarcerated juveniles have histories of mental illnesses. One challenge is that not all correctional facilities are equipped to manage these individuals. The fact that we are incarcerating a large number of adolescents with mental illnesses, however, is not a new phenomenon. Two decades ago, as many as 77% of juveniles admitted to correctional facilities had mental health problems (Robertson, Dill, Husain, & Undesser, 2004). The Teplin et al. (2006) study above reported similarly high percentages.

Similar to juveniles in the general population, there is a strong relationship between substance abuse, suicide attempts, and completed suicides in correctional settings. Chapman and Ford (2008) reported that traumatic stress and substance abuse were the best indicators of suicide risk in detained youth. There are also striking similarities between youth who have co-occurring disorders (mental health problems and substance abuse) and completed suicides in residential placements (Huizinga, Loeber, & Thornberry, 1995; Hayes, 2004; Roberston et al., 2004). Hayes (2004) found, for example, that almost 90% of suicide victims in juvenile correctional facilities had a history of substance abuse.

Juveniles completing suicide inside residential facilities are often victims of emotional abuse. Emotional abuse can be broadly defined to include verbal abuse, neglect, excessive punishment, and general family dysfunction (Hayes, 2004). Previous studies indicate that nearly 60% of youth in the juvenile justice system have been emotionally abused (Cocozza, 1991). Furthermore, incarcerated and delinquent youth suffer from high rates of post traumatic stress disorder (PTSD) (Steiner, Garcia, & Matthews, 1997). PTSD in children typically stems from witnessing traumatic events such as assaults or abuse. Steiner and colleagues (1997) found that over 50% of incarcerated youth were suffering from some form of PTSD. Additional studies have confirmed that almost 60% of juveniles who committed suicide while incarcerated had been emotionally abused (Hayes, 2004). Emotional abuse can be particularly difficult to identify because shy or reserved adolescents may not be willing or inclined to share these problems with staff members.

Self-Harm and Suicide

In general, many individuals (both youth and adults) attempt suicide at least once before completing suicide (Gould et al., 2003; Malone, Haas, Sweeny, & Mann, 1995). Moreover, many juveniles exhibit self-harm behaviors prior to attempting suicide (Penn, Esposito, Schaeffer, Fritz, & Spirito, 2003). Self-harm (which often involves some form of self mutilation) and suicidal behavior can be differentiated by three characteristics: lethality, repetition, and ideation.

Self mutilation is typically low in lethality, but can be repetitive (Walsh & Rosen, 1988). Self mutilation often takes the form of cutting and most practitioners and residents call these acts "slashing." Not all juveniles who harm themselves, however, are suicidal. Some youth who engage in self-harm do so to manipulate staff (e.g., "If I don't get a visit, I will slash up") or to get attention. Anecdotal accounts from staff members who work in juvenile corrections, for example, suggest that these acts tend to be "infectious" and that if one youth engages in self-harm, others model that behavior. One of the problems associated with this form of acting-out, however, is that sometimes youth who do not intend on committing suicide accidentally kill themselves.

Suicidal ideation is rare in those who self-harm. A study conducted by Morris and colleagues (1995) discovered that approximately 22% of incarcerated juveniles had considered suicide, 20% planned an attempt, 16% actually attempted, and 8% were injured during their suicide attempt. Later reports indicated that almost 72% of persons who committed suicide in juvenile detention had a history of suicidal behavior (Hayes, 2004). Almost

188

one-third of these suicide victims had a history of suicidal ideation and almost one-quarter were involved in self mutilation prior to their deaths.

Isolation

Placing a youth in an isolated environment inside of correctional facilities greatly increases the chance of a suicide. Isolation in a single cell or room—often a hardened cell that has few amenities—was historically used as an intervention to reduce the risk of suicide because the youth has access to fewer items that could be used to harm herself. In addition, it is sometimes easier to watch these youth since their movements are restricted. Such policies and practices, however, tend to increase the feelings of isolation. Moreover, the stark and dreary environment of these settings contributes to a youth's depression.

Residents in juvenile facilities are frequently removed from the rest of the population if they become physically combative or disruptive (Parent et al., 1994). During this isolation, feelings of alienation increase and so do the opportunities and odds for a completed suicide. Hayes (2004) found that almost three-quarters of suicide victims inside juvenile correctional facilities lived in single occupancy rooms. Other research has indicated that death by suicide rises by a factor of seven (or 660%) in facilities that lock juveniles in their sleeping rooms (Gallagher & Dobrin, 2006a). Not only may the locked rooms intensify the feelings of isolation, but perhaps more importantly, the locked rooms enhance the opportunity for attempts.

As stated previously, juveniles residing in correctional facilities often have histories of mental, physical, emotional, and substance abuse. Removing these troubled youth from human contact tends to amplify feelings of isolation and hopelessness. Thoughts of despair and desperation increase suicidal tendencies. Perhaps the following quote from Boesky (2002) best sums up the problem of isolating disturbed juveniles: "[w]hen placed in a cold and empty room by themselves, suicidal youth have little to focus on—except all of their reasons for being depressed and the various ways that they can attempt to kill themselves" (p. 210).

Suicide Prevention

Suicide in corrections is preventable. An in-depth study conducted by Hayes (2004) examined 110 adolescent suicides occurring in detention and treatment centers, as well as correctional facilities between 1995 and 1999. This report focused on many critical shortcomings within these institutions, including problems with intake and screening, staff training, and the length of confinement. There are also some noteworthy similarities and differences between completed juvenile suicides in these types of facilities compared to adult suicides in jails and prisons.

Intake Screening

Surprisingly, not all facilities screen their admissions for suicide risk. Screening involves a series of questions that ask a youth about his current mental health including feelings of depression, his likelihood of engaging in self-harm (e.g., "Are you thinking about hurting yourself?"), if the youth has a plan to harm himself, the lethality of the plan, and his prior history (e.g., "Have you, a close friend, or a family member ever attempted suicide?"). These queries are sometimes part of a series of questions that screen for physical and mental health problems.

In the event that a youth reports feelings of depression, hopelessness, or has a plan to harm himself, he is typically referred to a medical or mental health professional for further assessment and treatment—although this is sometimes difficult if the youth is admitted during the evening or week-end—which is the norm for detention facilities.

According to Sickmund (2006) approximately 70% of all juvenile correctional facilities reported screening all of their residents for the threat of suicide. An additional 17% of facilities screen some of the incoming youth for suicide ideation. Hayes (2004) reported, however, that over 20% of the facilities that experienced a completed suicide had no type of screening at intake.

Research has indicated that the most prudent way to reduce the number of attempts and completed suicides in juvenile facilities is to screen all adolescents for suicidal behavior when they are first admitted (Gallagher & Dobrin, 2005). If such a policy is not feasible at intake, ideally some measure of screening should occur before the youth is moved from the admissions unit to a housing unit. Although facilities with large populations of residents were more likely to screen all youth (Sickmund, 2006), larger institutions were also more likely to have serious suicide attempts (Gallagher & Dobrin, 2005). Such a finding, however, is not a cause for alarm because it should not be surprising that a facility with more troubled adolescents has more suicide attempts than a center with fewer residents.

In adult jails and prisons, a majority of completed suicides had historically occurred within the first 24 hours of the inmate entering the facility and almost 33% of the suicides occurred within the first three hours of arrival (Hayes, 1989). Recent statistics show, however, that while almost one half of all suicides in local jails from 2000-2002 happened during the first week, slightly fewer than 14% of all jail suicides occurred during the first day (Mumola, 2005, p. 8). For arrestees admitted to a jail for the first time, fear and an uncertain future may be powerful incentives to take one's life. Furthermore, many of these persons are under the influence of drugs or alcohol and their inhibitions may be low (Tartaro & Lester, 2008). Thus, the first few hours of admission—especially for a first-time arrestee—are generally perceived to be a higher risk for self-harm or suicide, but arrestees admitted to adult jails are safer today, in part because of increased awareness on the part of correctional officers about the risk.

Although one's admission to a facility has historically represented a time of great risk, recent statistics show that actual suicides during the first hours after a youth's intake have decreased. Livsey, Sickmund, and Sladky (2009) examined suicides that occurred in juvenile facilities in 2004. They found that only one of the 16 suicides had occurred within a day of the youth's admission to the facility, and that 13 of these suicides had occurred after the residents had been incarcerated for more than two weeks. Livsey, Sickmund, and Sladky (2009) reported that "not until 75 days after admission were half of the reported suicides accounted for" (p. 14). It is possible that increased awareness of these risks has actually reduced the likelihood of suicide in the first hours after a youth has been admitted.

A person sentenced to a long-term disposition may be overcome with feelings of desperation and anger and seeking a way out of his or her current situation. In a study of 850 suicides that occurred in jails and prisons, Hayes (1989) found that 60% of the victims placed in isolation were dead within 48 hours of their arrival in the facility. Additionally, almost 90% of the youth who completed suicides within 48 hours were intoxicated at the time of incarceration—again reinforcing the link between lowered inhibitions, withdrawal, and incidents of self-harm or suicide. Placing a depressed, despondent, or suicidal person in isolation, whether in a juvenile or adult facility, has consistently demonstrated to increase the odds of a completed suicide.

As an alternative to placing a depressed inmate in isolation, many adult correctional systems have used trained inmate observers (also called inmate buddies in some jurisdictions) to constantly monitor the suicidal prisoner and notify staff members if the at-risk inmate engages in any form of self-harm. Jurisdictions that use such inmate volunteers usually report that the approach is effective (Tartaro & Lester, 2008) and represents a significant change in strategy compared to placing depressed and suicidal individuals by themselves in isolation cells that will enhance their feelings of despair. While research does not indicate any jurisdictions that are using juvenile observers in juvenile residential settings, such an approach might be very effective in suicide reduction.

Incarceration and Suicide Risk

Historically, practitioners regarded the first few hours after admission as the greatest time of risk for suicide. Research demonstrates, however, that juvenile suicides were widely distributed throughout a 12-month period of confinement (Hayes, 2004). There were just as many suicides (ten) in the first three days after admission as there were after a year-long incarceration period. While 70% of juvenile suicides occurred within four months of the admission, these figures still differ from the patterns of adult suicide in jails and prisons. Thus, practitioners in adult facilities that hold juveniles (e.g., local jails or prisons) should be aware of these differences.

A number of factors might influence when a suicide occurs. For instance, a juvenile might commit suicide shortly after being admitted to a detention facility because of feelings of despair and uncertainty. Others admitted to a training school may feel that they cannot serve their entire sentence. Some youth might harm themselves on the anniversary date of a loved one's death or during the holidays such as Christmas or Thanksgiving if they cannot be with their families. Last, a small number of juveniles may commit suicide shortly before their release dates because they fear their community reentry.[1] Altogether, there are a number of factors that contribute to a resident's likelihood of harming herself, so staff in juvenile correctional facilities must be aware of changes in the moods and behavior of their residents, and know what to do when they encounter these changes.

Operational Factors

Deploying competent, well trained, and caring staff and having written suicide prevention policies are the best strategies to reduce suicides. Parent and colleagues (1994) established four specific suicide prevention measures to be adopted by detention centers:

- Intake screening of all youth,
- Written procedures detailing how staff should help suicidal juveniles,
- Close observation of suicidal youth, and;
- Training the staff to manage suicidal juveniles. (p. 162)

Further studies indicated that facility staff members should have at least eight hours of suicide prevention training before working with incarcerated youth and an additional two hours of training every year afterward (Hayes, 2004).

Not all jurisdictions, however, have the resources to provide suicide prevention training. Smaller and county operated facilities usually provide less initial and on-the-job training (OJT) for staff members than state correctional agencies. Hayes (2004) discovered that 43% of juvenile correctional facility employees received no pre-service, annual, or periodic suicide prevention training. Additionally, of those who had received some training, 65% had training which lasted two hours or less.

Furthermore, not all facilities have professional mental health staff who are trained to help troubled youth. In many youth detention centers, for instance, mental health officials did not have advanced professional training and were not supervised by a certified professional (Wassermann et al., 2003). In fact, 15% of those deemed to be mental health professionals had only a bachelor's degree or less formal education. If juvenile suicides in correctional facilities and detention and treatment centers were rare events, such a systematic lack of prevention training and relying upon paraprofessional staff members would be less disconcerting. The high rate of suicides in these residential facilities, however, belies these facts.

Characteristics of Suicides in Juvenile Corrections

Methods of Death

Correctional facilities have a limited range of items that can be used to commit suicides (e.g., there are no firearms or automobiles and it is difficult to access lethal doses of medications). The lack of these devices forces suicidal individuals to use hanging as the most common method of committing suicide. Although some detainees have hanged themselves from exposed pipes in ceilings, doorknobs or bed frames have also been used; asphyxiation can occur in a relatively short period of time. Essentially, all a youth needs to commit suicide is a noose—which can be fabricated out of cloth, wire, or even a plastic garbage bag—and a fixed object upon which to tie this noose. Hayes (1989) found that over 93% of suicide victims in correctional facilities hanged themselves, while White and Schimmel (1995) found that almost 80% of suicides relied on some sort of hanging or strangulation.

Hanging is also the most common form of suicide in detention and treatment centers. Hayes (2004) found all but one of the suicides in adolescent correctional facilities was completed via hanging. Over 70% of the victims relied on some sort of bedding to hang themselves, although belts, clothing, and shoelaces were also used. Even in suicide resistant rooms, youth have used toilets, sinks, and window frames as anchoring devices for a noose. Due to the lack of other viable alternatives used to commit suicide, it should not be surprising that hanging is the most prevalent form of suicide in residential facilities. While belts, shoelaces, and other immediately recognizable instruments of hanging and strangulation should be confiscated from those deemed suicidal, it is not reasonable or even possible to remove every type or form of hanging material from potentially suicidal adolescents.

In order to reduce the likelihood of self-harm or suicide, a number of companies have designed suicide resistant clothing. Some facilities, for instance, have purchased anti-suicide smocks, which are one-piece garments that are made of heavy quilted material, which cannot be torn or fashioned into a noose. Other correctional facilities, by contrast, will use paper gowns, which are disposable items that are light enough that they cannot be made into a noose. In addition, staff members in most correctional facilities have access to specially designed knives to rescue a hanging resident (one example is called a hook knife—which enables a staff member to cut through the noose without endangering the resident).

Victim Characteristics

As previously stated, most adolescents in the general population who take their own lives are White and male. These figures are similar compared to the juveniles who complete suicide while incarcerated. Hayes (2004) found almost 80% of the victims were male and almost 70% were White. Recent numbers from the BJS, which compiled the number of deaths in state operated correctional facilities from 2002 to 2005 revealed almost 90% of the suicides were male; however, only 37% were White (Mumola & Noonan, 2008). Contrary to the history of juvenile suicide in the United States, the majority of the cases from the BJS research (almost 42%) were Black. Other studies have, however, noticed an increase in the completed suicides of Black adolescents over the past few years (Gallagher & Dobrin, 2006b). One of the limitations of our understanding of suicide is the reason for this change and further study into this trend is needed.

Time of Day and Suicide Checks

Some experts have observed that suicides in adult jails and prisons are more likely to occur in the early morning hours when supervision is low (Hayes & Rowan, 1988). Studies into this matter, however, have reported mixed results. Hayes and Rowan (1988) indicated that approximately 30% of adult suicides occurred between midnight and 6:00 a.m. The same study found that almost 29% of suicides happened between 6:00 p.m. and midnight. White and Schimmel (1995) found that only 22% of completed adult suicides in jails and prisons occurred between midnight and 6:00 a.m., as opposed to almost 39% of suicides between 6:00 p.m. and midnight.

Similar to the Hayes and Rowan (1988) and White and Schimmel (1995) studies, completed juvenile suicides in custody do not appear to happen in the middle of the night when the staff to resident ratio is the lowest. Hayes (2004) discovered that over half of the completed adolescent suicides occurred from 6:00 p.m. to midnight, while only 11% took place from midnight to 9:00 a.m. Staff may be more inclined to relax during the late evening periods or may be distracted by paperwork and other end-of-shift activities (e.g., many evening shifts end at midnight). Perhaps the staff members believe that residents are more likely to attempt suicide during the early morning hours, so they are more vigilant.

Written policies detailing how frequently a suicidal adolescent should be checked vary by institution. The most common check for an at-risk or suicidal youth is at least once every 15 minutes. Studies have indicated, however, that almost half of completed suicides in both adult and juvenile facilities occur while the victims are being observed at least once every 15 minutes; for example, Hayes (2004) found that over 40% of completed youth suicides occurred while the juvenile was being monitored once every 15 minutes. Approximately 84% of all completed adolescent suicides happened when staff observations were done hourly. One study of suicides in adult facilities reported that about 42% of the victims were under observation once every 15 minutes and almost 90% were being supervised at least once per hour (Hayes & Rowan, 1988). While 24-hour, constant supervision might be ideal, the reality of staffing difficulties and costs makes such a policy unrealistic for some facilities. Even closed circuit video observation would require at least one set of eyes to be constantly monitoring the screen without interruption.

Cross-National Concerns with Incarcerated Juvenile Suicide

The linkages between mental illness, substance abuse, delinquency, and suicide are not unique to America. Studies from the United Kingdom and Australia have demonstrated similar findings in regards to the rates of adolescent suicides in residential settings. In recent years, Australia's youth suicide rate has been one of the highest in the industrialized world (Cantor, 2001). Furthermore, suicide rates among incarcerated Australian youth are four times higher than their national average (Kosky, Sawyer, & Gowland, 1989). Four separate evaluations over a 12-year span have indicated consistent relationships between mental illness, substance abuse, delinquency, and youth who committed suicide in Australian facilities (Howard, Lennings, & Copeland, 2003).

Studies in the United Kingdom (U. K.) have found higher rates of completed suicide among those juveniles with histories of self-harm (Sakinofsky, 2000). Failure to screen juveniles at intake for suicidal ideation, as well as inadequate staff training to detect and treat deliberate self-harm also occur in the U. K. (Morgan & Hawton, 2004). It seems there are significant problems worldwide with a lack of intake screening and staff training in regards to recognizing and preventing suicides. Failing to respond to these shortcomings creates environments that foster suicides. It might be possible that the fear of litigation has, in part, made American correctional facilities more responsive to these problems (Tartaro, 2005).

Conclusions

Juvenile suicide in the United States is a persistent problem. While reasons for each suicide might be different, there are very strong relationships between completed suicides and rates of mental illness; physical, sexual, and emotional abuse; delinquency; and a history of self-harm and suicidal behavior. Attempts to curb suicides inside some juvenile correctional facilities, however, are not particularly encouraging and progress at improving these conditions seems to be proceeding slowly.

Intake screening, written policies, and staff training specifically aimed at identifying those in need of suicide prevention are not mandatory in all jurisdictions. If training is offered, the number of hours is not adequate to fully prepare the staff members to work with suicidal youth. Occasionally, the interventions occurring inside the facilities (such as placing a depressed youth alone in an isolation cell) only exacerbate the possibility of a suicide. Furthermore, once a youth's high risk of self-harm is recognized, there need to be skilled clinicians who can work with the youth to reduce his risk. Youth confined in smaller or rural facilities may be at additional risk if these mental health care professionals are not accessible.

While juvenile suicide prevention measures have been taking place inside correctional facilities and detention and treatment centers over the last 30 years, there is still significant room for improvement. Until there are consistent and mandatory policies requiring intake screening and staff training, as well as mental health professionals who are accessible to the facility, adolescents will continue to commit suicide.

It is possible that litigation will force the development of more comprehensive suicide prevention interventions. Tartaro (2005) reported that Section 1983 lawsuits—where the families of persons who have committed suicide in custody have sued the agency in order to force improvements—have sometimes led to correctional agencies providing better training for officers and developing more effective prevention procedures. Furthermore, agencies that are accredited with the American Correctional Association or the National Commission on Correctional Health Care have suicide prevention protocols in place. Suicides in custody are preventable and a first step after acknowledging the problem is to recognize that failures by the staff are often a significant contributing factor to these tragedies.

On a final, alarming note, some residential placements have no mandatory, suicide reporting policies (Hayes, 2004). Moreover, there is no centralized body that collects data about suicides in group or foster homes or other privately operated juvenile facilities (those that may not receive any government funding). Simply put, if an adolescent commits suicide, a governing or regulatory body is not contacted and statistics are not gathered. The result of incomplete reporting policies means it is quite possible that many suicides go unreported. These reporting policies leave one with the impression that there is no problem, whereas these tragedies could be increasing each year.

Endnote

1. Studies of juvenile offenders released from correctional facilities show high rates of mortality (Teplin, McClelland, Abram, & Mileusnic, 2005).

References

Abram, K. M., Choe, J. Y, Washburn, J. J., Teplin, L. A., King, D. C., & Dulcan, M. K. (2008). Suicidal ideation and behaviors among youth in juvenile detention. *Child & Adolescent Psychiatry, 47*, 291-300.

Anderson, R. N. (2002). Deaths: Leading causes for 2000. *National Vital Statistics Reports, 50*(16). Hyattsville, MD: National Center for Health Statistics.

Boesky, L. (2002). *Juvenile offenders with mental health disorders: Who are they and what do we do with them?* Landham, MD: American Correctional Association.

Brent, D. A. (1995). Risk factors for adolescent suicide and suicidal behavior: Mental and substance abuse disorders, family environmental factors, and life stress. *Suicide and Life-Threatening Behavior, 25*(supplemental), 52-63.

Brent, D. A., Baugher, M., Bridge, J., Chen, T., & Chiappetta, L. (1999). Age- and sex-related risk factors for adolescent suicide. *Journal of the American Academy of Child and Adolescent Psychiatry, 38*(12), 1497-1505.

Brent, D. A., Perper, J. A., Goldstein, C. E., Kolko, D. J., Allan, M. J., Allman, C. J., et al. (1988). Risk factors for adolescent suicide: A comparison of adolescent suicide victims with suicidal inpatients. *Archives of General Psychiatry, 45*(6), 581-588.

Brent, D. A., Perper, J. A., Moritz, G., Allman, C. J., Friend, A., Roth, C., et al. (1993). Psychiatric risk factors for adolescent suicide: A case-control study. *Journal of the American Academy of Child and Adolescent Psychiatry, 32*(3), 521-529.

Cantor, C. (2001). *Drop in suicide rates for 1999.* Melbourne: Australian Institute of Family Studies

Cavaiola, A. A., & Lavender, N. (1999). Suicidal behavior in chemically dependent adolescents. *Adolescence, 34*(136), 735-744.

Centers for Disease Control and Prevention. (1991). *An epidemiological surveillance system to monitor the prevalence of youth behaviors that most affect health.* Atlanta, GA: Author

Chapman, J. F., & Ford, J. D. (2008). Relationships between suicide risk, traumatic experiences, and substance use among juvenile detainees. *Archives of Suicide Research, 12*(1), 50-61.

Cocozza, J. (1991). *Responding to the mental health needs of youth in the juvenile justice system.* Seattle, WA: National Coalition for the Mentally Ill in the Juvenile Justice System.

Drake, R. W., Gates, C., Cotton, P. G., & Whittaker, A. (1984). Suicide among schizophrenics: Who is at risk? *Journal of Nervous and Mental Diseases, 172*(10), 613-617.

Farand, L., Chagnon, F., Renaud, J., & Rivard, M. (2004). Completed suicides among Quebec adolescents involved with juvenile justice and child welfare services. *Suicide and Life-Threatening Behavior, 34*(1), 24-35.

Feldman, R. P. (1984). Some special aspects of suicide in adolescence and youth. In N. Linzer (Ed.), *Suicide: The will to live vs. the will to die,* (pp. 101-112). New York: Human Services Press.

Fergusson, D. M., Horwood, L. J., & Lynskey, M. T. (1996). Childhood sexual abuse and psychiatric disorder in young adulthood, II: Psychiatric outcomes of childhood sexual abuse. *Journal of the American Academy of Child and Adolescent Psychiatry, 35*(10), 1365-1374.

Fergusson, D. M., & Lynskey, M. T. (1995). Childhood circumstances, adolescent adjustment, and suicide attempts in a New Zealand birth cohort. *Journal of the American Academy of Child and Adolescent Psychiatry, 34*(5), 612-622.

Flaherty, M. G. (1980). *An assessment of the national incidence of juvenile suicide in adult jails, lock-ups, and juvenile detention centers.* Washington, DC: Office of Juvenile Justice and Delinquency Prevention.

Gallagher, C. A., & Dobrin, A. (2005). Deaths in juvenile justice residential facilities. *Journal of Adolescent Health, 38,* 662-668.

Gallagher, C. A., & Dobrin, A. (2006a). Facility-level characteristics associated with serious suicide attempts and deaths from suicide in juvenile justice residential facilities. *Suicide and Life-Threatening Behavior, 36*(3), 363-375.

Gallagher, C. A., & Dobrin, A. (2006b). Deaths in juvenile justice residential facilities. *Journal of Adolescent Health, 38*(6), 662-668.

Garrison, C. Z., McKeown, R. E., Valois, R. F., & Vincent, M. L. (1993). Aggression, substance use, and suicidal behaviors in high school students. *American Journal of Public Health, 83*(2), 179-184.

Gould, M. S., Greenberg, T., Velting, D. M., & Shaffer, D. (2003). Youth suicide risk and preventive interventions: A review of the past 10 years. *Journal of the American Academy of Child and Adolescent Psychiatry, 42*(4), 368.

Groholt, B., Ekeberg, O., Wichstrom, L., & Haldorsen, T. (1997). Youth suicide in Norway, 1990-1992: A comparison between children and adolescents completing suicide and age- and gender-matched controls. *Suicide and Life-Threatening Behavior, 27*(3), 250-263.

Hayes, L. (1989). National study of jail suicides: Seven years later. *Psychiatric Quarterly, 60*(1), 7-29.

Hayes, L. (2004). *Juvenile suicide in confinement: A national survey.* Washington, DC: Officer of Juvenile Justice and Delinquency Programs.

Hayes, L. M., & Rowan, J. R. (1988). *National study of jail suicides: Seven years later.* Alexandria, VA: National Center on Institutions and Alternatives.

Holland, S., & Griffin, A. (1984). Adolescent and adult drug treatment clients: Patterns and consequences of use. *Journal of Psychoactive Drugs, 16*(1), 79-88.

Howard, J., Lennings, C. J., & Copeland, J. (2003). Suicidal behavior in a young offender population. *Crisis, 24*(3), 98-104.

Huizinga, D., Loeber, R., & Thornberry, T. (1995). *The prevention of serious delinquency and violence: Implications from the program of research on the causes and correlates of delinquency.* Washington, DC: Office of Juvenile Justice and Delinquency Programs.

Johnson, J. G., Cohen, P., Gould, M. S., Kasen, S., Brown, J., & Brook, J. S. (2002). Childhood adversities, interpersonal difficulties, and risk for suicide attempts during late adolescence and early adulthood. *Archives of General Psychiatry, 59*(8) 741-749.

Kosky, R. J., Sawyer, M. G., & Gowland, J. C. (1989). Adolescents in custody: Hidden psychological morbidity? *Medical Journal of Australia, 153*(1), 24-27.

Livsey, S., Sickmund, M., & Sladky, A. (2009). *Juvenile residential facility census, 2004: Selected findings.* Washington, DC: Office of Juvenile Justice and Delinquency Prevention.

Malone, K. M., Hass, G. L., Sweeney, J. A., & Mann, J. J. (1995). Major depression and the risk of attempted suicide. *Journal of Affective Disorders, 32*(3), 173-185.

Marttunen, M. J., Aro, H. M., & Lonnqvist, J. K. (1992). Adolescent suicides: Endpoint of long-term difficulties. *Journal of the American Academy of Child and Adolescent Psychiatry, 31*(4), 649-654).

Memory, J. M. (1989). Juvenile suicides in secure detention facilities: Correction of published rates. *Death Studies, 13*(5), 455-463.

Morgan, J., & Hawton, K. (2004). Self-reported suicidal behavior in juvenile offenders in custody: Prevalence and associated factors. *Crisis, 25*(1), 8-11.

Morris, R. E., Harrison, E. A., Knox, G. W., Tromanhauser, E., Marquis, D. K., & Watts, L. L. (1995). Health risk behavioral survey from 39 juvenile correctional facilities in the United States. *Journal of Adolescent Health, 17*(6), 334-344

Mumola, C. J., & Noonan, M. E. (2008). *State juvenile correctional facility deaths: 2002-2005.* Retrieved November 5, 2008, from http://www.ojp.gov/bjs/dcrp/juvenileindex.htm

Parent, D. G., Leiter, V., Kennedy, S., Livens, L., Wentworth, D., & Wilcox, S. (1994). *Conditions of confinement: Juvenile detention and corrections facilities.* Washington, DC: Office of Juvenile Justice and Delinquency Programs.

Penn, J. V., Esposito, C. L., Schaeffer, L. E., Fritz, G. K., & Spirito, A. (2003). Suicide attempts and self-mutilative behavior in a juvenile correctional facility. *Journal of the American Academy of Child and Adolescent Psychiatry, 42*(7), 762-769.

Robertson, A., Dill, P. L., Husain, J., & Undesser, C. (2004). Prevalence of mental illness and substance abuse disorders among incarcerated juvenile officers in Mississippi. *Child Psychiatry and Human Development, 35*(1), 55-74.

Robertson, A., & Husain, J. (2001). *Prevalence of mental illness and substance abuse disorders among incarcerated juvenile offenders.* Jackson, MS: Mississippi Department of Public Safety and Mississippi Department of Mental Health.

Sakinofsky, I. (2000). Repetition of suicidal behavior. In K. Hawton & C. van Heeringen (Eds.), *The international handbook of suicide and attempted suicide,* (pp. 385-404). Chichester: Wiley.

Shaffer, D., Gould, M. S., Fisher, P., Trautman, P., Moreau, D., Kleinman, M., et al. (1996). Psychiatric diagnosis in child and adolescent suicide. *Archives of General Psychiatry 53*(4), 339-348.

Sickmund, M. (2006). *Juvenile residential facility census, 2002: Selected findings.* Washington, DC: Office of Juvenile Justice and Delinquency Programs.

Steiner, H., Garcia, I. G., & Matthews, Z. (1997). Posttraumatic stress disorder in incarcerated juvenile delinquents. *Journal of the American Academy of Child and Adolescent Psychiatry, 36*(3), 357-365.

Tartaro, C. (2005). Section 1983 liability and custodial suicide: A look at what plaintiffs face in court. *Californian Journal of Health Promotion, 3,* 114-123.

Tartaro, C., & Lester, D. (2008). Saving lives through suicide prevention. In R. Ruddell & M. Tomita (Eds.) *Issues in correctional health,* (pp. 147-166). Richmond, KY: Newgate.

Teplin, L. A., McClelland, G. M., Abram, K. M., & Mileusnic, D. (2005). Early violent death among delinquent youth: A prospective longitudinal study. *Pediatrics, 115,* 1586-1593.

Thompson, M. P., Kingree, J. B., & Ho, C. H. (2006). Associations between delinquency and suicidal behaviors in a nationally representative sample of adolescents. *Suicide and Life-Threatening Behavior, 36*(1), 57-64.

Walsh, B. W., & Rosen, P. M. (1988). *Self-mutilation: Theory, research, and treatment.* New York: Guilford.

Wassermann, G. A., Jensen, P. S., Ko, S. J., Cocozza, J., Trupin, E., Angold, A., et al. (2003). Mental health assessments in juvenile justice: Report on the consensus conference. *Journal of the American Academy of Child and Adolescent Psychiatry, 42*(7), 752-761.

White, T., & Schimmel, D. (1995). Suicide prevention in federal prisons: A successful five-step program. In L. Hayes (Ed.), *Prison suicide: An overview and guide to prevention,* (pp. 46-57). Washington, DC: National Institute of Corrections.

CHAPTER 11
BALANCING ACT: STAFF MEMBERS IN A JUVENILE CORRECTIONAL FACILITY

Michelle Inderbitzin

O riginally designed with the intention to serve as a surrogate parent to delinquent, dependent, and neglected children, today's juvenile court has moved far away from its foundation of *parens patriae*. In many states, juvenile court judges no longer have the time or inclination to act as "kind and just parents" (Ayers, 1997) to the children brought before them; instead, they are now regulated by sentencing guidelines and have little discretion in deciding the treatment/punishment of troubled youth. While some undoubtedly care deeply about what happens to juvenile delinquents, judges have relatively little contact with the individual offenders who pass through their courtrooms.

If the philosophy of *parens patriae* survives at all in the juvenile justice system, it is most likely to be found in the correctional facilities that house adolescent juveniles for the months and years of their incarcerations. For more than 150 years, the United States has sent its wayward and delinquent youth to reformatories and training schools in hopes that they might learn hard work and conforming values (Platt, 1977). As people-changing organizations, juvenile correctional facilities generally strive to bring about change by using the strongest tools at their disposal—their staff members and the relationships they build with the juveniles and with each other (Feld, 1977). The staff members working the front lines of such institutions take on many roles, becoming the surrogate parents, corrections officers, counselors, and guardians of the state's most serious problem children.

Working in a maximum security juvenile correctional facility offers a variety of challenges each and every day. While some argue their first and most important duty is to protect the community from their population of criminal adolescents, staff members are also charged with caring for and raising the young men and women sentenced to serve time for their delinquent acts. Because the cottage living unit is "the architectural and organizational focal point" (Snyder & Sickmund, 1999, p. 289) of juvenile institutions, staff members play a critical role in the state's attempts to re-socialize young offenders into more conforming, less dangerous adults. In very real ways, the staff members help to define the institutional experience for the juveniles, setting the tone for virtually every aspect of life inside:

> As in a family, it is the tone (of a training school) that is the subtle but pervasive quality crucial to all else. Tone bespeaks whether an institution is humane or degenerate, constructive or vengeful, growing or stagnant. It stems from the sum of the staff members' attitudes toward themselves, their purposes, their degrees of understanding of their objectives and their commitment to them. (O'Neil, 1988, p. 194)

As a group, the cottage staff must learn to work together and to work with and utilize the powerful influence of their juvenile leaders to maintain order in the living unit and to keep everyone safe from physical harm (Bartollas, Miller, & Dinitz, 1976; Inderbitzin, 2006b). Like their counterparts working in adult prisons, staff members face enormous challenges stemming from their lack of resources and training and the many structural constraints inherent in the institution and the job. Despite these challenges, staff members generally embrace their positions as prosocial role models, counselors, coaches, mentors, and keepers of teenagers deemed too dangerous to be out in the community. They work to balance philosophies of treatment and control, doing the best they can with their limited resources (Inderbitzin, 2007).

In a change from earlier times (Feld, 1977), staff members in juvenile institutions are now generally assigned to work in specific cottages or locations and they do not get to choose with whom they work; they can only choose the kind of workers and role models they will be in doing their job. By their own accounts, the key to their successes and their satisfaction in the job is in the strength of the relationships they build. In this chapter, the complex roles and relationships of cottage staff members in a maximum security juvenile correctional facility are described and analyzed.

The importance of the setting cannot be overemphasized. The juveniles are confined to a total institution (Goffman, 1961) where loss of their physical freedoms is only one aspect of the punishments they face. While serving their sentences, the entirety of young offenders' lives is lived in the company of others, others they did not and almost certainly would not choose. The institution and the people in it become their society (Sykes, 1958) and their world for a period of months and years, with only the television and the occasional visit or telephone call from family and friends to provide glimpses of life on the outs (e.g., in the community or free world, as some residents describe the community). Because their confinements and their isolations are so nearly complete, building relationships with the people with whom they interact in the institution becomes an important survival strategy (Inderbitzin, 2005, 2006a).

The relationships between staff members and the residents of the cottages are ongoing and are built and rebuilt every day. While previous research has suggested that "staff and cottage subcultures are, in fact, quite insulated from each other" (Polsky, 1962, p. 136), that is not generally the case in the cottage central to this study. The lives of the juveniles and the staff are intertwined during their respective time in the institution. For the juveniles immersed in a world ruled by monotony, punishment, and deprivation, their relationships with staff members substitute for many others. The adults in the relationship take on a number of roles, serving as correctional officers, parents, counselors, coaches, friends, and guardians. Conflicting or cooperative, the relationships between staff members and the young offenders are key to daily life in the cottage.[1]

Participant Observation in a Juvenile Correctional Facility

Singer (1996) has observed that the very confidentiality put in place to protect juvenile delinquents can also work against juvenile justice systems (p. 196). Singer (1996) argued for more public discussion of juvenile justice issues: "By opening the doors of juvenile justice, we can learn more about its real purpose in preventing and controlling serious delinquent behavior" (p. 196). This study provided an inside view of the deep end of juvenile corrections (Lane, Lanza-Kaduce, Frazier, & Bishop, 2002) to better understand the handling of serious delinquents and to think seriously about the utility of juvenile correctional facilities. As such, this research entails an ethnographic study of a cottage of violent offenders in the state's end-of-the-line juvenile correctional facility—or training school as it is more euphemistically called. Because much of the research that is conducted on juvenile correctional institutions is survey- or interview-based, this chapter adds to our understanding of these closed worlds by introducing a participant-observer into the daily life of one cottage. Spending time in the cottage allows for observation and reveals information and perspective from both staff members and juveniles. As the researcher's relationships with individuals grew, more sensitive topics could be addressed.

The data for this chapter were collected over a period of approximately fifteen months. Because the young male juveniles and many of the staff members were initially suspicious of a female outsider, formal interviews were avoided; instead, the research relies on less obtrusive means of gathering information. This included hundreds of hours in the Blue cottage observing and interacting with the young residents of the cottage (the institution's preferred term) and the staff members assigned to supervise them. After leaving the institution, documents were developed to record the day's events, activities, and conversations in detailed field notes. The time in the cottage allowed for extensive interaction and fostered relationships with approximately 20 of the residents and 12 staff members.

Attempts to get to know the staff members included talking with them and asking questions, observing them interacting with each other and the residents in the cottage, and listening to them when they were on the phone. A great deal of time was spent in the small staff office with them (and, in particular, Luke) after the youth had been locked down for the night. It was a quiet time in the cottage as they prepared to end their shifts and they could and often would reflect on that particular night and the larger issues they faced on the job. Other time was spent outside of the institution with two staff members, Kyle and Eddie, discussing their roles, hopes, and frustrations. Information learned about the staff members' families included: how they were raised, the values they learned from their parents, and how they were raising their own children. At one point, Eddie said to me, "Sometimes after talking to you, I am amazed at the things I tell you." This comment seemed to indicate that while I would never fully be an insider, I had gained a level of trust with at least some of the staff members.

The Setting

Located in a rural area, far from where most of the boys grew up and committed their crimes, the training school in this study was a maximum security juvenile correctional facility, complete with razor wire fences around the perimeter, bars on the windows, and locked rooms within locked cottages. There was a full time security staff, an Intensive Management Unit (where the most volatile youth would spend 23 hours a day in locked single cells), and drug dogs that would occasionally be brought around the cottages to search the campus for contraband.

This training school housed approximately 200 of the state's most serious problem children—chronic and violent male offenders between the ages of 15-20 years. Most of these young men had previously served time in other juvenile institutions; for nearly all of them, this would be their last stop in the juvenile justice system. Their sentences ranged from several months to juvenile life: if sentenced to juvenile life, the individual would be released on his twenty-first birthday. On average, residents spent approximately two years in the training school.

The Blue cottage had 16 rooms and held between 18-26 young men at any given time. After attending school, working in the institution, going to recreation in the gym, and eating their meals in the central cafeteria, the Blue cottage was home base to its population of violent offenders. In their free time, they hung out in the cottage lounge watching television or playing cards or they spent time in the cottage game room providing commentary for and about others while waiting for their turn to play pool or a video game.

The Blue cottage had 10-12 staff members assigned to it and between two and four individuals worked each shift. The Blue staff was predominantly male and relatively young. In their daily activities, Blue cottage staff members had the difficult job of trying to balance a number of contradictory tasks, including "guiding, mentoring, facilitating, developing, and watching inmates" (Hemmens & Stohr, 2000, p. 327). When the residents got into trouble at the institution's school or in the main cafeteria, the complaints came to the Blue staff; they were then responsible for dealing with their problem children. Teachers and other workers in the institution expected the living unit staff to maintain order and to keep their population in control at all times. In almost every way, the Blue cottage and the Blue staff defined the institutional experience for the youth assigned there. Any strides the young offenders made were at least somewhat attributable to the relationships they built with the staff members who literally helped to raise them. As Bell (2000) has argued:

> The key to any good secure confinement facility is the quality of the line staff and their immediate supervisors. Properly trained and supervised staff usually exercise good judgment and provide safe, caring, and humane confinement. It is widely known throughout the field that any examination of a well-run facility reveals excellent staff. (p. 203)

Staff and Juvenile Perspectives

This study began as an attempt to look at how a group of young men had ended up in one state's end-of-the-line juvenile institution—what they had done to be included amongst the handful of worst juvenile offenders in the state and sentenced to its most severe placement. The staff's perception on this point was clear: the vast majority of their problem children came from troubled families. I sat with the cottage supervisor one day, going over a list of the current residents and discussing the parents of each. Of the 25 youth in the cottage at that time, he estimated that three of them had two parents that still called, visited, or showed any real concern for them. Staff members explained that many of the young men in the cottage were severely abused as children, physically or mentally. Some were sexually abused. One 16-year-old boy's mother would frequently call him when she was drunk or high, leaving him visibly angry and frustrated after such conversations. Staff members paid close attention when he was on the phone and attempted to deescalate (Kivett & Warren, 2002) his temper before violence erupted.

The residents' life histories, chronicled in thick files in the Blue office, told their stories for them. Many of the residents had parents who were addicted to drugs and/or alcohol; some of their parents had worked as prostitutes or drug dealers; some were incarcerated. Several of the youth in the cottage were wards of the state and they had grown up in and out of various foster homes. When they were released from their current sentences before they were legally adults, the system—most notably the youth's counselor in the cottage and his parole officer in the community—was forced to rush to place them in group homes or other creative living situations. The cottage supervisor said in one such case, "Let's see if we can pull a rabbit out of a hat," as he began phoning distant relatives of the boy to see if any would be willing to take him in.

I frequently heard more about the residents' histories from the staff than from the residents themselves. Staff members would often give me a brief description of a particular resident's crime and his problems. Occasionally, they shared this information to warn me about particularly dangerous offenders, but, more often, the background facts were offered as a rationale for the youths' behavior and bad choices. Perhaps because part of their job was to try to re-socialize the juveniles in their care into more conforming citizens, they (more than the boys) seemed to attribute the youths' crimes to the lack of positive socialization they had received while growing up.

The more treatment oriented staff members or "people workers" (Farkas, 2000) shared stories of boys in the cottage who had a "history of severe and sometimes bizarre abuse" (Currie 1998, p. 83). They told of residents who had been beaten and drop-kicked by their stepfathers and their mothers' boyfriends. One of the most charismatic young men in the living unit grew up with abusive foster parents after his own mother was imprisoned for killing his sister. In the stories of these boys, it seemed clear to staff members that many of the offenders' parents had significant problems, which were then transferred to their children. One boy's mother apparently suffered from severe psychological problems; she repeatedly abused her son, leaving permanent physical and emotional scars. He had learned to distrust adults and there was concern in the institution about whether he would be able to adapt to life in a relatively open living unit. The staff took special care to slowly ease him into the Blue cottage, bringing him in for visits while he was still assigned to the more restrictive intensive management unit.

The staff worried that many of the youth in the cottage were in danger of becoming institutionalized. Staff members explained that the institution provided the first real structure and consistency that many of the residents had ever known. Even as they helped the boys adjust to living in the cottage, they hoped that they would not become too comfortable with institutional life. Staff members made extra efforts to mentor the boys assigned to their caseloads, to try to teach them conforming values during their time inside. They worked with them to help them deal with their anger and to make preliminary plans for the future. There was no question that time in the institution would put its stamp on the boys; the staff hoped that some of the skills the youth developed would open new opportunities for them and help them to cope with challenges after they were released.

The institution in this study is the end-of-the-line state training school and many of the residents had previously served time in other juvenile facilities. The pathway to this institution is often littered with sentences to three or four of the other state schools or group homes. The boys spoke knowledgeably about the people and places at other institutions, discussing staff whom they liked and disliked and the pros and cons of each place. One resident, Ben, offered his insights when he wrote a letter to me expressing his feelings about his experience with the juvenile justice system and what he felt might be done to improve it. He basically argued that the system itself does little for the youth going through it, but that good people can make a difference. He suggested that the system should prioritize hiring more staff members who care and who can empathize with the youth they deal with, teaching them to work through their problems.

Relationships in the Cottage

The Blue cottage staff faced unique challenges and recurring problems every day when they came into work. Working with incarcerated teenage males proved to be frustrating, dangerous, amusing, and occasionally rewarding. It was a job that required a great deal of energy and flexibility because the staff never knew quite what the day would bring. Goffman (1961) uses the concept of involvement cycles to describe how staff members' energy waxes and wanes in total institutions. Such involvement cycles occur when a staff member becomes close to some juveniles, retreats, then builds warm relationships again. Luke, a young Caucasian staff member, told me explicitly that the energy and the mood of the place was sometimes cyclical for him — how at times he really liked the residents and wanted to work with them and help them and at other times he would get "fed up with all of their crap." There were days, he explained, that he didn't really want to deal with the boys beyond what was absolutely necessary. His sentiments echoed almost exactly Weber's (1961) on cottage parents and their struggles in dealing with institutionalized kids:

> Some cottage parents felt discouraged, disheartened and hopeless about their efforts to 'treat' delinquents. When they were discouraged or despondent, they worked in a listless, perfunctory, and routine way. Some made an effort to disguise their discouragement, but others did not. As these feelings intensified, cottage parents became more disinterested and did only the most necessary things to maintain the routine of the cottage. (p. 206)

Dealing with the role conflict (Hemmens & Stohr, 2000, p. 331) of having to serve as both counselors and corrections officers sometimes took its toll on the relationships staff members had with the residents. Some of the youth asked to switch counselors when they had conflicts with the individual they had been assigned to, claiming that that person "had it in for them." The staff of the Blue cottage usually tried to take such complaints seriously and to come up with creative solutions. More difficult, still, were the residents for whom nothing seemed to work. Luke had one problem child who was particularly annoying to most members of the staff; Luke sometimes got frustrated with him, as well, but he made an effort to stay flexible and he tried multiple approaches with the boy, hoping for a breakthrough.

One of the things that Luke tried to do with all of the residents in the cottage was to give them choices and allow them to feel like they had at least some control over their lives. One night, for example, the problem child mentioned above was in a dispute with other residents over a chair in the television area. Luke told him he had two choices—move to another chair or go to his room. The youth did not move. A minute later, Luke got up and ordered him to go to his room. The boy dragged his feet and Luke started a verbal countdown. The boy finally left the room, reluctantly, and Luke decided to give him some time to cool off before going down to deal with him. Luke eventually went down to the boy's room to talk things over with him in private and the incident passed.

Luke and other workers on the Blue staff often came up with creative sanctions rather than just giving the young men disciplinary checks (penalties placed on youth that reduced their privileges): on one occasion, two of the residents opted to do an extra cleaning detail in the cottage rather than take a check. As part of the trade-off, the details that Luke came up with were purposely unpleasant. One of the guys had to go clean out the seats in the lounge area. The chairs had blue cushions and, over time, a lot of garbage fell into or was crammed into the cracks in the seats. His job was to dig out the objects from around the cushions. The other resident was stuck cleaning the toilet, a task made more challenging by the fact that they could not find a toilet brush for him to use. He finally set about the task with a toothbrush, a decent sized scrubbing pad, some tape, and rubber gloves, telling me in an aside that he would just fake it and get the pad "hella dirty." Luke seemed satisfied with their efforts and the residents did not get checks that night.

In another example of implementing creative sanctions, one of the residents was required to write an essay in order to regain his privileges in the cottage. He had received three checks that week, which would normally drop his privilege level in the cottage. The last check was because he had called Judy, the only female staff member assigned to Blue at the time, an "old bitch." His letter gave his perspective on what happened to lead up to the incident and then said that he was sorry and should have handled it differently. Luke, his counselor, laughed when he read the essay and said that it was the reality of the situation, but that the youth needed to improve his social skills. Kyle, in his role as cottage supervisor, also read the essay and then asked the resident what he had learned from the whole thing. The boy gave a somewhat generic, but socially acceptable response; he was allowed to keep his level.

Eddie, a well liked African-American staff member in his thirties, told me that he employed a different style of counseling than many other staff members. He did not like to give checks and instead he tried to work with the residents in other ways. He said that he tried to treat them as reasonable beings and to gain their cooperation through means other than punishment and sanctions. He explained that he generally tried to use his mind and his mouth, rather than strict disciplinary measures, to show up the guys and put them in their places when necessary. In fact, one of the particularly recalcitrant youth had asked him on occasion to "just give a check rather than fuck with him." A former elite athlete, Eddie grew up in a rough neighborhood and was able to relate with the residents at their own levels; he commanded their respect by listening to them and knowing what was up.

Staff members who were least flexible seemed to have the hardest time in the Blue cottage; they seemed to find it a particularly difficult assignment within the institution. Robert, for example, was transferred from the intake unit to work in the Blue cottage for a period of time. His military background may have influenced the approach he took with the job and his interactions with the residents (Hemmens & Stohr, 2000, p. 343). Robert was a middle-aged African-American male with a friendly, but very strict countenance. He was a stickler for the rules—a hard liner (Farkas, 2000) or hardass, according to the youth. He would chastise the boys for swearing and carefully monitor their behavior, even telling them not to flail their arms when talking. The young men deeply resented such "triviality of the official's control" (Sykes, 1958, p. 73) and breathed a collective sigh of relief when Robert was transferred to the Red cottage.

The different styles and philosophies of individual staff members made it more or less pleasant for them to work together. There was general camaraderie and respect amongst the staff, but friction between co-workers occasionally surfaced, making the job much more difficult at those times. Ron, a middle-aged Caucasian staff member, told me that after three years of working at the institution, he never got tired of the kids, but that he sometimes had problems with other staff members who made the job much harder and more frustrating. He thought that he and Eddie worked best together, a sentiment with which Eddie agreed. Eddie told me that Ron was a "straight-shooter, a good, honest man" and that they were both good at deescalating volatile situations. In addition, the two of them watched each other's backs and generally looked out for each other, telling the other to go home when he was sick or when a shift dragged on long past its scheduled hours.

There was also real affection between Eddie and Luke and they told me more than once how much they enjoyed working with each other, how the two of them worked really well together. Luke said that their combined style worked 95% of the time — that they were more apt to talk to and reason with the kids rather than throw checks up on the board and sanction them. He said that they would punish the youth and give checks when warranted, but it was never their first choice. Instead, they tried to lead by example, willingly taking on the role of surrogate parents, big brothers, and coaches for the kids in their care, offering advice and counsel on a wide range of topics.

Day-to-Day Life in the Blue Cottage

By all accounts, the Blue cottage seemed to be more adaptable than its counterparts in the institution and the staff members who had the most success in the cottage were the workers, like Luke and Eddie, who were flexible in approach and made efforts to come up with creative solutions to problems. This was the tone of the Blue cottage. Rather than calling the security staff or sending their residents to the Intensive Management Unit, the Blue staff worked together to figure out ways to reach individual kids. They would analyze the youth and the situation and try to come up with the best solution for that moment. They sometimes found, for example, that putting boys on U-level (Un-invested in the program) — in which they were locked in their rooms in the cottage for most of the day — was not a painful enough sanction to encourage them to work to improve their privilege level. Staff members would then discuss, "What else can we take away from him?" in order to make it unpleasant or boring enough to get the resident to work within the living unit's rules. Sometimes they took away the youths' radios or their photographs, leaving them with little to do while confined in their rooms but to think about their actions and learn about consequences.

Flexibility was key, too, in the staff's daily work as it was sometimes necessary for them to implement a system of give and take—for example, they would sometimes send the higher-level residents to bed earlier than their scheduled time if they were short on staff, but they would promise to make it up to the youth, saying, "We'll pay you tomorrow and let you stay out late." Along with having to care for the residents, staff members also had to have the patience and the grace to deal with parents, guardians, and girlfriends who would call in with questions, complaints, and fears. Ron was particularly good on the phone, unfailingly polite to all who called, and at times seemingly blessed with extra doses of patience. When one new resident was transferred to the institution, Ron spent several minutes on the phone talking with his parents, letting them know that their son had arrived safely and explaining the program and the way that the days were scheduled. He offered answers and a comforting voice of reason for the boy's parents who lived across the state.

Even when staff members are working with the best of intentions, however, Goffman (1961) describes such intimate contact with the juvenile's family and friends as contaminative contact. Talking to the residents' girlfriends and relatives on the phone and glancing at their mail before sending it out was undoubtedly one of the ways that the staff got to know so much about the young men's personal lives. I was always surprised at how much staff members could—and would—tell me about me the guys in the cottage. Reflecting the intimacy in staff-prisoner relationships (Crawley, 2004), they knew a great deal about the residents' histories from reading their files and time spent in their counseling sessions, but they also knew a lot about the youths' current relationships and future plans. While adults may have resented the loss of privacy, it actually seemed helpful to some of the boys as the door was opened for them to go to staff members for advice.

The daily interactions between the staff and the residents were generally tempered by good-natured humor and teasing. In the Blue cottage, humor helped to neutralize the stress and unite staff members, while at the same time allowing the boys to express emotions and affection within the masculine culture and context of the living unit (Kivett & Warren, 2002; Nurse, 2001). It was clear which staff members the residents liked and respected by whom they felt comfortable enough to tease. The staff they disliked, they either ignored or ridiculed behind their backs. Face-to-face teasing seemed to come with a dose of affection. Many of the residents enjoyed teasing and making fun of the younger staff members, especially calling them names and sometimes hitting or playfully slapping them with a conspicuously innocent "did that hurt?" expression. While horseplay was strictly forbidden in the institution, when a friendly staff member was involved, that rule was generally ignored (Kivett & Warren, 2002).

On one occasion, Luke was issued a challenge by a group of the boys; he and Alex, one of the residents, ended up full-out wrestling for a few minutes while several other residents stood around "oohing" and "ahhing" and applauding the impressive moves on display. When the impromptu wrestling match ended, Luke came into the office and went into the staff bathroom to examine his exposed flesh. He spent a minute looking at his hands and arms; when he realized that his finger was cut and bleeding, he said, "Oh, I'm glad that it's me," meaning that he was glad that the blood he saw was his and not Alex's or one of the other residents. Although he tried to play it cool and hide his discomfort, Alex was also in mild pain, suffering from rug burns on his knees. When Luke came back out to the lounge area, they laughed and joked together for several more minutes, showing affection and good sportsmanship.

With so much time on their hands, the residents found other ways to play with the staff. They liked to tease staff members about their clothes and their haircuts, making fun of Ron's tight jeans and Kyle's ratty shoes. Ron usually ignored them, but without a strong defense, Kyle could only laugh along as the residents discussed taking up a collection in the cottage to buy him a decent pair of shoes. On another occasion, when Eddie went to start the day's session of his anger-management counseling group, one of the boys joked with him that maybe he needed to attend for a refresher course. He illustrated his anger-management problem by playfully slapping Eddie on the back of the head. Eddie laughed and joked with him before sending him down to his room where he would be less of a distraction.

The staff members were not merely the recipients of the teasing—many of them played along and tried to give as good as they got. Kyle, for example, enjoyed trying to disrupt the residents' plays (attempting to form relationships with girls living in the community) on the phone—his favorite trick was to hold out the phone and ask very loudly which girl the recipient of the call thought was on the line. The guys who were considered game (smooth with the opposite sex) outside of the institution received a lot of phone calls and sometimes had difficulty correctly identifying the female on the phone. In another example, after a large bust where about half of the kids in the cottage lost their privilege levels for having dirty UA's (urinalysis tests), some of the staff members joked with each other and the boys about the residents' marijuana use. Kyle took to calling two of the leaders Cheech and Chong in relation to drug related movie plots and other staff members made sly comments about how the residents in the cottage seemed particularly mellow and how they all had the munchies.

While being a woman in the male world of Blue cottage held special challenges, female staff members who could think on their feet and make clever comebacks won some level of respect from the young male residents. Judy, an older Caucasian woman who filled something of a grandmother role, was flashed one day by one of the kids serving time for a sex offense. She apparently put him in his place by saying that it was "No big deal," implying he had a small penis and amusing the other boys. In another example, when a younger female staff member was transferred to Blue, she won some points by responding to a resident's "Fuck you," with a cool, "In your dreams." It was undoubtedly a much more effective response with the Blue population than getting offended or angry.

One of the strangest stories between the residents and the staff was the possible history between Luke and Zac, a 19-year-old Latino youth. The two of them had lived in the same neighborhood and, as they compared notes, it seemed clear that Zac had broken into Luke's truck while he was still a practicing burglar. One day when we were all sitting in the office, Luke told me that Zac was probably the one who had broken into his truck and Zac agreed, saying, "That was my area." Zac and Luke discussed the specifics of the crime—including some of the strange and memorable items stolen from the truck that day—and both of them laughed at the memory and the oddity of the coincidence. It was a pretty good-natured conversation, all things considered. Zac said that he used to leave a screwdriver in the car as his calling card and that he never left any fingerprints because he always wore gloves. Luke said that he did indeed have a screwdriver stuck in his passenger's seat and Zac laughed a little sheepishly. It seemed clear that their paths had crossed before. Later, perhaps as informal restitution for this offense, or perhaps as a sign of respect, I heard Zac telling Luke that he could help him get a system in his truck that would be impossible to break into or steal.

Reaching Outside the Walls

Many members of the staff of the Blue cottage seemed to go above and beyond their official duties in order to help the youth in their care. Eddie, for example, had developed a strong relationship with Kody, a 19-year-old African-American, who was arguably the most powerful and charismatic resident in the institution. Eddie had literally watched Kody grow up during his four years of incarceration. They both laughed when they remembered how young and small Kody was when he first came to the training school. Eddie said that he thought he was some staff member's kid and was just visiting...until he opened his mouth. While most of the staff thought that Kody would likely end up going to prison shortly after being released from the juvenile institution, Eddie frequently spoke to Kody about his future, discussing his options and helping him to consider the costs and benefits of his actions.

To try to further increase his legitimate opportunities and his chances for a legal lifestyle, Eddie tried to use his own connections to set up a job for Kody in the community as his release date neared. As part of the deal, he warned Kody that he needed to be responsible and not to mess up because it was Eddie's name on the line and he could ruin it for other guys down the road. He joked that he would have spies in the community checking up on him and reporting back on his progress. Eddie's extra efforts were clearly the exception rather than the rule; while many staff members cared about these residents while they were in the institution, most would not carry their relationships beyond the institution's walls. In fact, the administration of the training school discouraged staff members from keeping contact with the young men once they were released. The feeling seemed to be that they should do their best for them while the residents were incarcerated and then cut the cord upon their release, as Kyle explained. There was also the real fear that, once in the community, the more volatile and violent youth could come after staff members or their families to settle old scores. Blue cottage staff members explained that they did not want the kids to know their last names because they did not want them to be able to look them up once they were on "the outs" (in the community). As one example of their ongoing concern over this issue, a number of staff members were upset when the institution's school newspaper profiled new staff and inadvertently printed their full names.

Although it was against the norms of the institution, Eddie and a couple of the Blue staff members did try to keep in touch with some of the young men on their caseloads after they were released. This was often a difficult task as many of the residents seemed to vanish once they left the institution, leaving the staff to wonder about them and how they were doing. Some graduates of the training school called the cottage on occasion to update the staff and their still-incarcerated friends on their lives and their progress. The staff read about others in the newspaper, learning about new crimes, new sentences, and deaths.

Some caring members of the staff took on the extra responsibility of checking up on their "sons" to see how they were doing after they were released. Ron, for example, periodically called two of his boys, Tony and Alex, to check in and offer fatherly advice and pep talks. When Alex spoke of his plans to get married shortly after being released, Ron warned him against getting married so young (age 19) and so soon after returning to the community. He let Alex vent his frustration about his job search and then encouraged him to persevere through the tough times, taking "shitty" jobs for a while, if that was what needed to be done. He continued to be a mentor for him after Alex was released and encouraged him to build other mentoring relationships with strong father figures in the community.

Luke, too, went out of his way to help the kids in the cottage prepare for their return to the community. He helped many of them fill out applications for entrance into community college and helped them sort through the paperwork for financial aid. He encouraged them to take advantage of summer job programs for delinquent and at-risk youth. When one of the boys on his caseload was released and then returned to the institution several times for parole violations, Luke spent a great deal of time and effort trying to help him figure out how to best change his life. Luke counseled with the young man, even bringing his mother and his pregnant girlfriend into the institution for sessions, and he helped them finally decide to move to another state so that the boy's mother could have more family support and the boy could get away from his neighborhood and his gang affiliations.

Another of the residents on Luke's caseload was repeatedly turned down for transfers to group homes and was refused acceptance to a job-training program at the last minute. This particular resident was serving juvenile life (until his 21st birthday); in the years that he had already served, he had completed high school and he was eager to take college courses and/or learn new vocational skills if the opportunities were made available to him. He was an exceptionally bright and artistic young man—a published poet and the cottage's artist of choice—and he claimed that he wanted to go to college and study to be a criminologist. Luke recognized that the institution had little left to offer this resident and he made it a personal goal to get him sent to one of the state's forestry camps, where he might learn new skills, for the remainder of his sentence.

Efforts like these demonstrated that at least some members of the staff cared about these young men above what the job description entailed and what the pay warranted. It was clear in witnessing the interactions and in talking to the boys in the cottage that the kids recognized which members of the staff sincerely cared about them and they learned to appreciate the staff members' concern and their efforts.

Discussion and Conclusions

Whatever remnants of the *parens patriae* ideology that remains in the juvenile justice system are largely sustained by the staff members working in the trenches with the state's most serious delinquent offenders. Judges and administrators may support the idea of rehabilitation (Caeti, Hemmens, Cullen, & Burton, 2003), but their interaction with juvenile offenders is limited. While Bernard (1992) has argued that "there is no place in a modern juvenile justice system for large, custody oriented juvenile institutions"(p.

178), it seems that such institutions may be where true efforts at rehabilitation and resocialization take place. Staff members who work with incarcerated delinquents on a daily basis — listening to their concerns, dealing with their behavioral problems, even teaching the young men in their care to shave for the first time — come closest to putting into practice the ideals of the juvenile justice system first articulated by the child-savers (Platt, 1977).

It is a difficult job and the occupational stress of cottage staff members (Mitchell, MacKenzie, Styve, & Gover, 2000) seemed to be on the rise by the end of this study because Blue cottage staff perceived that their young population needed more parenting and care than ever. During their tenure, staff members saw many young men come and go, paying for their crimes by spending part of their adolescence incarcerated in the Blue cottage. They shared their concerns that the youth coming into the institution had changed; they seemed to be getting younger, mouthier, and more needy. The Blue staff members were well aware of the fact that younger juveniles often have a harder time adjusting to confinement and are more likely to act out (Gover, MacKenzie, & Armstrong, 2000) and they saw their jobs becoming ever more challenging.

While serving their sentences, the world of the adolescent juvenile shrinks. Whatever sense of home and family they can claim at the institution is generally centered in their cottage living unit. Staff members and older juveniles become their role models and their best sources of interactive advice. Researchers of total institutions have long recognized the importance of staff and juvenile relationships in the state's attempts to re-socialize offenders before sending them back out into the community. Four decades ago, Studt, Messinger, and Wilson (1968) argued that:

> Resocializing agencies have a double interest in social relationships. They aim to encourage clients to change the ways in which they relate to others. And in this effort their proper tools — if not their only tools — are relationships among persons: among staff members and among clients, and between the clients and their communities. (p. 257)

While they hoped to impart wisdom and conforming values to the young people in their care, staff members also benefited from the relationships they built in the cottage. Staff members working in the Blue cottage undoubtedly took the lessons learned at the training school with them back into the community. For those who aspired to other occupations, time in the institution provided invaluable experience. Brandon, for example, was planning to complete his degree in order to become a teacher and coach. His father told him that his experiences working with young offenders at the institution would be a blessing when it came to dealing with angry or difficult children; reflecting on what he had learned on the job, he thought his father was probably right.

Staff members also adopted different and contradictory views of teenagers, in general, after working in a juvenile detention facility. The labels that they embraced and the potential fear that they felt for the incarcerated juveniles they worked with were extended to cover all adolescents (Gordon, Moriarty, & Grant, 2003). As one example, the Red cottage supervisor told me that he would never again look at a group of teenagers in the same way—he would regard them with deep suspicion for the rest of his life. His young female colleague disagreed, however, and said that after getting to know the knuckleheads in the same cottage, she would never be afraid of juvenile criminals again. She would see them as youngsters making incredibly bad decisions rather than the superpredators depicted in the media. Neither Red staff member claimed that the youth had significantly changed; instead, what had changed were their own attitudes about them.

Many members of the Blue cottage staff started their careers with high hopes of saving these kids—these problem children. As the months passed and the residents came and went, the failures eventually wore on them. The cynicism of many of the staff members built over the years, fueled by the dashed hopes they invested in promising young men, who left the institution full of excitement but went on to re-offend, to kill, or be killed. Ultimately, staff members must send all of their "sons" back out into the community. They hope for the best and they try to move on. Before he was released, one young man asked Ron if he was going to miss him. Ron never quite answered the question, but he did respond wearily that for each one who leaves, he gets two more problem children. The youth change, but the problems remain.

In spite of the disappointments, however, most of the staff members of the Blue cottage hold tightly to their good intentions, staying guardedly optimistic for the youth in their care. Some have adapted their strategies, choosing to save their best hopes and efforts for the young men who show the most promise. One thing they know for sure is this: the institution will go on, more kids will be sent their way, and the cycle will continue. The staff members will continue to serve as guardians, correctional officers, and surrogate parents for the troubled youth the state has deemed too dangerous to be in the community and has locked away.

Knowing that the young offenders in their care will return to the community in a matter of months and years impels staff members to keep building caring and mentoring relationships with their state-assigned "sons." Consistent with the notion of *parens patriae* embraced by the original juvenile court, it is their mission to guide the troubled young men in their care through "the immense journey of adolescence, a journey of peril and possibility" (Ayers 1997, p. 138). The perils are clear for incarcerated adolescents; caring staff members can help them to see the possibilities as well.

Endnote

1. Editors' Note: This chapter, in comparison to others in the volume, trades breadth for depth. Here, the author delves into the day-to-day activities within a particular secure facility for juveniles. This snapshot focuses on the critical dimensions of relationships within such facilities and, while not representative of all facilities, it sheds light on the dynamics within this particular setting. Professor Inderbitzin highlights the many dilemmas of correctional work with juveniles: the variation between different staff members, the balance between rehabilitation and holding youth accountable (e.g., the example of the youth who "flashed" the staff: in many jurisdictions the resident might face criminal charges for that act). Overall, this analysis is an important addition to the book because it articulates the dilemma of treating youth with equal doses of compassion and ensuring fairness and consistency—something that many of these youth never received at home. Some of the workers depicted in this chapter may have acted (at times) in a manner inconsistent with "best correctional practices," but the common theme underlying this chapter is the importance of the relationships between the staff members and youth—which is a key factor in their rehabilitation. One of the limitations of our understanding of juvenile corrections is a lack of qualitative studies where we learn what actually occurs in these places.

References

Ayers, W. (1997). *A kind and just parent: The children of juvenile court*. Boston: Beacon Press.

Bartollas, C., Miller, S. J., & Dinitz, S. (1976). *Juvenile victimization: The institutional paradox*. New York: John Wiley & Sons.

Bell, J. (2000). Throwaway children: Conditions of confinement and incarceration. In V. Polakow (Ed.), *The public assault on America's children: Poverty, violence, and juvenile injustice*, (pp. 188-210). New York: Teachers College Press.

Bernard, T. J. (1992). *The cycle of juvenile justice*. New York: Oxford University Press.

Caeti, T. J., Hemmens, C., Cullen, F. T., & Burton, V. S. (2003). Management of juvenile correctional facilities. *The Prison Journal, 83*, 383-405.

Crawley, E. M. (2004). Emotion and performance: Prison officers and the presentation of self in prisons. *Punishment & Society, 6*, 411-427.

Currie, E. (1998). *Crime and punishment in America*. New York: Henry Holt & Company, Inc.

Farkas, M. A. (2000). A typology of correctional officers. *International Journal of Offender Therapy and Comparative Criminology, 44,* 431-449.

Feld, B. C. (1977). *Neutralizing inmate violence: Juvenile offenders in institutions.* Cambridge, MA: Ballinger Publishing Company.

Goffman, E. (1961). *Asylums.* New York: Anchor Books.

Gordon, J. A., Moriarty, L. J., & Grant, P. H. (2003). Juvenile correctional officers' perceived fear and risk of victimization. *Criminal Justice & Behavior, 30,* 62-84.

Gover, A. R., MacKenzie, D. L., & Armstrong, G. S. (2000). Importation and deprivation explanations of juveniles' adjustment to correctional facilities. *International Journal of Offender Therapy and Comparative Criminology, 44,* 450-467.

Hemmens, C., & Stohr, M. K. (2000). The two faces of the correctional role: An exploration of the value of the correctional role instrument. *International Journal of Offender Therapy & Comparative Criminology, 44,* 326-349.

Inderbitzin, M. (2005). Growing up behind bars: An ethnographic study of adolescent inmates in a cottage for violent offenders. *Journal of Offender Rehabilitation, 42,* 1-22.

Inderbitzin, M. (2006a). Lessons from a juvenile training school. *Journal of Adolescent Research, 21,* 7-26.

Inderbitzin, M. (2006b). Negotiating cooperation and control: Inmate leadership in a juvenile institution. *Corrections Compendium, 31,* 6-7, 33-34.

Inderbitzin, M. (2007). A look from the inside: Balancing custody and treatment in a juvenile maximum security facility. *International Journal of Offender Therapy and Comparative Criminology, 51,* 348-362.

Kivett, D. D., & Warren, C. A. B. (2002). Social control in a group home for delinquent boys. *Journal of Contemporary Ethnography, 31,* 3-32.

Lane, J., Lanza-Kaduce, L., Frazier, C. E., & Bishop, D. M. (2002). Adult versus juvenile sanctions: Voices of incarcerated youth. *Crime & Delinquency, 48,* 431-455.

Mitchell, O., MacKenzie, D. L., Styve, G. J., & Gover, A. R. (2000). The impact of individual, organizational, and environmental attributes on voluntary turnover among juvenile correctional staff members. *Justice Quarterly, 17,* 333-357.

Nurse, A. M. (2001). The structure of the juvenile prison: Constructing the inmate father. *Youth & Society, 32,* 360-394.

O'Neil, C. F. (1988). Training school potential: Fulfilling the expectation. In R. L. Jenkins & W. K. Brown, (Eds.), *The abandonment of delinquent behavior: Promoting the turnaround.* New York: Praeger.

Platt, A. M. (1977). *The child-savers: The invention of delinquency.* Chicago: University of Chicago Press.

Polsky, H. W. (1962). *Cottage six – The social system of delinquent boys in residential treatment.* New York: Russell Sage Foundation.

Singer, S. I. (1996). *Recriminalizing delinquency: Violent juvenile crime and juvenile justice reform.* Cambridge: Cambridge University Press.

Snyder, H. N., & Sickmund, M. (1999). *Juvenile offenders and victims: 1999 national report.* Washington, DC: Office of Juvenile Justice and Delinquency Prevention.

Studt, E., Messinger, S. L., & Wison, T. P. (1968). *C-Unit: Search for community in prison.* New York: Russell Sage Foundation.

Sykes, G. M. (1958). *The society of captives: A study of a maximum security prison.* Princeton University Press.

Weber, G. H. (1961). Emotional and defensive reactions of cottage parents. In D. R. Cressey, (Ed.), *The prison: Studies in institutional organization and change,* (pp. 189-228). New York: Holt, Rinehart and Winston, Inc.

CHAPTER 12
CORRECTIONAL HEALTH CARE

Matthew O. Thomas

T here are approximately 100,000 youth held in local and state operated juvenile correctional facilities within the United States (West & Sabol, 2008). In addition to engaging in impulsive, risky, and delinquent behaviors, this group is likely to have elevated rates of communicable diseases, high levels of mental disorders or learning difficulties, involvement in substance abuse, and poor histories of community health care. This population is also at high risk of violence and suicide, both within a correctional facility and in the community. These factors shape the type of medical and mental health care that these youth (also called wards, minors, residents, or youthful offenders) require when they are incarcerated.

Various types of institutions and organizations provide residential services for delinquent youth, including detention facilities, group homes, boot camps, reception centers, state correctional facilities (also called training schools), and ranches. Considerable diversity exists in the types of programs that are offered and a blend of public, private, and faith-based organizations offer residential programs. Significant differences abound in the style, security, and programming at these various facilities, but they are all expected to provide appropriate health care for their residents. Historically, health care was an afterthought in many places and some evidence suggests that training schools and ranches were less likely to conform to standards of care (Parent et al., 1994). There is, however, an increasing awareness between the relationships of physical and mental health care services and institutional behavior. Moreover, providing effective health care services for incarcerated youth may also contribute to success in the community once they are released.

Juvenile Health Care

In general, youth entering secure detention facilities face more serious health issues than the general youth population. Incarcerated youth in Milwaukee reported high rates of chronic illnesses, including asthma, high rates of previous hospitalization, surgery, medication use, and some level of violent victimization (Matson, Bretl, & Wolf, 2000). Oregon youth entering the adult corrections system indicated very high levels of chronic illnesses (77%) , mental health disorders (87%), substance abuse issues (77%), and past suicide attempts (33%) — making for a high health-risk group (Gilhooly, Simon, Tsu, & Sells, 2001). Clearly, delinquent youth pose serious challenges due to the variety of health issues that they present and these challenges can be exacerbated by their placement in juvenile correctional facilities.

For example, a study of Washington State juveniles found significant differences in the medical needs and care of juveniles in state versus county facilities. Those in county facilities had higher rates of emergency room visits, a greater number of acute health issues (such as pregnancy or sexually transmitted infections [STI]), and more suicide watches than those in state facilities. Conversely, juveniles in state institutions were more likely to have chronic health needs, such as dentistry, dermatology, or nutrition (Anderson & Farrow 1998). There are several reasons for this difference in services. Juveniles in state facilities tend to stay longer and their health care needs are more likely to be identified. Moreover, because most state governments draw from a larger tax base, they may be able to provide a better standard of care.

A youth's admission to a correctional facility begins with establishing the legality of her detention or sentence, as well as an assessment of her current emotional and physical functioning. Information about the youth is also used to determine an appropriate classification. Classification enables officials to assign residents to units with levels of security based on several criteria: the youth's current and prior offenses (e.g., whether he or she is a violent offender), age and gender, previous institutional behavior, and whether he or she has any significant physical or mental health concerns. This is not an option for all facilities though: smaller institutions may not have the capacity to segregate their residents due to their size. As a result, these facilities sometimes mix adolescent males and females, as well as youngsters and more mature adolescents on the same unit, thus creating further challenges to their supervision.

An initial medical assessment is critical for several reasons, including the need to identify communicable diseases and also because juveniles who are taken into custody may be under the influence of drugs or alcohol. Intoxicated or impaired youth should be carefully evaluated and monitored by medically trained personnel because they are at some risk of overdose or poisoning (Roush, 1996). In addition, newly admitted youth need to be checked for injuries or existing health problems. The American Correctional Association (ACA) sets a one hour standard timeframe for intake assessments and staff conducting these evaluations should have comprehensive training in suicide assessment and medical care (Parent et al. 1994) because the first few hours of incarceration are a time of high risk of self-harm or suicide.

In addition to the ACA, the National Commission on Correctional Health Care (NCCHC) also sets comprehensive standards for juvenile health care. Correctional agencies wanting to be accredited are required to meet a set of health-related standards, such as health screening and assessment, availability of trained personnel, and the availability of emergency and recreational services. Few detention facilities, however, meet these standards. Gallagher and Dobrin (2007) reviewed data from over 700 juvenile halls and found facilities that provided better care tended to "have longer average lengths of stay, are larger, and are government owned" (p. 991).

The quality of health screening often depends on the type of facility to which the juvenile is placed. Juvenile hall admissions often occur during hours when full time medical staff members are unavailable, so a cursory screening is done and cases where only minor care is required are referred to a nurse or physician the next day. If immediate care is required, by contrast, the youth is often taken to an emergency department in the community. Most youth stay for only a few days in juvenile detention and this fact influences the types of health care they receive. Health assessment in state correctional facilities, by contrast, tends to be more comprehensive because youth will be there much longer. Therefore, they are often screened for communicable diseases, chronic health conditions, and pregnancy.

In the most recent *Juvenile Residential Facility Census*, for example, it was reported that "68% of facilities reported providing physical health examinations to all youth" (Livsey, Sickmund, & Sladky, 2009). Larger facilities tended to provide more extensive health screening and assessments. Livsey and colleagues (2009) also reported that fewer facilities offered specialized health screening:

Exam type:	All youth	Some youth	No youth
Dental	46%	46%	8%
Vision	38	51	12
Gynecological	18	70	12

Last, these investigators found that a greater number of facilities test all youth for tuberculosis (46%) compared to pregnancy (16%), sexually transmitted infections (14%), hepatitis B (10%) or HIV (4%) (p. 12).

One issue that juvenile correctional officers often encounter is the problem of malingering. Youth in confinement may exaggerate their health care conditions or needs. In some cases, the adolescent may have an ulterior motivation, such as missing educational classes to get some sympathy from a health care provider or the desire to break the routine. Unfortunately, because of issues with malingering, youth correctional officers will occasionally fail to investigate the cause of a youth's complaints of pain or distress, thus leading to tragedies. In addition, correctional officers do not always cooperate with the health care providers. They may fail to abide by treatment plans, follow-up on medical advice or ensure that youth receive their medications. As a result, tensions may exist between the security and medical staff (Roush, 1996).

A nutritionally sound diet is an important component for all individuals, especially juveniles. For example, improper diets can lead to health problems, exacerbate existing medical conditions, and may be associated with acting-out behaviors. Youth with chronic illnesses such as diabetes, prenatal care, or obesity may require special diets. Some residents, however, may be reluctant to comply with such diets; nutritionists or nurse-educators can provide counseling to them. Adding to the problem, correctional food is also notorious for being unhealthy and many facilities provide meals that are high in fat and starch content and offer few fresh fruits or vegetables. One study found that while 12% of admitted youth were obese at intake (with another 2% classified as overweight), the time in confinement led to dramatic changes—after three months of confinement, the percentage of obese or overweight juveniles increased to two-thirds (Robinson et al., 2006). Some of the weight gain is attributable to prescribed psychotropic medications (prescription medications that are intended to modify psychological functioning) and the access to food, which might not be as available to youth outside confinement (Robinson et al., 2006). As a result, some scholars call for the implementation of individualized diet plans for incarcerated youth (Feinstein, Gomez, Gordon, Cruise, & De Prato, 2007).

Other factors associated with healthy conditions in juvenile corrections include cleanliness and taking precautions to reduce the transmission of infectious diseases (Bick, 2005). This is worsened by the fact that juveniles often resist efforts to increase their hygiene. In some cases, youth might have very poor social skills and must be educated about hygiene and healthy lifestyles. Providing youth with clean clothing, bedding, and showers is typically a responsibility of the correctional staff because access to these amenities is often restricted. Moreover, the control over access to daily recreation, exercise, and fresh air rests with the security staff and idleness often results in higher rates of misconduct.

Incarcerated juveniles tend to have high rates of asthma, hypertension, diabetes, tuberculosis, and dental problems (Committee on Adolescence, 2001). These youth also exhibit higher rates of risk behaviors, including alcohol and tobacco use, assaultive behavior, gang membership, and sexual activity (Roush, 1996). A sample of detained youth in Maryland found that 45% reported having a medical condition (with the majority suffering physical abuse), while many had reported having previous injuries, including stab and gunshot wounds; more than a tenth never received treatment for these injuries (Shelton, 2000).

Secure facilities face other obstacles in providing health care, not the least of which includes an inability to easily move people in and out of the institution – many of which are located in rural and remote areas. Because of these impediments, the National Commission on Correctional Health Care (NCCHC) issued guidelines for the acquisition and use of emergency equipment, like Automated External Defibrillators (AEDs). AEDs require additional training for staff, but when properly utilized provide an on-site option to deal with cardiac arrest—an option that would otherwise take valuable time to clear through the secure measures of the facility (NCCHC, 1999), as well as ambulance crews traveling to the facility. This example shows how the development of guidelines and standards, paired with technological innovations, can improve health care conditions for incarcerated youth.

Health Care Challenges Within Juvenile Corrections

Confidentiality

Little privacy exists in a secure detention facility. Staff work very closely with one another and some may be privy to confidential health care information. Roush (1996) reports that this can cause problems if juveniles are fearful of discussing health care issues, such as their HIV status, when correctional staff members are present. The Health Insurance Portability and Accountability Act of 1996 (HIPAA) resulted in significant changes in the manner that health-related information could be disseminated within a youth detention or correctional facility. In some cases, health care providers are not legally able to disclose to other facility staff or parents about the health status of the juveniles in their care (Nicoletti, 2003). Bizzell (2003) suggests that even though some of the HIPAA guidelines are relaxed in correctional facilities, staff members who disclose the confidential health information of inmates without proper authorization may be placing themselves in jeopardy of being sued or prosecuted.

Despite the fact that some medical care information cannot be shared, it is critical that facilities develop comprehensive information systems that track health-related issues and that medical staff have access to this information. Some state correctional systems have developed quality management and peer review processes where health care is monitored to ensure that it is consistent with national standards. In California, for instance, the Division of Juvenile Justice within the California Department of Corrections and Rehabilitation (CDCR) has implemented Quality Management Committees to review the medical care delivered to juveniles in their care (CDCR, 2006). Under their guidance, physicians working within this correctional system engage in peer review of practice (when physicians review the work of other doctors) to ensure that quality care is maintained.

Dental Care

Providing appropriate dental care in juvenile correctional facilities is challenged by a number of factors. Many youth fear dental exams, have poor dental hygiene, and may ignore what appear to be minor dental problems. The emergence of meth mouth, a condition brought on by methamphetamine abuse, raises considerable concern for dentists who practice in correctional facilities (American Dental Association, 2006; Rhodus & Little, 2005). Dental emergencies such as impacted wisdom teeth or injuries resulting from recreational activities, unintentional causes, or assaults also occur behind bars. Because incarcerated youth are unlikely to have received any kind of comprehensive dental care in the community, it is important that juveniles who reside in these facilities for longer periods of time receive some preventative care and, if possible, health education about proper dental care.

Medical Care Expenditures

Providing appropriate correctional health care for juveniles is costly. According to a study that examined these expenditures, fixed costs (such as medical staff contracts and laboratory supplies) represent the greatest portion of health care outlays (Tennyson, 2003). But intermediate costs (e.g., emergency care and dentistry) and variable costs (e.g., prescriptions) are also rising and are less predictable than fixed costs. Mental health care expenditures are also costly and can be three times the amount of general medical expenses (Tennyson, 2003). Variable costs represented 11% of the budgets in Tennyson's (2003) study and as items such as prescriptions increase in cost, the ability of administrators to adequately budget for medical expenditures decreases. A single case of HIV/AIDS, for example, represents a cost of $13,900 to $36,500 for medication per year (Infectious Diseases in Corrections Report, 2006). Another study, looking at juvenile correctional health care, found that even when a facility attempts to manage or decrease costs, by holding nurses salaries constant and by decreasing laboratory equipment spending by half, costs increased by 17% over a five year period (Tennyson, 2004). One of the more dramatic increases came in optical care, which increased by 200%; while one variable cost (ambulance transportation) decreased over this period, all other variable costs increased (Tennyson, 2004).

Juvenile correctional facilities must provide comprehensive health care treatment that tackles the problems of chronic medical conditions, past injuries, psychological problems, and dental and optometric services. Residents of these facilities also require emergency care, including access to nursing or health care staff at sick call (the term used when an inmate requests medical care). Not all juvenile correctional facilities provide appropriate care. At a minimum, facilities must treat the most obvious or emergent conditions, bring immunizations up-to-date, and provide educational information about risk behaviors affecting the minor. The short-term nature of juvenile detention, for instance, may be an ideal place to deliver basic health education and promotion information to high risk populations. One problem with delivering these educational programs, however, is that many juvenile halls have failed to partner with local public health agencies to deliver such courses.

One of the more recent attempts to combat rising health care costs in juvenile facilities is telemedicine. Telemedicine, or the use of telephones, Internet services, or television conferences, allows specialized health care professionals to assist in the diagnosis of patients without having to transport the youth from the facility or require a costly "house call" from a physician. Furthermore, these approaches reduce the stigma associated with transporting a youth in restraints (e.g., handcuffs and/or leg irons) to a medical appointment in the community. While this technology holds some promise, a recent study of youth detention facilities in Tennessee determined that even though telemedicine decreased costs associated with the transportation of youth, the overall use of telemedicine significantly increased overall medical costs (Fox, Somes, & Waters, 2006). The authors of the study concluded that telemedicine needs an appropriate economy of scale before it becomes more financially prudent than traditional health care; as a result, the practice may be suitable for larger consortiums of facilities (Fox et al., 2006).

Blood Borne Pathogens and Infectious Diseases

Controlling the spread of blood borne pathogens and infectious diseases is a key issue in the operation of youth facilities. Communicable diseases such as sexually transmitted infections (STIs), HIV/AIDS, and hepatitis must be detected and treated. Because inmates are usually housed in close quarters, the likelihood of transmission is increased. In addition, some of the negative behaviors of youth in custody (such as engaging in consensual sex, assaults, and rape) increase the risk of transmitting diseases.

But it is behavior outside of residential facilities that is of some concern to researchers. Juvenile delinquents in the Chicago area reported very high rates of sexual activity (over 90% of the males were sexually active and over

60% of those had multiple partners), high rates of receiving tattoos and drug use (although intravenous drug use was rare); this indicates a variety of risky behaviors (Teplin, Mericle, McClelland, & Abram, 2003). Risky sexual activity often co-occurs with drug use, especially the use of marijuana (Rosengard et al., 2006). Gang members, in particular, are significantly more likely to engage in risky behaviors, such as unprotected sex or sex with multiple partners, increasing their exposure to STIs (Voisin et al., 2004). Juveniles in general are less likely to use condoms and are less knowledgeable about AIDS transmission, while bisexual male juveniles are more likely to engage in prostitution, leading to increased risk of exposure (Lichtenstein, 2000).

AIDS education can increase juveniles' willingness to be tested and increase their levels of fear about the disease, but, unfortunately, education does not appear to significantly impact decision-making to engage in risk behaviors (Morris, Baker, Valentine, & Pennisi, 1998). Another study finds that while more juveniles are willing to be tested for HIV/AIDS, some youth who fall into high risk categories are not being tested, leaving the possibility open of undiagnosed cases (Pugatch, Ramratnam, Feller, Price, & Riggs, 1999). Perhaps most importantly, a diagnosis of HIV/AIDS requires significant medical attention—both during the incarceration period and after release. Post release treatment is insufficient in most instances, but the Centers for Disease Control and Prevention (CDC)/Health Resources and Services Administration (HRSA) intervention program is showing some promise in these areas (Robillard et al., 2003).

Chlamydia trachomatis (CT) and gonorrhea are two common STIs that affect sexually active juveniles. In a study of juvenile detention facilities that screened for these infections, researchers found that females experienced significantly higher rates than males; both males and females tested positive for both over 50% of the time (Kahn et al., 2005). Complicating the diagnosis of these STIs, a large percentage of juveniles do not present with visible symptoms of the STIs (Pack, DiClemente, Hook, & Oh, 2000). More and more facilities are moving to a urine-based screening test for CT and gonorrhea, which decreases costs and increases participation (Oh, Smith, O'Cain, Kilmer, Johnson, & Hook, 1998). In California, urine-based screening detected a 12.9% prevalence among females and a 6% prevalence among males; those affected reported low levels of access to regular health care in the previous year (Chartier et al., 2004). Another study, conducted in San Antonio, TX, found that almost one-quarter of females and 8.7% of males suffered from CT, making it a serious health concern for the detention facility, as well as an educational priority (Kelly, Blair, Baillargeon, & German, 2000).

A cross-sectional survey of incarcerated juveniles, aged 13 to 18 years, investigated the risk factors for STI contraction, specifically CT and gonorrhea (Robertson, Baird, St. Lawrence, & Pack, 2005). Females experienced higher rates of infection for both diseases; demographic characteristics such as age and race accounted for over half of the variation and behavior accounted for one-third (Robertson et al., 2005). Screenings for CT are more common for female detainees (Lofy, Hofmann, Mosure, Fine, & Marrazzo, 2006), but expanding screenings to sexually active male adolescents has increased the success rate in identifying and treating CT (Tebb et al., 2005).

Rates of hepatitis are higher in correctional populations than in the community. This is a problem because the illness is associated with long-term rates of adult liver failure (Murray, Richardson, Morishima, Owens, & Gretch, 2003). A variety of risky behaviors increase one's exposure to hepatitis and these include engaging in unprotected sex and having multiple sexual partners. Additionally, intravenous drug use, tattooing, and body piercing add to these numbers. One study of incarcerated juveniles found relatively low rates of hepatitis infection; the greatest rate was among intravenous drug users (Feldman et al., 2004). The study's authors advocated increased testing and intervention in order to keep hepatitis infections at a low level (Feldman et al., 2004). Murray and colleagues (2003) confirmed that incarcerated juveniles have lower hepatitis infection rates than the adult population, but have a higher hepatitis prevalence rate than the non-incarcerated juvenile population and are more likely to engage in high risk behaviors.

The risks associated with spreading blood borne pathogens and communicable diseases are significant for the youth who reside in juvenile facilities, as well as the staff who work within them. As a result, in most jurisdictions staff members receive orientation training about blood borne pathogen containment as well as annual training updates. Furthermore, some juvenile correctional systems have established infection control committees and hired public health practitioners to investigate, control, and prevent the spread of infections (CDCR, 2006). Unfortunately, many correctional systems have been slow to implement these types of interventions.

Special Health Needs of Female Juveniles

Females present unique challenges for the juvenile justice system and, as their numbers increase, the demand for female-specific programming has also grown (Budnick & Shields-Fletcher, 1998). One long-standing concern is that correctional health care has typically been delivered on models created for male populations and male youth entering correctional facilities are in significantly poorer health than other male youth (Forrest, Tambor, Riley,

Ensminger, & Starfield, 2000), but females require a greater degree of services. One cross sectional survey of incarcerated female juveniles found high percentages of sexually transmitted infections (Robertson et al., 2005), past pregnancies, suicide attempts, and substance abuse (Crosby et al., 2004). Reproductive health care and pregnancy are female-specific conditions that require significant health care treatment (Fitzgibbon, 2004). In addition, some disorders such as anorexia, bulimia, suicide attempts, and depression disproportionately affect incarcerated females (Roush, 1996). Females are also more likely to suffer from coexisting disorders and are 15 times more likely to have been the victims of unwanted sexual advances (Alemagno et al., 2006).

A recent survey examined the lifestyle characteristics of detained females (Lederman et al., 2004). Respondents (those admitted to a correctional facility for the first time) indicated the presence of the following family problems: mental health (21%), alcohol abuse (27%), drugs (26%), and criminal justice system involvement (58%). Respondents who had been admitted more than once, by contrast, reported higher percentages of the same problems. Lederman and colleagues (2004) also found that in addition to coming from dysfunctional families, a vast majority of female detainees experienced a major trauma, such as witnessing a death or being threatened with a weapon. High percentages of respondents also reported having mental health or substance abuse problems and being sexually active. Last, youth admitted for the first time (22%) and minors admitted more than once (29%) also reported being the victims of sexual abuse.

As juvenile justice policy makers come to realize the importance of gender differences in health care, some facilities are introducing gender specific education programs in the area of health. Girl Talk-2, a newly developed program delivered on a peer-to-peer basis, shows promise of increasing health care awareness and behavior modification (Kelly, Martinez, & Medrano, 2004). Juvenile corrections educators continue, however, to face higher percentages of youth with learning disabilities than do educators in traditional settings, and this may present another obstacle for delivering these types of programs (Shelton, 2006).

Conclusions

Providing physical health care is a critical responsibility within the entire continuum of juvenile corrections—from detention to placement in state correctional facilities. The effort is often costly, but strategies that focus on prevention are cost effective if viewed over the long-term. By taking a proactive health promotion approach with incarcerated juveniles, serious health problems may be avoided. Some health education programs, for instance, are short in duration and could be delivered to groups of residents, even those detained for a few days.

Accreditation standards place clear timeframes for medical professionals working within juvenile justice facilities to complete initial and ongoing physical and psychological assessments. Careful attention should be paid by regulatory bodies to ensure that these standards are met in all types of facilities. In reality, Gallagher and Dobrin (2007) found, however, that only a small percentage of youth facilities comply with NCCHC accreditation standards. Again, compliance with these national standards may prove expensive in the short-term, but once a facility has developed an accredited program, it is much easier to maintain.

Delivering constitutionally appropriate juvenile correctional health care is challenged by a number of issues. Concerns about privatization, confidentiality of health care information, changes in drug markets (e.g., the rising use of methamphetamines), the disproportionate population of minority youth in correctional facilities, growing numbers of females admitted to detention, and long-term periods of incarceration each represent unique challenges for the juvenile justice system. Yet, each of these issues is also an opportunity for health promotion strategies and public health interventions that may have a significant long-term impact on the mental and physical well being of the residents in juvenile correctional facilities.

Delivering health care interventions in juvenile residential placements is a complicated and costly endeavor; providing services that comply with the Americans with Disabilities Act, the IDEIA, HIPAA, as well as the Constitution are a challenge to cash-strapped juvenile halls and state correctional systems where youth sometimes become lost in the shuffle. DeMuro (2003) wrote about the importance of using best practices and observes how it is easier to deliver services in a well operated and managed facility. Research about these best practices provides juvenile justice policy makers with an array of successful programs that can aid in the assessment of mental health, the treatment and control of infectious diseases, controlling institutional behavior, treatment of chronic health care, and providing services and support for the youth once they are returned to the community.

References

Alemagno, S. A., Shaffer-King, E., & Hammel, R. (2006). Juveniles in detention: How do girls differ from boys? *Journal of Correctional Health Care, 12,* 45-53.

Anderson, B., & Farrow, J. A. (1998). Incarcerated adolescents in Washington state. Health services and utilization. *Journal of Adolescent Health, 22,* 363-367.

American Dental Association. (2006). *Meth mouth can leave users toothless*. Retrieved April 14, 2007, from http://www.ada.org

Bick, J. (2005). Infection control in the correctional setting. *Infectious Diseases In Corrections Report, 8*, 1-6.

Bizzell, W. D. (2003). *The protection of inmate's medical records: The challenge of HIPAA privacy regulations*. Retrieved April 14, 2007, from: www.corrections.com

Budnick, K. J., & Shields-Fletcher, E. (1998). *What about girls?* Washington, DC: Office of Juvenile Justice and Delinquency Prevention.

California Department of Corrections and Rehabilitation. (2006). *Division of juvenile justice health care remedial plan*. Sacramento, CA: Author.

Chartier, M., Packel, L., Bauer, H. M., Brammeier, M., Little, M., & Bolan, G. (2004). Chlamydia prevalence among adolescent females and males in juvenile detention facilities in California. *Journal of Correctional Health Care, 11*, 79-97.

Committee on Adolescence. (2001). Health care for children and adolescents in the juvenile correctional care system. *Pediatrics, 107*, 799-803.

Crosby, R., Salazar, L. F., DiClemente, R. J., Yarber, W., Caliendo, A. M., & Staples-Horne, M. (2004). Health risk factors among detained adolescent females. *American Journal of Preventive Medicine, 27*, 404-410.

DeMuro, P. (2003). Good news from Toledo: Real improvements in detention. *Journal for Juvenile Justice and Detention Services, 18*, 79-91.

Feinstein, R. A., Gomez, R., Gordon, S., Cruise, K., & De Prato, D. (2007). Prevalence of overweight youth among a population of incarcerated juveniles. *Journal of Correctional Health Care, 13*, 9-44.

Feldman, G. M., Sorvillo, F., Cole, B., Lawrence, W., & Mares, R. (2004). Seroprevalence of Hepatitis C among a juvenile detention population. *Journal of Adolescent Health, 35*, 505-508.

Fitzgibbon, J. J. (2004). Health care for adolescents in juvenile facilities: Increasing needs for adolescent families. *Journal of Pediatric and Adolescent Gynecology, 17*, 3-5.

Forrest, C. B., Tambor, E., Riley, A. W., Ensminger, M. E., & Starfield, B. (2000). The health profile of incarcerated male youths. *Pediatrics, 105*, 286-291.

Fox, K. C., Somes, G., & Waters, T. M. (2006). The use of telemedicine technology and restructured referral patterns to reduce health care costs in a juvenile justice system. *Journal of Correctional Health Care, 12*, 214-221.

Gallagher, C. A., & Dobrin, A. (2007). Can juvenile justice detention facilities meet the call of the American Academy of Pediatrics and National Commission on Correctional Health Care? A national analysis of current practices. *Pediatrics, 119*, 991-1001.

Gilhooly, J. A., Simon, E., Tsu, R., & Sells, C. W. (2001). A look at the health of Oregon's adolescents in the adult correctional system. *Journal of Correctional Health Care, 8*, 55-65.

Infectious Diseases in Corrections Report. (2006). News and literature reviews: HIV costs have decreased. *Infectious Diseases in Corrections Report, 9*, 8.

Kahn, R. H., Mosure, D. H., Blank, S., Kent, C. K., Chow, J. M., Boudov, M. R., Brock, J., & Tulloch, S. (2005). Chlamydia trachomatis and Neisseria gonorrhea:

Prevalence and coinfection in adolescents entering selected U. S. juvenile detention centers, 1997-2002. *Sexually Transmitted Diseases, 32,* 255-259.

Kelly, P. J., Blair, R. M., Baillargeon, J., & German, V. (2000). Risk behaviors and the prevalence of Chlamydia in a juvenile detention facility. *Clinical Pediatrics, 39,* 521-527.

Kelly, P. J., Martinez, E., & Medrano, M. (2004). Gender specific health education in the juvenile justice system. *Journal of Correctional Health Care, 11,* 45-58.

Lederman, C. S., Dakof, G. A., Larrea, M. A., & Li, H. (2004). Characteristics of adolescent females in juvenile detention. *International Journal of Law and Psychiatry, 27,* 321-337.

Lichtenstein, B. (2000). HIV risk and healthcare attitudes among detained adolescents in rural Alabama. *AIDS Patient Care and STDs, 14,* 113-124.

Livsey, S., Sickmund, M., & Sladky, A. (2009). *Juvenile residential facility census, 2004: Selected findings.* Washington, DC: Office of Juvenile Justice and Delinquency Prevention.

Lofy, K. H., Hofmann, J., Mosure, D. J., Fine, D. N., & Marrazzo, J. M. (2006). Chlamydial infections among female adolescents screened in juvenile detention centers in Washington State, 1998-2002. *Sexually Transmitted Diseases, 33,* 63-67.

Matson, S. C., Bretl, D., & Wolf, K. (2000). Health care needs of detained youth. *Journal of Correctional Health Care, 7,* 245-261.

Morris, R. E., Baker, C. J., Valentine, M., & Pennisi, A. J. (1998). Variations in HIV risk behaviors of incarcerated juveniles during a four-year period: 1989-1992. *Journal of Adolescent Health, 23,* 39-48.

Murray, K. F., Richardson, L. P., Morishima, C., Owens, J. W. M., & Gretch, D. R. (2003). Prevalence of Hepatitis C virus infection and risk factors in an incarcerated juvenile population: A pilot study. *Pediatrics, 111,* 153-157.

National Commission on Correctional Health Care. (1999). Use of automated external defibrillators in correctional settings. *Journal of Correctional Health Care, 6,* 139-144.

Nicoletti, A. (2003). Teens, confidentiality, and HIPAA. *Journal of Pediatric and Adolescent Gynecology, 16,* 113-114.

Oh, M. K., Smith, K. R., O'Cain, M., Kilmer, D., Johnson, J., & Hook, E. W. (1998). Urine-based screening of adolescents in detention to guide treatment for gonococcal and chlamydial infections. *Archives of Pediatric and Adolescent Medicine, 152,* 52-56.

Pack, R. P., DiClemente, R. J., Hook, E. W., & Oh, M. K. (2000). High prevalence of asymptomatic STDs in incarcerated minority male youth: A case for screening. *Sexually Transmitted Diseases, 27,* 175-177.

Parent, D. G., Lieter, V., Kennedy, S., Livens, L., Wentworth, D., & Wilcox, S. (1994). *Conditions of confinement: Juvenile detention and corrections facilities.* Washington, DC: Office of Juvenile Justice and Delinquency Prevention.

Pugatch, D., Ramratnam, M., Feller, A., Price, D., & Riggs, S. (1999). HIV testing, drug use, and STD Prevalence among juveniles entering a Rhode Island correctional facility. *Journal of Correctional Health Care, 6,* 197-205.

Rhodus, N., & Little, J. W. (2005). Methamphetamine abuse and meth mouth. *Northwest Dentistry, 84,* 29, 31, 33-37.

Robertson, A. A., Baird, C., St. Lawrence, J. S., & Pack, R. (2005). Predictors of infection with Chlamydia or Gonorrhea in incarcerated adolescents. *Sexually Transmitted Diseases, 32,* 115-122.

Robillard, A. G., Garner, J. E., Laufer, F. N., Ramadan, A., Barker, T. A., Devore, B. S., Myers, J. J., Porterfield, J., & Wood, P. H. (2003). CDC/HRSA HIV/AIDS intervention, prevention and continuity of care demonstration project for incarcerated individuals within correctional settings and the community. *Journal of Correctional Health Care, 9,* 453-486.

Robinson, K. M., Haupt-Hoffman, D., Stewart, B., Schneider, F., Hamm, N., & Garrison, V. (2006). Is obesity a problem in a juvenile correctional facility? *Journal of Correctional Health Care, 12,* 175-180.

Rosengard, C., Stein, L. A., Barnett, N. P., Monti, P. M., Golembeske, C., & Lebeau-Craven, R. (2006). Co-occurring sexual risk and substance use behaviors among incarcerated adolescents. *Journal of Correctional Health Care, 12,* 279-287.

Roush, D. W. (1996). *Desktop guide to good juvenile detention practice.* Washington, DC: Office of Juvenile Justice and Delinquency Prevention.

Shelton, D. (2000). Health status of young offenders and their families. *Journal of Nursing Scholarship, 32,* 173-178.

Shelton, D. (2006). A study of young offenders with learning disabilities. *Journal of Correctional Health Care, 12,* 36-44.

Tebb, K. P., Pantell, R. H., Wibbelsman, C. J., Neuhaus, J. M., Tipton, A. C., Pecson, S. C., Pai-Dhungat, M., Ko, T. H, & Shafer, M. B. (2005). Screening sexually active adolescents for *Chlamydia trachomatis*: What about the boys? *American Journal of Public Health, 95,* 1806-1810.

Telpin, L. A., Mericle, A. A., McClelland, G. M., & Abram, K. (2003). HIV and AIDS risk behaviors in juvenile detainees: Implications for public health policy. *American Journal of Public Health, 93,* 906-912.

Tennyson, D. H. (2003). The high cost of health care within the juvenile justice system. *Journal of Correctional Health Care, 10,* 89-108.

Tennyson, D. H. (2004). Juvenile correctional system health care costs: A five-year comparison. *Journal of Correctional Health Care, 10,* 257-271.

Voisin, D. R., Salazar, L. F., Crosby, R., DiClemente, R. J., Yarber, W. L., & Staples-Horne, M. (2004). The association between gang involvement and sexual behaviors among detained adolescent males. *Sexually Transmitted Infections, 80,* 440-442.

West, H. C., & Sabol, W. J. (2008). *Prisoners in 2007.* Washington, DC: Bureau of Justice Statistics.

CHAPTER 13
STATIC AND DYNAMIC SECURITY
IN JUVENILE CORRECTIONS

Tommy Norris and Rick Ruddell

The primary mission of juvenile corrections is the long-term protection of the public and a key element of that role is ensuring a safe and secure correctional environment. From that foundation of safety, rehabilitative efforts will be more effective—which, in turn, decreases recidivism. When a juvenile is returned to the community, one goal of the facility staff is that they have prepared that youth to be a law-abiding citizen. That task is made more difficult if the youth's experiences in corrections were shaped by fear, violence, or abuse—or if he is negatively influenced by negative associations, such as joining a gang. This chapter introduces the concepts of static and dynamic security and how the staff members working in juvenile correctional facilities have used these measures to create a foundation of safety.

Throughout the past 30 years, there have been significant changes in juvenile corrections. Every jurisdiction has increased the sanctions for youthful offenders by making it easier to transfer them to adult court and lengthening dispositions (Kupchik, 2006). Since the mid-1990s, however, rates of youth violence have decreased (Snyder, 2008) and there appears to be a softening of public and political opinions toward juvenile offenders (Bishop, 2006). The notion of rehabilitating juveniles seems to be more popular and there is considerable interest in research that demonstrates the effectiveness of different rehabilitative strategies (e.g., evidence-based interventions).

Yet, for the superintendents and staff working within juvenile correctional facilities, there are a number of significant challenges to rehabilitating the youth in their care. First, there are increasing numbers of juveniles who are gang-involved and some facility officials report that over half of their population has some degree of gang affiliation (Thomas & Thomas, 2007). Some of these gang-involved juveniles might actively undermine the staff authority and attempt to derail the rehabilitative efforts of the staff, using force or the threat of violence. Second, there are a significant number of youth who have mental health problems in juvenile corrections, including those with psychological barriers to learning (Skowyra & Cocozza, 2006).

Furthermore, some youth are serving very long dispositions in correctional facilities and it is difficult to keep these adolescents focused on positive goals for years at a time. One of the challenges of working with juveniles is that they typically have a short-term view of their circumstances (e.g., here and now or live for the moment) rather than a future orientation.

There are other challenges of ensuring that the youth placed in the care of the county or state are safe. Many juvenile correctional facilities, for example, are antiquated and do not take advantage of new architectural designs that enable better supervision, increase the interactions between staff members and the youth, and reduce violence. Second, recruiting and retaining juvenile correctional officers (also referred to as counselors, youth workers, or juvenile detention officers) who can balance the roles of security and rehabilitation is difficult. Working with juvenile offenders is challenging because these youth can require more attention than their adult counterparts. Often, juvenile correctional officers are paid the same as officers working with adults, at least in state systems, and the psychological demands on adult correctional officers may be less burdensome. Last, the increased severity of sanctions in some jurisdictions has led to overcrowding in some facilities and correctional systems (Livsey, Sickmund, & Sladky, 2009). As a result, some of the creativity and resourcefulness of correctional administrators is devoted to managing the crowding crisis instead of developing new forms of rehabilitative programs.

Static and Dynamic Security

The history of juvenile corrections in the United States extends back to the Houses of Refuge, which were established almost two centuries ago. Throughout that time, there has been a long history of violence (both resident-on-resident and staff-on-resident) and abuse, as well as serious incidents such as escapes, disturbances, and riots. In addition, our best efforts to reform juveniles have often failed (Bernard, 1992). For the most part, facility superintendents and their staff members have gained more control over their facilities. The challenge, however, is to balance that security and control while still allowing for rehabilitation to occur (Inderbitzin, 2007). In the following pages, we outline several ways at looking at security and safety in juvenile corrections and how this has led to reductions in violence and has set the stage for more effective rehabilitative efforts.

There are two dimensions to security: static (or physical) security and dynamic security (the activities of the staff members). These two descriptions of security are popular in Commonwealth nations, such as Australia, Canada, or the United Kingdom, but less so in the United States where they are more apt to be known as active or passive security. In either case, they provide a useful way to describe correctional security (Bryans, 2007).

Static (or physical/passive) security focuses upon the physical structure and layout of a facility and the use of technology to enhance the ability of the counselors and staff to supervise residents. Accordingly, this would include the razor wire fences, riot gates, iron bars, internal and perimeter fences, and all other physical means of controlling the residents, including closed circuit television monitors. Architects have long recognized that the structure of a facility shapes the frequency and quality of interactions between the officers and residents. Modern correctional facilities—whether they house adults or juveniles—are designed to increase the supervision of the residents (see Chapter 2).

Dynamic security, on the other hand, refers to the activities of the juvenile correctional officers (JCO) and support staff in maintaining order, resolving resident-on-resident conflicts (or disruptive behaviors) before they escalate, helping them develop better problem-solving skills, assigning youth to the most appropriate facility and housing unit (e.g., one that best matches their needs for safety and security), and ensuring that these residents have enough meaningful activities to keep them constructively occupied.

Two issues are of particular importance here. First, there is an emerging philosophy in juvenile corrections that youth should be treated, whenever possible, in the least restrictive environment (Skowyra & Cocozza, 2006). Using this approach, however, means that some serious or potentially violent juvenile offenders may receive out-of-home placements that are ill suited to their security needs if improperly classified.

Second, adolescents require more structure and planned activities than their adult counterparts in order to keep them constructively occupied. As such, levels of supervision are generally much higher. Where one correctional officer might supervise 50 or more adult prisoners, in many jurisdictions, the ratio of juvenile correctional officers and staff to youth is closer to ten residents for each staff position (although this is less in some jurisdictions). Another feature of juvenile corrections that influences the ratio of staff to residents is the need for rehabilitative staff members. In keeping with the rehabilitative philosophy of juvenile correctional systems, there are generally a greater number of teachers, life skills coaches, vocational preparation staff, nurses, and counselors than there are in adult facilities of similar size.

Dynamic security involves the daily activities of the juvenile correctional officers in maintaining institutional security: doing the routine activities such as resident and cell searches, population counts, as well as following agency protocols for supervising the youth. Pathak (2005) defines dynamic security as:

Adaptable, flexible, resilient and elastic. They rely less on technology and more on people. Dynamic systems do not need additional programming and new costs each time the threat and situations change. They are also the most expensive. People are not cheap, yet it has been proven time and time again, you get what you pay for. (p. 570)

It is important to acknowledge that both dynamic and static security are interdependent because most correctional facilities cannot be operated without fences and brick and mortar buildings to house the residents (the exceptions are low security camps and community-based placements, such as group homes).

There is wide acknowledgement that even the most secure operations will not be effective unless the JCOs are well trained, alert, and observant (also called situational awareness), have above average interpersonal and communication skills, high levels of integrity, are positive role models for the youth, and follow all of the safety and security protocols and procedures. In order to achieve these goals, facility superintendents must recruit good officer candidates and provide them with adequate training, supervision, and leadership. Of course, this is easier said than done; historically, salaries for juvenile correctional officers were low. Furthermore, small and rural juvenile halls might find it difficult to recruit and retain staff members because the number of qualified applicants may be very small.

Juvenile detention facilities and state correctional systems (and their privately operated counterparts) have become safer places for the residents and staff members because of the steps that administrators and juvenile correctional officers have taken to increase order, including abiding by ACA accreditation standards. One of the problems of understanding the extent of violence in juvenile corrections, as highlighted in Chapter 9, is that there is no national-level baseline measure of violence, so we do not know if the violence that occurs in one facility is above or below average.

Most violence reduction programs can be attributed to an integrated approach to security where every leadership, institution, and community position, whether that employee is an officer or supports the activity of the officers, works together to meet the primary goal of the facility, which is to provide a safe and secure environment.

Atherton and Phillips (2007) outlined nine elements of a healthy security system in adult corrections:

- Fundamental and clear understanding of the agency's and institution's mission by all staff and sufficient resources to carry out that mission.

- A well structured and well staffed headquarters organization (that supports the activities of the facilities).
- A comprehensive institution program, which provides all necessary supporting services to staff and residents.
- A high-quality personnel management structure, which includes efficient selection, supervision, and staff development functions.
- Careful matching of the institution (layout, design, age, and level of maintenance) with a given type of resident and a specific staffing level.
- The availability of appropriate equipment, including locking devices, door and window hardware, perimeter security devices, and other items used for monitoring and control.
- The availability of programs that enhance security by involving residents in productive use of their time.
- The availability of information management systems to assist in security operations (e.g., computerized systems that collect information on residents, incidents, and costs).
- The existence of a variety of security systems that act jointly to prevent violence, control contraband, and prevent escapes. (p. 2)

Although these goals were established for adult operations, they are equally important in juvenile facilities. Some of these goals, however, will take on more importance, such as activities or programs that provide youth with the opportunity to productively use their time.

Another area where the philosophies of adult and juvenile systems diverge is that there is more attention paid to the rehabilitative needs of the residents in juvenile operations. Security sets the foundation for the rehabilitative programs and the case and release planning that goes on with each youth. While local detention facilities may have comparatively fewer rehabilitative opportunities, most offer a school program and some life skills or similar developmental programs, which is more than most local jails offer adult detainees. As the responsibility for managing these security programs rests upon the shoulders of the facility superintendents, the juvenile correctional officers are those who play a primary role in carrying out the operations of an institution.

Dynamic Security

Juvenile Correctional Officers: The Foundation of Dynamic Security

Dynamic security rests upon the talent of the facility administrators, supervisors, the JCOs, and the staff members who support the officers. Historically, the salary, benefits, and selection standards for staff members working in juvenile corrections were low and still are in some jurisdictions. Mendel (2001) observed that:

> Day-to-day supervision of juvenile offenders in most train-ing schools is provided by low-paid workers without college education or in-depth training in youth development. Thus, even if quality education and counseling services are pro-vided for a few hours each day, confined youth spend the bulk of their waking hours overseen by staff without the skills or motivation to maintain a positive therapeutic envi-ronment. (p. 40)

The description above is not the norm in many jurisdictions today, but the low wages paid in some counties and states leads to a number of problems. First, most juvenile halls or state facilities experience high levels of employee turnover because many staff members stay for a year or two and then move on to other positions (Matz, 2008). A second problem is that the low pay may have drawn persons into the job who might not have been hired if salaries were more competitive. Generally speaking, as salaries improve, facility superintendents are able to recruit and retain more professional staff mem-bers (e.g., better educated or better skilled). It is also difficult to recruit and retain nurses, teachers, and psychologists. Professionals are often reluctant to work with offenders in institutions because there is more status, higher salaries, and less professional isolation working with more sympathetic clients in the community.

In some places, getting a job in a youth facility is a relatively straightfor-ward task: applicants are interviewed and the employer conducts a rudimen-tary background check (e.g., checks for prior criminal convictions and conduct reference checks). In other jurisdictions, candidates are investigated more carefully and it is not unusual for applicants to undergo a physical fitness test and psychological examination. Moreover, background investiga-tions in some jurisdictions are more extensive and investigators conduct personal interviews with references; they also scrutinize the applicant's financial status, driving record, and educational credentials. This enhanced scrutiny reduces the possibility that candidates with low levels of personal integrity and problematic past behaviors can negatively influence vulnerable youth. One characteristic of corrections, whether it is adult or juvenile systems, is that agencies that pay greater salaries can generally attract better candidates and screen them more carefully.

In the past, most JCOs learned their profession on the job and they re-ceived only minimal formal training, perhaps only a few days of orientation, before they started working with youth. This approach is shortsighted because these staff members do not have the knowledge of institutional rules, routines, or policies that they needed to make sound decisions. In addition, the residents of these facilities are often manipulative and prey on the inexperience of new officers (see Cornelius, 2001). Elliot and Verdeyen (2002), for instance, highlighted a number of different strategies that offenders use to manipulate correctional officers. While residents in juvenile facilities are generally not as sophisticated as their adult counterparts, many have led difficult lives on the streets and have the ability to manipulate unwary or naïve staff members. While there are a number of defenses to falling victim to manipulative behavior, one of the foremost is being prepared for the job and receiving effective support and supervision once officers are working with these youth.

Today's juvenile correctional officers, especially those working in state systems, are likely to attend a month or more of full time academy training before working their first shift (although some jurisdictions offer a blend of academy and "on the job" training). The California Department of Corrections and Rehabilitation (Division of Juvenile Justice), for instance, provides a 16-week academy based training program for juvenile correctional officers and youth correctional counselors. Although the training content and the length of academy vary between states, an overriding goal is to give these officers the knowledge, skills, and abilities they need to ensure the safety and security of a facility.

Officers working in local detention facilities, by contrast, often do not receive as much training and this not only places them at a disadvantage, but also decreases facility safety. In some respects, working with detained populations can pose more challenges than with juveniles serving a disposition in a state correctional facility. Juveniles in detention, for instance, are more likely to be experiencing withdrawal from the alcohol or drugs that they used on the streets, are frightened about their forthcoming court appearances, and are unsettled if experiencing their first placement outside the home (and for some youngsters, this could be their first time away from their families). Moreover, since the average stay in most juvenile halls is measured in days, these youth do not have a lot of time to become accustomed to institutional rules or routines. These conditions make it likely that they may be less settled and more aggressive than youth in long-term placements.

Most juvenile academies start with increasing the cadet's knowledge of adolescent behavior and how factors such as impulsivity, poor decision-making skills, and lack of control contribute to incidents in correctional settings (Taylor, Kemper, & Kistner, 2007). Another factor that differentiates the training between juvenile and adult officers is a greater emphasis on rehabilitative strategies such as case management, a topic addressed in the pages that follow. The Kentucky Division of Juvenile Justice (2008), for instance, provided the following training to cadets in their seven-week academy:

- Conflict resolution
- Cultural diversity
- Behavior management
- Crisis prevention
- Physical skills
- First aid/CPR
- De-escalation
- Self awareness and team building
- Gang awareness
- Contraband and searches
- Human sexuality
- Report writing
- Group dynamics
- Safety
- Adolescent substance abuse
- Universal precautions
- Adolescent development
- Communications
- Administration

Training enhances the new officer's confidence and gives him a better range of skills than previous generations of youth correctional staff who learned through trial and error. Juvenile correctional officers typically serve a probationary period for the first six months or year and, in some cases, correctional field training officers mentor them. Providing this training, mentoring, and support is an essential part of preparing officers for their careers and reducing stress, uncertainty, and turnover (Hesse, 2008). Retaining staff members is a key concern for correctional administrators because of the costs associated with recruitment, conducting background checks, orientation, and training.

To the outsider, many of the daily tasks of a JCO look mundane and routine and include activities such as:

- Conducting room searches (as well as searches of common areas and living units),
- Initiating "pat downs" and searches of residents,

- Carrying out perimeter patrols,
- Logging (or recording) resident movement,
- Conducting resident counts,
- Confronting wards about their behavior,
- Leading resident self help groups such as positive peer culture,
- Controlling the use of tools and restricted items,
- Gathering information about gangs and other threats,
- Screening visitors (and searching them when necessary), and
- Monitoring, searching, and censoring incoming mail.

These activities are critical at reducing the number of weapons (such as shanks — objects fashioned into makeshift knives — or clubs) or other contraband (including drugs, tobacco, or pornography) in circulation and ensuring that the physical security of the facility (e.g., the locks, security systems, interior barriers, doors, and the interior and exterior fences) has not been compromised.

Officers who have been on the job for several years are likely to have mastered the rules, routines, and security procedures. Perhaps more importantly, however, they have also developed the interpersonal skills important for de-escalating conflict, sanctioning juveniles, as well as having a greater degree of situational awareness (in other words, developing a sense for potential incidents long before they occur). Last, more senior officers and staff members generally have a better ability to build relationships with the youth. All of these factors are associated with increasing order and security, which ultimately reduces the likelihood of serious incidents.

To ensure that JCOs develop their skills, most institutions offer some form of ongoing training. In fact, operations that are accredited by the American Correctional Association, for example, must provide a minimum of 40 hours of on-going training each year.[1] This on-going training is important in honing the officer's skills and ensuring that they remain up-to-date on use of force (including verbally de-escalating potentially violent situations), are in compliance with first aid and cardio pulmonary resuscitation certification, and keep up-to-date on changing policies and procedures and the correct use of new equipment. While most of this staff training is delivered in-house, many facilities will send staff members to annual meetings of organizations such as the Correctional Security Network, National Juvenile Detention Association, the National Partnership for Juvenile Services, or the American Correctional Association to receive advanced training and keep up-to-date on the newest security innovations and emerging trends in the field.[2]

Some juvenile officers take on specialized roles within their facilities, such as gang investigator, canine handler, or corrections emergency response team member (CERT). All of these roles are important for the security of a facility and these staff members receive additional training in order to be successful in these roles. One specialized staff role that has recently taken on more importance is gang investigator. Gangs have a corrosive effect on correctional functioning by increasing resident-on-resident violence, encouraging racism (as most gangs form along ethnic or racial lines), engaging in criminal activities, undermining efforts at rehabilitation, and reducing public safety when these gang members return to the community (Colon, 2004).

A significant challenge confronting corrections staff, particularly in juvenile facilities, is that adolescents are drawn to gangs. Gangs provide acceptance, a sense of belonging, access to desirable contraband (e.g., drugs, alcohol, or weapons), excitement, protection, and increase the youth's status (Eghigian & Kirby, 2006). These factors make membership in these criminal organizations very desirable, especially for adolescents coming from communities with few positive role models or legitimate opportunities. The problem is that gang membership greatly increases youth violence, both within correctional institutions and in the community.

Populations of gang members in some juvenile correctional facilities are very high and some practitioners claim that over half of their residents are somehow involved with gangs (Thomas & Thomas, 2007), although their allegiance to the gang may be fleeting. For the most part, formal interventions to suppress gang activities within juvenile corrections are based on collecting information and, in some jurisdictions, sanctioning youth who are gang-involved (e.g., restricting their movements, program participation, or privileges). In many jurisdictions, officials from juvenile correctional facilities share information and intelligence with law enforcement officials, including representatives from jails and prisons. Such interventions are important; Trulson (2007) found that gang-involvement in youth corrections was significantly associated with serious incidents, such as "assaulting staff, assaulting residents, and possessing a weapon" (p. 27).

Classification

One of the most important staff functions in juvenile corrections are the case managers, case workers, counselors, or JCOs, who are responsible for classifying inmates to ensure that they are placed in facilities or housing units that best match their needs for security. A basic definition of classification is the process of placing residents in the most appropriate facility and living unit. There is sometimes a distinction between the classification that occurs in a county operated juvenile facility compared to youth admitted to a large state correctional system. Classification in smaller institutions tends to be less formal and in some of the smallest facilities — those with only one living unit where all residents are mixed — it may be non-existent. In these smaller facilities, the staff members have to be much more careful about the placement of a youth; a high risk youth, for instance, should be placed in a single rather than a shared room.

Most large juvenile correctional systems first classify offenders at reception centers where juveniles go after they are adjudicated. During a youth's placement at a reception center, which is generally a period of weeks, evaluations are conducted of his or her physical and psychological functioning as well as his or her social and legal background. Conducting these comprehensive investigations into the youth's functioning and need for security is a significant improvement over earlier forms of classification. The failure to use formal or objective classification procedures may contribute to serious incidents and assaults.

Austin (2003) outlined that in the past, most correctional systems used subjective classification (or gut feelings, intuition, or the best judgment of an officer or committee) to place inmates in housing units and establish the appropriate security levels for them. Austin, Johnson, and Weitzer (2005) cautioned, however, that "classifying youth should not be arbitrary" (p. 6). Instead, objective instruments should be used that are designed to evaluate the actual risk of misconduct. Factors that are considered in developing a classification score often include the current offense and the detention or disposition length, previous criminal history, prior institutional history (e.g., disciplinary actions or misconduct in prior out-of-home placements), age at first arrest, gang involvement, and individual factors (including educational or employment history or drug and alcohol use). Some jurisdictions might even consider family related factors in the development of a classification system (e.g., levels of parental support or family dysfunction).

Most classification systems utilize a numerical score and the higher the resident's score, the more likely he will be placed in a unit or facility with a greater degree of security. Austin, Johnson, and Weitzer (2005) highlighted the four components of custody classification for youth and they are summarized as follows:

- **Initial screening.** Trained intake staff should screen youth immediately after their assignments to secure confinement. The most common type of screening instrument is a checklist with questions regarding the youth's medical and mental health needs, substance abuse history, and other information that might indicate the need to place the youth in a special housing unit for further assessment and observation by medical, mental health, and classification staff. The major objective of this review is to ensure that youth with severe mental health, medical, and other management issues are identified so they can be separated from the general confinement population until a more careful assessment can be done.

- **Initial classification.** Classification staff members determine a youth's custody level using an initial classification form that includes standard risk factors for escape or institutional misconduct. Because many youth are experiencing their first admission to a custodial setting, initial classification places emphasis on their current offenses, prior juvenile records, successes or failures on probation, and various measures of community stability (e.g., age, school attendance, and family structure). If youth have been confined previously, their earlier institutional conduct should also play an important role in the initial assessments.

- **Reclassification.** The reclassification form is used to reassess the youth's initial classification designation through a review of his or her conduct during the first 60 to 90 days in a facility. Consequently, it places more emphasis on institutional behavior and less on the youth's prior offenses and criminal history. Because most youth will not become involved in serious misconduct, the reclassification process allows youth with positive behavior patterns to be placed in lower custody levels and thus will conserve expensive high security bed space.

- **Program needs assessment.** The final component of a custody classification system requires that each youth's need for services and treatment be assessed in a more in-depth manner than during the initial screening. The resulting data are used to assign a youth to a facility, housing unit, or program that provides the most appropriate and most needed services commensurate with the youth's custody level. For example, if a needs assessment reveals a youth's heavy involvement with alcohol and/or drugs, his or her placement in a residential substance abuse wing or program would be appropriate. (pp. 10-11)

In addition to determining the youth's facility assignment, which is the process of external classification, the classification staff members also determine housing unit and program participation for the juvenile, which is called internal classification.

Altogether, the adoption of formal classification has gone a long way in better understanding risk and serious incidents in juvenile corrections (Taylor, Skubic Kemper, & Kistner, 2007). One challenge that correctional officials must face, however, is that policy makers often direct that youthful offenders be placed in the least restrictive setting, which in turn enables youth to gain access to a greater number of rehabilitative opportunities. Achieving this without compromising public safety is a difficult balance because the least restrictive correctional environments are generally community-based placements that provide the least amount of supervision. As a result, one strategy is to use objective case management and reclassify youth in two to three months based on their institutional behavior and the degree to which they are working toward meeting goals outlined in their case plans, which is a function of the case management process described in the following paragraphs.

Case Management

The case management process begins shortly after juveniles are admitted to housing units (and upon their transfer from reception centers). With the exception of some youth who have been charged as adult offenders—and if convicted are held in adult facilities—most juveniles who have been adjudicated delinquent and placed outside the home will return to the community within a year or two, although in most jurisdictions the resident can be held until his or her 21st birthday (and his or her 25th birthday in California). Planning for the youth's release generally starts shortly after the juvenile's admission to a facility. The goal of this approach is to get the youth to focus on his release and enhancing his knowledge or skills in order to reduce his time in custody as well as the likelihood of future recidivism. While youth sometimes have ambivalent feelings toward continuing their education or participating in different rehabilitative opportunities, such as Alcoholics Anonymous, they see these steps as important to reducing their security status (and transferring to a less secure unit), and earning an earlier release. In order to achieve these goals, most correctional systems employ case managers or youth correctional counselors to monitor the youth's progress in meeting his case plan goals. The following paragraphs describe the case management process and some typical challenges for youth in correctional settings. It is important to understand that when youth are positively engaged in their case plans, they will be more likely to work toward their rehabilitation and less likely to engage in institutional misconduct.

There are a number of different case management models, but they all have a similar set of goals. Healy (1999) outlined how the following activities are typically used in corrections:

* Assessing the client's needs,
* Developing a service plan,
* Linking the client to appropriate services,

- Monitoring client progress, and
- Advocating for the client as needed. (p. 2)

All of these activities are important. Assessing a juvenile offender's treatment needs, for instance, is often done through a needs assessment instrument. These instruments assist the case manager in identifying problems such as substance abuse, anger management, negative peer associations (such as gangs), and psychological and medical health problems.

Having established the juvenile's need for treatment, the case manager and youth work together on developing a case plan (also called a case management, service plan, or treatment plan). These plans outline and prioritize the services that the youth requires. One of the difficult aspects of developing these plans is that youth are often resistant to participating in interventions, such as a substance abuse program, if they feel their drinking or drug use does not contribute to their delinquency. Furthermore, substance abuse might also be part of the youth's identity, making it more difficult for her to stop drinking or using drugs.

Some of these programs, such as anger management and social and life skills development, are associated with violence reduction because they teach the resident better methods of responding to frustration or difficult social situations. In some cases, the lifestyles that youth have developed are a consequence of imitating the behaviors of their parents, who were poor role models. In adult corrections, policy makers and practitioners often refer to the rehabilitation of offenders, but in the case of juveniles, we sometimes use the term habilitation because some youth have so few skills.

Some treatment, such as participating in sex offender programming, may be ordered by the court. As a result, it is important that the case manager and youth work together to ensure that these expectations are met. A key role of the counselor is to help the youth identify and acknowledge her problems. Moreover, the counselor helps her understand the relationship between concerns identified in the needs assessments or predisposition reports (reports based on investigations by probation officers about the youth's involvement in an offense) and her involvement in crime.

While linking the juvenile to the appropriate resources sounds straightforward, there are a number of challenges. Treatment resources in juvenile corrections are often scarce and case managers are often hesitant to refer a youth to a treatment program if the youth is not fully committed to participating. Moreover, an important question is when the juvenile should participate in a program: shortly after her admission to a facility or just prior to her return to the community? Either has an implication for the youth's release. If the youth starts treatment earlier, for example, she might be transferred to a facility or housing unit with a lower level of security (such as a community-based group home) or be released sooner.

One shortfall of correctional case management is that once case plans are established, they are sometimes neglected. As a result, most facilities establish timelines for the development of a youth's case plan (e.g., within the first month of admission) and regularly scheduled meetings to evaluate the resident's progress on meeting his goals, such as formal reviews that take place every three months. In some cases, goals are revisited and new case plans established that take into account the youth's progress. By ensuring that the case plan is constantly being monitored, however, both the youth and the case manager are actively preparing the youth for his return to the community.

Last, the case manager is also responsible for advocating on behalf of the youth. Healy (1999) reported that case managers have testified or made recommendations in court on their client's behalf, secured priority placements at programs with waiting lists, negotiated *pro bono* services for their clients, overcome bureaucratic obstacles, and advocated for changes that impact all juvenile offenders, including those living in the community or placed outside the home (pp. 3-4).

In conclusion, both classification and case management strive to enhance the safety of an institution and better prepare the youth for a law-abiding life in the community. This cannot occur, however, without the efforts of staff members in all job descriptions who are dedicated, professional, and highly skilled.

Programs and People

Atherton and Phillips (2007) observed that "the most critical components of a successful, highly secure institution are the programs and the people. The key to management, regardless of custody level, is reducing idleness and involving inmates in programs" (p. 61). While referring to adult populations, the same principles apply to juveniles in residential settings. Not all juveniles, however, are involved in activities that constructively occupy their time. In local detention facilities, for example, the average stay is measured in days, so the facility managers have little incentive to develop long-term rehabilitative programs and providing these services is not within their mandate. As mentioned above, most county operated detention facilities offer little more than a school program during the weekdays and other short-term programs. These programs are more important for youth who may reside in these facilities for a longer period of time (e.g., a youth accused of committing a serious offense may reside in a local juvenile hall for months while the case works its way through the court).

Treatment programs in long-term settings, such as state operated training schools, are more comprehensive. Most programs focus on five basic areas: (a) educational programs; (b) substance abuse treatment; (c) vocational training (including job preparation, correctional industry programs, and institutional work assignments); (d) life skills (including interventions that confront criminogenic thinking and anti-social values, parenting, hygiene, and social skill development); and (e) recreation and spiritual (or cultural) needs. The first three programs respond to the needs of most residents who tend to be undereducated, drug- and/or alcohol-addicted, and often have no history of legitimate employment. Recreation and spiritual programs, on the other hand, provide a positive outlet for minors to constructively use their time, maintain their fitness (and therefore reduce long-term health care costs), and sustain a positive and prosocial attitude. This is not, however, a comprehensive list of rehabilitative opportunities and some jurisdictions offer more extensive programs.

One hazard of juvenile corrections is that it is often easier to get youth to participate in recreational activities than it is to engage them in more formal rehabilitative programs. As a result, facility superintendents and their deputies have to be aware of how much time these youth actually devote to their formal educational, vocational, or treatment programs; they also have to ensure that their staff members are providing a meaningful rehabilitative program.

Some of the programs offered in institutions are more specialized. Sex offender treatment programs, for instance, are an important intervention in some state-run facilities. In California approximately 16% of all the wards in the Division of Juvenile Justice in 2006 had mandated sex offender treatment and another 7% had a non-mandated offense or elevated sex offender referral document score (Ruddell, 2006). Since a high proportion of the juvenile population require these programs, interventions must be based on what the evidence demonstrates is effective at reducing recidivism. Such programs must be staffed with professionals and their work must be supported by the security staff members.

One of the challenging aspects of providing rehabilitative services in corrections is that many residents have histories of failure with school systems and are sometimes resistant to classroom learning (see Chapter 14). As a result, the educational and treatment staff members who work with offenders must have much patience, excellent interpersonal skills, and the ability to encourage and motivate students. To add further complexity to their jobs, the rehabilitative staff members may sometimes come into conflict with security staff. Sometimes there is a difficult balance between rehabilitation and security, but all other factors being equal, ensuring the facility's safety and security overrides all other considerations.

Another challenge for juvenile correctional administrators is to provide an environment that is consistent with rehabilitation. Staff members who have been trained in core correctional practices may be able to create such an environment. According to Dowden and Andrews (2004), core correctional practices refer to the "effective use of authority, anticriminal modeling and reinforcement, problem-solving, use of community resources, and quality of interpersonal relationships between staff and client" (p. 204). By using this approach, the staff members are positive role models who consistently model and reinforce prosocial behavior. Furthermore, these officers will also challenge the negative behaviors of youth in a constructive manner. These interventions, however, can only occur if there is a positive relationship between the staff members and the youth.

To summarize, dynamic security is fashioned on the knowledge, skills, and abilities of the juvenile correctional officers and the staff who support them. Correctional administrators rely upon the expertise of the officers to conduct the day-to-day supervision of offenders, and engage in activities that reduce the possibility of violence (e.g., reducing the amount of contraband in a facility). While the security staff in an institution have a primary role in ensuring safety, the activities of the educational, rehabilitative, vocational, religious (e.g., Chaplain), and other treatment staff cannot be minimized. Their activities keep inmates constructively engaged and focused on positive goals. Yet, without hardened facilities, fences, and security equipment, the JCO, treatment and rehabilitative staff, and superintendents could not do their jobs very effectively.

Static Security

Architectural Design

There have been significant changes in the design of juvenile correctional institutions over the past three decades. Some large detention centers and training schools constructed at the turn of the 20th century were imposing structures, built of brick or stone. Other juvenile facilities were smaller, dormitory-like or cottage structures. These early types of facilities suffered from a number of limitations that contributed to higher numbers of incidents. Many, for instance, had numerous blind spots that made it hard for the staff members to supervise residents. Furthermore, these facilities are also expensive to heat and cool and most jurisdictions are replacing these inefficient operations with housing units based on the new generation design that was first introduced in adult corrections in the 1970s.

Newly constructed juvenile correctional facilities have a much different look than the traditional institutions. Instead of rooms arranged in long corridors with a day room at one end of the hallway, the new generation model utilizes rooms that are arranged around the perimeter walls of the housing unit. The center of the unit is a multipurpose area and is used for recreation, meals, group meetings, and education (see the examples in Chapter 8). In addition to providing more open space, this design enables the youth to be housed more efficiently, officers are able to supervise the juveniles more closely, and staff members can engage in more effective problem-solving with the residents. These living units and enhanced staff-resident interaction are associated with less disruptive behavior and fewer assaults (Wener, 2006).

The security of most high security juvenile correctional facilities is often incorporated into the architectural design. Windows are made using thick layers of Lexan or similar glass and this has eliminated the need for iron bars. Furnishings that were once used as weapons, such as tables or chairs, are now bolted to the floor. Fixtures such as sinks and toilets that were once constructed of porcelain are now made of stainless steel. While residents have the ability to flush their toilets or turn on their lights, in many facilities officers can turn off electricity or water to an individual room if a juvenile is disruptive (e.g., is trying to flood his or her room by blocking the toilet). In the latest census of juvenile correctional facilities, Livsey, Sickmund, and Sladky (2009) observed that static or physical security generally increases with the size of the institution: residents are locked in their rooms at night, locked doors confine youth to their housing units, and these large facilities are more likely to be surrounded with razor wire fences (pp. 5-6).

Low security youth sometimes live in dormitory settings. While dormitories enable officials to house a large number of residents in a relatively small space, there are some limitations. First, these arrangements may contribute to misconduct if the juveniles are not carefully monitored. Second, many youth actually prefer to be housed in a single or shared room because it increases privacy and reduces the likelihood that they will be assaulted.

There is a growing emphasis today on placing juveniles in small cottage-style living units with a maximum of ten to fifteen residents. Often, these facilities have furniture similar to that found in homes, in contrast to the institutional furniture described above. Missouri's Division of Youth Services, for example, has developed a network of these small facilities throughout that state (see Chapter 15). What they lose in economies of scale (cottages are more expensive per resident to operate than larger facilities), they have recouped in less aggressive behavior and lower rates of recidivism. Other jurisdictions are adopting similar models and it is likely that this trend will continue if these operations successfully reduce recidivism.

Some of the security in a juvenile facility depends on the levels of classification for the minors. As outlined earlier, many low security residents live in dorms, cottage-style facilities, or sleep in bunks in living units that are constantly monitored by facility staff members. Juveniles who require a higher level of control are often placed in individual rooms. In addition, out-of-control or disruptive youth are placed in isolation cells. Most correctional facilities have at least one of these single-room hardened cells (e.g., bare concrete walls and stainless steel fixtures) for the temporary control of disruptive youth and they are sometimes called segregation or isolation rooms or units.

Despite the fact that the option to place youth by themselves in a hardened room or cell exists, isolating these youth is often considered a last resort in dealing with a difficult-to-manage resident. Isolating a youth has many potential negative effects, including a higher risk of self-harm (see Chapter 10). As a result, most facilities have strict policies on the use of these rooms and a primary goal is to return the youth back to his or her unit as soon as possible.

Technology and Security

In addition to the architecture of a correctional facility, there have been a number of technological changes that have reduced costs and serious incidents, increased security, and made it easier to supervise the residents. Some technological innovations in security, such as using cameras to monitor living units, may reduce the possibility of violence by creating a deterrent to planned disruptive behavior (Allard, Wortley, & Stewart, 2008). Devices that help officers conduct less intrusive searches on residents and visitors, by contrast, decrease the amount of contraband entering a facility, which reduces the possibility of conflict and violence. Altogether, technology has increased the ability of officers to supervise the juveniles in their care, reduce conflict, and deter violent behavior.

Closed circuit television or video, for example, has also enabled JCOs to increase security, order, and safety. Some of these systems have become so sophisticated that they can be programmed to detect the types of movements associated with assaults or to warn officers if there are too many people in a room. In addition, the fact that incidents are recorded may deter some violent acts because both staff and inmates know that their actions are being recorded. Video surveillance also allows officers to monitor the internal and external perimeters of the facility and this reduces the need for perimeter patrols — freeing staff members for other activities.

Some correctional facilities have taken advantage of various types of detection equipment to reduce the amount of contraband entering a facility or transfers of contraband within an institution. Handheld metal detectors (also called wands), for instance, have long been used to search for metal objects, but walk-through metal detectors (similar to those used in airports) are a more recent introduction and are often used at entry points to larger facilities. Some larger operations also have scanning equipment that enables officers to quickly check for contraband hidden in incoming mail or packages and this technology can also be used to scan fully clothed inmates for contraband. Atherton and Phillips (2007) reported that "a highly sensitive metal detector configured as a chair with an oral sensor accessory is used across the country to detect metallic objects hidden in the anal, vaginal, and oral or nasal cavities" (p. 64).

Although very expensive, new generations of backscatter X-rays enable officers to conduct unobtrusive searches for both hard and soft materials; it is likely that these machines will become more prevalent in corrections — at least in the largest facilities — as these instruments become cheaper. In addition to enabling quicker and more efficient searches, these methods are less intrusive compared to a pat down or strip search. This is an important consideration when one considers that many incarcerated juveniles, both males and females, have histories of sexual abuse (Mason, Zimmerman, & Evans, 1998).

Some technological interventions are controversial. Many high security facilities, for instance, have the ability to monitor a resident's phone calls (the exception being privileged communication between the youth and her attorney, ombudsman, or political representative) in order to reduce the flow of contraband into a facility, gang-involvement, and crime. Calls can also be recorded using digital technology and then replayed afterward: officers on the night shift or those deployed for perimeter security can then listen to these recordings for plans of illegal or disruptive activities. When evidence of an undesirable act is uncovered, it can be referred to the security staff, gang investigator, or the superintendent.

In order to reduce the flow of contraband into a facility, many administrators have placed restrictions on incoming mail and packages. Some jurisdictions require incoming items to come from a select list of vendors: family members pay for these approved goods (e.g., personal hygiene items, food, or reading materials) and they are sent directly to the facility without passing through unauthorized hands. Other organizations are experimenting with services that charge family members to send emails to a resident; the emails are then printed out for residents in the institution (the residents do not have access to the Internet). This has reduced the need to search envelopes for drugs, money, or other contraband. Moreover, since the officers have electronic access to the incoming mail, they can conduct searches for words that are related to illegal activity (e.g., such as guns, drugs, or gang terminology).

As computerization becomes cheaper, there is an increasing use of radio frequency identification devices (RFID), which is an electric label or transmitter that can be read by computers or other sensors. Residents in some larger facilities are required to wear tamper-proof wristbands with these embedded transmitters. These transmitters enable officers to continuously track resident movement and they can also be used to confirm when youth receive medications or meals. This technology has also been used to track controlled items in correctional facilities, such as weapons, keys, tools, or computer equipment. By tracking restricted materials and residents more quickly and efficiently, these tools enable officers to reduce contraband and increase accountability and security.

A significant problem in adult and juvenile corrections is the proliferation of unauthorized cell phones in the hands of the residents. These phones can represent a serious threat to facility and public safety because calls can be used to intimidate witnesses in the community, conduct unlawful activities (such as arranging drugs to be brought into a facility), arrange escapes, or other institutional misconduct. Moreover, gang-involved residents can carry out their operations using these phones. In response, there are a number of corporations that are developing devices to identify these unauthorized phones and some jurisdictions are experimenting with canines that can detect these phones.

Some facility administrators are also taking advantage of innovations in computer technology that make it easier to identify residents and process their movements (e.g., admissions to the facility and transfers within the institution). Automated fingerprint readers (such as Livescan) enable staff members to identify new admissions or current residents quickly and with less mess than ink fingerprinting. Furthermore, many correctional systems have automated case file systems that allow officers to access information quickly without the need for a paper file. In some cases, information about a juvenile could be matched with the RFID technology mentioned above. This allows admissions, transfers, and discharges to occur more quickly, and with fewer errors.

Some security devices directly increase correctional officer safety. In almost all facilities, JCOs have access to intercoms and they carry radios. In addition, in larger and high security facilities, staff members are issued personal alarms that can be activated in emergencies (Southerland, 2008).

Using non-lethal methods for the emergency control of aggressive or acting out youth is controversial. Commonly used in adult correctional facilities, chemical agents help officers manage or control the residents while reducing the need for physically subduing them. While pepper spray (oleoresin capsicum or OC) is the best known of these agents, officers in correctional facilities have used chemical agents such as CN/CS (also called tear gas) to control disruptive residents. In some jurisdictions, such as California, these agents can be used in launchers (such as PepperBall guns) or grenades. These devices are generally preferred to weapons such as batons because they reduce the use of physical force and injuries for both the staff members and the youth.

While not a technological innovation *per se*, some jurisdictions have reduced the use of handcuffs and shackles to restrain youth who are acting out or apt to harm themselves or others. One method of immobilizing residents is called "The Wrap Restraint System," which envelops the person in soft restraints. Another option, used by some jurisdictions, is the restraint chair, which holds the resident in a padded chair with a series of belts. Both of these approaches are safer than immobilizing a youth through force (e.g., when staff members physically hold the youth) and pose a reduced risk of the youth succumbing to positional asphyxia, which sometimes occurred when they were "hog-tied" (when a youth's hands and feet are restrained with handcuffs and shackles and then the hands and feet are tied together using a strap or handcuff).

One of the common themes in the literature about technology in juvenile corrections is that it deters serious or violent incidents. If a youth realizes that her actions will be documented on videotape, she might be less willing to engage in a planned attack that would result in internal sanctions or additional criminal charges. Yet, we have to remember that youth are often impulsive and act without thinking and it is likely that these measures are more likely to reduce the possibility of staff misconduct.

Altogether, most managers are careful not to rely too heavily on technological solutions to the challenges of working with juveniles in correctional settings because technology can fail. In the end, it is the dedicated efforts of the juvenile correctional officers and staff members who maintain order and reduce violence in juvenile corrections. As highlighted in this and other chapters, the relationships that the staff members develop with the residents are an important key to ensuring institutional safety.

Conclusions

Juvenile correctional systems in some jurisdictions have had considerable success in creating a climate more suitable for rehabilitation. These accomplishments are a consequence of improved resident classification, more effective case planning, changes in facility design, the use of technology, and recruiting and retaining skilled juvenile correctional officers, counselors, teachers, and staff members who support these professionals. These security programs rest upon static and dynamic security: static security being the physical or fixed methods of reducing misconduct, while dynamic security refers to the interpersonal, communication, and security skills of the juvenile correctional officers and staff in ensuring security. Both of these factors are important and they rely upon one another; but without skilled and knowledgeable officers, even the most secure facility would have higher levels of misconduct.

Endnotes

1. Accreditation, when a correctional agency is expected to meet national standards of care, is becoming more prevalent in U. S. corrections. According to the American Correctional Association (2008), the benefits of accreditation include: improved staff training and development, assessment of program strengths and weaknesses, establishment of measurable criteria for upgrading operations, defense against lawsuits, safer environments for staff and inmates, and improved staff morale and professionalism (see Chapter 17).
2. The Performance-based Standards (PbS) initiative provides support, technical assistance, and training to youth correctional facilities (see Chapter 17).

References

Allard, T. J., Wortley, R. K., & Stewart, A. L., (2008). The effect of CCTV on prisoner misbehavior. *The Prison Journal, 88,* 404-422.

American Correctional Association. (2008). *Standards and accreditation.* Retrieved Feb. 4, 2008, from http://www.aca.org/standards/benefits.asp

Atherton, E. E., & Phillips, R. L. (2007). *Guidelines for the development of a security program.* Alexandria, VA: American Correctional Association.

Austin, J. (2003). *Findings in prison classification and risk assessment.* Longmont CO: National Institute of Corrections.

Austin, J., Johnson, K. D., & Weitzer, R. (2005). *Alternatives to the secure detention and confinement of juvenile offenders.* Washington, DC: OJJDP.

Bernard, T. J. (1992). *The cycle of juvenile justice.* New York: Oxford University Press.

Bishop, D. (2006). Public opinion and juvenile justice policy: Myths and misconceptions. *Criminology & Public Policy, 5,* 653-664.

Bryans, S. (2007). *Prison governors: Managing prisons in a time of change.* Cullompton, Devon: Willan Publishing.

Colon, T. (2004, April). *Gang members in juvenile detention: A California story.* Presented at the Behavioral and Social Sciences Research Symposium, CSU Chico.

Cornelius, G. (2001). *The art of the con: Avoiding offender manipulation.* Alexandria, VA: American Correctional Association.

Dowden, C., & Andrews, D. A. (2004). The importance of staff practice in delivering effective correctional treatment. *International Journal of Offender Therapy and Comparative Criminology, 48,* 203-214.

Eghigian, M., & Kirby, K. (2006). Girls in gangs: On the rise in America. *Corrections Today, 68,* 48-50.

Elliot, B., & Verdeyen, V. (2002). *Game over! Strategies for redirecting inmate deception.* Lanham, MD: American Correctional Association.

Healy, K. M. (1999). *Case management in the criminal justice system.* Washington, DC: National Institute of Justice.

Hesse, M. (2008). One juvenile facility's answer to retention: Training and mentoring. *Corrections Today, 70,* 58-60.

Inderbitzin, M. (2007). A look from the inside: Balancing custody and treatment in a juvenile maximum-security facility. *International Journal of Offender Therapy and Comparative Criminology, 51,* 358-362.

Kentucky Division of Juvenile Justice. (2008). *Academy trainee schedule, Academy 60.* Richmond, KY: Author.

Kupchik, A. (2006). *Judging juveniles: Prosecuting adolescents in adult and juvenile courts.* New York: New York University Press.

Livsey, S., Sickmund, M., & Sladky, A. (2009). *Juvenile residential facility census, 2004: Selected findings.* Washington, DC: OJJDP.

Mason, W. A., Zimmerman, L., & Evans, W. (1998). Sexual and physical abuse among incarcerated youth. *Child Abuse and Neglect, 22,* 987–995.

Matz, A. K. (2008). *Analysis of turnover and turnover intentions among juvenile justice staff at the Kentucky Department of Juvenile Justice.* Unpublished thesis.

Mendel, R. A. (2001). *Less cost, more safety: Guiding lights for reform in juvenile justice.* Washington, DC: American Youth Policy Forum.

Pathak, J. (2005). Risk management, internal controls and organizational vulnerabilities. *Managerial Auditing Journal, 20,* 569-577.

Ruddell, R. (2006). *Gap analysis and training needs assessment: Positive approaches to sexual treatment (sexual offender treatment program).* Chico, CA: Author.

Skowyra, K., & Cocozza, J. J. (2006). *A blueprint for change: Improving the system response to youth with mental health needs involved with the juvenile justice system.* Delmar, NY: National Center for Mental Health and Juvenile Justice.

Snyder, H. (2008). *Juvenile arrests, 2006.* Washington, DC: OJJDP.

Southerland, R. (2008) What works: Wireless protection. *Access Control & Security Systems, 50,* 18-20.

Taylor, J., Skubic Kemper, T., & Kistner, J. A. (2007). Predicting institutional maladjustment in severe male juvenile delinquents from criminal history and personality/clinical subtype. *Criminal Justice and Behavior, 34,* 769-780.

Thomas, R., & Thomas, L. (2007, October). *Juvenile gangs behind fences.* Presented at the 2007 Correctional Security Network, Cincinnati, OH.

Trulson, C. R. (2007). Determinants of disruption: Institutional misconduct among state-committed delinquents. *Youth Violence and Juvenile Justice, 5,* 7-34.

Wener, R. (2006). Effectiveness of the direct supervision system of correctional design and management. *Criminal Justice and Behavior, 33,* 392-410.

West, H. C., & Sabol, W. J. (2008). *Prisoners in 2007.* Washington, DC: Bureau of Justice Statistics.

CHAPTER 14
EDUCATIONAL PROGRAMS

Carolyn Eggleston

A t-risk and delinquent youth have traditionally had difficult relationships with community educational systems. Frequent moves, truancy, inconsistent parenting, and a lack of parental support for education may interact with individual factors, such as physical or psychological disabilities or substance abuse that makes it difficult for these students to succeed in community schools. When a youth is placed in a correctional setting, it is unlikely that her negative feelings toward school have changed. As a result, one of the challenges of correctional administrators is that they must provide these youth with an educational program that best meets their needs in classroom settings that leave much to be desired: in crowded facilities, serving youth with a diverse range of educational needs, and with teachers who often have inadequate resources and very high rates of turnover. This chapter explores the challenges of providing effective correctional education, including recruiting and retaining educators, complying with recent legislation, such as No Child Left Behind (NCLB) and the Americans with Disabilities Act (ADA), and ends with a review of promising educational programs in corrections.

Mary Carpenter — a 19th century prison reformer who worked with juveniles and women offenders — felt that the experiences youth faced while incarcerated were usually detrimental to their success after leaving the institution (Carpenter, 1974). This issue, although modernized with better teacher preparation and technology, continues in youth corrections today. Educational experiences should facilitate improvement and growth, not simply repeat earlier school experiences.

The struggle for educators in juvenile corrections centers on the need to provide school programs that are different from the experiences of their community or kindergarten through grade 12 (K-12) schools. This is not to say that educators should not or cannot select innovations from K-12 schools. However, juveniles in corrections may have had bad school experiences during the times they actually did attend school. All of them did have community school experiences and some call juvenile offenders "recidivists" from the K-12 public school, while Tyack (1974) called some juveniles "push-outs" instead of drop-outs from the K-12 schools. A poor K-12 school experience contributes to the wariness with which students approach institutional schools. As a result, correctional education instruction has to be different from the traditional public school curriculum because that has already failed.

The students placed in correctional classrooms experience a much higher level of learning and behavior problems, oftentimes unidentified in their prior K-12 classroom. Research has shown that special education students in the juvenile system have significantly lower academic skills than non-delinquent students at equivalent age levels and that male juvenile offenders have lower academic skills than female juvenile offenders (Zabel & Nigro, 2001). Moreover, many of the youth who are placed in correctional settings have a range of emotional problems (Teplin, Abram, McClelland, Mericle, Dulcan, & Washburn, 2006). Despite these challenges, correctional educators are rarely prepared to work in alternative settings. They must translate the training designed for K-12 schools and learn on the job, generally from veteran teachers. This can work if the veteran teacher is dedicated and committed to teaching wards in correctional schools; this is disastrous if the veteran is burned out or disengaged.

Education Staff in Youth Corrections

Educators often come to the field of youth corrections prepared as elementary school teachers or subject matter teachers, such as mathematics or English. They have studied their discipline, learning the major contributors and theories, and have practiced the strategies of their field. This preparation, however, often proves inadequate for the correctional classroom. Newly appointed teachers must adapt to correctional education and often they receive little assistance.

This problem is even more pronounced when adding the dimension of special education. There is a shortage of special education teachers and the idea of teaching in a correctional school may be alien to these teachers. In addition, the laborious processes that state systems often use for hiring is a real disincentive to prospective teachers, even if they found the idea of teaching in a correctional system attractive. Anecdotal accounts suggest that teachers who can be hired in other settings may lose interest in teaching in a correctional setting long before the state hiring system completes the process.

All this leads to the issue of a lack of professional identification as correctional educators. Many do not consider themselves to be professional correctional educators with life-long careers in the field. Instead, they identify with their community school counterparts and a few may actually feel more connected to the institutional security staff. At worst, they consider themselves mere "sojourners" in the institution—there until a better job comes along. As a result, turnover rates are often high. Platt (2007) reported that in Florida, the "Department of Juvenile Justice had a 49% teacher turnover rate in 2003-2004" and "the statewide rate in the K-12 System was 16%" (p. 2).

Learning what skills and characteristics are necessary to be successful, correctional educators address the issue of teacher turnover rate. Correctional educators need to learn how to adapt the curriculum and how to maintain their own educational excellence in the environment of a juvenile facility. There is a body of research that has identified the skills and characteristics of correctional educators (Gehring, Eggleston, & Ashcroft, 1992). Experienced correctional educators (including academic and vocational instructors and educational administrators from varied juvenile and adult correctional settings) have been asked what they consider the most important things correctional educators need to know to be successful. According to a DACUM (designing a curriculum) exercise done by the National Juvenile Detention Association (1999), a juvenile facility educator "develops, implements, supports, coordinates, researches, and assesses educational programs (i.e., academic, vocational, self/career awareness, GED, and social skills) for students in juvenile correctional facilities emphasizing the creation of a safe, secure and supportive educational environment" (p. 1).

In addition to the specific skills highlighted above, other personal characteristics are important as well. For example, it is essential for a correctional teacher to have a sense of humor, not to take oneself too seriously, have interests outside of work, and continue to learn and study so that the difficult environment does not make one jaded and disinterested.

Training for Educators in Juvenile Institutions

As noted above, there continues to be a substantial need for teacher preparation specific to correctional facilities. Educators come to corrections with licensure in elementary education, secondary education, special education, or with vocational certificates. They rarely, if ever, have been trained to work in the environment in which they find themselves. A system of pre- and in-service training must be developed to facilitate skills in teaching in a correctional environment.

For most K-12 public schools, the emphasis for instruction is on knowledge, skills, and attitudes. This is consistent with child development. For students in youth corrections, a different approach is needed. They are adolescents or young adults, already provided with developmental instruction. They have shown that they have had problems in the community. Instead, they need a curriculum that first emphasizes attitudes, and then skills, and knowledge (Gehring, Eggleston, & Ashcroft, 1992). Although they may have academic deficits, the lack of particular academic skills is not the reason they became incarcerated. There is a growing body of research, for example, that highlights how the antisocial and criminogenic thinking of offenders must be challenged in order to reduce recidivism (Bonta & Andrews, 2007).

In addition, correctional educators must understand that these students have had life experiences that they bring to the classroom or clinical setting. Although some of their stories may give professionals nightmares, those experiences need to be acknowledged and appreciated. This does not mean that educational content should be substantially different from the public school. Every effort should be made to assist in high school completion and students in the correctional setting deserve the same level of content as their public school counterparts. But, correctional educators also need to adapt the curriculum to the student and the environment and not simply repeat instructional strategies that were not successful the first time around.

The issue of teacher preparation for educators in correctional settings is one that must be addressed by every system. Current in-service activities in institutional schools often have little to do with this necessary training—they tend to focus on maintaining clean classes, filling out forms properly, or repeated trainings on how dangerous the students are.

Professional development efforts for correctional educators have often centered on either subject matter curriculum or security issues related to the institution. They rarely directly address the unique needs of working with incarcerated youth. Good teaching is good teaching, but there are dimensions of instruction within the correctional facility that make things different. Without knowledge of the foundation of correctional education—where we came from, who our major contributors were/are, and how to survive in the institution—we become vulnerable to non-education forces. If one asks a correctional teacher why he or she is leaving the field, it is rarely problems with students and most often problems with the system.

There are few pre-service programs available to correctional or alternative education trainees. Most preparation, if it exists at all, comes on the job. Universities are not generally interested in providing a specialization in colleges of education because they have a K-12 emphasis. Colleges of Criminal Justice, if they offer content in correctional education, usually focus on the correctional aspect and not teaching strategies (Eggleston, 1991). In addition, it must be said that pre-service programs that train undergraduates to teach may not be best for correctional education because there is a maturation dimension which must be considered. Youth corrections may not be the best place for an immature college graduate to practice his or her first teaching experience.

Special Education Teachers and Related Services Provision

Youth correctional facilities often have difficulty hiring qualified special education personnel. This is an area of shortage for community schools, so the two systems are often competing for those same professionals. It remains challenging to recruit qualified teachers when many of the larger, long-term facilities are located in rural areas, where administrators draw from a smaller pool of applicants. When they are hired for corrections, teachers may not be prepared for work in an institutional environment. They require additional in-service training (especially in terms of safety and security procedures) to be successful. As Platt (2007) noted:

> Along with the other challenges such as a lack of teacher preparatory programs in the area of correctional education, as well as prevailing misconceptions concerning both the value and reinforcing qualities of teaching in juvenile correctional facilities, makes recruitment and retention of teachers a daunting task. (p. 2)

Last, it does take some time to become accustomed to working in an institutional environment and turnover rates of juvenile justice staff members are high during the first year (Matz, 2008). As a result, some jurisdictions are attempting to develop better mentoring and supports for first year juvenile correctional officers and staff.

Related services in special education include counseling, speech services, occupational therapy, and physical therapy. Correctional schools often do a poor job of providing the appropriate services because they are unsuccessful in hiring and keeping qualified specialists, many of whom are very marketable. Many identified services remain unmet or under-met in correctional systems. Indeed, there is a tendency to not identify certain services a student needs when the school knows such services are unavailable.

Some places have developed some innovative ways to overcome these constraints — sometimes by having a traveling team of professionals working at several school sites, hiring public school professionals to come in after their regular workday, or contracting with local agencies to provide services. These strategies work best in areas where several institutional schools are located in close proximity to one another or are in urban environments. Such efforts have improved the situation to some degree, but it can be said that many correctional systems continue to have problems in this area.

There is a significant problem with collaboration, or the lack thereof, between agencies and disciplines. This problem occurs within the institution as well as with outside agencies. Some specialized services should be provided through interagency agreements because they may not be fully available in all settings. Within the institution, there is often a problem with turf issues and with professionals not cooperating as well as they should. Each unit and discipline is dedicated to provision of that particular service, but may not consider others as important. In addition, the outside agencies are often reluctant to work with an institutional population or to provide quality services after a youth's release. They frequently are overburdened and understaffed and, as a result, released students have multiple issues and need extensive services.

Educational Programs in Youth Corrections

The school programs offered in juvenile schools feature academic and career exploration or vocational instruction and special education. Schools for students in youth corrections may take many forms: classes held in (a) alternative settings managed by the community school system, (b) the local juvenile hall, (c) state correctional schools, and (d) alternative settings once a youth is released (e.g., aftercare). The model for these programs often closely follows the K-12 public school model, centering on hour-long academic courses with movement between classes. These programs often focus on prevocational skills development rather than vocational training. Other schools employ more of an adult education model, where academic efforts are directed toward general equivalency diploma (GED) preparation rather than high school degrees. Adult education model schools generally offer more entry-level vocational training programs.

Despite the fact that there were over 2,800 residential facilities for youth in the United States in 2004 there had been very little research about the types of programs that are available in these settings, what programs are effective, or the quality of instruction. The most recent *Juvenile Residential Census*, however, shows that 83% of facilities screened all residents for grade level prior to the end of their first week (Livsey, Sickmund, & Sladky, 2009). According to Livsey and colleagues, in 2004:

> The vast majority of facilities (89%) that screened some or all youth for grade level and educational needs used previous academic records. Some facilities also administered written tests (70%), or conducted an education-related interview with an education specialist (62%), intake counselor (43%), or guidance counselor (27%). (p. 9)

In addition to screening youth and conducting assessments, Livsey, Sickmund, and Sladky (2009) also found that "89% of facilities reported that at least some youth in their facility attended school" (p. 10). Residents in smaller facilities were less likely to attend school than youth living in larger institutions. Livsey, Sickmund, and Sladky (2009) also reported that "most facilities also reported offering special education services (79%) and GED preparation (70%). A much smaller proportion of facilities provided vocational or technical education (38%) and post-high school education (25%)" (p. 10).

While these programs exist, there is little assurance that they are responsive to the educational needs of the residents. An Office of Juvenile Justice and Delinquency Prevention report in 1994 reported that while 57% of the facilities that were reviewed had educational programs that met basic criteria of programming, there was no assessment of the quality of those programs (Wilson, p. 6) and it was recommended that the quality of juvenile correctional education be studied (p. 12). In a recent meta-analysis study (where the results of a number of studies are combined to produce one set of results), Foley (2001) found a wide variety of educational programming among juvenile facilities. Although not universal, there were examples of effective instructional strategies, cooperative learning, and well designed programs (pp. 5-6). The sample used in this study, however, was small and Foley (2001) did not generalize the findings to other states.

Schools in juvenile corrections offer some degree of special education, as mandated by federal and state laws, even in juvenile hall programs. Implementation of special education programs, however, may range in comprehensiveness. Some facilities offer a full range of assessment and educational programs; others provide only rudimentary services for the youth. The services that a youth receives are often the product of the type of facility in which he or she resides (e.g., a juvenile hall will offer fewer services due to the short-term nature of these programs), its location (in urban or rural locations), and the commitment of the organization's leaders to providing a full range of rehabilitative services to the youth in its care. Over the past few decades, however, several pieces of legislation were enacted to ensure that the learning needs of youth in facilities were met.

Complying with No Child Left Behind

The requirements of the Title I Act, No Child Left Behind, (NCLB), have caused particular problems for correctional settings. Both public school and correctional systems are having difficulty certifying that teachers have appropriate subject matter competence. Provisions such as teacher licensure in specific subjects and collaboration with home community schools, for example, are very difficult to implement (Cramer Brooks, 2008). The Improving Teacher Quality aspect of the legislation, for instance, requires that educators be highly qualified in the subjects that they teach. Many correctional educators, however, teach three or four subjects and would have to take years of additional coursework in order to meet the requirements. According to Platt (2007):

> Too often a teacher will look for another position rather than go through the overwhelming task of having to encounter endless years of additional study, while still being faced with the challenges of a teaching position for which he/she had no pre-service preparation...Correctional education administrators are faced with a no-win situation. If they support the needed staff training to comply with NCLB, as they must by law, they are faced with the likelihood that they will lose this teacher to the K-12 system. They are also faced with the reality that such training is not geared to the curriculum that is needed by delinquent youth. (p. 3)

Thus, while the intent of NCLB is to improve the quality of education, in the case of juvenile corrections, it has had the opposite impact.[1] It is possible, however, that other legislation will have a more significant long-term impact upon juvenile corrections.

Programs for Juveniles with Disabilities in Corrections

Soon after the passage of the Education of All Handicapped Children Act (EHA) in 1975, it became clear that services for students with disabilities were overrepresented and underserved in correctional settings (Morgan, 1979; Murphy, 1986; Robinson & Rapport, 1999; Rutherford, Nelson, & Wolford, 1985). This problem has continued through the reauthorizations of Individuals with Disabilities Act (IDEA) of 2004 and 2007 (Zenz & Langelett, 2004). Research indicates that the number of students in juvenile corrections with identifiable disabilities is much higher than in the community population. The K-12 schools, for example, report that between 11% and 13% of the school population possesses educational disabilities, while the range reported in the literature for incarcerated populations is from 30% to 70% (Rutherford et al., 1985; Robinson & Rapport, 1999; Zenz & Langelett, 2004). Morris and Thompson (2008) recently found that 33.4% of youth in correctional schools had some type of disability (p. 175). In spite of a significant amount of litigation in the area, however, not all special education students are being properly served.

Disability Categories in Juvenile Corrections

There are 13 categories of disabilities identified by the IDEA legislation.[2] No doubt that all of them are reflected among juveniles in youth corrections, although the most frequently occurring are sometimes called "The Big Three," which include specific learning disabilities, mental retardation, and emotional disturbance. However, there are also juvenile offenders with oppositional defiant disorder, autism, those who are deaf and hard of hearing, and those who are visually impaired. Youth with these problems are encountered less often and correctional systems sometimes have difficulty providing appropriate services for these residents (Cohen, 2008; O'Rourke & Gordon, 2003).

For students with specific learning disabilities (SLD), the nature of the disability creates additional challenges inside these facilities. Beyond the problems the disability creates in the academic setting, there is also a social dimension. Residents with SLD often do not appropriately understand social situations. A significant challenge is that misreading social cues in a correctional facility may lead to problems with security staff or, at its worst, dangerous consequences with other youth (Eggleston, 1995). It can be a matter of life or death to misinterpret an interaction with other wards in the institution. For this reason, if no other, residents with learning disabilities should be given special consideration when they are placed on housing units.

There may be a few students with each disability in the institution, but at varying levels of severity. The range and nature of the different disabilities creates significant problems. The focus for most programs in the institution is a "one size fits all" model. This model is less expensive to administer and requires less consistent change. But wards with disabilities do not often fit nicely into standard programs. When the correctional system does develop specialized programs for wards with disabilities, there is not always an understanding of the distinctions between type and severity of the disabilities.

Services to Students with Disabilities

The basic tenets of special education law addressed problems with special education students in K-12 schools. Prior to the enactment of the EHA in 1975, some states provided relatively sound programs, but there was no clear requirement to do so. The programs were often hit or miss. In the following paragraphs, a number of challenges of providing services to incarcerated juveniles are highlighted, including providing free appropriate public education, parental notification, offering services in the least restrictive environment, confidentiality, abiding by legislative timelines, assessment and evaluation, and transition to the community. Altogether, correctional educators are required to abide by many statutory requirements.

One of the challenges with special education implementation is the availability of programs and not all children with special needs are served. The EHA and IDEA require that special education services be provided and cannot be limited because of financial constraints. School districts must actively attempt to locate and serve eligible special needs students through a process called Child Find, where school systems must actively search for students who need special education and do not simply wait until a student or parent comes forward to request special help. The original legislation included the statement that children, "wherever they are found, including corrections," must be served (20 USC 1412 sec 612 2 c 30). Child Find obligations set the foundation that students in any setting are eligible for special education, including custodial facilities. The lack of Child Find efforts in juvenile facilities has recently been cited as a deficiency in a lawsuit launched against the Ohio Department of Youth Services (Cohen, 2008).

Definitions of the disability categories are provided in the regulations, so that a multidisciplinary team has criteria for making eligibility decisions. Once a student is identified for special services, the development of an educational plan specific to that child's individual student needs must be developed. This Individualized Education Plan (IEP) has strict guidelines and timelines for service delivery and a built-in process of reevaluation.

An area of particular importance to a youth corrections population is transition services. This problem was not addressed in the first wave of special education law, but was in IDEA. Awareness that students with special needs required extra help in transitioning from the school to community led to requirements for transition programming before leaving the school environment. This is particularly relevant to youth corrections, which has serious aftercare needs.

Free Appropriate Public Education

The underlying concept in special education implementation is the provision of a Free, Appropriate, Public Education (FAPE). This requires that proper education and related services be provided to each student identified as eligible for special education services. Although services have improved for providing FAPE in juvenile corrections, a number of problems continue. For example, students in special or restrictive housing are often not provided appropriate education. These students may receive reduced or no educational services. The movement of students within and between correctional facilities makes continuity of service very difficult: transfers often occur for reasons that relate to discipline or custody, not education.

A particular problem is providing the total amount of service indicated on the student plan. That may be caused by employee absences, competition for student time, or even school closures. It is one of the most disturbing aspects of institutional services because it occurs with such frequency. O'Rourke and Gordon's (2003) report on the California Youth Authority (that later became the Division of Juvenile Justice) found the following in various California facilities:

- Classes are routinely cancelled when teaching staff are sick or on vacation.
- A six-month review indicates that an average of 27% of the classes were closed each day for a variety of reasons.
- Class cancellations due to security issues, teacher absences, and lack of available substitute teachers constitute a significant problem.
- Administrators confirm that living unit staff routinely pull wards out of school for non-school related reasons.
- A review of one special education teacher's attendance file revealed that a classroom had been closed for almost one month while the teacher was on vacation.
- Classes were cancelled when an entire unit was placed on lockdown status.
- Classes are frequently cancelled because of teacher vacancies, absences, and the inability to employ substitute teachers. (p. 13-14)

Such disruptions in an educational program make it difficult for the youth to stay engaged in his studies. If the correctional facility doesn't appear interested in delivering a full time educational program, the youth might have a similar reluctance to participate.

Parental Involvement

Parental involvement is a cornerstone of special education law, but this requirement presents particular problems in youth corrections. Although it is clear that the corrections agency must have parental consent to evaluate a student for special education, for IEP development, and for any changes in program, some systems are not rigorous in efforts to find the natural parent or legal guardian. It can be difficult for a corrections system to find parents because they may be incarcerated or not involved in the resident's life. However, unless parental rights have been removed legally, attempts must be made to find parents. When the efforts to find a natural parent or legal guardian have been exhausted, a surrogate parent must be appointed.

The provision that a student may serve as his or her own parent after the age of 18 years has been implemented by youth correctional systems, sometimes to the student's detriment. Some correctional systems have implemented programs for students to serve as their own guardians, but may not provide the required support and training. Students may be encouraged to sign themselves out of special education altogether, which makes life easier for the system but can be a disservice to the students. The effect of this policy can be seen not only during incarceration, but after release as well. Special education students who have signed themselves out of services may not be able to access programs they need once they return home.

Least Restrictive Environment

Complying with the least restrictive environment (LRE) requirement in special education can be a problem in youth corrections, which are the most restrictive environments. The intent of the law is that students with special education needs will not be educated in environments that are more restrictive than their non-disabled peers (Morris & Thompson, 2008). This has been interpreted to mean non-disabled juveniles within the institution. It has been determined that as long as students with disabilities within the institution are not housed in more restrictive environments than other correctional students because of their disability, the obligation of LRE has been met. Where this continues to be a problem is for students with mental illnesses or severe emotional disturbances. The behaviors exhibited by this group often place them in more restrictive housing units and educational opportunities are often limited in these settings. As a result, students with severe mental illnesses may need to concentrate on therapeutic efforts rather than formal educational experiences for a period of time.

Confidentiality of Records

Confidentiality requirements for special education sometimes seem to conflict with those in correctional systems. Although both corrections and special education have clear confidentiality requirements, corrections may overlay its procedures to the point that access is restricted to youth correctional educators who should read these records.

Public schools in the community often are not forthcoming with student records. Correctional students may have been out of a community school for a long time or have attended a number of schools and identifying the proper school district can be difficult. Sporadic school attendance may also require that a correctional educator attempt to get records from several schools or even several states. The community K-12 school may inhibit legitimate access by their own confidentiality rules. Youth corrections often has to wait a long time for records and, in some cases, K-12 public schools do not recognize correctional schools as real schools, so they are unwilling to submit records.

Timelines

Another requirement of special education in which corrections systems commonly fail is meeting timelines for special education implementation. Special education requirements, by both federal and state statutes, have clear timelines for when evaluation, identification, IEP program development, and services must be accomplished. These timelines were developed to address the problem of a public school that dragged its feet in developing a special education program for a child because of expense or the lack of services. However, the timelines do not account for the physical movement that many correctional students make—from detention to an evaluation center (commonly called reception and diagnostic centers or receiving units in large juvenile systems), to a facility, and then perhaps another long-term institution. A youth may be moved any number of times before settling in at one facility due to security concerns, custodial level, gang considerations, or bed space availability. The emphasis is rarely related to educational needs. If a student is found eligible for special education at a diagnostic center, services must be provided within a very short time, and the student may not have a permanent placement for several weeks. To make matters more difficult, the length of stay at an institution may vary a great deal.

Many states provide the required comprehensive evaluation procedures at central receiving units, a procedure which concentrates the staffing for psychologists, educational evaluators, social workers, and other professionals. The problem of meeting timelines becomes critical when the identification is made but school services are not available within the unit. An alternative that some states have explored is to have all evaluation services— eligibility, reevaluation, and IEP development for special education—occur at the actual placement site. This requires that the full range of diagnostic services be available at each site, which is more expensive even though it better meets student needs.

Assessment and Evaluation

Assessment for eligibility for special education and progress in the program often is not comprehensive in youth corrections. The full range of screening and testing services and an appropriate multidisciplinary team for special education are not always available, especially in smaller facilities. One or two people may complete the evaluation at best and the requirement of observing a student in several educational settings may not occur. Furthermore, inappropriate assessment materials may be used. When a student is identified and the educational program is developed, the services articulated may be influenced by the knowledge of what services are available at the sites instead of the actual needs of the residents.

Continuum of Educational Placements

Continuum of educational placements requires that students be provided those services needed to meet individual needs in the most appropriate setting. This also relates to the least restrictive environmental issue, in which the student is required to be served in the environment least restrictive to meet his or her specific educational needs. For example, a student who requires only a few hours of support services should be placed in a regular educational classroom with a special education teacher providing resource help. The educational needs of this student are not best met if placed in a special day class simply because that is the only option available at that particular school.

Many students who require increased special education services may be provided a program through part time resource help by a special education teacher because there are not enough special education teachers to serve all students. This leads to the problem often cited by state Departments of Education and in lawsuits when the appropriate level of compensatory education has not been provided for all students with disabilities. Appropriate level can mean both placement options and the number of hours served by special education.

When considering low incidence disabilities such as services for the deaf or visually impaired, providing qualified educational and support staff becomes even more difficult. In addition, the correctional educators who are licensed in regular educational areas, such as elementary or secondary education, usually consider the special education student to be the sole obligation of the special education teacher (Moody, 2003). The collaboration between regular and special education, psychologists, and other providers can sometimes be difficult in a system that fragments services.

Community Transition

Transition services, in spite of being one of the most important efforts for the correctional student, remain poorly implemented in many systems. According to Morris and Thompson (2008):

> This also presents a challenge to correctional facilities in comparison to public schools, because rather than, for example, preparing students for a postsecondary education or employment setting, correctional facilities often need to prepare incarcerated juveniles for return to (and survival in) their respective community settings, and possibly prepare them to return to their respective public education setting. (p. 183)

The challenge is that the school in the institution usually is not funded to provide any kind of transition service beyond a short prerelease program required for all residents.

Transition (community reentry) services are generally considered a function of the custodial or casework staff. Sometimes, there is a state prohibition against institutional employees having contact with students once they leave the facility, which makes follow-up impossible. Furthermore, there is sometimes a lack of collaboration between educational personnel and treatment staff regarding reentry, making the efforts of both ineffective. The central issue seems to be a general lack of understanding about what transition is and should be, even though it is so very important. As a result, a "one size fits all approach" is often used. The transition efforts for purposes of special education should be a significant part of the overall treatment plan for transition from the institution. Educational transition efforts may include transition from the institutional school to the general population of the institution, to educational services on the outside, or even to commitment to an adult prison.

In a review of 12 years of research studies on special education student transition from institutions, Baltodano, Mathur, and Rutherford (2005) found that there were indicators that lead to success after release: planning prior to release, an emphasis on community member support, follow-up educational services, and recognition of differences in gender needs (p. 123). More collaborative work needs to address this area of need and, in response to this challenge, some states, such as Missouri, have hired case managers who are responsible for the youth while they are placed in a facility and after they return to the community. This integrated case management approach increases continuity of care and is associated with lower rates of recidivism (see Chapter 15).

Promising Programs in Youth Corrections

Although most national studies of educational programs in youth corrections have focused on the type of program rather than the quality of program, it should not be meant to imply that there is not good education happening in most correctional schools. Most days, students in youth corrections attend classes and have the opportunity to change their lives through education. There is a great deal of anecdotal evidence about school success, although correctional educators are sometimes reluctant to write about their programs or subject them to empirical examination (Costelloe, 2007; Lewis, 2006). Despite this limitation, there is a growing body of research that demonstrates the effectiveness of educational programs in juvenile corrections.

Steurer, Smith, and Tracy (2001), for instance, found in their recidivism study of three states that participation in correctional education is one of the main indicators of success after release. The more the student participates in education, the less likely he or she is to return to the institution. Education provides one of the most significant opportunities for change and this change also extends into the community.

A program in Pennsylvania has attempted to integrate students to community life while on probation (DeAngelo, 2006). Probation efforts center on serving the youth in the community instead of a corrections location. A collaborative approach is taken that incorporates education, after school programs, and community activities to look at the entire student and his or her life (p. 20).

A Kansas program, by contrast, has established collaborative learning communities to better address the lifelong needs of the student (Kollhoff, 2002). This includes real life activities using the Internet to help students learn content as well as skills for successful reentry. In Oregon, recognizing the need for collaboration has led to an innovative partnership. The Oregon Department of Education and the Oregon Youth Authority provide collaborative services in youth corrections in that state (Conlon et al., 2008). The focus is on career and technical education and transition to the community. Conlon and colleagues stated that "protecting the public will always be the top priority in this field, but a close and interrelated second should be accepting incarcerated youth for who they are and working consistently and patiently toward success for each of them" (p. 52). Last, in New York City (NYC), education for juveniles at Riker's Island is provided by the NYC Department of Education. The correctional education unit has developed a collaborative pilot program for transition back to the community (Lisante,

2008). This intensive service program, called the Community Prep High School, provides specialized services for returning youth. Although the program is expensive because of the high levels of academic, vocational, and counseling services, it addresses the aftercare problem that has long been identified by practitioners. It assists youth who want to continue to make positive changes with practical skills to be successful upon release.

Gehring and Muth (2008) have identified the nine elements of successful programs identified by the literature. They state that successful programs contain common elements of (a) pedagogy/andragogy (addressing adult educational needs for juveniles in corrections); (b) vocational education; (c) social education; (d) cultural education; (e) shared responsibility for decision making; (f) inclusion; (g) technology; (h) access to libraries; and (i) administrative organizational structure (p. 3). Thus, the roadmap to effective correctional educational programs has been developed and future research will help further refine these elements.

Conclusion

Education in youth corrections is frequently quite good, in spite of continuing problems. Students who attend schools in youth corrections are often disenchanted with education and may possess disabilities. There can be expectations by the community that years of academic problems will be eliminated by participation in short-term institutional programs. Correctional educators can be their own worst advertisement because they may be embarrassed about teaching in such an environment instead of displaying pride in working with one of the most difficult populations.

For many correctional educators, however, there is the best-kept secret of correctional education; that it is the best teaching environment possible. It is one in which real gains can be made and lives can be changed forever. For example, learning to read for the first time creates a life choice that did not exist before. That still leaves the option to continue on the same path, but it does provide a real choice—for the first time. Teaching in correctional education is truly the last frontier of teaching. It should attract and keep the best, most innovative teachers and offer hope to an environment that can be harsh.

Endnotes

1. One area of NCLB that will never be met by correctional systems is that of school choice (Leone & Cutting, 2004). Even though the neglected and delinquent portion of the Act is specific to juvenile corrections, most provisions cannot fully be implemented. Since placement in a correction-

al institution, detention facility, or alternative school is not based on education, but criminal conviction, choice of school is not an option.

2. According to the National Center for Learning Disabilities (2008), the following are the 13 categories: "autism, deaf-blindness, deafness, emotional disturbance, hearing impairment, mental retardation, multiple disabilities, orthopedic impairment, other health impairment (e.g., asthma, attention deficit disorder or attention deficit hyperactivity disorder, diabetes, epilepsy, heart condition, hemophilia, lead poisoning, leukemia, nephritis, rheumatic fever, sickle cell anemia and Tourette syndrome), specific learning disability, (e.g., Perceptual Disabilities, Brain Injury, Minimal Brain Dysfunction, Dyslexia, Developmental Aphasia), speech or language impairment, traumatic brain injury, visual impairment (including blindness), and developmental delay."(p. 1)

References

Baltodano, H., Mathur, S., & Rutherford, R. (2005). Transition of incarcerated youth with disabilities across systems into adulthood. *Exceptionality, 13*, 103-124.

Black, S. (2005). Learning behind bars. *American School Board Journal, September*, 50-52.

Bonta, J., & Andrews, D. A. (2007). *Risk-need-responsivity model for offender assessment and rehabilitation.* Retrieved October 6, 2008, from http://www.ps-sp.gc.ca/res/cor/rep/_fl/Risk_Need_2007-06_e.pdf

Carpenter, J. E. (1974). *The life and work of Mary Carpenter.* Montclair, NJ: Patterson Smith.

Conlon, B., Harris, S., Nagel, J., Hillman, M., & Hanson, R. (2008). Education: Don't leave prison without it. *Corrections Today, February*, 48-51.

Costelloe, A. (2007). Researching correctional education: Why we must advance from "Research on" to "Research on and for" and ultimately "Research on, for and with." *The Journal of Correctional Education, 58*, 205-212

Cramer Brooks, C. (2008). The challenge of following education legislation in confinement education programs. *Corrections Today, February*, 28-46.

DeAngelo, A. (2006). Competency development and evidence-based programs in the juvenile justice system. *Corrections Today, October*, 19-20.

Eggleston, C. (1991). Correctional education professional development. *Journal of Correctional Education, 42*, 88-90.

Eggleston, C. (1995). *Learning disability and the justice system. Their world.* New York: National Center for Learning Disabilities.

Foley, R. (2001). Academic characteristics of incarcerated youth and correctional education programs: A review. *Journal of Emotional & Behavioral Disorders, 9*, 248-264.

Gehring, T., Eggleston, C., & Ashcroft, R. (1992). *Correctional teacher skills, characteristics, and performance indicators.* Riverside, CA: Robert Presley Institute of Corrections Research and Training.

Gehring, T., & Muth, B. (2008). What works and why? And what doesn't work and why? The search for best practices in correctional education. *Applying Ken*

Wilber's ideas and models to professionalize correctional education. San Bernardino: CSUSB University Press.

Kollhoff, M. (2002). Reflections of a Kansas juvenile corrections educator. *Journal of Correctional Education, 53* (2), 98-99.

Leone, P. (2001, November). *Accommodating the needs of inmates with developmental disabilities in the California Department of Corrections.* Presented at the American Association of Criminology Annual Meeting, Atlanta GA.

Leone, P., & Cutting, C. (2004). Appropriate education, juvenile corrections, and No Child Left Behind. *Behavioral Disorders, 29,* 260-265.

Lewis, J. (2006). Correctional education: Why it is only "promising." *Journal of Correctional Education, 57,* 286-296.

Lisante, T. (2008, March 5). *Community prep high school.* New York: Unpublished brochure and personal interview.

Livsey, S., Sickmund, M., & Sladky, A. (2009). *Juvenile residential facility census, 2004: Selected findings.* Washington, DC: Office of Juvenile Justice and Delinquency Prevention.

Matz, A. (2008). *Analysis of turnover and turnover intentions among juvenile justice staff at the Kentucky Department of Juvenile Justice.* Eastern Kentucky University: Unpublished thesis

Moody, B. (2003). Juvenile corrections educators: Their knowledge and understanding of special education. *Journal of Correctional Education, 54,* 105-107.

Morgan, D. (1979). Prevalence and types of handicapping conditions found in juvenile correctional institutions: A national survey. *The Journal of Special Education, 13,* 283-295.

Morris, R. J., & Thompson, K. C. (2008). Juvenile delinquency and special education laws: Policy implementation issues and directions for future research. *The Journal of Correctional Education, 59,* 173-188.

Murphy, D. (1986). The prevalence of handicapping conditions among juvenile delinquents. *Remedial and Special Education, 7,* 7-17.

National Center for Learning Disabilities. (2008). *IDEA terms to know.* Retrieved October 3, 2008, from http://www.ncld.org/content/view/921/456099/

National Juvenile Detention Association. (1999). *Occupational profile: The juvenile facility (correctional, detention, residential) educator.* Retrieved October 3, 2008, from http://dacum.eku.edu/archivelist.php

O'Rourke, T., & Gordon, R. (2003). *Education program review of California Youth Authority.* Retrieved October 3, 2008 from http://www.prisonlaw.com/pdfs/CYA3.pdf

Platt, J. (2007). *JJETSTREAM.* Unpublished document.

Robinson, T., & Rapport, M. (1999). Providing special education in the justice system. *Remedial and Special Education, 20,* 19-26.

Rutherford, R., Nelson, M., & Wolford, B. (1985). Special education in the most restrictive environment: Correctional special education. *Journal of Special Education, 19,* 59-71.

Rutherford, R., Quinn, M. M., & Mathur, S. (2004). *Handbook of research in emotional and behavioral disorders.* NY: Guilford Press.

Steurer, S., Smith, L., & Tracy, A. (2001). *Three state recidivism study.* Lanham, MD: Correctional Education Association.

Teplin, L. A., Abram, K. M., McClelland, G. M., Mericle, A. A., Dulcan, M. K., & Washburn, J. J. (2006). *Psychiatric disorders of youth in detention.* Washington, DC: Office of Juvenile Justice and Delinquency Prevention.

Tyack, D. (1974). *The one best system: A history of American urban education.* Cambridge: Harvard University Press.

U. S. Department of Education. (1996). *Survey of state correctional education systems: Analysis of data from 1992 field test.* Washington, DC: Office of Correctional Education.

Wilson, J. (1994). *Conditions of confinement: Juvenile detention and corrections facilities.* Washington, DC: Office of Juvenile Justice and Delinquency Prevention.

Zabel, R., & Nigro, F. (2001). The influence of special education experience and gender of juvenile offenders on academic achievement scores in reading, language, and mathematics. *Behavioral Disorders, 26,* 164-172.

Zenz, T., & Langelett, G. (2004). Special education in Wisconsin's juvenile detention system. *Journal of Correctional Education, 55,* 60-68.

CHAPTER 15
REFORMING REFORM SCHOOL

Richard A. Mendel

This chapter presents a detailed description of the State of Missouri's unusual and highly successful approach to juvenile corrections, which has been touted by many experts as a national model. Unlike the vast majority of states, which rely on large, congregate care training schools, Missouri relies exclusively on smaller facilities to house juvenile offenders and employs a unique treatment oriented correctional regime to reverse the delinquent behavior of troubled teens. The program has become so successful that in September 2008, the Division of Youth Services (DYS) was awarded an Innovations in American Government Award from the Ash Institute for Democratic Governance and Innovation at Harvard University (Ash Institute, 2008). This chapter details the evolution of the Missouri system, describes many of its key features, and documents the evidence of its effectiveness.

The Need to Reform Juvenile Corrections

In most states, the largest piece of the juvenile justice budget is spent on correctional facilities; most committed youth are sent to training schools, large correctional units typically housing over 100 youth. Nationwide, for example, over 46% of juveniles confined in 2004 were held in facilities with more than 101 residents (Livsey, Sickmund, & Sladky, 2009).

Most of these training schools—historically known as reform schools—are located in rural areas. Inside the facilities, young offenders (mostly minorities from urban areas) spend months or years housed in small rooms far from their families and neighborhoods, disconnected from the social forces that drove them to criminality and to which they will one day return.

Training schools employ teachers and (in most cases) certified mental health counselors, but in many states youth spend much of their time under the supervision of juvenile correctional officers, many with no post secondary education, some with little training in or affinity for counseling or youth development. If youth misbehave, they may be locked down in isolation cells. In other states, direct staff members have blended counselor-security roles (see Chapter 11), are better educated, and take an active role in the youth's rehabilitation.

Decades of research has found that large training schools are not effective in rehabilitating youthful offenders or steering them from crime (Howell, 2004). Indeed, veteran juvenile justice scholar Barry Feld (1999) has concluded, "Evaluation research indicates that incarcerating young offenders in large, congregate care juvenile institutions does not effectively rehabilitate and may actually harm them... A century of experience with training schools and youth prisons demonstrates that they are the one extensively evaluated and clearly *ineffective* method to 'treat' delinquents" (p. 143).

Training school confinement is often justified as a necessary step to protect the public. Yet, only 24.6% of incarcerated youth nationwide have been found guilty of a violent index offense (murder, sexual assault, robbery, or aggravated assault, see Sickmund, Sladky, & Kang, 2008). Most have committed only property or drug crimes, disorderly conduct, or sometimes only misdemeanors or status offenses (like truancy or alcohol possession) that would not be crimes if committed by an adult. Nonetheless, recidivism studies routinely find that half or more of training school youth are convicted of a new offense within three years of release (Mendel, 2000, 2003).

In addition, training schools have also suffered frequently with substandard conditions of confinement, overcrowding, and even resident abuse (Armstrong & MacKenzie, 2003; Parent et al., 1993). Nationwide, 13,000 cases of abuse were reported in juvenile institutions from 2004 to 2007; in 2006 and 2007, the U. S. Department of Justice conducted investigations, issued findings, and entered and/or monitored formal consent decrees or other settlement agreements involving conditions of confinement in juvenile detention and correctional facilities in 16 states and two territories (CNN, 2008).

Evolution of Reform

Like other states, Missouri's juvenile corrections system also long relied on training schools. From 1887 until 1983, the Boonville Training School, a 158-acre campus of two-story brick residence halls, was Missouri's primary correctional facility for boys, holding up to 650 teens at a time. Though its stated mission was rehabilitative, the reality at Boonville was often brutal. Soon after losing his job in 1949, for instance, former Boonville superintendent John Tindall described the facility in the *St. Louis Post Dispatch*: "I saw black eyes, battered faces, broken noses among the boys," Tindall wrote. "The usual corrective procedure among the guards was to knock a boy down with their fists, then kick him in the groin...Many of the men were sadists" (Abrams, 2003). Three boys died inside the facility in 1948.

Conditions remained problematic from the 1950s through the 1970s, reports University of Missouri law professor Douglas Abrams, who recently completed a history of the state's juvenile courts (Abrams, 2003). A 1969 federal report condemned Boonville's quasi-penal-military atmosphere, particularly the practice of banishing unruly youth to "the Hole"—a dark, solitary confinement room atop the facility's administration building (Abrams, 2003). Investigative reporter Kenneth Wooden wrote that during his visit to Boonville in 1973, youth complained about "staff members having sexual relations with the children, beating them, throwing them into solitary confinement for no substantial reason, [and] pushing drugs" (Abrams, 2003). In 1983, Missouri shut down the Boonville training school. In the 1970s, Missouri's Division of Youth Services (DYS) had begun to experiment with smaller and more therapeutic correctional programs. Liking the results and tired of the endless scandals at Boonville, the state donated the facility to the state's Department of Corrections, which turned it into an adult penitentiary.

In place of Boonville, as well as a training school for girls in Chillicothe that closed in 1981, DYS secured smaller sites across the state—abandoned school buildings, large residential homes, even a convent—and outfitted them to house delinquent teens. The largest of the new units housed only three dozen teens. Today, Missouri operates 42 juvenile corrections facilities statewide; all but four of them house fewer than 40 youth. In June 2008, the largest facility was the W. E. Sears Youth Center, with a population of 61 residents (Anderson, 2008); this is a sharp contrast to the larger secure facilities in most states.

The Importance of Facility Size

According to both Missouri insiders and national justice experts, Missouri's switch to smaller facilities was crucial to improving its juvenile corrections system. Paul DeMuro, a veteran juvenile justice consultant, suggests that "the most important thing in dealing with youthful offenders is the relationships, the one-on-one relationships formed between young people and staff. And not just the line staff. It's critical that the director of the facility know every kid by name" (Mendel, 2003).

Ned Loughran, executive director of the Council of Juvenile Correctional Administrators, warns that "the kids coming into juvenile facilities need a lot of specialized attention, and they need to develop a relationship with staff" Loughran added, "A small facility allows the staff to get to know the kids on a very individual basis. The kids interact better with peers and staff." Large facilities routinely suffer with high rates of staff turnover and absenteeism, "so the kids spend a lot of time sitting in their rooms... With large [facilities] it's like going to a large urban high school. Kids get lost, and these kids can't afford to get lost" (Mendel, 2003). David Alschuler (1999) has argued that "it is exceedingly difficult to successfully punish, deter, and treat incarcerated juvenile offenders in large, locked, secure training schools that are operating over capacity; yet this is the norm in juvenile corrections nationwide."

Smaller facilities are not a magic bullet for juvenile corrections reform, however. Kentucky has long housed delinquent teens in small facilities rather than larger training schools, but a federal investigation in 1995 found that Kentucky was ignoring abuse complaints, using isolation cells excessively, and providing substandard education and mental health programming (see *U. S. v. Commonwealth of Kentucky, 1995*). Since then, Kentucky has beefed up staff training and closed its worst facilities. In fact, Division of Juvenile Justice (DJJ) correctional officers now receive seven weeks of classroom training within their first year (see Chapter 13).

In Missouri, small facilities likewise produced no immediate miracles. Initially, chaos reigned inside many of the new sites, recalls Gail Mumford, who began working with DYS in 1983 and now serves as the division's deputy director for treatment services. "It was really crazy," says Mumford. "We didn't know what we were doing. The boys ran us ragged [at first]. They were acting up every day, sometimes every hour" (Mendel 2003). But, conditions in Missouri's small facilities have improved dramatically since the early 1980s because DYS built a continuum of care to address the needs of youth with varying risk and need profiles and — thanks to a series of interrelated reforms — developed an effective and comprehensive youth treatment system.

The Missouri Juvenile Treatment Continuum

As in every state, only a small fraction of youth adjudicated in Missouri's juvenile courts are ever sentenced to the state youth corrections agency. The vast majority of juveniles are released, placed in juvenile court diversion programs, or — in large jurisdictions like Kansas City and St. Louis — placed in locally operated youth corrections facilities. In 2006, for instance, of the 39,496 Missouri youth referred to juvenile courts for law violations, just 1,137 (or slightly less than three percent) were placed under DYS custody (Missouri Division of Youth Services, 2007). While DYS does not operate diversion or local youth corrections programs, its budget does include $4.15 million in the 2009 budget to help support intensive probation, day treatment, group counseling, and other community programs (Anderson, 2008).

Risk Assessment

Whenever a youth is placed into DYS custody, the first step is to determine the proper placement. For this process, DYS uses a formal risk assessment instrument, which uses a point system to evaluate both the seriousness of the offenses committed and the risk of reoffending. The 23-point scale is based upon three questions: the seriousness of the current offense (up to ten points), the seriousness of prior adjudications (up to ten points), and the youth's behavior in previous residential placements (up to three points). Because ten points is the cut-off for a most serious designation, any youth ever adjudicated for murder, first degree assault, forcible rape or sodomy, first degree robbery, or drug distribution is designated as most serious, while those with lesser offending histories can receive moderately serious or less serious designations.

The 23-point risk of reoffending scale is based on ten questions concerned with the youth's prior offending and placement history, age at first referral, and problems in peer relations, family disruption, school failure, and substance abuse. Here, too, youth are grouped into high, moderate, and low risk categories.

Continuum of Care

As detailed in Chart 1 below, the youth are analyzed on a placement grid and referred to community-based supervision, non-secure group homes, moderately secure facilities, or secure care.

Day Treatment and Other Community-based Supervision

DYS places committed youth with the least serious offending histories and the lowest likelihood of re-offending into community-based supervision programs. Statewide, approximately ten percent of DYS youth are placed directly in these non-residential programs.

Most youth placed in community supervision are assigned to day treatment centers where they spend from 8:00 a.m. to 3:00 p.m. every weekday in a combination of academic education and counseling. After school, many participate in community service, academic tutoring activities, or in individual or family counseling. The ten-day treatment programs, which can serve up to 171 youth on any given day, also serve as a step down for many youth following their time in residential programs.

Chart 1. Placement and Length of Stay (LOS) Grid.

S E R I O U S N E S S	*Most Serious* *10+*	Moderately Secure Residential LOS = 6-9 months	Secure Residential LOS = 9-12 months	Secure Residential LOS = 9-12 months
	Moderately Serious *6-9*	Community-Based Residential LOS = 4-6 months	Moderately Secure Residential LOS = 6-9 months	Secure Residential LOS = 9-12 months
	Least Serious *2-5*	Non-Residential LOS = 1-6 months	Community-Based Residential LOS = 4-6 months	Moderately Secure Residential LOS = 6-9 months
		Lowest Risk *2-10*	*Moderate Risk* *11-17*	*Highest Risk* *18-22*
		Risk of Re-Offending		

A small number of youth in community-based supervision are monitored by trackers—community residents or college students pursuing a degree in social work or a related discipline who maintain close contact with delinquent young people and their families and offer support, mentoring, and troubleshooting assistance. Trackers are often part of aftercare supervision for teens following residential placement. Throughout the state, there were 156 persons available to deliver tracking services to youth in June 2008 and they provided these services to about 250 youth (Anderson, 2008).

Residential Confinement

For the remaining 90% of youth sentenced to DYS custody, the first placement is to a residential facility. However, most of the residential beds overseen by DYS are not in locked, secure-care facilities. Instead, all of the five DYS regions operate group homes and moderately secure facilities. Typically, these facilities are not surrounded by a perimeter fence. Resident youth are not under 24-hour/day lock and key and they participate in many outside activities in the community.

Table 1. Missouri Department of Youth Services Levels of Care.

Level of Care	Number of Facilities/ Programs	Total Beds/Slots	Participant Profile	Typical Length of Stay
Day Treatment	10	171	First-time, non-serious offenders or youth on aftercare following a stay in residential DYS pro-grams	1-6 months
Community-Based Residence	7	70	Less serious offenders, often with high needs	4-6 months
Moderately Secure Care	18	424	Youth with multiple or serious (but mostly non-violent) offenses	6-9 months
Secure Care	7	192	Chronic and/or serious youth offenders	9-12 months

Source: Missouri Division of Youth Services.

Group Homes

Youth with low seriousness and re-offending risk scores are referred to one of the six non-secure group homes scattered throughout the state. Each of these group homes typically houses 10-12 youth who have committed status offenses or misdemeanors — young people who pose little danger to the community but require more structure, support, and supervision than their families can provide. Group home youth attend school onsite, not in public schools, but they spend considerable time away from their facilities in jobs, group projects, and other community activities. Within the facilities, they participate in extensive individual, group, and family counseling.

Moderately Secure Facilities

Youth with somewhat more serious offending histories or higher risk levels are placed into one of the state's 18 moderately secure residential facilities located in residential neighborhoods, state parks, and two college campuses. Though many youth sent to these facilities are felons, they also spend time in the community. Closely supervised by staff, residents regularly go on field trips and undertake community service projects. Those who make progress in the counseling component of the program and demonstrate trustworthiness are often allowed to perform jobs with local nonprofit or government agencies as part of a $678,000 per year DYS work experience program.

Secure Care

For the most serious offenders referred by Missouri juvenile courts, DYS operates six secure care residential facilities, each with a maximum capacity of 33 residents or less. These youth seldom participate in activities outside the facility, but in other ways their daily activities are similar to youth in less secure residential settings.

Youth Transferred to Criminal Court

While DYS secure care facilities house the toughest offenders adjudicated in Missouri's juvenile courts, the state's most serious youth offenders are transferred out of juvenile jurisdiction and tried in adult courts. As amended in 1995, Missouri's juvenile transfer laws require a judicial transfer hearing for any youth accused of drug distribution or serious violent crimes (murder, rape, robbery, or aggravated assault) and they grant judges the discretion to transfer youth accused of lesser offenses.

As DYS's reputation for success has spread, however, judges have transferred fewer and fewer youth to adult courts—just 120 youth in 2007, which is down from 302 youth in 1996. As in other states, some Missouri youth transferred to stand trial in adult courts are never convicted of crimes and others are placed on probation. When youthful offenders are sentenced as adults to serve time behind bars, they receive one of two types of sentences.

Blended Sentences

Authorized under Missouri's 1995 juvenile reform law, this option allows youth sentenced to long adult prison terms to serve the first years of their sentences under the care of DYS. When youth reach 18 years of age, the court can either transfer them to adult prison or retain them in DYS custody for continued treatment. Then, as youth still in DYS care approach the age of 21 years, the court holds a second hearing to decide whether to: (a) stay the remaining years of their sentences and return youth to the community (under continuing probation supervision); or (b) send them on to prison to complete the full sentence. As of June 2008, DYS had supervised 64 youth sentenced in this manner, since the inception of the program, 19 of whom remained in DYS custody (Anderson, 2008).

Of the first 22 blended sentence youth who left DYS care, five did not make substantial attitudinal and behavioral changes while in DYS care and were transferred to adult prisons. DYS recommended that the other 17 be released to the community based on their progress in juvenile custody and the courts accepted the recommendation in every case (Steward, 2004). As of 2004, DYS was aware of only two cases in which youth have had their probations revoked following release; it knew of no case in which a dual sentenced offender has committed a new violent felony.

Adult Prison

Serious youth offenders who are not offered a dual sentence must serve out their full sentences in adult prisons lacking any type of juvenile programming or services. Thanks to the limited number of adult court transfers in Missouri and the availability of the blended sentence, however, the number of youth serving time in Missouri prisons appears quite small. While Missouri does not keep records on the number of offenders convicted in adult courts and imprisoned for crimes committed before their 17th birthdays, state records show that as of September 2004, only three youth under 17 years of age were in state prisons.

The Missouri Treatment Model

Regardless of custody level, all DYS residential facilities employ a similar correctional strategy. This approach relies on group process and personal development, rather than punishment and isolation, as the best medicines for delinquent teens and it is strengthened by a host of innovations and enhancements developed and refined by DYS over two decades. The model has several key features, all of which are discussed below: a regional approach, group treatment, case management, a humane environment, highly trained staff, double coverage, education and training, individual and family therapy, the treatment room, maintenance of physical and emotional safety, and aftercare.

A Regional Approach

DYS has divided the state into five regions, each of which operates independently and provides a full array of services. Thus, youth in DYS custody almost always remain in their home regions, close to their homes and families. This enables DYS staff to remain in close contact with family members and to involve them in all phases of the treatment process.

Group Treatment

At every DYS residential facility, youth spend virtually all of their time in treatment groups of 10-12 residents, living together in a dormitory and participating together in academic classes and group therapy sessions. The teams eat together, sleep together, study together, and participate in recreation together—always under the supervision of DYS youth specialists (or teachers during the school day). At least five times per day, the teams check in with one another, telling their peers and the staff how they feel physically and emotionally. And at any time, youth are free to call a circle, in which all team members must stand facing one another, to raise concerns or voice complaints about the behavior of other group members. Thus, at any moment the focus can shift from the activity at hand (education, exercise, clean up, a bathroom break) to a lengthy discussion of behaviors and attitudes. Staff members also call circles frequently to communicate and enforce expectations regarding safety, courtesy, and respect.

Case Management

From the moment they enter DYS custody, all youth are assigned to a service coordinator, a single case manager who oversees their cases before, during, and after their time in DYS facilities. This service coordinator conducts the risk assessment (and also a needs assessment and individual treatment plan) as soon as a teen is placed under DYS supervision and recommends an appropriate placement.

Once a young person is placed in a residential facility, the service coordinator meets with him or her at least once per month; the service coordinator also conducts outreach to the parents and other family members. As the youth approaches the end of a residential program, the service coordinator, in consultation with facility staff and parents, takes the lead in determining the release date as well as the appropriate next placement (for youth whose families may not have a suitable home for the youth).

Finally, once youth are released from a residential DYS facility, the service coordinator meets with them regularly; at least weekly for the most risky offenders, bi-weekly for those with moderate risk profiles, and monthly for those at lowest risk. If the young person fails to follow rules and behave appropriately while on aftercare, the service coordinator has authority to revoke the aftercare status and place the youth back into residential care. For those who remain on track in aftercare, the service coordinator decides when to close the case and release the young person from DYS supervision.

A Humane, Youth Friendly Environment

Although youth inside DYS facilities are under constant staff supervision, the atmosphere even in secure care facilities is far from prison-like. There are no cells inside most DYS facilities; in fact, other than a metal detector at the front door, there are few locked doors and little security hardware of any type—just video cameras linked to monitors in the central office. As in group homes and moderately secure facilities, secure care residents joke easily with staff, whom they address on a first name basis. Furnishings are new and cheerful in the facilities. Colorful bulletin boards cover most of the walls featuring youths' work or positive messages written and designed by the youth. The atmosphere is more like a home or college dormitory than like the typical juvenile correctional center.

Highly Trained Staff

As DYS struggled to impose order in its new network of small facilities in the 1980s, one of its key policy changes was to upgrade the quality of direct care staff. Rather than requiring only a high school diploma, DYS began staffing its facilities primarily with college-educated youth specialists, rather than traditional corrections officers. In addition, DYS developed an ambitious in-service training regimen to steep all new hires in its new treatment oriented correctional philosophy. Today, all DYS staff must complete 120 hours of in-service training during their first two years on the job.

Double Coverage

According to DYS veterans, the single most important change made by the agency to improve the safety and therapeutic environment in its facilities came in the early 1990s when it began requiring double coverage, which means that two DYS staffers must be present with every group at all times. Among groups of delinquent teens, the potential for mischief, fighting, and other negative behaviors is always present. DYS found that by keeping two sets of eyes and two calming influences present with the groups at all times, it could minimize these risks and maintain an atmosphere of safety and respect that allows participants to stay focused on their work and positive in their behaviors. Due to budget shortfalls, DYS is no longer able to maintain double coverage on all cases, particularly during night shifts in low security programs. However, double coverage remains the rule at all times in secure care facilities.

Education and Training

Youth confined in DYS facilities attend six 50-minute periods of academic instruction every weekday all year round. They break into small groups for GED instruction or class work toward their high school diplomas, work together on special projects or current events, or do individual lessons in a computer learning lab. Teachers are certified, but they are employed directly by DYS rather than working for the public schools. DYS also employs a special education teacher in almost every facility (and contracts for special education services in the remaining facilities). DYS also provides extensive work and community service experience for many teens, particularly those in the less secure facilities, through its work experience program.

Individual and Family Therapy

Like a growing number of states, Missouri employs mental health counselors to work with youth and their families; the state also partners with outside psychiatrists to ensure that confined youth receive appropriate psychotropic medications. DYS places strong emphasis on family therapy and the regional approach keeps most teens close to their families. Roughly 40% of DYS youth participate in family therapy. In some cases, this therapy involves only a handful of sessions prior to release, while in other cases the therapy process is more intensive. Unlike mental health care provided in many other states, DYS therapists do not need to be licensed counselors or social workers. Most are former direct care staff members who express interest in counseling and undertake 150 hours of additional in-house training.

The Treatment Room

While many states concentrate their treatment efforts in occasional therapy sessions provided by mental health professionals, Missouri operates under a philosophy that treatment occurs 24 hours per day and it strives to infuse treatment into the fabric of its programming. At every DYS facility, each group meets for an hour each afternoon to talk about their personal histories, their future goals, and the roots of their delinquent behavior.

Some days, the teens participate in "group-builders" which are shared activities designed to build camaraderie and help teens explore issues like trust, perceptions, and communication. But in many meetings, one particular teen will talk to the group about his or her life. The first of these sessions is a "who am I?" exercise in which youth list their favorite people, foods, cars, and movies. In subsequent sessions, the topics become more personal. In the life history, teens are asked to — and often do — talk about wrenching experiences in their lives: domestic abuse, violence, sexual victimization, and family negligence. They are also encouraged to speak about their crimes and other misdeeds.

In the genogram, teens produce and then explain a coded family tree detailing the incidence of domestic violence, alcoholism, drug addiction, criminality, illiteracy, and other pathologies in their families as a first step toward exploring the historic roots of their own behavior problems. In the "line of body," confined adolescents trace their bodies onto a large sheet of paper and then write in the physical and mental traumas they have suffered during their young lives. These instruments are particularly useful for juveniles because they visually show patterns of behavior.

Maintaining Physical and Emotional Safety

According to former DYS deputy director Vicky Weimholt, convincing delinquent teens to open up about their troubled pasts is critical in reversing behavior problems. The key to getting teens to talk is physical and emotional safety. "Our staff are always there, and they will not let you get hurt," Weimholt said, "And on the emotional side, you can't underestimate the power of group work... There's safety in knowing that I'm not the only one going through this" (Mendel, 2003). In promoting safety, DYS shuns the tactics commonly used in training schools. DYS youth are almost never held in isolation and DYS staff members do not employ hog ties or four-point restraints.

Aftercare

The small scale and therapeutic, family oriented atmosphere distinguish Missouri's juvenile facilities from training schools common in most states. However, the differences do not end when Missouri teens walk out the doors of a DYS facility. More than most states, Missouri supports youth through the tricky transition when they leave facilities and return home.

"Large, locked, secure training schools frequently fall prey to an institutional culture in which the measures of success relate only to compliance with rules and norms," writes David Altschuler, the nation's foremost expert on aftercare for juvenile offenders. "Progress within such settings is generally short-lived, unless it is followed-up, reinforced, and monitored in the community. [In most cases, the institution and its staff have] no responsibility, authority, or involvement with anything other than institutional adjustment and progress" (p. 240). As outlined in Chapter 14, in some jurisdictions, facility staff members are prohibited from contact with youth once they have been released.

Missouri has made aftercare a core component of its correctional approach. Typically, youth leaving DYS care are placed on aftercare status for three to six months. During this period, they meet frequently with their service coordinators and follow an aftercare plan developed prior to their release. Many youth—about 40% of those on aftercare—are also assigned a tracker, who meets with them several times per week, monitors their progress, counsels them informally and helps them find jobs. Some aftercare youth are placed temporarily into day treatment programs, often as a bridge period to maintain their educational progress before they can return to a public school at the start of a new semester.

Unlike parole officers employed by most states, DYS service coordinators already have longstanding relationships with teens when they head home, which is a result of their involvement with the youth and families during the period of out-of-home placement. The service coordinators have authority to decide when the young person will leave residential care and to revoke aftercare and return young people to residential care if they break rules or deviate severely from their aftercare plans.

Organizational Strength

In addition to its reliance on small facilities, its impressive continuum of programs and services, and its unique and comprehensive treatment approach, Missouri juvenile corrections efforts have also been bolstered by unique organizational strengths within the Division of Youth Services. In particular, the agency has been blessed with unusually stable leadership and a rare degree of deep, bi-partisan political support.

Organizational Stability

Nationwide, directing a state juvenile corrections agency is typically a high turnover job. In most states, agency leaders come and go with each new governor or with each new scandal. Missouri, by contrast, had the same director from 1988 through 2005: Mark Steward. Steward's continuing presence, along with his firm commitment to youth oriented treatment, provided crucial stability for DYS, which allowed the agency to develop a strong organizational commitment to its treatment oriented correctional philosophy and to steadily refine its programs and procedures to make that philosophy effective.

In addition, the stability of DYS has been strengthened by the agency's staff — both at state and regional administrative offices and in the division's facilities. Beginning with the Director himself, nearly every key administrator and every facility manager began their careers at DYS working directly with youth in one of the agency's facilities. As a result, DYS leaders statewide share a common understanding of the agency's mission and a shared commitment to seeing it accomplished.

Bipartisan Political Support

In his years as DYS Director, Mark Steward carefully cultivated a network of prominent supporters statewide, including leaders in both political parties. Before his untimely death in 2000, former Democratic Governor Mel Carnahan frequently invited Steward to bring DYS youth for visits to his office in the state capitol. Likewise, conservative state Supreme Court Judge Stephen Limbaugh, a cousin and close confidant of conservative commentator Rush Limbaugh, is also a longtime DYS supporter.

As one of his first steps after taking over DYS in the late 1980s, the Director created a state advisory board and filled it with top leaders. By inviting advisory board members, judges, state legislators, and other key leaders to tour its facilities and by allowing youth to guide these tours and describe in their own words the value of the DYS treatment process, the Director and DYS have earned support across the political spectrum. Also, by placing dozens of facilities throughout the state, it has built a powerful base of grassroots support to maintain its decentralized programming. Since

Steward's departure in 2005, DYS has retained its stability as other long-time agency staffers have taken the reigns.

Exceptional Outcomes

Over the years, DYS has sponsored countless facility tours for influential leaders from all over Missouri. In recent years, as word has spread, juvenile justice leaders from across the nation have come to tour DYS facilities and learn about the state's unconventional approach to youth corrections. In these visits, outsiders often respond with surprise, even amazement, at the feeling of safety and optimism inside the facilities and at the ability of Missouri youth to articulate a positive message and dispel the negative stereotypes that typically surround delinquent teens.

After touring DYS facilities in the Kansas City area in September 2003, Maryland Juvenile Services Secretary Kenneth Montague reported, "What impacted me most was the atmosphere that existed there. The staff knew these kids very well. They conveyed an attitude of continual support for them, and the kids were really responding to that. That's the kind of environment we all want" (Mendel, 2004).

Linda Leubbering, a long-time senior official with the Missouri Division of Budget and Planning, vividly recalled her first visit to a DYS facility. "I was surprised that I was walking into a facility like that—these were hard-core kids—and I was completely comfortable to go up and talk to them about their treatment," Luebbering said. "I ended up in a long conversation with a very well-spoken young man. Only afterward did Mark [Steward] tell me that this kid had committed murder. It made a big impression on me" (Mendel, 2003).

Low Recidivism

Teaching youth to speak articulately and behave well inside correctional institutions is not the Division of Youth Services' core mission, however. The Division's statutory purpose is "the prevention and control of juvenile delinquency and the rehabilitation of children" to minimize the future offending of delinquent teens. The evidence shows that Missouri is succeeding. An in-depth DYS recidivism report, compiled in February 2003, found that 70% of youth released in 1999 avoided recommitment to a correctional program within three years.

Of 1,386 teens released from DYS custody in 1999, just 111 (8%) were sentenced to state prison or a state-run 120-day adult incarceration program within 36 months of release; 266 (19%) were sentenced to adult probation. The report also showed that 94 youth were recommitted to DYS for new offenses following release (Mendel, 2003). Another 134 youth returned to DYS residential facilities temporarily for breaking rules while on aftercare, but DYS does not consider these cases failures or include them in its recidivism data. The most recent DYS recidivism data, obtained from Anderson (2008), provide less detail, but indicate that recidivism rates are largely unchanged since 2003.

Compared to states that measure recidivism in similar ways, these success rates are exceptional. For instance, a 2000 recidivism study in Maryland found that 30% of youth released from juvenile corrections facilities in 1997 were incarcerated as adults within three years (Iyengar, 2000). In Louisiana, 45% of youth released from residential programs in 1999 returned to juvenile custody or were sentenced to adult prison or probation by mid-2002 (Mendel, 2003). In Florida, 29% of youth released from a juvenile commitment program in 2000–2001 were returned to juvenile custody or sentenced to adult prison or probation within 12 months; the comparable figure in Missouri is just nine percent (Florida Department of Juvenile Justice, 2003).

Moderate Costs

Missouri's lower recidivism rates do not come with a high price tag. The total DYS budget for 2002 was $58.4 million—equal to $103 for each young person statewide between the ages of 10 and 16 years. By contrast, Louisiana spends $270 per young person aged 10–16 years, Maryland spends roughly $192 for each youth aged 10–17 years, and Florida spends approximately $271 (Mendel, 2003). Although juvenile courts in Maryland and Florida have jurisdiction over youth up to age 17, Missouri and Louisiana juvenile laws cover youth only up to the age of 16. According to Anderson (2008), the average cost of programs for fiscal year 2007 was $115.13 per day in community residential programs, $122.29 in moderate care facilities, and $161.83 for secure care programs (or $59,069 per year).[1] Missouri's cost per youth is much cheaper than the $175,616 that it cost to house a resident in the California Department of Corrections and Rehabilitation (CDCR) Division of Juvenile Justice in 2007 (CDCR, 2008).

Other Positive Outcomes

Not a single Missouri teen has committed suicide under DYS custody in the 20 years since Boonville closed. Lindsay Hayes, a researcher with the National Center on Institutions and Alternatives, reports that 110 youth suicides occurred nationwide in juvenile facilities from 1995 to 1999 (Mendel, 2003) and another 21 youth killed themselves in state operated juvenile training schools between 2002 and 2005 (Mumola & Noonan, 2008).

Missouri's educational outcomes are also promising. Though DYS youth are in the 26th percentile of Missouri students in reading and the 21st percentile in math, and many have not attended school regularly for year, three-fourths made more academic progress than a typical public school student in 2002 and 222 DYS youth earned their GEDs (Mendel, 2003).

Conclusions

Based on these positive outcomes, it is clear that Missouri's approach to juvenile corrections should be a model for the nation. Its success offers definitive proof that states can protect the public, rehabilitate youth, and safeguard taxpayers far better if they abandon incarceration as the core of their juvenile corrections systems. "I think it's a great system," says Barry Krisberg, president of the National Council on Crime and Delinquency. "More than any other state in the country, Missouri provides a positive, treatment oriented approach that's not punitive or prison-like" (Mendel, 2003).

Endnote

1. According to Anderson (2008), the costs to house a juvenile do not include fringe benefits of employees, most capital improve-ments/maintenance costs, most technology maintenance and up-dates, nor medical costs for youth eligible for Medicaid. Because of the differences in calculating the per diem costs, it is very difficult to accurately compare costs between jurisdictions.

Case Cited

U. S. v. Commonwealth of Kentucky, Civ. No. 3:95CV-757-S (W.D. Ky.)

References

Abrams, D. (2003). *A very special place in life: The history of juvenile justice in Missouri.* Jefferson City, MO: Missouri Juvenile Justice Association.

Altschuler, D. (1999). Trends and issues in the adultification of juvenile justice. In P. M. Harris (Ed), *Research to results: Effective community corrections,* (pp. 233-271). Lanham, MD: American Correctional Association.

Anderson, S. (2008). Personal communication.

Anderson, S. (2008a). *DSS division among 50 top programs chosen for 2008 Innovations in American Government Award.* Missouri Department of Youth Services Press Release. Retrieved May 28, 2008, from http://www.dss.missouri.gov/press/2008/041508a.htm

Ash Institute for Democratic Governance and Innovation. (2008). *Division of Youth Services, State of Missouri: Really rehabilitating juveniles.* Retrieved November 9, 2008, from http://dss.mo.gov/dys/pdf/iaga.pdf

California Department of Corrections and Rehabilitation. (2008). *Summary fact sheet.* Retrieved June 15, 2008, from http://www.cdcr.ca.gov/Reports_Research/summarys.html

CNN. (2008). *Sex abuse, violence alleged at teen jails across the United States.* Retrieved May 5, 2008, from: http://www.cnn.com/2008/CRIME/04/04/juvenile.jails/

Feld, B. (1999). *Bad kids: Race and the transformation of the juvenile court.* New York: Oxford University Press.

Florida Department of Juvenile Justice. (2003). *2003 outcome evaluation report.* Tallahassee, FL: Florida Department of Juvenile Justice.

Gregg, D. (2004). Personal communication.

Iyengar, L. (2000). *Recidivism rates for youths released in fiscal year 1997 by major programs for one, two, and three years after release.* Baltimore, MD: Department of Juvenile Justice.

Livsey, S., Sickmund, M., & Sladky, A. (2009). *Juvenile residential facility census, 2004: Selected findings.* Washington, DC: Office of Juvenile Justice and Delinquency Prevention.

Mendel, R. (2000). *Less hype, more help: Reducing juvenile crime, what works – and what doesn't.* Washington, DC: American Youth Policy Forum.

Mendel, R. (2001). *Less cost, more safety: Guiding lights for reform in juvenile justice.* Washington, DC: American Youth Policy Forum.

Mendel, R. (2003). *Small is beautiful.* Baltimore, MD: Annie E. Casey Foundation.

Mendel, R. (2004). Show & tell: Missouri's Division of Youth Services acts as a national model. *Corrections Today, 66,* 56-59.

Missouri Division of Youth Services. (2002). *Juvenile court statistics.* Jefferson City, MO: Author.

Missouri Division of Youth Services. (2003). Unpublished data provided to author.

Missouri Division of Youth Services. (2007). *Juvenile court statistics.* Jefferson City, MO: Author.

Missouri Division of Youth Services. (2008). *Education.* Retrieved November 9, 2008, from http://www.dss.mo.gov/dys/ed.htm

Mumola, C. J., & Noonan, M. E. (2008). *Deaths in custody statistical tables.* Retrieved October 6, 2008, from http://www.ojp.usdoj.gov/bjs/dcrp/dictabs.htm

Sickmund, M., Sladky, T. J., & Kang, W. (2008). *Census of juveniles in residential placement databook.* Retrieved May 31, 2008, from http://www.ojjdp.ncjrs.org/ojstatbb/cjrp/

Steward, M. (2004). Personal communication.

CHAPTER 16
AFTERCARE

Gaylene Armstrong, Bitna Kim and Rick Ruddell

E very day, staff members working in juvenile correctional facilities aim to help youth prepare for their release to the community. When these youth entered the facility, they brought a host of challenges and issues; the hope is that when the youth are discharged, they will have a new set of problem-solving, social, and communication skills to assist them in building a prosocial life that is free of delinquency. Many of the youth will have participated in educational and vocational programs and are better prepared to return to community schools or to look for jobs. Some youth will have confronted addictions or renounced gang memberships. Even a relatively short-term placement in detention can stabilize a youth's behavior, interrupt potentially disastrous problems (e.g., substance abuse), and provide some structure in their lives. Although the problems of insufficient medical and mental health care have been well documented throughout this book, many are able to get care that wasn't available in the community.

Yet, there is growing awareness that the transition from juvenile corrections to the community (also called reentry or reintegration) is a time of great uncertainty for many youth—especially for those who have been incarcerated for longer periods of time. Rates of recidivism are generally very high, especially for those youth who have been incarcerated on numerous occasions. Anecdotal accounts suggest that rates of self harm and suicide, as well as accidental death and other misadventures are also high amongst those released from correctional facilities.[1]

While we often have high expectations for the success of youth, they return to the community having to confront a number of challenges, both the ones they were faced with before their incarceration and sometimes new ones as well. Almost all youth will return to the same disadvantaged schools and neighborhoods from which they came and will continue to lack positive role models or career opportunities within these environments. In addition, most youth return to live within the same family dynamics, which often includes a parent(s) who has his or her own problems with addictions, mental health issues, unemployment, and a lack of coping or problem-solving skills. Last, youth frequently gravitate toward the same delinquent peers with whom they committed the offenses that led to their original incarcerations. Altogether, youth must confront these challenges; to do this, they need community-based supports.

The question of how to reduce the impact of environment and lifestyle hinges upon the aftercare provided to youth upon their release. Yet, while almost everybody agrees that aftercare is important for youth returning to the community, there is less agreement on how it should be managed or who should pay for continued intervention. This chapter examines some of the characteristics of aftercare programs, provides examples of programs that have reduced recidivism, and highlights an agenda for future research.

The Importance of Aftercare

Programming for juveniles emphasizing a punitive or pure supervision orientation is not likely to be successful in reducing recidivism (Altschuler & Brash, 2004; Howell, 2003; Wells, Minor, Angel, & Stearman, 2006). Many institutions provide treatment and rehabilitation programs to juvenile offenders. However, these programs are offered in an institutional setting that may do little to help juvenile offenders integrate into the communities the lessons learned during incarceration (Kurlychek & Kempinen, 2006; Travis, 2000).

During the past decade, increasing interest developed in aftercare services for juvenile offenders has led to the broad based implementation of aftercare programs across the country (Kurlychek & Kempinen, 2006; Wells et al., 2006). Supporters of these programs believe that aftercare provisions may hold the key to the effective reentry of juvenile delinquents and significant reduction of subsequent recidivism levels (Anderson, Dyson, & Burns, 1999; Meisel, 2001). Aftercare programs aim to provide services and supervision that assist juveniles who are released from out-of-home placements in effectively reintegrating into their communities. Often, this is done though establishing collaborative linkages with the full range of public and/or private sector organizations and individuals in the community (Altschuler & Armstrong, 2001; Gies, 2003; Kurlychek & Kempinen, 2006; Wells et al., 2006).

Aftercare programs are differentiated from traditional post release programs in that the primary concern of aftercare is the rehabilitative or continuity of care philosophy of justice, whereas juvenile parole is primarily concerned with crime control and public protection (Meisel, 2001). In practice and in theory, aftercare is concerned with incorporation of a broad range of services and intensive intervention that begins before release; it continues after the youth is released into the community (Gies, 2003). In comparison, parole tends to focus primarily on supervising offender behavior in order to protect the public from crimes committed by the youth.

All of the youth adjudicated in a juvenile court will eventually return to the community. Whether that youth's disposition will last a month or a more lengthy stay through their 21st birthday, planning for their release to the community is a key component of the case management process. Case management, as highlighted in Chapters 13 and 15, involves the setting of rehabilitative goals that a youth will work toward during his or her stay in a residential setting. A resident and his or her case manager will examine the youth's criminal history, patterns of offending, the information reported in predisposition reports (PDRs), needs assessments (instruments that identify a youth's treatment needs), and psychological assessments. From that information, they will establish a set of rehabilitative goals.

The rehabilitative goals that a youth establishes typically centered upon upgrading his or her education, working toward a general equivalency diploma (GED), career preparation (e.g., vocational courses), or addressing substance abuse. In some cases, the rehabilitative goals might be directly related to the offense(s) that was committed. Sex offender treatment, for instance, is commonly delivered in secure settings; many larger facilities have specific living units for juvenile sex offenders (Underwood, Robinson, Mosholder, & Warren, 2008).

Some youths' educational skills are so poor that they have to start with basic literacy and numeracy. Furthermore, most case managers will work with youth on their social skills, including anger management, skills streaming (where appropriate behaviors are demonstrated and practiced by the residents), and addressing areas of basic living such as developing good hygiene.

Today, there is also growing awareness that the youth's pro-criminal, anti-social, or criminogenic thinking must also be targeted. Bonta and Andrews (2007) highlighted a number of areas to be addressed, including:

- Antisocial personality pattern (Impulsive pleasure seeking behaviors);
- Pro-criminal attitudes (Rationalizations that support crime);
- Social supports for crime (Criminal friends and isolation from prosocial others);
- Substance abuse;
- Family/marital relationships (Inappropriate parental monitoring and disciplining);
- School/work (Poor performance and low levels of satisfaction); and
- Prosocial recreational activities. (p. 6)

In order to address some of these anti-social attitudes, some juvenile facilities, for example, have offered moral reconation therapy, reasoning and rehabilitation, and cognitive behavioral approaches. Wilson, Bouffard, and MacKenzie (2005) found that these programs were effective at reducing future criminal behavior.

All of this suggests that there has been a movement to provide more holistic services that address all of the youth's needs. It is pointless, for instance, to provide interventions that address a youth's pro-criminal attitudes if they have unmet needs for a chronic physical health problem such as diabetes and a diagnosis of attention deficit hyperactivity disorder. All of these needs must be addressed and often the youth finds it difficult to see how their physical, mental health, and other challenges are related to his or her delinquent behaviors. While work generally starts on responding to these deficiencies during correctional placement, once the resident leaves a facility, the treatment often stops.

As a result, there is now a growing recognition that a youth's work toward his or her rehabilitation does not end when he or she is released from a residential placement. This brings us to the challenge of aftercare; the following section addresses the different types of aftercare.

Forms of Aftercare

The type of aftercare that a youth receives will be a product of the jurisdiction where he or she was incarcerated and the type of placement where he or she was held. Some jurisdictions offer very little aftercare or reentry services. Historically, for example, no facilities provided aftercare for detention, but some jurisdictions have introduced reentry planning for these youth. Residents who served long terms of incarceration in a training school tended to receive higher levels of community supervision. Last, residents of boot camps may have received comparatively more supervision—at least in later generation operations—because aftercare was considered integral to the intervention.

In Chapter 6, the hazards of placing a youth in a detention facility were addressed. There is growing recognition that the longer a resident is placed in these facilities, the greater his or her needs for reentry planning and services. MacDonald, Mitchell, and Moeser (2007) reported that aftercare can fulfill the following goals:

- Maintaining continuity in educational programming;
- Supporting continuity of communication with other juvenile justice programs and services;
- Including, involving, and respecting the family and other significant relationships as partners in the ultimate goal of successful reentry; and

- Gathering and disseminating information that can be used by those involved in the case planning for a youth. (p. 68)

Such goals are based on two principles: (a) to reduce the disruptions in the youth's life (e.g., by ensuring continuity of his or her community schooling and appointments for medical or psychological services) and (b) gathering information and building relationships that support the case management process.

One challenge of providing aftercare is that detention services are not typically treatment oriented; instead, these agencies are charged with providing supervision until a youth's court appearances are completed. Because of this, local policy makers are often hesitant to provide much funding for rehabilitative services for these youth. This is, however, a short-sighted approach and detention should be viewed as part of the entire juvenile justice continuum (MacDonald, Mitchell, & Moeser, 2007).

Most of the aftercare literature focuses on youth being released from longer-term placements. As these youth are typically adjudicated on more serious offenses, have a greater number of problems, and have been away from the community for a longer amount of time, their transition to the community tends to be more problematic. As described above, the case management process attempts to identify and target their needs and risks. Yet, many of these youth find themselves with few community supports when they return home.

Bouffard and Bergseth (2008), for example, identified two dominant aftercare approaches, the Intensive Aftercare Program and Serious and Violent Offender Reentry Initiative, noting that:

> Each model calls for the coordination of case management and rehabilitative/reintegrative services over (a) an institutional or prerelease planning and services phase, (b) a reentry preparation or short term post release phase, and (c) a community-based services phase after release from placement. (p. 296)

Most aftercare services require that juvenile offenders first be placed in intensive supervision programs and then gradually moved toward regular supervision until their dispositions or sentences are served (Anderson et al., 1999). In some jurisdictions, a juvenile may receive a vast array of aftercare services including formal needs assessments, orientation to the community, involvement of families and the parole agent, cognitive behavior therapy, substance abuse treatment, drug and alcohol follow-up services, job training, job placement, education, housing assistance, problem-solving skills, anger management, psychiatric services, antisocial peer association counseling, medical services, and life skills counseling (Anderson et al., 1999; Baltodano et al., 2005; Kurlychek & Kempinen, 2006).

Effective aftercare requires a continuum of community services to prevent the recurrence of antisocial behavior; it can involve public-private partnerships to expand the overall capacity of youth services (Gies, 2003). Despite the fact that aftercare has shown promising results in reducing recidivism, many jurisdictions have failed to support youth in their return to the community. The cost of providing such services is often a barrier in many jurisdictions. Griffin (2004), for instance, reported that an intensive aftercare program in Pennsylvania cost between $6,000 and $7,000 for every participant. Even though such services are expensive, they are a short-term expense; the long-term savings in terms of reduced crime, the costs to victims, and less need for institutionalization are much greater. Cohen and Piquero (2009), for instance, calculated the benefits of preventing further delinquency, reporting that the monetary value of saving a high-risk 14-year old from a life of crime was $2.6 to 5.3 million (p. 25).

Aftercare programs also provide supervision to youth upon release and the levels of surveillance may vary significantly (Chung, Schubert, & Mulvey, 2008). As a result, some aftercare programs that emphasize intensive supervision may fail to provide an adequate amount or dosage of intensive services (Anderson et al., 1999). Maruna and LeBel (2003) noted that deficit based practice, which emphasizes an ex-convict's problems, has often been applied in juvenile settings. There is increasing interest, however, in building on the strengths of the youth, rather than focusing on his or her weaknesses.

Barton (2006) has advocated for juvenile justice policies and practices, including aftercare, which focus on strengths within the offender, family, or communities. The strengths perspective places more focus on the steps that juvenile offenders can take to make amends and a contribution to the community, rather than on what must be done to supervise and control their behavior (Barton, 2006; Saleebey, 2002). Barton (2006) also suggested that the incorporation of a strengths based approach to intensive juvenile aftercare programs has the potential to engage youth in actively adopting prosocial roles in their communities, to connect them to supports in communities, thus reducing the likelihood of recidivism.

On release to aftercare services, the responsibility of monitoring these youth shifts from correctional institutions to the departments of parole and probation, although there can be differences between jurisdictions. In some states, for instance, the probation officer who prepared the initial predisposition report may work for a county; the facility case manager and parole agents who supervise the youth in the community might work for the state government. In their studies, Bourque, Han, and Hill (1996) discovered that there is often little or no communication between these agencies. The overall effectiveness of aftercare provision depends on constant and effective communication between agencies involved in the process (Anderson et al., 1999; Bourque et al., 1996).

Incorporating Aftercare: Examples from the Boot Camp Literature

The authors of Chapter 5 described how juvenile boot camp programs gradually disappeared. These interventions, however, are important to acknowledge because aftercare is frequently incorporated into these programs. The newest generations of juvenile boot camp programs implemented aftercare components to supplement the boot camp experience of juvenile participants with the goal of increasing offender accountability and decreasing recidivism. Researchers have compared the recidivism levels of juvenile boot camp graduates who participated in a systematic aftercare phase to the recidivism of a matched control group of juvenile graduates receiving standard custody or traditional parole. Overall, evaluation research conducted to date demonstrates the importance of subsequent quality aftercare provisions for boot camp graduates (Kurlychek & Kempinen, 2006; MacKenzie, 2006; Wells et al., 2006).

The studies reported above show that juvenile boot camps have generally failed to reduce recidivism, except for the boot camps followed by enhanced aftercare components (Bottcher & Ezell, 2005; MacKenzie, 2006; Kurlychek & Kempinen, 2006; Lutze, 2006; Tyler, Darville, & Stalnaker, 2001; Stinchcomb & Terry, 2001; Wells et al., 2006). For example, measuring the recidivism effects of juvenile boot camp placement with and without aftercare programs, Kurlychek and Kempinen (2006) found that participation in boot camp followed by quality aftercare services both reduces the overall risk of recidivism and, for those who do recidivate, lengthens the time to failure as compared to participating in boot camp followed by traditional parole. While the addition of an aftercare component appears to elevate boot camps to a promising strategy, additional research suggests that even relatively well developed juvenile boot camps followed by an intensive aftercare program are unlikely to reduce recidivism rates among participants if the aftercare intervention is only short term—or if aftercare provisions do not focus on individual needs or provide intensive treatment services (Bottcher & Ezell, 2005; Wells et al., 2006).

Challenges in Providing Aftercare Services

Despite the fact that research has demonstrated that aftercare is a key component in reducing recidivism, numerous challenges need to be overcome, including the youth's educational and housing needs, health care, and ensuring continuity of care from the institution to the community. As highlighted in the previous paragraphs, many of these challenges ultimately come down to funding and who will assume responsibility for the costs of helping youth in their transitions back to the community. In an era of shrinking budgets, however, these questions become very problematic.

In terms of correctional health, for instance, it is often difficult to maintain treatment for the juvenile in the community. While the youth is incarcerated it is relatively easy to make sure that he or she will attend his or her medical or mental health appointments, guarantee that his or her medications are being taken according to the physician's instructions, and since the youth was in the care of the state, there was little debate about who would pay for these services. Once he or she is released into the community, however, these factors become significant barriers.

Youth in rural communities, for example, might find it difficult to travel to the city to attend an appointment with a mental health professional or a physician. Other youth may fail to show up for these meetings, especially if they were not enthusiastic about receiving care in the first place. While parents are supposed to support these youth and ensure that such appointments are kept, they are not always reliable.

Another significant problem is ensuring that youth continue to take the medications that were prescribed. When facilities discharge a youth, they often give enough prescription medications for a few days. This places the responsibility upon the youth for refilling prescriptions. Most of these parolees have no health insurance. Gupta and colleagues (2005) noted:

> Although Medicaid is the most likely source of insurance for health coverage after release, enrollment in Medicaid is often terminated...Thus, youth leaving correctional facilities on parole are often uninsured and not eligible for immediate benefits. (p. 1079)

As a result it might be difficult for a youth to obtain medications. Even if youth do have an adequate supply of medications, he or she might not take them according to the prescription; or, in the case of psychotropic medications such as Ritalin (commonly prescribed for attention deficit hyperactivity disorder), youth might sell them. In some cases, the parents might use their children's medications for recreational use. These challenges are greater if youth are in independent living situations or their parents are unreliable.

This leads to the issue of providing an appropriate residential placement once the youth is released from a facility. While most youth want to live with their mothers and fathers, this is not always possible nor is it in their best interests. Sometimes, their parents are deceased, separated or divorced, incarcerated, detached, or too dysfunctional to provide a stable home setting. Furthermore, some youth (particularly sex offenders) may not be able to live within the same residence as their victims, which might exclude them from returning home. Thus, finding an appropriate place for a youth to reside upon release is often very challenging.

Often youth who cannot live with their parents stay with extended family members such as grandparents. Yet, this is also problematic because some of these family members cannot provide proper supervision. While independent living is an option for some older youth, this is often a last resort because there are few supports with those arrangements and most juveniles lack the financial resources to live independently. As a result, some youth go into group or foster homes. Ultimately, however, research shows that youth who have unstable post incarceration placements are at higher risk of recidivism (Baltodano, Platt, & Roberts, 2005).

Chapter 14 highlighted the challenges of ensuring the continuity of educational services for youth leaving correctional facilities. Many community schools, it was noted, are not enthusiastic about having these youth return. But, it is important to acknowledge that students who are eligible for services under the Individuals with Disabilities Education Improvement Act must receive transitional services (Morris & Thompson, 2008). Despite this mandate, Baltodano, Platt, and Roberts (2005) found that the following barriers existed: insufficient resources or personnel, a lack of clear guidelines and responsibilities for transition, and the fact that "no single agency is responsible for providing transition records or services" (p. 375).

In the case of detained youth who were away from the community for only a few weeks, teachers or case workers in detention facilities could ensure that their schoolwork was being done. For youth returning from a long period of incarceration, by contrast, these transitions are more difficult, especially if the schools within the actual institutions do not meet the needs of the youth (Cohen, 2008). As Baltodano and colleagues (2005) noted:

> It is imperative that secure care facilities, public schools, families, and others charged with assisting youth transition to the community include the youth in developing their individualized transition plans and include them at all stages of the transition process. By doing so, youth are more likely

> to be successful upon their return to home, school, employ-
> ment, and the community. (p. 386)

Since most youth who have been in long-term placements do not finish their high school education, providing them with vocational training prior to their release may be an important component of their release plans (Mears & Travis, 2004).

Juveniles who are returning to the community must also find ways to constructively use their leisure time. This factor is shaped somewhat by their living arrangements, whether they are working or attending school, and their neighborhoods. As mentioned earlier, most youth return to their home communities and are often welcomed back by delinquent peers and shunned by youth with more conventional values. Yet, we know that the likelihood of recidivism increases if these youth are spending more time with delinquents; this risk increases substantially if their associates are gang members.

Altschuler and Brash (2004) noted that the importance of leisure time and recreational interests are often overlooked (p. 83), especially given that many of these youth have spent a considerable amount of their adolescence incarcerated and might not know how to constructively use their time. Furthermore, many of these youth have long histories of substance abuse and "drinking and drugging" was how they passed their time. As a result, providing youth with healthy and constructive alternatives to idle time is seen as an important element in reentry planning.

Another significant challenge is the lack of integrated facility-community case management services. In many jurisdictions, an incarcerated youth might have a facility case manager and may not meet their community parole officer or agent until their release or shortly before their community reentry. In some cases, youth can get lost in the shuffle because they are transferred between facilities and then into the community. Furthermore, as staff turnover in facilities is often high, the youth might have a number of facility case managers before being released. As a result of these limitations, some jurisdictions are providing integrated case management services, in which one case manager helps with the youth's case management needs while they are incarcerated and when they return to the community.

One advantage of an integrated case management approach is that it enables the youth and the case manager to establish a long-term relationship. Additionally, as the case manager has an understanding of the services and resources in both the community and the facilities, they may be able to be more effective at helping the youth access these supports. Mendel (2003, see also Chapter 15) described how the Missouri Department of Youth Services has used this approach with considerable success.

Altogether, there are many challenges confronting those who want to implement effective aftercare programs. While some of these approaches appear to be working, there is increasing interest in using research to demonstrate the effectiveness of criminal justice interventions, including aftercare. The following pages outline several considerations in establishing a research agenda for aftercare.

Establishing a Research Agenda

There are a number of challenges with research into the effectiveness of aftercare. Bouffard and Bergseth (2008) reported that "research on juvenile aftercare has been plagued by a predominance of null findings for program effect, as well as small sample sizes, implementation difficulties, and little consistency in program implementation and/or evaluation methodology" (p. 297). Research on recidivism often fails to establish clear findings about the effectiveness of aftercare programs. For instance, it may be hard to disentangle the different impacts of: (a) the quality of the rehabilitation programs within residential placements, (b) the differential risks of the youth returning to the community, and (c) the effectiveness of the aftercare program.

One of the challenges with correctional research is programs that are said to exist—and that youth have graduated from—are sometimes less rigorous than was intended by the persons who developed the programs. This is the problem or challenge of program fidelity. Urban (2008) observed how "failing to adhere to the original plan, original dose, or original philosophy has resulted in failure to reach goals in multiple circumstances" (p. 100). Practitioners delivering an intervention may adapt it to the needs of their operation, limit services in response to excessive costs, or tailor a program to a special needs population. In addition, programs may be implemented without adhering to the original design and the staff members may not receive the proper training. All of these factors illustrate the challenge of ensuring program fidelity—that the intervention delivered is actually what the developers of the program intended (Aos, Lieb, Mayfield, Miller, & Pennucci, 2004).

MacKenzie and Armstrong (2004) observed that the programmatic philosophies and service delivery strategies of aftercare programs vary significantly. In other words, jurisdictions may implement different aftercare models. It is important to investigate these diverse models to determine which type of aftercare programs or components of the programs are more effective in reducing recidivism (Kurlychek & Kempinen, 2006; MacKenzie, 2006).

One of the factors that juvenile justice systems have historically overlooked is the issue of gender differences and whether approaches such as aftercare are more successful with females. Previous studies have indicated that gender differences exist in the manner in which juveniles are processed and treated within the juvenile justice system (Belknap, Holsinger, & Dunn, 1997; Chesney-Lind & Shelden, 2004). These differences could be present in aftercare services as well. Meisel (2001) suggests that the impact of aftercare components may vary by gender. In recognition that there are gender differences in the types of services that offenders need as they return to the community, the National Institute of Corrections has developed gender responsive approaches for aftercare. Berman (2005) highlighted how the special needs of women were taken into account in the development of the transitioning from prison to the community (TPC) model. While there is no evidence that this model is currently being used for juvenile offenders, such approaches might prove fruitful.

In addition to our lack of knowledge about the success of females returning to the community, to date there is little information about the effectiveness of aftercare programs for minority youth (Vaughn, Wallace, Davis, Fernandes, & Howard, 2008). One factor that policy makers and researchers have to consider, however, is that it is often very difficult to determine whether the differences in programs are ultimately responsible for differential outcomes based on gender or race (e.g., some programs may be more effective than others). As a result, additional research on these interventions is needed.

Conclusions

It has long been recognized that aftercare is an important component of residential services for youth. In 1917, Alan Philips wrote that:

> Surely that the state sins when it turns a homeless and jobless boy out of an institution with no place to go, often, but to a broken home, and nothing to do, often, but to loaf. A safe conclusion is that the problem of juvenile delinquency will never be solved only through and by the means of an institution. Protective social agencies must extend themselves into the field, and must give help to the boy before delinquency ever comes, or after delinquency has received correction. (p. 272)

What is striking about that observation is that in the past 90 years, many jurisdictions still have not yet adopted comprehensive, long-term aftercare programs. In some places, aftercare exists, but most of the resources are channeled into supervision and surveillance. In order to provide quality aftercare, it is important to assure that adequate community resources and service linkages are allocated or exist within aftercare programs (Anderson et al., 1999).

An additional challenge facing the juvenile justice system is a growing number of female juvenile offenders in custody (Bloom, Owen, Deschenes, & Rosenbaum, 2002; Budnick & Shields-Fletcher, 1998). One problem, however, is that little or no consideration of developing and funding gender specific aftercare services has occurred (Bloom et al., 2002; see also Chapter 8). The need to develop and implement appropriate gender based aftercare services for females that address their distinct needs and the complex issues faced by this population should be a priority (Bloom et al., 2002; Budnick & Shields-Fletcher, 1998).

Endnote

1. Studies of juvenile offenders released from correctional facilities show high rates of mortality (Teplin, McClelland, Abram, & Mileusnic, 2005).

References

Altschuler, D. M., & Armstrong, T. L. (2001). Reintegrating high risk juvenile offenders into communities: Experiences and prospects. *Corrections Management Quarterly, 5*(1), 79-95.

Altschuler, D. M., & Brash, R. (2004). Adolescent and teenage offender confronting the challenges and opportunities of reentry. *Youth Violence and Juvenile Justice, 2,* 72-87.

Anderson, J. F., Dyson, L., & Burns, J. (1999). *Boot camps: An intermediate sanction.* New York: University Press of America.

Aos, S., Lieb, R., Mayfield, J., Miller, M., & Pennucci, A. (2004). *Benefits and costs of prevention and early intervention programs for youth.* Olympia, WA: Washington State Institute for Public Policy.

Baltodano, H. M., Platt, D., & Roberts, C. W. (2005). Transition from secure care to the community: Significant issues for youth in detention. *Journal of Correctional Education, 56*(4), 372-388.

Barton, W. H. (2006). Incorporating the strengths perspective into intensive juvenile aftercare. *Western Criminology Review, 7*(2), 48-61.

Belknap, J., Holsinger, K., & Dunn, M. (1997). Understanding incarcerated girls: The results of a focus group study. *The Prison Journal, 77*(4), 381-404.

Berman, J. (2005). *Women offender transition and reentry: Gender responsive approaches to transitioning women offenders from prison to the community.* Retrieved November 9, 2008, from http://nicic.org/Downloads/PDF/Library/021815.pdf

Bloom, B., Owen, B., Deschenes, E. P., & Rosenbaum, J. (2002). Moving toward justice for female juvenile offenders in the new millennium: Modeling gender-specific policies and programs. *Journal of Contemporary Criminal Justice, 18*(1), 37-56.

Bonta, J., & Andrews, D. A. (2007). *Risk-need-responsivity model for offender assessment and rehabilitation.* Retrieved October 25, 2008, from http://www.ps-sp.gc.ca/res/cor/rep/_fl/Risk_Need_2007-06_e.pdf

Bottcher, J., & Ezell, M. (2005). Examining the effectiveness of boot camps: A randomized experiment with a long-term follow up. *Journal of Research in Crime and Delinquency, 42*(3), 309-332.

Bouffard, J. A., & Bergseth, K. J. (2008). The impact of reentry services on juvenile offenders' recidivism. *Youth Violence and Juvenile Justice, 6,* 295-318.

Bourque, B., Han, M., & Hill, S. M. (1996). *A national survey of aftercare provisions for boot camp graduates.* Washington, DC: National Institute of Justice.

Budnick, K. J., & Shields-Fletcher, E. (1998). *What about girls?* Washington, DC: Office of Juvenile Justice and Delinquency Prevention.

Chesney-Lind, M., & Shelden, R. (2004). *Girls, delinquency, and juvenile justice.* Pacific Grove, CA: Brooks/Cole.

Chung, H. L., Schubert, C. A., & Mulvey, E. P. (2008). An empirical portrait of community reentry among serious juvenile offenders in two metropolitan cities. *Criminal Justice and Behavior, 11,* 1402-1426.

Cohen, F. (2008). *Final fact-finding report: S.H. v. Stickrath.* Retrieved January 22, 2008, from http://www.dys.ohio.gov

Cohen, M. A., & Piquero, A. R. (2009). New evidence on the monetary value of saving a high risk youth. *Journal of Quantitative Criminology, 25,* 25-49.

Gies, S. V. (2003). *Aftercare services.* Washington, DC: Office of Juvenile Justice and Delinquency Prevention.

Griffin, P. (2004). *Aftercare: The sequel.* Retrieved October 26, 2008, from http://www.pccd.state.pa.us/pccd/lib/pccd/pubs/progress/progressdecember2004.pdf

Gupta, R. A., Kelleher, K. J., Pajer, K., Stevens, J., & Cuellar, A. (2005). Delinquent youth in corrections: Medicaid and reentry into the community. *Pediatrics, 115,* 1077-1083.

Howell, J. C. (2003). *Preventing & reducing juvenile delinquency: A comprehensive framework.* Thousand Oaks, CA: Sage.

Kurlychek, M. C., & Kempinen, C. (2006). Beyond boot camp: The impact of aftercare on offender reentry. *Criminology & Public Policy, 5*(2), 363-388.

Lutze, F. E. (2006). Boot camp prisons and corrections policy: Moving from militarism to an ethic of care. *Criminology & Public Policy, 5*(2), 389-400.

MacDonald, S., Mitchell, D. E., & Moeser, J. (2007). Defining reentry for short-term stays. In C. Rapp Zimmerman, G. Hendrix, J. Moeser, & D. W. Roush, (Eds.), *Desktop guide to reentry for juvenile confinement facilities,* (pp. 65-77). Annapolis, MD: American Correctional Association.

MacKenzie, D. L. (2006). Aftercare following a correctional bootcamp may reduce recidivism. *Criminology & Public Policy. 5*(2), 359-362.

MacKenzie, D. L., & Armstrong, G. S. (2004). *Correctional boot camps: Military basic training or a model for corrections?* Thousand Oaks, CA: Sage Publishers.

Maruna, S., & LeBel, T. P. (2003). Welcome home? Examining the "Reentry Court" concept from a strengths-based perspective. *Western Criminology Review, 4*(2), 1-17.

Mears, D. P., & Travis, J. (2004). *The dimensions, pathways, and consequences of youth reentry.* Washington, DC: Urban Institute.

Meisel, J. S. (2001). Relationships and juvenile offenders: The effects of intensive aftercare supervision. *The Prison Journal, 81*(2), 206-245.

Mendel, R. (2003). *Small is beautiful.* Baltimore, MD: Annie E. Casey Foundation.

Morris, R. J., & Thompson, K. C. (2008). Juvenile delinquency and special education laws: Policy implementation issues and directions for future research. *The Journal of Correctional Education, 59*, 173-188.

Phillips, A. A. (1917). A study of the after-career of 408 delinquent boys who were committed from the King County (Washington) juvenile court to the boys' parental school and the state training school during the five-year period 1911-1915. *Journal of the American Institute of Criminal Law and Criminology, 8*, 270-272.

Saleebey, D. (2002). *The strengths perspective in social work practice.* Boston: Allyn & Bacon.

Stinchcomb, J. B., & Terry, W. C. (2001). Predicting the likelihood of rearrest among shock incarceration graduates: Moving beyond another nail in the boot camp coffin. *Crime & Delinquency, 47*(2), 221-242.

Teplin, L. A., McClelland, G. M., Abram, K. M., & Mileusnic, D. (2005). Early violent death among delinquent youth: A prospective longitudinal study. *Pediatrics, 115*, 1586-1593.

Travis, J. (2000). *But they all come back: Rethinking prisoner reentry.* Washington, DC: National Institute of Justice.

Tyler, J., Darville, R., & Stalnaker, K. (2001). Juvenile boot camps: A descriptive analysis of program diversity and effectiveness. *Social Science Journal, 38*, 455-471.

Underwood, L. A., Robinson, S. B., Mosholder, E., & Warren, K. M. (2008). Sex offender care for adolescents in secure Care: Critical factors and counseling strategies. *Clinical Psychology Review, 28*, 917-932.

Urban, L. S. (2008). Issues in juvenile program implementation: A case study. *American Journal of Criminal Justice, 33*, 99-112.

Vaughn, M. G., Wallace, J. M., Davis, L. E., Fernandes, G. T., & Howard, M. O. (2008). Variations in mental health problems, substance use, and delinquency African American and Caucasian juvenile offenders: Implications for reentry services. *International Journal of Offender Therapy and Comparative Criminology, 52*, 311-329.

Wells, J. B., Minor, K. I., Angel, E., & Stearman, K. D. (2006). A quasi-experimental evaluation of a shock incarceration and aftercare program for juvenile offenders. *Youth Violence and Juvenile Justice, 4*(3), 219-233.

Wilson, D. B., Bouffard, L. A., & MacKenzie, D. L. (2005). A quantitative review of structured, group-oriented, cognitive-behavioral programs for offenders. *Criminal Justice and Behavior, 32*, 172-204.

CHAPTER 17
ENSURING ACCOUNTABILITY

Rick Ruddell

T hus far, the contributors to this book have identified a series of challenges associated with incarcerating juveniles in community-based settings (such as therapeutic foster homes, wilderness or challenge programs, and boot camps) and institutional corrections. In some of these operations, there is very little oversight or regulation: private individuals or corporations run these programs with no state funding, so they can operate as they desire (U. S. Government Accountability Office, 2007). State and locally operated facilities, by contrast, are now subject to higher levels of scrutiny from the courts, regulatory bodies, advocacy groups, and the media. This chapter examines how juvenile correctional administrators have become more accountable for their operations.

If a facility is effectively managed, the likelihood of illegal, unethical, or other undesirable conduct is decreased. As a result, managers are the first line of defense to follow the vision and mission of the organization and to ensure that staff members are held accountable for their actions. Research has demonstrated that juvenile correctional administrators tend to have a much greater interest in the rehabilitation of the youth in their care compared to their adult counterparts (Caeti, Hemmens, Cullen, & Burton, 2003). Yet, despite the fact that there are professional, well motivated, and dedicated facility superintendents, directors, or other managers does not guarantee that a facility will operate without problems.

There are hundreds of short- and long-term residential placements within the United States, ranging in size from those holding a dozen or so youth in a community-based program to facilities that hold hundreds. Each type of facility has its own set of challenges, but this chapter focuses primarily upon secure placements. Superintendents in these facilities require a broad set of knowledge, skills, and abilities in order to successfully lead hundreds of employees and manage multi-million dollar budgets while ensuring a safe and secure environment. Making the job even more challenging are increasing expectations for rehabilitation; greater numbers of difficult-to-manage residents; the challenge of recruiting, training, and retaining staff; and accomplishing these tasks in an era of diminishing budgets.

Similar to other leadership positions, the role of superintendent is strongly influenced by changes in the internal and external environments. In some cases, the goals of the employer may be in sharp contrast to the positions of community activists, residents' families, attorneys, the local providers of health and educational services (e.g., mental health services or community schools), and other stakeholders. Furthermore, given the prospects of litigation, the activities of unions or associations of correctional officers, and the media, superintendents have come under increasing scrutiny. Kaftan (2007) noted, "superintendents operate in highly political and complex environments" (p. 1-1). The complexity of leading a juvenile correctional facility is enhanced by the fact that many jurisdictions are operating with budget restrictions and all managers are being asked to "do more with less."

The first part of this chapter examines correctional litigation and how lawsuits have shaped the operations of juvenile corrections. The second component explores different methods of improving accountability and performance in juvenile correctional facilities. Many jurisdictions, for example, have introduced Ombudsman or Children's Advocacy units to give youth a voice without having to resort to the courts. According to Puritz and Scali (1998), "Ombudsmen can monitor conditions and service delivery systems, investigate complaints, report findings, propose changes, advocate for improvements, access appropriate care, and help to expose and reduce unlawful deficiencies in juvenile detention and correctional facilities" (p. 9). One positive aspect of these programs is that they teach youth how to bring up issues in a constructive and positive manner; the interventions of the Ombudsmen or Children's Advocate occur much quicker than litigation, which may take months or years before an issue is resolved.

Other agencies have undertaken a different approach in order to increase their accountability. Many state juvenile corrections systems, for example, are undergoing voluntary accreditation with bodies such as the American Correctional Association (ACA) or the National Commission on Correctional Health Care (NCCHC). Abiding by national-level standards is one way of demonstrating that the agency is concerned about the treatment of their residents.

This chapter ends with an introduction of a promising method of improving the accountability and effectiveness of juvenile correctional institutions through performance monitoring. Use of Performance-based Standards (PbS), introduced by the Council of Juvenile Correctional Administrators (CJCA), enables an agency's manager to increase both efficiency and accountability by using data that is collected about key institutional goals such as security, safety, education, and health care. This system also enables correctional managers to compare their facility operations with national-level averages. Moreover, there are supports built into this system so that juvenile detention or training school superintendents can learn from other jurisdictions. This approach has been championed as a way of increasing accountability and the conditions of confinement (Loughran, 2007).

Accountability in Juvenile Corrections

The Impact of Litigation on Juvenile Corrections

When a juvenile or adult is taken into custody, detained prior to their court dates, or sentenced to a term of incarceration, local or state governments assume responsibility for their care. Our contributors have highlighted the fact that there are clear standards for complying with standards of health care, access to education, and compliance with legislation such as the Americans with Disabilities Act (ADA). These requirements have placed significant demands on residential programs. This was not, however, always the case. The courts had historically taken a "hands-off" approach to correctional populations — meaning that they were reluctant to become involved in the correctional treatment of juveniles or adults. The *Ruffin v. Commonwealth* decision of the Virginia Supreme Court in 1871, for instance, defined prisoners as slaves of the state with no constitutional or legal rights or forum to raise grievances except what correctional systems decided to provide. This decision shaped correctional care for almost 100 years because it signaled the court's reluctance to be involved in the day-to-day operations of correctional facilities.

For the most part, the history of juvenile corrections leaves much to be desired. Many juveniles who were temporarily detained were held in adult jails, especially in rural counties that did not have separate juvenile halls. Jail inspectors such as Joseph Fishman (1923) documented the abuses that these youth experienced when mixed with adult offenders in local jails. Not only were these youth exposed to the negative influences of older and sophisticated offenders, but they were also physically, emotionally, and sexually abused (MacCormack, 1949) and at very high risk of suicide or self-harm (Schwartz, 1989).

The *Ex parte Hull* decision of the Supreme Court in 1941 granted adult prisoners access to the courts. However, they had little success getting cases into the federal courts prior to the *Cooper v. Pate* decision in 1964 that declared that jail or prison inmates could seek redress or damages if their rights were violated due to correctional policies or the actions of individual officers under Title 42, Section 1983, of the Civil Rights Act of 1871. These cases, often called Section 1983 lawsuits, can be brought directly before the courts and are applicable to juvenile corrections. Section 1983 lawsuits allege that the staff members within a correctional facility have violated the civil rights of a juvenile, although in most juvenile cases, a lawsuit is filed on behalf of all residents within a detention facility or the juvenile correctional system. Some of these lawsuits seek damages, while most seek some type of remedy, such as a change in policy.

The *Pate* decision occurred at about the same time as the due process revolution in the juvenile court with decisions such as *Kent v. U.S.* (1966) and *In re Gault* (1967) that provided more due process protections for juveniles.[1] There was broad recognition that the rights of juveniles who became involved with the police, courts, or corrections were often disregarded or ignored. Soler (1988) noted that there was a "flood of civil rights litigation on behalf of inmates in prisons and jails" (p. 194). Soler provided a history of cases that specifically related to the removal of juveniles from adult jails, but he also observed that many of the juvenile cases that came before the courts were initiated as class action lawsuits, which are on behalf of all youth in a correctional system. Support for these lawsuits became more aggressive since 1976, when the losing party was responsible for paying the attorney's fees. Soler (1988) observed that "the new statute provided a strong fiscal incentive to attorneys to bring actions on behalf of jailed children" (p. 198).

While some of these juvenile cases were resolved through the award of monetary damages, in most juvenile cases, attorneys sued on behalf of all residents to improve the living conditions within a specific facility or the entire system. Since the 1970s, many correctional administrators (and their attorneys) have entered into court supervised consent decrees where they agreed to remedy the problem(s) that led to the litigation. Current examples, mentioned in Chapter 1, include the California Department of Corrections and Rehabilitation's Division of Juvenile Justice (*Farrell v. Tilton*) and the Ohio Department of Youth Services (*S.H. v. Stickrath*). Both of these state correctional agencies entered into court monitored agreements to respond to the specific concerns brought up in the litigation. In these cases, advocacy groups, rather than individual attorneys, initiated these lawsuits on behalf of all youth residing within these systems. The Youth Law Center, for example, represents youth held in the Ohio Department of Youth Services and they have acted on behalf of juveniles in 63 cases, from 19 states, Washington D. C., and the U. S. Virgin Islands (Youth Law Center, 2009). In California, by contrast, the Prison Law Office represents the youth placed in the Division of Juvenile Justice. Since the attorneys working within these organizations have such extensive experience in these cases, they are more likely to ensure that agreements are carried out.

In lawsuits involving an entire youth correctional system where it would be difficult to determine whether changes were actually occurring, a special master is sometimes appointed by the court to ensure that the terms of these agreements are being upheld. In the California litigation, the special master produces a lengthy quarterly report (in February 2009, it was 220 pages long including appendices) detailing the progress that the Division of Juvenile Justice has made in resolving the problems identified in the litigation. There have been cases where correctional officials have been held in contempt of court if federal judges felt that they were failing to carry out the conditions outlined in the decree (Sturm, 1993).

A review of the actual court documents shows that in some of the cases where litigation involves entire juvenile correctional systems, there is a common set of problems. In the *S.H. v. Stickrath* case in Ohio, for instance, the report of a consultant detailed dozens of deficiencies (Cohen, 2008), but they centered on a smaller number of key issues: providing a safe environment (including the excessive use of force on residents and the overuse of isolation); access to mental, dental, and physical health care; offering more comprehensive educational programs; the development of a better resident grievance system; and changes to the disciplinary systems. In the California case, the most significant issues in that lawsuit related to general conditions (safety, staff use of force, and use of segregation), access to health care, sex offender treatment programming, complying with the Americans with Disabilities Act, education, and mental health care and substance abuse treatment. Overall, there appear to be more similarities than differences in the needs of youth incarcerated in these two states. Regardless of the reasons, however, litigation is expensive and some juvenile correctional agencies and systems have been forced to pay millions of dollars to comply with consent decrees (Kleinknecht, 2008).

The Influence of CRIPA on Juvenile Corrections

Litigation is not the only mechanism whereby youth and their advocates can attempt to improve conditions in juvenile corrections. In 1980, the federal government introduced the Civil Rights for Institutionalized Persons Act (CRIPA). This legislation gave the federal government the authority to protect the rights of institutionalized persons, including people with mental illness, those in jails and prisons, and incarcerated youth (Abrams, 2005). According to the U. S. Department of Justice (DOJ) (2008):

> Investigations, and the subsequent settlements reached in most cases, have focused on a number of important federal rights of juveniles, including rights guaranteed by the Individuals with Disabilities Education Act, the Americans with Disabilities Act, and youths' constitutional rights to reasona-

ble safety, adequate medical and mental health care, rehabilitative treatment and education. Several of the cases have
involved allegations of staff abusing juveniles, preventable
youth-on-youth violence, and excessive use of restraints and
isolation. The Section has made a priority of ensuring adequate access to mental health treatment and has focused attention on the special needs of very young juveniles,
juveniles with special medical problems, and on the myriad
of problems created by crowding in juvenile facilities. (p. 1)

The DOJ (2008) reported having investigated over 100 different juvenile
facilities, including at least eight state correctional systems. If the DOJ finds
that conditions within a facility do not comply with federal laws, they send a
letter outlining the violations and identify measures to remedy the problems
prior to involving the courts.

Rosenbaum (1999), an official with the DOJ, observed that the federal
government strives for collaborative relationships and focus upon solving
problems and improving the conditions of confinement:

In practice, we make every effort to reach an agreement with
the jurisdiction about how to correct the problems we found
before we ever resort to litigation. We view this process as
joint problem-solving for a common purpose. State authorities often voluntarily comply with the remedies we suggest.
When we see steady improvement and genuine effort we
will continue to work with the state. As a result, most CRIPA
matters end before contested litigation ever begins. (p. 1)

Although Rosenbaum presents a friendly, problem-solving approach, it is
likely that few juvenile justice officials would want the federal courts to
become involved in the daily operations of their facilities.

It is important to acknowledge that the interventions of the DOJ and advocates to access the federal courts to improve conditions of confinement are
often positive acts. Many correctional officials, for instance, reported that
when conditions for the residents are better, they improve for the staff as
well (Schlanger, 2003). Furthermore, better access to medical and psychological health care, education, violence reduction, and rehabilitation—which are
common themes of most litigation—have long-term benefits for public
safety. Perhaps the greatest change in juvenile corrections, however, is that
residents now have a greater voice and can raise issues about abuse, living
conditions that threaten their health or safety, or stand up to arbitrary
rulings of correctional officials. Some of the limitations of litigation and

CRIPA, however, are that change or reform using these approaches generally takes a long time and is intended to respond to egregious cases.

Ombudsmen and Youth Advocacy

One way that youth can constructively address issues of their treatment within a correctional facility is to bring them to the attention of an Ombudsman or Children's Advocate. A number of state and local governments have funded these operations in order to provide youth with a legitimate method of bringing up their concerns. Ombudsman programs originated in Sweden, but they are commonly encountered in English speaking Commonwealth nations, such as Australia, Canada, or New Zealand and increasingly in the United States. These agencies developed as independent government funded investigative bodies that respond to public complaints about wrongdoing in government agencies.

We sometimes forget that youth in correctional settings do not always have the verbal or written skills to constructively raise a concern. In some cases, residents who try to bring up an issue end up escalating the situation: sometimes to their detriment. As a result, most juvenile correctional facilities have formal mechanisms so that youth can initiate complaints. Typically, this is called a grievance system. Grievances are handled by a staff member, such as a supervisor or manager, who investigates the complaint and acts on substantiated complaints. Youth in the facility, however, may not always view this process as fair when an individual investigates wrongdoing within their agency. As a result, external investigators might be more effective at responding to the concerns of youth.

Most juvenile correctional facilities are closed environments and decisions made about consequences for misconduct (e.g., also known as disciplinary infractions in many facilities) or engaging in illegal behavior are sometimes arbitrary. Correctional officers sometimes make decisions about safety and security that might not make sense to residents or their families. In addition, youth in residential placements occasionally become involved in conflicts with juvenile correctional officers when they question treatment or the implementation of a policy, as their interpersonal skills are often poorly developed and they may escalate rather than de-escalate situations. Having the support of an Ombudsman or Advocate also helps the youth to build their interpersonal skills. In addition, the access to an advocate may force juvenile correctional officers to act less arbitrary and more consistent with policies.

Jones and Cohn (2005) observed that there were a number of reasons why Ombudsman programs have become more popular in juvenile corrections:

- Large numbers of cases and delays make the grievance process cumbersome; there is little time for proper investigation of complaints.
- Some disputes are very complex and need more attention than a cursory review can provide.
- Reliance on internal resolution of complaints may lead the public to perceive that fact finders are not really neutral.
- Service providers cannot be insulated from the pressures of their agencies and may not be truthful in expressing grievances or complaints; they may not have the skill or will to judge critically what is wrong or make recommendations.
- Some internal investigators, in fact, may be serving their agencies' desire to keep complaints "under control" (Davidson, 1994).
- By reviewing complaints over time, patterns can be detected that a specific agency may not have recognized. (p. 2)

The power that an Ombudsman or Children's Advocate has varies by jurisdiction.[2] In most places, these offices can initiate investigations and make recommendations. An Ombudsman might make recommendations for resolving a specific case, such as the excessive use of force in one incident. These agencies also address broader problems in juvenile corrections, including a lack of staff development or training that negatively impacts upon all youth.

The issue of agency or staff inaction might be just as important for the Ombudsman to investigate. For instance, most youth in long-term correctional facilities have some type of treatment or case plan. Although there are different forms of case plans in various jurisdictions, these documents specify the tasks that youth should accomplish before they are released, such as participating in alcohol and drug treatment or anger management courses (see Chapter 13). The problem is that without active staff involvement in encouraging the youth, preparing them to participate in these interventions, and making appropriate referrals, these plans sometimes fail. As a result, youth might not receive the rehabilitative interventions that they need and they may spend more time in facilities if their treatment needs were unmet. Because Ombudsmen or Children's Advocates typically work with youth from the entire correctional system, they might recognize broad patterns of inaction, such as a lack of attention to case management and planning. Thus, investigators from these agencies may be able to make a series of recommendations that highlight a problem before it worsens.

In February 2008, the National Conferences on State Legislatures (NCSL) reported that "29 states currently have either ombudsman or offices of the child advocate with duties and purposes related to the welfare of children" (p. 1). The funding and mission of these advocacy groups differ according to state mandates, but all are charged with looking out for the interests of children and youth by receiving and investigating complaints. While little research about the effectiveness of these agencies has been published, they give incarcerated youth a positive outlet for complaints. This might increase the sense of fairness and legitimacy toward the juvenile justice system, which may in turn promote law-abiding behavior (Tyler, 1990).

Correctional Accreditation

Historically, correctional facilities operated with very little oversight or outside review. That means that with the exception of youths' families and a small number of reporters, few really monitored what occurred in foster homes, juvenile halls or training schools. In the paragraphs above, we learned that juveniles did not have much access to the courts, so very few people knew what occurred in residential placements and most did not care. Over time, more agencies started to monitor what occurred in both adult and juvenile corrections and the federal courts became responsive to prisoner lawsuits. Reporters gained entry into correctional institutions and family members became more critical and vocal about the treatment of their children. As the operations of the youth justice system came under more scrutiny, there was an increased interest in making facilities that held juveniles more professional.

One way that agencies could demonstrate to the outside world that they operated according to a set of professional standards was to obtain accreditation. Today, accreditation has become very important in adult jails and prisons and juvenile corrections are likely to follow the same trend. On October 1, 2008, for instance, a review of the American Correctional Association's (ACA) Web site revealed that 252 juvenile correctional facilities or agencies were accredited (ACA, 2008). In fact, entire juvenile correctional systems in states such as Idaho, Indiana, Kentucky, New York, and Ohio are fully accredited. Accreditation means that an agency abides by an extensive set of standards—an approach that is very common in health care and educational institutions. Starting in the 1970s, the ACA began to offer accreditation to agencies that voluntarily applied. The ACA is one of the largest accrediting bodies, although the National Commission on Correctional Health Care accredits correctional health programs; the Commission on Accreditation of Rehabilitation Facilities and Council on Accreditation also accredit juvenile facilities. Accreditation has been described as the "Good Housekeeping Seal" for correctional agencies (Gibbons & de B. Katzenback, 2006) and many administrators ensure that their facilities meet the requirements of these accrediting bodies.

Correctional agencies must pay to have auditors from the ACA visit their facilities every three years to conduct an audit of the facility operations. According to the ACA (2008), the following are reasons why a facility should be accredited:

- Improved staff training and development,
- Assessment of program strengths and weaknesses,
- Defense against lawsuits,
- Establishing measurable criteria for upgrading operations,
- Improved staff morale and professionalism,
- Safer environment for offenders and staff,
- Reduced liability insurance costs, and
- Performance based benefits. (p. 1)

In order to be awarded accreditation, the agency must meet a set of national-level standards. These standards may include the educational requirements of a facility's superintendent, the hours of pre-service training that staff must receive, levels of medical services, cleanliness and sanitation of the facility, use of segregation, crowding, the percentage of residents participating in rehabilitative programs, and basic services such as how many calories youth receive per day and their access to the outdoors. The strength of tracking these issues is that facility managers can monitor the progress or performance of their operations.

In terms of juvenile corrections, ACA (2008) standards exist for community-based residential facilities, training schools, probation and aftercare services, detention facilities, day treatment operations, and boot camps. In some cases, privately operated correctional facilities must be accredited in order to win contracts with state correctional agencies or the federal government. Thus, some organizations have a strong incentive to maintain accreditation.

The accreditation process is lengthy, including a self evaluation completed by the facility's managers, a review of documentation by the facility's managers, and a three day audit by three corrections professionals from the ACA, which is followed by a hearing (Gibbons & de B. Katzenback, 2006). To be accredited by the ACA, a facility must meet or exceed all of the mandatory standards (roughly ten percent of the standards are mandatory) and meet 90% of the remaining, non-mandatory standards (Gibbons & de B. Katzenback, 2006). Once a facility is accredited, it lasts for three years and facilities must annually certify their continued compliance. Furthermore, in the event of a significant incident (e.g., a death in custody) the facility administrator must provide the accrediting agency with detailed information about the event.

Despite the fact that most corrections professionals agree that accreditation is a positive strategy, Gibbons and de B. Katzenback (2006) outlined a number of criticisms. First, they noted that only policies are monitored and that there is no guarantee that the policy is actually being followed. ACA officials, however, have challenged this criticism and maintain that the auditors check policy, procedure, and practice (Flowers, 2008). ACA auditors, for instance, participate in detailed facility tours and interview officials from the facility as well as offenders. As all of the auditors have extensive "on the job" experience (a minimum requirement is that they served as a supervisor in a correctional facility for three years) they are savvy about correctional practices.

Another criticism of accreditation is that, in many cases, the standards are set low and as long as the minimum requirement is met, the agency meets the accreditation standard. Yet, these standards are also dynamic and are updated on a regular basis. There is a standards committee that meets at the annual meetings of the ACA and they review existing standards and determine whether they are consistent with current legislation and best correctional practices. Furthermore, agencies can submit proposals to modify existing standards and some advocacy groups have used this mechanism to promote changes in the way that correctional facilities operate (Flowers, 2008).

Performance Measures in Juvenile Corrections

There has been growing interest in the use of performance measures in juvenile justice systems (Mears & Butts, 2008). One method of measuring the effectiveness of the operation of a facility is using Performance-based Standards (PbS). This approach establishes high standards for institutional functioning and then collecting data about the institution's performance on seven key goals of juvenile care. This information is used to learn how conditions within a facility are changing (e.g., if things are getting better or worse) and the data allows for comparisons with other juvenile correctional institutions throughout the nation.

One example is resident-on-staff assaults, which is a key indicator of safety. Using a PbS approach, the facility collects data about these incidents over a period of years. By reviewing these data, the staff members can see if these violent acts are increasing or decreasing and they can compare their facility with other institutions. As a result, the superintendent and staff will know if their institution is safer than others. Furthermore, if there are more assaults, they can develop interventions to reduce these incidents. Because PbS is based on a network approach, a facility manager can get help from other jurisdictions about practices that have been successful in reducing violence.

Loughran (2007) outlined how the PbS model is based on collecting information about seven different goals of juvenile corrections:

- Safety: To engage in management practices that promotes the safety and well being of staff and youths.
- Order: To establish clear expectations of behavior and an accompanying system of accountability for youths and staff that promote mutual respect, self discipline and order.
- Security: To protect public safety and to provide a safe environment for youths and staff, an essential condition for learning and treatment to be effective.
- Programming: To provide meaningful opportunities and services to youths to improve their educational and vocational competence, to effectively address underlying behavioral problems and to prepare them for responsible lives in the community.
- Justice: To operate the facility in a manner consistent with principles of fairness and that provides the means of ensuring and protecting youth's and family's legal rights.
- Health and Mental Health: To identify and effectively respond to residents' health, mental health, and related behavioral problems throughout the course of confinement through the use of professionally appropriate diagnostic, treatment, and prevention protocols.
- Reintegration: To prepare youths for successful reintegration into the community while they reside at the facility. (pp. 21-22)

These seven goals are then broken down into a series of standards and outcome measures upon which the data are collected. In addition, PbS lists a number of expected practices that facility managers can use to ensure that the outcome measure is met and processes that support those practices. While this description seems complicated, the example below shows that it is quite simple in practice.

For instance, one of the PbS standards for order (one of the seven main goals) is to maximize the opportunities for a resident's participation in activities and programs within the institution. We know that incarcerated youth must be kept busy or they will be more likely to engage in misconduct. As a result, most facilities try to keep youth engaged throughout the day in some form of recreational activity, working on their school work, rehabilitative plans, or doing assigned chores. In the PbS approach, keeping the residents busy relates to the goal of order and the CJCA (2008) example below shows the following standard: "To establish clear expectations of behavior and an accompanying system of accountability for youth and staff that promote mutual respect, self discipline and order" (p. 11). The outcome measure is the number of hours a youth is idle and the expected practices provide a number of examples for reducing idle time.

**Table 1. Example of PbS Order Standard,
Expected Practices, and Processes.**

(1) Outcome Measures	(3) Expected Practices	(2) Processes
O12: Average number of idle hours youth spend in their rooms or dorms not including 8 hours for sleeping.	OEP18: Programs, services, and activities are held on schedule.	OP14: There is a current and robust schedule of weekly programs, services and activities.
	OEP19: Youths are engaged in meaningful, healthy, and age-appropriate activities during waking hours with adequate staff supervision.	OP15: Policy exists requiring that schedule for daily and weekly programs, services and activities be posted in various conspicuous places within the programming, recrea-tional and residential areas.
	OEP20: Facility and agency managers routinely observe activities, particularly during evenings, holidays and weekends and cross-reference observations with the published schedule.	

Source: CJCA (2008). PbS Goals, Standards, Expected Practices and Processes.

Using this standard, the superintendent ensures that data is collected about the number of hours that a youth is idle per day and determines if that amount changes over time. Furthermore, he or she could compare the number of idle hours at their facility to other institutions to determine differences. If there are more hours of idle time, for instance, there may be a relationship with incidents (e.g., youth getting into trouble when there are fewer hours of structured programming). Altogether, there are 105 outcome measures for long-term institutions compared with 59 outcome measures for detention facilities. Because detention facilities house youth for a shorter period of time, they have fewer standards and outcome measures for health, programming, and community reintegration. Table 2 shows the differences between standards in juvenile corrections and detention facilities.

Table 2. Standards and Outcome Measures in Corrections and Detention Facilities.

Area	Corrections	Detention
Safety	14	14
Order	12	12
Security	7	7
Health	14	7
Programming	27	12
Justice	7	7
Reintegration	24	0
Totals	27 Standards	19 Standards
	105 Outcome Measures	59 Outcome Measures

Source: Loughran (2007). Performance-based Standards for Youth Correctional and Detention Facilities.

Even though there are fewer outcome measures for health care or programming in detention facilities, Table 2 shows that the goals of safety, order, justice, and security are identical in both types of institutions. Just and safe facilities are a cornerstone of healthy correctional institutions and Loughran (2007) noted that a guiding principal of the PbS approach is that "facilities should be places we'd feel comfortable sending our own children" (p. 6).

Although a relatively new method of increasing accountability in juvenile corrections, the Performance-based Standards approach is becoming more widely used. In October 2007, Loughran said that there were "196 sites in 29 states, and that total included 124 correction, 62 detention, and 10 assessment centers that held over 14,000 youths" (p. 9). This total represents approximately 15% of all youth incarcerated in local detention or state facilities. Moreover, more state correctional systems have been added since that time. As the number of participating agencies increases, it will enhance the ability of managers to network with each other and better understand the strategies that are effective in reducing incidents and increasing the effectiveness of safety, security, and rehabilitative interventions.

In addition to PbS, other approaches to performance monitoring exist. Mears and Butts (2008) identified several others, including the National Performance Measures Demonstration (Report Card) project and the Reclaiming the Futures Project. Regardless of the individual approach, these methods provide facility managers with an additional tool to monitor their operations and improve the effectiveness of their organizations.

Conclusions

A number of internal practices (such as PbS) as well as external forces (e.g., Ombudsmen or litigation) have made juvenile correctional administrators more accountable for the youth in their care. External sources of oversight, such as litigation and CRIPA, have had the most significant impact on changing the conditions of confinement in most juvenile facilities. Managers of youth correctional systems and local juvenile halls have found themselves working with federal officials and court appointed special masters to ensure that the quality of care in their facilities meets constitutional standards. Many of these shortfalls, however, are a consequence of a lack of funding and many facility superintendents and directors are restricted by an inability to hire the professional staff they need to properly fulfill their missions or provide support and training to the staff members already employed.

Other forms of external oversight are the Ombudsman or Children's Advocate agencies that are independent, government funded organizations that investigate unreasonable actions or inactions in child welfare and juvenile corrections. These agencies can be found in more than one half of all states and are important because they give a voice to youth who have little influence. Furthermore, these organizations are also situated to make broad recommendations about the care and treatment of youth given their ability to investigate all of the facilities within a correctional system.

In response to these external organizations and pressures, many juvenile corrections leaders are choosing to voluntarily comply with national-level standards of accreditation with the American Correctional Association or participate in the Performance-based Standards model that was introduced by the Council of Juvenile Correctional Administrators. Participation in either approach demonstrates that the agencies have made a considerable investment in providing a more accountable service to the youth in their care.

Although the PbS model is a relatively new approach, it has the advantage of setting high standards and the ability to compare measures against a facility's performance over time, as well as making comparisons to national-level norms. Facilities that have implemented the PbS approach have reported reductions in violence, suicide, and staff misconduct (Loughran,

2007). In addition, since these facilities set relatively high standards, they have become less vulnerable to CRIPA investigations because CRIPA focuses on compliance with the minimum constitutional standards. One of the hallmarks of the success of PbS is its adoption by an increasing number of large state correctional systems. While the evidence showing the success of this approach has thus far been limited (New Amsterdam Consulting, 2007), it appears to be a very promising approach to making juvenile facilities safer and saner places to live and work.

Endnotes

1. The *Kent* decision in 1966 was the first juvenile case heard by the U. S. Supreme Court and the Court found that the waiver to adult court order of a juvenile court was unconstitutional. The *Gault* case, by contrast, extended a number of due process protections to youth, including the right to counsel, the right against self incrimination, and the right to confront witnesses. Prior to these decisions, attorneys were generally not involved in juvenile court proceedings and they were widely considered to be informal events (e.g., there were no transcripts of the proceedings) with the goal of providing treatment and rehabilitation rather than holding youth accountable.
2. The role of youth advocate also varies by jurisdiction. Russell (2008) noted that "the primary role is to help the young person put forward his or her view or wish about a particular matter even if the advocate does not believe it to be in the child's 'best interests.' It is the young person's view that counts" (p. 13).

Cases Cited

Cooper v. Pate, 378 U.S. 546 (1964)
Ex Parte Hull, 312 U.S. 546 (1941)
Farrell v. Tilton
In re Gault, 387 U.S. 1 (1967)
Kent v. United States, 383 U.S. 541 (1966)
Ruffin v. Commonwealth (62, Va. 790, 1871)
S.H. v. Stickrath

References

Abrams, D. E. (2005). Reforming juvenile delinquency treatment to enhance rehabilitation, personal accountability, and public safety. *Oregon Law Review, 84,* 1001-1092.

American Correctional Association. (2008). *Standards and accreditation.* Retrieved October 7, 2008, from http://www.aca.org/standards/

Butterworth, B. (1995). *Limits sought on frivolous inmate lawsuits.* Retrieved May 11, 2008, from http://myfloridalegal.com

Caeti, T. J., Hemmens, C., Cullen, F. T., & Burton, V. S. (2003). Management of juvenile correctional facilities. *The Prison Journal, 4,* 383-405.

Cohen, F. (2008). *Final fact-finding report: S.H. v. Stickrath.* Retrieved January 22, 2008, from http://www.dys.ohio.gov

Council of Juvenile Correctional Administrators. (2008). *PbS goals, standards, outcome measures, expected practices and processes.* Retrieved May 10, 2008, from http://pbstandards.org/DocLib/PbS%20Standards_April%202008.pdf

Fishman, J. F. (1923). *Crucibles of crime: The shocking story of the American jail.* New York: Cosmopolis Press

Flowers, M. (2008, October). *American Correctional Association accreditation.* Presented at the Correctional Security Network Conference, Cincinnati, OH.

Gibbons, J. J., & de B. Katzenback, N. (2006). *Confronting confinement: A report on the Commission on Safety and Abuse in America's prisons.* New York: Vera Institute of Justice.

Jones, J., & Cohn, A. W. (2005). *State ombudsman programs.* Washington, DC: Office of Juvenile Justice and Delinquency Prevention.

Kaftan, S. (2007). Management is not leadership. In P. Withrow (Ed.), *"A view from the trenches:" A manual for wardens by wardens,* (pp. 1-1-1-7). Annapolis Junction, MD: American Correctional Association.

Kleinknecht, W. (2008). Judge ends court supervision of Essex County juvenile detention center. *The Star-Ledger.* Retrieved October 7, 2008, from http://www.nj.com

Loughran, N. (2007, October). *Performance-based standards (PbS) for youth correction and detention facilities.* Presented at the Correctional Security Network Conference, Cincinnati, OH.

MacCormick, A. H. (1949). Children in our jails. *Annals of the American Academy of Political and Social Science, 261,* 150-157.

Mears, D. P., & Butts, J. A. (2008). Using performance monitoring to improve the accountability, operations, and effectiveness of juvenile justice. *Criminal Justice Policy Review, 19,* 264-284.

National Conference of State Legislatures. (2008). *Children's ombudsman offices.* Retrieved May 9, 2008, from http://www.ncsl.org/programs/cyf/ombuds.htm

New Amsterdam Consulting. (2007). *Performance-based standards for youth correction and detention facilities: A research report.* Scottsdale, AZ: Author.

Puritz, P., & Scali, M. (1998). *Beyond the walls: Improving conditions of confinement for youth in custody.* Washington, DC: Office of Juvenile Justice and Delinquency Prevention.

Rosenbaum, S. H. (1999). *Remarks of Steven H. Rosenbaum, Chief, Special Litigation Section, Civil Rights Division, United States Department of Justice.* Long Beach, California, May 16, 1999. Retrieved May 9, 2008, from http://www.usdoj.gov/crt/split/documents/juvspeech.htm

Russell, F. (2008). Advocacy in young offender institutions. *Prison Service Journal, 177,* 13-15.

Schlanger, M. (2003). Inmate litigation. *Harvard Law Review, 116*, 1555-1706.

Schwartz, I. (1989). *(In)justice for juveniles: Rethinking the best interests of the child.* Lexington, MA: Lexington Books.

Soler, M. (1988). Litigation on behalf of children in adult jails. *Crime & Delinquency, 34*, 190-208.

Sturm, S. P. (1993). The legacy and future of corrections litigation. *University of Pennsylvania Law Review, 142*, 639-738.

Tyler, T. R. (1990). *Why people obey the law.* New Haven, CT: Yale University Press.

U. S. Department of Justice. (2008). *Civil rights of incarcerated persons.* Retrieved May 10, 2008 from: http://www.usdoj.gov/crt/split/cripa.htm

U. S. Government Accountability Office. (2007). *Residential treatment programs: Concerns regarding abuse and death in certain programs for troubled youth.* Washington, DC: Author.

Youth Law Center. (2009). *YLC in action.* Retrieved June 25, 2009, from http://www.ylc.org/ylcInAction.php

CHAPTER 18
CHALLENGES AND OPPORTUNITIES
IN JUVENILE CORRECTIONS

Rick Ruddell

T he authors in the previous 17 chapters highlighted a number of challenges confronting juvenile justice systems, especially as they relate to the treatment of youth in residential placements. Youth placed in the care of the state had historically been at increased risk of violence, contracting illnesses or diseases, and self-harm or suicide. Furthermore, they were also susceptible to the negative influences of other youth and many nonviolent youth placed in detention or other placements have been lured into gangs and other negative peer associations. In addition, staff members in some facilities had neglected, abused, or otherwise harmed youth due to their actions or inaction. In some cases, parents who thought that their youngsters would emerge from residential placements with a more positive or prosocial attitude instead had to bury them after died from suicide, assaults, illnesses, or unintentional injuries. Other youth were released with higher levels of antisocial or criminogenic attitudes and beliefs: instead of being corrected, the youths' experiences in correctional facilities pushed them further into crime and delinquency.

Until the 1970s, the treatment of youth in many correctional facilities had not evolved much beyond the way that residents were treated in the Houses of Refuge or Reform Schools a century earlier. Status offenders were placed with hard-core delinquents, boys mixed with girls, and residents with severe mental health problems were placed with ordinary delinquents. Because correctional officials did not fully understand or appreciate gender differences, including the different pathways to offending, young women typically received the same type of interventions as males. Youth with learning disabilities or other learning problems attended the same classes as other residents and received little additional support. Furthermore, we had very unsophisticated approaches to case management or using the power of small groups of residents to solve issues. Instead, threats of physical violence and placing the residents in isolation were used to control behavior. Since there were few mechanisms of oversight, this standard of care was the norm for decades and these facilities were often underfunded, overcrowded, and

333

staffed with workers whose knowledge, skills, and abilities working with juvenile offenders left much to be desired.

Much in the world of juvenile corrections has changed and our strategies of working with juveniles in residential placements have improved. Some jurisdictions have successfully reduced violence and have established high standards of care. In most places, the overriding goal of juvenile corrections has become the preparation of youth for their reentry into the community and to be good students, workers, and ultimately parents and taxpayers.

The Future of Juvenile Corrections

The following pages highlight a number of emerging trends in juvenile justice and provide a framework for discussing the future of juvenile corrections. While any attempt to predict the future is always problematic (especially the further into the future that one attempts to foresee) the following will be significant issues in the field of juvenile corrections in the next decade.

A Growing Focus on Rehabilitation

Bernard (1992) identified several distinct periods in U. S. juvenile justice policy where tough-on-juvenile-crime policies were replaced with more forgiving juvenile justice practices. He suggested that this pattern will continue to repeat itself and it is possible that we are emerging from a two decade long tough-on-crime era. Part of the reason for softening attitudes toward juvenile offenders is the growing recognition that there is a developmental basis for some youthful misconduct.

Teenagers are different than adults, especially in terms of brain development. Studies have shown that the frontal lobes, the parts of the brain responsible for reasoning and problem-solving, are not fully developed until young men and women reach their twenties. The American Bar Association (2004) noted that "even as they become fully capable in other areas, adolescents cannot reason as well as adults" (p. 2). Fully understanding these developmental explanations for adolescent immaturity led to the *Roper v. Simmons* decision of the Supreme Court in 2005 that made the death penalty unconstitutional for youth who were under the age of 18 years at the time of the offense.

Public opinion polls, mentioned in Chapter 1, highlighted how there has been a softening of punitive feelings toward juvenile offenders and taxpayers have expressed an interest in paying higher taxes to ensure that juveniles receive treatment and rehabilitation rather than punishment (Mears, Hay, Gertz, & Mancini, 2007). Consistent with this approach seems to be a growing acceptance for restorative justice practices such as family group counseling, in which a victim and offender meet in a planned and structured manner that is intended to repair the harm that the offender did to the individual and community when he or she committed an offense (Braithwaite, 1989). These programs are popular in Commonwealth nations such as Australia, Canada, New Zealand, and the United Kingdom, but have been comparatively slow to be adopted in the United States (where such initiatives are based on a philosophy called balanced and restorative justice [BARJ]).

The increasing interest in restorative justice may represent a transition to a kinder and gentler juvenile justice system and this may have an impact upon juvenile corrections by removing nonviolent youth from institutions. There is growing consensus that youth should be treated in the least restrictive environment consistent with public safety (Underwood, Robinson, Mosholder, & Warren, 2008). Of course, that leaves the serious, persistent, and violent residents. This population may require a different management approach with higher levels of supervision and staff-to-resident ratios. Furthermore, this population may require new or different types of interventions (e.g., suppressing gang activities or new methods of assessing and intervening in the lives of residents).

One emerging type of sentence is the blended juvenile/adult sentence—also called extended juvenile jurisdiction (EJJ)—that attempts to blend the rehabilitation of the juvenile justice system with the threat of adult sanctions if the youth continues to break the law (Brummer, 2002). In Minnesota, for instance, a youth who commits a serious offense as a juvenile can be sentenced as an adult. But, that sentence is stayed and the youth remains in the juvenile justice system. If he or she commits any further offenses during their juvenile disposition or violates the conditions of probation, they are returned to the adult court and the outcome could include the imposition of the original adult sentence (Backstrom, 1998). Sometimes the consequences for failure on these blended sentences are severe. Uggen (2008) described how a youth who failed on EJJ was sentenced to serve the 72-year sentence that was originally imposed. While blended sentences give a youth one more chance to succeed, the consequences of a single failure can be catastrophic and thus puts pressure on the juvenile justice system to reform these youth.

Developing New Models of Institutional Management

Most juvenile facilities attempt to regulate the behavior of their residents by rewarding desirable behaviors. Two such examples are level systems and token economies. Level systems are based on providing more privileges for residents who consistently abide by facility rules and their success in meeting their case plan goals, such as doing well in the educational program and participating in treatment. Generally, these systems have three or four different levels and the youth can move up a level after a set amount of time—for instance, a week of positive behavior at Level 1 will earn the resident a Level 2 rank; the resident moves down the level system if they are involved in a serious infraction, such as a fight. Examples of additional privileges that a resident earns include later bedtimes or the ability to spend a greater amount of money at the canteen or commissary each week. As such, this system rewards residents who can consistently demonstrate positive behavior.

Another approach to rewarding positive behavior is through the use of a token economy, which provides a tangible reward (a token) that residents can earn and then use to buy goods or privileges. This approach might be more successful with youth who have a shorter attention span and need more immediate and tangible indicators of success. Variations of level systems or token economies are used in most facilities, but suffer from a number of limitations. Many young people, for example, may have difficulty attaching cause and effect and find it difficult to stick with these programs over the long term. Learning difficulties or injuries to the central nervous system, such as fetal alcohol spectrum disorders (FASDs), may make it more difficult for some youth to abide by these methods of behavioral management. Finally, these approaches only work if the staff members consistently implement them and this is sometimes difficult to achieve.

A third way of regulating the behavior of residents is through self governance approaches, which use the positive influences of the youth in group settings to ensure that the program operates smoothly, that behavioral expectations are being met, and that problems in the living unit are being resolved before they escalate. There are a number of different models and two that are widely used are positive peer culture (PPC) and guided group interaction (GGI). These models have been around for decades (articles about guided group interaction were published in the 1950s) and such approaches rely upon frequent group meetings—supervised by staff members—where the residents solve problems on the unit and sometimes impose sanctions on group members. A similar approach, described in Chapter 15, is used in Missouri with much success.

The self governance approach has a number of strengths, including developing a youth's problem-solving and communication skills. Yet, not all residents will respond positively to these approaches: youngsters who are mixed with older residents, for example, sometimes have trouble meeting the expectations of the older youth. Moreover, the staff members overseeing these group meetings have to carefully monitor them to ensure that the group's power is not being misused. While some facilities still use these approaches, their use has decreased. Thus, therapeutic communities (a more sophisticated extension of GGI or PPC) have been used in substance abuse treatment, their use has not generally expanded to general populations in juvenile corrections, creating opportunities for new approaches to intervening with youth.

Juvenile Assessment and Intervention System

One strategy of assessment and behavioral management that is attracting increasing attention is the Juvenile Assessment and Intervention System (JAIS), an approach to youth treatment based on an automated comprehensive risk assessment that is combined with case planning and also includes a set of strategies that best responds to the needs of four distinct groups of juveniles. The National Council on Crime and Delinquency (2008) developed this model and one of the strengths of the approach is that youth in residential placements are treated in a manner that best matches their behavioral needs:

Selective Intervention
The lives of Selective Intervention (SI) juveniles tend to be distinguished by positive, prosocial adjustment and the absence of significant behavior problems prior to an abrupt onset of delinquency. There may be a rapid decline in school attendance and achievement and a marked shift in peer group from prosocial to delinquent. Initially, delinquent behavior in this group is in response to an external stressor or to an internal, neurotic need. Once delinquency is established as a coping mechanism, however, it may continue even after the stressor is resolved.

Casework Control
The Casework Control (CC) group is characterized by general instability and chronic adjustment problems. Home situations are likely to be chaotic, including residential and emotional instability, chemical abuse, and inconsistent or exaggerated attempts at discipline by the parents. Physical, emotional, and/or sexual abuse are frequently noted. These problems often result in a negative self perception and general intolerance and hostility toward most others on the part of the juvenile. Chemical abuse and emotional instability are frequently seen among members of this group. Negative attitudes toward authority usually result in adjustment problems in school, even though intellectual functioning may be

adequate. When residential instability is a factor, it is generally due to frequent family relocation or multiple foster placements.

Environmental Structure
The Environmental Structure (ES) group is characterized by a lack of social and survival skills and poor impulse control. Members of this group have difficulty understanding the motives of others and are often used and exploited. Delinquency tends to take place when ES juveniles are influenced by more sophisticated and criminally-oriented peers. Due to their lack of social skills, juveniles in this group often experience social isolation. The resulting desire for acceptance, coupled with a general lack of foresight, can result in susceptibility to the influence of others. Members of this group are generally eager to please and want to be liked. These characteristics can be used as an advantage in the course of supervision since these youth are often equally susceptible to positive as to negative influence.

Limit Setting
Juveniles in the Limit Setting (LS) group tend to be motivated by power, money, and excitement. Their value structures are generally so antisocial or sufficiently weak that they readily engage in delinquency for thrills. LS juveniles find their role models among criminals or other delinquents whom they perceive as successful, powerful, or glamorous and often seek out association with these individuals. LS juveniles tend to have strong self concepts and see no real need to change their values or behaviors except to avoid getting caught. (p.1)

One goal of the JAIS approach is to separate youth based on these different classifications. Proponents of this model argue that we shouldn't mix youth from the Environmental Structure group (who tend to be followers) with residents who require strict Limit Setting because those youth tend to be leaders and negatively influence more impressionable residents (Baird & Gasper, 2008). Moreover, each group has somewhat different case management and supervision needs.

The automated risk assessment component of the JAIS approach is relatively new and while Baird and Gasper (2008) have reported promising results, research has not yet conclusively demonstrated that this model reduces institutional misconduct or recidivism. One of the limitations of adopting juvenile justice programs that have been demonstrated by research to be effective is that it sometimes takes years before a practice is thoroughly evaluated. Yet, the wait is worthwhile because basing interventions on solid research, rather than fads or "gut feelings," is a best practice in both adult and juvenile corrections (Gendreau, Goggin, Cullen, & Paparozzi, 2002).

Utilizing Evidence-Based Practices

Implementing any type of intervention in juvenile corrections is costly. Staff must be trained in new ways of working with youth and often there is resistance to change (see Lin, 2000 for an example in adult corrections). As a result, most facility superintendents are reluctant to implement new programs unless research can demonstrate that the new approach is substantially better than existing methods of working with youth.

One of the problems with juvenile corrections is that some interventions, such as Scared Straight programs (where at-risk youth are taken to prisons and the inmates inform them about the worst aspects of prison life in order to deter them from committing further crimes) are fads that research has shown are not effective at reducing crime (Drake, 2007). Latessa, Cullen, and Gendreau (2002) — three of the most prominent correctional researchers — proposed the idea of correctional quackery and the fact that many correctional programs are based on ideas about crime and offenders who are misguided. Often these views are based on stereotypes about offenders, a correctional administrator's gut feelings about criminals, or what treatment offenders, including juveniles, require. Latessa, Cullen, and Gendreau (2002) advocated for designing, developing, and implementing programs that are based on what the research demonstrates is effective at reducing undesirable behavior (such as institutional misconduct or recidivism), which is called evidence-based research. This approach is increasingly being used in criminal justice, health care, education, and child welfare (Aos, Miller, & Drake, 2006).

Aos, Miller, and Drake (2006) stated that sound evidence-based research uses all of the studies that have been published on a topic (e.g., the consistent evidence that shows the ineffectiveness of the Drug Abuse Resistance Education or DARE program in reducing drug use — see Rosenbaum, 2007) rather than just using studies that support the researcher's beliefs, including research that used control and comparison groups (e.g., youth who received DARE versus youth who didn't participate and studies that used real world groups, such as kids who are in ordinary schools); they discount the results from studies that were done by the developer of the program because they may be biased (p. 7).

To date, most studies of delinquency have used recidivism as a measure of evaluating success. In her study of the effectiveness of correctional interventions, MacKenzie (2006) examined different approaches to reducing recidivism. She compared the effectiveness of multi-systemic therapy (also known as MST, which uses a team of professionals to deliver a series of interventions to the youth and their families in the community) to traditional residential placement of juveniles and community supervision of youth on probation. MacKenzie (2006) found that MST had the most powerful impact on reducing recidivism and noted that "supervision programs that often focus on increasing the control over offenders are not effective in reducing recidivism" (p. 186).

One type of research that compliments recidivism research is cost-benefit analysis. These studies compare the cost of the intervention against the economic benefits. For instance, Drake (2007) reported that it costs $58 to deliver a Scared Straight intervention to a youth. While this is an inexpensive treatment, Drake (2007) found that there were no actual crime reduction benefits of these programs and participants might actually be involved in crimes at a higher rate, costing taxpayers $6,253 and crime victims $8,355 (p. 7). Yet, Drake (2007) also reported that the benefits of multidimensional treatment foster care, compared to regular group care, paid a dividend of $77,798 for $6,945 worth of treatment (p. 7). While critics of these analyses point to the fact that it is often easier to calculate the costs compared to the benefits (especially in terms of crime reduction), during times of economic crisis, it is likely that politicians and policy makers will pay more attention to this research.

A Growing Focus on Reentry and Aftercare

As outlined in Chapter 16, there is increasing interest in a youth's transition from a residential placement to the community, and how to better prepare him or her for this change (Bouffard & Bergseth, 2008). Preparation for release should start with the resident's admission to the facility, and a cornerstone of case management is getting the youth to actively work toward a number of rehabilitative goals prior to their release. Most incarcerated juveniles identify issues such as finishing their education, vocational preparation, completing anger management or substance abuse programs as important (if substance abuse or anger was associated with their offenses). Despite the fact that the resident might successfully participate in these rehabilitative activities, community reentry is often difficult because they go back to the same disadvantaged neighborhoods and schools, dysfunctional family relationships, neighborhood gangs, and negative peers.

Sometimes, the youth's experiences while incarcerated make it more difficult to successfully return to the community. Some youth are victimized by other residents or staff members and their physical or psychological injuries have long-term effects, such as post traumatic stress disorders. Other youth might contract a communicable disease while incarcerated. Another problem is the failure of staff to help the youth make a significant rehabilitative change: through a staff member's inaction, for example, a youth might not be referred to the treatment programs that he or she requires.

Some youth spend so much time living in correctional environments that they do not develop the skills to make independent decisions for themselves and their interpersonal skills decrease (e.g., learning how to use violence as a problem-solving skill), or the experience of being incarcerated has other negative influences on them. In adult prisons, this is called institutionalization (e.g., when a person becomes so accustomed to living within a structured and deprived environment that it reduces his or her ability to make independent decisions) or prisonization (e.g., when someone assumes the negative values or culture of a correctional facility). Inderbitzin (2006) attributed these outcomes to the fact that some youth experience stability and structure for the first time in their lives in these settings. The trouble is that these traits make the youth's return to the community more difficult. If, for example, aggressive and manipulative behaviors are learned while incarcerated, these attributes are likely to cause problems for the youth once he or she is released and working or attending school.

To counter some of the problems associated with community reentry, some juvenile correctional systems are developing more supportive transition and aftercare programs. Transitional programs for a long-term resident of a juvenile correctional system might involve a gradual reduction in security with more community involvement. In some jurisdictions, youth can earn a furlough or temporary release from the institution to the community to recondition themselves to community life and these temporary releases may be part of a comprehensive reentry plan.

Aftercare programs, by contrast, provide resources and supports for the youth while they are in the community. There is some evidence to suggest that jurisdictions with stronger reentry programs also have lower rates of recidivism (Bouffard & Bergseth, 2008). Yet, as outlined in Chapter 16, there is a wide variety of aftercare programs and some jurisdictions are more focused on the surveillance and control of the youth rather than supporting their return to the community.

Moeser and colleagues (2007) argued that it is important to change our approach to reentry so that institutionalized youth develop a set of skills necessary for success in the community rather than focusing on their deficits or limitations. Moeser et al. (2007) wrote, "institutions need to modify their programs to enable the youth and reentry team to learn the requisite skills to successfully transition to the less structured and more demanding community" (p. 58). Juvenile correctional officers, they observed, often fail to acknowledge the impact that out-of-home placements have on the residents. This renewed focus on reentry is necessary in both long-term placements as well as detention: the longer youth are held in these facilities, the greater their need for services. MacDonald, Mitchell, and Moeser (2007) identified the following areas for enhancing reentry services from detention: continuity in educational programs, communication with other juvenile justice programs, involving the family and other significant persons in the youth's return, and gathering and sharing information for case planning (p. 68).

There is growing consensus that preparing residents for their return to the community is critically important in reducing recidivism. For most of the history of juvenile corrections, community and institutional corrections were seen as distinct or different. Today, however, there is more agreement that both dimensions of the juvenile justice system must support each other. Rapp Zimmerman (2007) observed that "reentry is a difficult and often misunderstood and neglected concept, so struggling to gain public and political understanding and acceptance will be a difficult task, but one in which none of us can afford to fail" (p. 100).

Reducing Disproportionate Minority Contact (DMC)

One of the most challenging problems for justice systems is the large percentage of persons of color involved with the justice system. Populations in juvenile facilities generally have higher rates of Black residents, although rates of incarcerated Latino youth tend to be closer to their representation in the population (Sickmund et al., 2008). There are a number of possible reasons for this over-representation. Mays and Ruddell (2007) highlighted several, including a disproportionate involvement in crime (or at least certain types of crime), biased or discriminatory practices of the criminal and juvenile justice systems, and poverty (which tends to be correlated with race). Being poor makes it difficult for families to hire attorneys or pursue community-based alternatives to incarceration, such as wilderness experience programs funded through a family's health insurance. It is likely that some combination of these three factors is responsible for DMC. The troubling part is that arrests, placement in detention, and incarceration have a cumulative effect and can place these youth at significant risk of severe sanctions if they continue their involvement with the justice system (Mays & Ruddell, 2007).

Reducing DMC has been a challenge. The Office of Juvenile Justice and Delinquency Prevention (OJJDP) has been at the forefront of efforts to reduce

DMC and has provided financial support for states to study the problem. Kempf-Leonard (2007) observed, however, that "in 20 years of concerted DMC reform initiatives, scholars have learned that identifying, explaining, and remedying disparity problems is much more complicated than it initially appeared" (p. 72). Cabiness, Frabutt, Kendrick, and Arbuckle (2007) proposed that a number of promising strategies or practices might reduce DMC:

- Comprehensive review of data and the identification of where juvenile justice decision-making occurs (to recognize trends and patterns).
- Increasing the cultural competence (understanding racial, ethnic and cultural differences, as well as differences in communication) of juvenile justice system decision-makers.
- Developing community-based detention alternatives.
- Removing decision-making subjectivity (e.g., using objective risk assessment instruments to make decisions about detaining or incarcerating youths rather than relying upon a juvenile officer's gut feelings about a youth's risks).
- Reducing barriers to family involvement in juvenile justice.
- Legislating system-level change to reform juvenile justice systems. (pp. 395-399)

Some of these strategies will be familiar with practitioners who work within juvenile corrections. There has been, for example, an increasing emphasis placed on developing the cultural competence of practitioners and using this knowledge to involve family members in case and release planning. This is sometimes challenging if parents or family members are in the country illegally or their experiences in other nations have made them distrust justice system officials. Finally, there has been an increased use of risk assessment instruments to increase fairness and reduce subjective decision-making. There is clearly no single solution to the problem of DMC and entrenched problems generally take a long time to solve. The end result, however, of a juvenile justice system that is based on consistency and fairness is critical because when juveniles and their family members perceive that the system is fair, it will have a long-term crime reduction effect (Tyler, 2006).

Acknowledging the Special Needs of Girls in the Juvenile Justice System

As highlighted in Chapter 8, there has been increasing attention paid to the special needs of young women who are placed in residential settings. This has lead to the development of gender responsive programs and strategies. It is likely that this interest will continue to grow and will shape juvenile corrections in the future. A cornerstone of gender responsive programs is that they are structured differently than programs for males — acknowledging that girls are different, especially in terms of their pathways to delinquency and their need for a safe environment. For the most part, these programs emphasize gender and cultural sensitivity and provide interventions that acknowledge the physical, sexual, and emotional abuse and trauma experienced by most girls in juvenile justice systems. In addition, these programs are also responsive to the different health needs of young women.

Recent research has shown that girls in detention have a much higher rate of psychological problems than males (Teplin, Abram, McClelland, Mericle, Dulcan, & Washburn, 2006). In addition, rates of substance abuse and dependency in girls are almost as high as males. Girls also have a much higher need for medical care, especially as it relates to reproductive health. Furthermore, rates of sexually transmitted infections are also very high in these populations (McDonnell, Levy, & Morton, 2009). Often, there is a great need for health education because many of these girls have had poor histories of health care and many lived on the street prior to being admitted to residential placements. Some of these young women were also intravenous drug users and engaged in other risky behaviors. As a result, placement in a well run juvenile facility can provide safety, stability, and structure.

Zahn (2008) identified a number of common themes in correctional programs that are successful in reducing girls' delinquency:

- Building skills in order to succeed in life, including: leadership and life skills, self esteem enhancement, empowerment, mental health services, recreation, and education.
- Building successful relationships, including: family involvement, and increasing communication and relationship building skills.
- Attaching these girls to prosocial or supportive community networks: these interventions might include cultural programs for youths from minority groups, as well as programs that engage these girls in the community. These programs or groups are seen as important for building supports for these young women. (pp. 8-9)

Yet, in order for these types of interventions to be successful, they must be implemented appropriately (Bloom, Owen, & Covington, 2003). In many cases, the most optimistic of juvenile justice reforms fail at the implementation stage.

In some ways, this growing concern for the welfare of girls is an acknowledgement that the needs of this population in juvenile corrections have long been underserved (Chesney-Lind & Shelden, 2004). Yet, there is also concern that girls seem to be involved in juvenile justice systems in increasing numbers, especially for violent offenses (Zahn et al., 2008). There is considerable debate whether this reflects a change in the behavior of girls or if the responses of justice systems have changed. Steffensmeier (2008) has argued that changes in policies are more likely responsible for growth in girls' arrests for some offenses rather than any meaningful change in the behavior of young women.

A Growing Focus on Health Care and Health Promotion

Youth admitted into correctional facilities typically have a host of medical, dental, and psychological problems. Many of these youth have poor histories of health care and have been involved in risky behaviors and, in some cases, are suffering from untreated chronic diseases. A youth's placement incarceration may be the first time that they actually received regular medical or dental care. This places a significant financial burden on correctional facilities for health care services; and costs are predicted to increase.

One area that has the potential to create significant expenditures is complying with the Americans with Disabilities Act (ADA) requirements to provide services that meet the psychological needs of these residents. Many of the youth within juvenile justice systems have learning difficulties and residential placements are required to meet their educational needs in order to comply with federal mandates. Thus, a greater need for psychologists and teachers with special education credentials may be required, although it is often difficult to recruit and retain these professionals (Platt, 2007).

Historically, the focus on health care in corrections has been diagnosing and treating existing conditions. Ruddell and Tomita (2008) outlined that health promotion has been neglected in corrections. The Joint Committee on Health Education Terminology (1991) defined health promotion as the "aggregate of all purposeful activities, designed to improve personal and public health through a combination of strategies, including the competent implementation of behavioral change strategies, health education, and health protection measures" (p. 101). Examples of health promotion activities in corrections include classroom instruction in reducing the risk of contracting a communicable disease through unsafe sex or intravenous drug use. Other health promotion activities are lifestyle related and youth in facilities can benefit from learning about diet, exercise, or preventative dental care.

Many juvenile facilities, however, neglect health promotion. Food in some facilities is high in fat and starch. Robinson and colleagues (2006), for example, examined youth admitted to a long-term juvenile correctional facility and discovered that residents found to be overweight or obese increased from 38% to 66% in three months. These investigators attributed the weight gain to overeating, inactivity, and the side effects of taking psychotropic medications (medications that are given for psychiatric conditions). While a limitation of this study is that it focused on only one location, youth will often gain weight while incarcerated. For some, this is due to getting regular meals. One concern is that incarcerated youth are a captive population and if we cannot promote healthy lifestyles inside these facilities, it is unlikely that these youth will have better habits once they return to the community.

Short-term health promotion activities might be effective interventions in juvenile detention, where the average stay tends to be measured in days. Yet, one of the characteristics of adolescent behavior is that youth generally think they are invincible and tend to "live in the present." Thus, while it may be easy to deliver health education and promotion activities in juvenile corrections, the residents might not be very interested in the message.

Staff Recruiting, Retention, and Development

The strength of a juvenile correctional facility resides in the staff members. One of the common themes in the correctional literature, however, is that it is increasingly difficult to recruit and retain staff members with high levels of honesty, integrity, and who have the interpersonal skills to work with either adult or juvenile populations. There are a number of challenges of recruiting juvenile correctional officers. Employees in institutions, for example, work unsocial shifts (such as holidays, evenings, and nights) and must interact with youth in crisis and many of them are rude, challenging, and aggressive. Officers who start with the best of intentions of helping juveniles sometimes find that these youth are not very receptive to their caring, support, and assistance. Moreover, serious, violent, and persistent offenders tend to be confrontational and violent.

There are additional obstacles in recruiting staff for juvenile corrections that are not present in adult operations. In most state systems, for instance, salary and benefits for juvenile and adult correctional officers are very similar. But, the expectations placed on juvenile correctional officers tend to be higher. In most adult systems, for example, the correctional officers are only responsible for custody and control of the prisoners. In most juvenile facilities, by contrast, the officers (or counselors) are responsible for case management duties that their adult counterparts are not required to complete. Also, as highlighted in Chapter 11, there is sometimes a tension between rehabilitation and security working in juvenile facilities that does not exist in adult corrections, where issues tend to be more "black and white." Thus, juvenile correctional officers are generally responsible for doing more duties for similar pay.

In a survey of correctional systems, Hill (2006) reported that some of the biggest challenges of recruiting were the "failure to monetarily compete with other law enforcement agencies or the location of facilities in rural areas" (p. 15). In some cases, the lengthy screening and background check process also gets in the way of hiring candidates. Most correctional jobs, for example, take months before background checks and pre-employment testing is completed. Vanyur, Nink, Upchurch, Bodman, and Greenwald (2009) observed that background checks confirm a candidate's criminal record, educational qualifications, references, character, military service, reputation, and eligibility to work (pp. 168-169). It is critically important, however, to ensure that candidates who are not suitable to work with juveniles are screened out of the hiring process.

Hiring and training a new staff member is a costly proposition for a juvenile correctional facility. Yet, many quit or are terminated within the first year (Matz, 2008). Some realize that they are not suited for this type of career. Others lack the interpersonal or security skills needed to be effective in a correctional setting. Finally, some juvenile correctional officers use their experience as a stepping stone to other law enforcement jobs.

One significant goal in all law enforcement, but particularly in corrections, is to recruit and retain minority officers (Brisco, Forh, Haynes, & Wheeler, 2004). As noted throughout this book, juvenile correctional facilities have high populations of minority youth (Sickmund, Sladky, & Kang, 2008) and it is important to have staff members who can act as positive role models for them. In addition, minority officers sometimes have a better understanding of the challenges that these youth confront.

It is also difficult to recruit and retain physicians, nurses, teachers, and psychologists to work in juvenile correctional settings. These staff members generally have a greater range of career options and are actively recruited by other public and private sector agencies. Moreover, many professionals such as nurses and teachers, report feeling isolated from their peers and underappreciated by correctional officers (Ruddell & Tomita, 2008). In some cases, teachers and other rehabilitative staff members might feel that their efforts are undermined by the security staff, which is an indicator of poor facility management.

One of the issues raised by litigation in the Ohio system was that a considerable investment in staff training and development was required (Cohen, 2008). Officers in state agencies, however, often receive more pre-service training than their counterparts in local juvenile halls or privately operated placements (see the example of training topics in Chapter 13). In California, for instance, youth correctional officers or counselors must complete a 16-week paid training academy—although this is probably the lengthiest in the nation. This training is a key factor in reducing misconduct, increasing the effectiveness of the rehabilitative programs, and ensuring that all staff members are aware of the organization's mission and values.

Some staff members in local juvenile halls or a non-profit residential placement may only receive a few hours of orientation before their first shifts. This is problematic because these staff members do not always have the knowledge of adolescent development or institutional rules and regulations, as well as the ability to verbally deescalate youth or safely restrain them if required. While training is expensive for these agencies, it is also an important investment to ensure that the youth are treated in an appropriate manner and to ensure the safety of the facility.

Training can also be used for changing an organization's culture. Cohen (2008) reported that a culture of violence existed in the Ohio Department of Youth Services. Yet, changing such a culture is a long-term proposition and sometimes there is active resistance to these changes, especially in corrections (Lin, 2000). As a result, it often takes a considerable investment in staff training as well as political and legislative support in order to modify the culture of a large correctional system.

Delinquency Prevention

One of the outcomes of cost-benefit analyses is a growing recognition that delinquency can be prevented. There is increasing interest in identifying risk factors in individuals, families, schools, and communities and reducing these risks before youth engage in delinquency. The groundbreaking evaluation study conducted by Larry Sherman and his colleagues from the University of Maryland reported that many criminal and juvenile justice interventions were not effective at reducing crime. Instead, Sherman et al. (1998) found that home visits by nurses to at-risk families, classes with weekly home visits by preschool teachers, and family therapy for delinquent and at-risk pre-adolescents were all effective at reducing delinquency. These programs tend to be low cost and have a high long-term impact, but they are not considered very politically appealing.

A number of interventions are effective in reducing delinquency. Farrington and Welsh (2007) observed that "two main individual-based interventions of preschool intellectual enrichment (such as a modified Head Start program) and child skills training (e.g., increased social skills and self control on topics such as how to help, what to do when you are angry, and how to react to teasing) are effective in preventing delinquency and later criminal offending" (p. 106). Some studies followed the participants 20 years after receiving these interventions and they found fewer arrests, less illegitimate children, lower levels of substance abuse, and an increase in higher status jobs.

Dysfunctional families are highly associated with delinquency. Farrington and Welsh (2007) found that "two main types of family-based programs — general parent education (home visiting and parent education plus daycare services) and parent management — are effective in preventing delinquency or later criminal offending" (p. 122). Parent management refers to treatment programs in which parents are trained to alter their child's behavior at home. Again, these interventions occur long before youngsters start engaging in delinquent behaviors.

Delinquency prevention can also occur at the school, neighborhood, and community levels. Again, it has long been known that poorly functioning schools, neighborhoods with high levels of unemployment, female headed households, gang involvement, and poverty are associated with crime. Farrington and Welsh (2007) summarized the research literature and reported that successful interventions included: school and discipline management (e.g., increasing the competence of teachers, changing the school climate, and teaching study skills to students); classroom or instructional management (e.g., combining parent training, teacher training, and skills training for students); reorganization of grades or classes (e.g., providing specialized instruction to high risk students); and increasing the self control and social competency of students (e.g., using role-playing, feedback, and rehearsal to increase awareness about negative peer influences, responding to risky or harmful situations, and improving moral character) (pp. 138-144).

Despite the promising research reported above, one of the hazards of all criminal justice interventions, including ones initiated by correctional agencies, is that practices that are successful in one jurisdiction do not always do well when implemented in another place (Urban, 2008). This is the challenge of program implementation and follow-up (or copycat) programs do not always successfully replicate the original intervention. Gendreau, Goggin, and Smith (1999) outlined a number of challenges of implementing programs in corrections. Sometimes, the follow-up programs lack charismatic leadership, programs are implemented only partially (oftentimes due to a lack of resources), and some staff members are resistant to change.

Over the past few decades, juvenile justice systems in many jurisdictions have been closely associated with adult corrections, sometimes to the detriment of the youth in those systems. One way that more preventative programs might be introduced is to better integrate child welfare and juvenile justice systems. There is growing recognition that a youth who is abused and neglected is at significantly higher risk of being involved in delinquency. Shay Bilchik (2007), the former administrator of the OJJDP, argues for more integration between juvenile justice, child welfare, health, behavioral health, and educational systems (p. 2). In some places, a movement of juvenile justice systems closer to the child welfare heritage of the original juvenile court is occurring and this may represent more positive attitudes toward rehabilitation.

Juvenile Corrections: A Case for Cautious Optimism

Throughout this chapter, a number of trends were highlighted that may shape the future of juvenile corrections. One important factor, however, is that the operations of juvenile correctional facilities are inextricably linked with attitudes toward juvenile crime and offenders. During times when our feelings toward juveniles are positive and rehabilitative, it is likely that the treatment of these youth will be seen in a more favorable manner. As a result, legislators may be able to allocate more funding for educational and health programs for youth in juvenile corrections or provide training for staff working within juvenile justice systems. As noted earlier, punitive attitudes toward juveniles have softened lately: juveniles are no longer in jeopardy of the death penalty, the number of transfers to adult courts has decreased, and the population of juvenile corrections is remaining stable or decreasing. Yet, these indicators also mirror the fact that rates of involvement in serious and violent crimes have decreased significantly since 1993, although rates have been slowly edging upward again (Snyder, 2008).

Publicly operated juvenile correctional facilities are almost entirely responsive to the external environment. Detention facility directors have very little control over the police who take juveniles into custody, probation officers (or parole agents) who return youth to custody for violating the conditions of their probation or parole, or the juvenile court judges who detain a youth for a lengthy period of time. Thus a police crack-down on juvenile crime, the implementation of a zero tolerance probation program, or delays in juvenile court case processing (taking a longer period of time to resolve a case) might contribute to overcrowding in the local juvenile hall. From a similar perspective, the superintendents of state correctional facilities are also forced to find additional beds if those detained youth are ultimately sentenced to long-term dispositions.

As a result of these external pressures, juvenile justice leaders should strive, whenever possible, to develop stronger working partnerships with other government and non-profit agencies. Juvenile offenders are often students in local schools, receive services from mental health organizations, and their parents often receive some form of support from social service agencies. Often, service delivery is fragmented and some agencies create additional barriers for formerly incarcerated youth. It is important for stakeholders in juvenile corrections to look for opportunities to improve services through partnerships and collaboration instead of resisting such efforts.

A number of contributors to this book observed that the interventions that were historically used with juveniles were not very sophisticated, but this is changing. Again, external factors such as litigation and the activities of advocacy groups have overcome some of the inertia that some facility administrators displayed in terms of modernizing their programs. While acknowledging that new does not always mean better, the impact of basing interventions on evidence-based research has become a driving force in juvenile corrections. As a result, it is easy to be optimistic about the future of juvenile corrections. Youth held in residential placements today are apt to be treated more humanely and with more respect than in previous eras. Yet, it is important to guard against complacency.

We live in an era when attitudes toward juveniles and juvenile justice are dynamic and we are still left with the remnants of a tough-on-crime agenda that supports the life imprisonment of 13- and 14-year-olds (Human Rights Watch, 2005). A series of school shootings or other high profile juvenile crimes might toughen the public's attitude toward juveniles and produce more support for punitive juvenile justice practices. As a result, supporters of juvenile justice reform argue that this point in time represents the best hope for implementing broad-based delinquency prevention programs (Farrington & Welsh, 2007).

Thus, the directions that juvenile corrections take will be shaped, at least in part, by external forces: public opinion, legislative priorities, and litigation. Yet, the professionals who work within juvenile justice systems can also moderate some of these forces through creativity and basing their interventions on evidence-based models. Wherever there are challenges, there are also opportunities; our hope is that the readers of this book will be encouraged to work within juvenile justice systems to make a difference in the lives of young people. We cannot lose sight of the fact that delinquency is a predictable function of adolescent development; despite the fact that some juveniles have committed serious offenses, they will need our understanding, support, and compassion in order to save them from a life of crime—which in turn, makes us all a little safer.

References

American Bar Association. (2004). *Adolescence, brain development, and legal culpability.* Washington, DC: Juvenile Justice Center, American Bar Association.

Aos, S., Miller, M., & Drake, E. (2006). *Evidence-based public policy options to reduce future prison construction, criminal justice costs, and crime rates.* Olympia, WA: Washington State Institute for Public Policy.

Backstrom, J. C. (1998). *Extended juvenile jurisdiction "One more strike and you're out!" Minnesota's blended sentencing law.* Retrieved May 16, 2008, from http://www.co.dakota.mn.us

Baird, C., & Gasper, D. A. (2008, April). *Criminal and juvenile justice offender management strategies.* Presented at the North American Association of Wardens & Superintendents Training Conference, Cleveland, OH.

Bernard, T. (1992). *The cycle of juvenile justice.* New York: Oxford University Press.

Bilchik, S. (2007, October). *The intersection of the juvenile justice and child welfare systems: Implications for policy and practice.* Presented at the OJJDP Training Conference, Denver, CO.

Bloom, B., Owen, B., & Covington, S. (2003). *Gender-responsive strategies: Research, practice, and guiding principles for women offenders.* Washington, DC: National Institute of Corrections.

Bouffard, J. A., & Bergseth, K. J. (2008). The impact of reentry services on juvenile offenders' Recidivism. *Youth Violence and Juvenile Justice, 6,* 295-318.

Braithwaite, J. (1998). *Crime, shame, and reintegration.* New York: Cambridge University Press.

Brisco, W., Forh, C., Haynes, V., & Wheeler, B. (2004). Minority recruitment for the 21st century. *Corrections Today, 66,* 128-129.

Brummer, C. (2003). Extended juvenile jurisdiction: The best of two worlds? *Arkansas Law Review, 54,* 777-822.

Cabaniss, E. R., Frabutt, J. M., Kendrick, M. H., & Arbuckle, M. B. (2007). Reducing disproportionate minority contact in the juvenile justice system: Promising practices. *Aggression and Violent Behavior, 12,* 393-401.

Chesney-Lind, M., & Shelden, R. G. (2004). *Girls, delinquency, and juvenile justice.* Belmont, CA: Thompson Wadsworth.

Cohen, F. (2008). *Final fact-finding report: S.H. v. Stickrath.* Retrieved January 22, 2008, from http://www.dys.ohio.gov

Drake, E. (2007). *Evidence-based juvenile offender programs: Program description, quality assurance, and cost.* Olympia, WA: Washington State Institute for Public Policy.

Farrington, D. P., & Welsh, B. C. (2007). *Saving children from a life of crime: Early risk factors and effective interventions.* New York: Oxford University Press.

Gendreau, P., Goggin, C., Cullen, F. T., & Paparozzi, M. (2002). The common sense revolution and correctional policy. In J. McGuire (Ed.), *Offender rehabilitation and treatment: Effective programs and policies to reduce re-offending,* (pp. 360-386). Chichester, UK: Wiley.

Gendreau, P., Goggin, C., & Smith, P. (1999). The forgotten issue in effective correctional treatment: Program implementation. *International Journal of Offender Therapy and Comparative Criminology, 43,* 180-187.

Hill, C. (2006). Staff recruitment/Work force issues. *Corrections Compendium, 31,* 15-32.

Human Rights Watch. (2005). *The rest of their lives: Life without parole for child offenders in the United States.* New York: Author.

Inderbitzin, M. (2007). A look from the inside: Balancing custody and treatment in a juvenile maximum-security facility. *International Journal of Offender Therapy and Comparative Criminology, 51,* 358-362.

352

Joint Committee on Health Education Terminology. (1991). Report of the 1990 Joint Committee on Health Education Terminology. *Journal of Health Education, 22,* 97-108.

Kempf-Leonard, K. (2007). Minority youths and juvenile justice: Disproportionate minority contact after nearly 20 years of reform efforts. *Youth Violence and Juvenile Justice, 5,* 71-87.

Latessa, E. J., Cullen, F., & Gendreau, P. (2002). Beyond correctional quackery: Professionalism and the possibility of effective treatment. *Federal Probation, 66,* 43-49.

Lin, A. C. (2000). *Reform in the making: The implementation of social policy in prison.* Princeton: Princeton University Press.

MacDonald, S., Mitchell, D. E., & Moeser, J. (2007). Defining reentry for short-term stays. In C. Rapp Zimmerman, G. Hendrix, J. Moeser, & D. W. Roush, (Eds.), *Desktop guide to reentry for juvenile confinement facilities,* (pp. 65-77). Annapolis, MD: American Correctional Association.

MacKenzie, D. L. (2006). *What works in corrections: Reducing the criminal activities of offenders and delinquents.* New York: Cambridge University Press.

Matz, A. K. (2008). *Analysis of turnover and turnover intentions among juvenile justice staff at the Kentucky Department of Juvenile Justice.* Unpublished thesis.

Mays, G. L., & Ruddell, R. (2007). *Making sense of criminal justice.* New York: Oxford University Press.

McDonnell, D. D., Levy, V., & Morton, T. J. (2009). Risk factors for Chlamydia among young women in a Northern California juvenile detention facility: Implications for community intervention. *Sexually Transmitted Diseases, 36,* 196-206.

Mears, D. P., Hay, C., Gertz, M., & Mancini, C., (2007). Public opinion and the foundation of the juvenile court. *Criminology, 45,* 223-258.

Moeser, J., Thomas, R. L., Walsh, T. B., Chakley, K., Mollner, J., New, P., & Jackson, S. R. (2007). Equipping for reentry success: Building partnerships, coalitions, and independence. In C. Rapp Zimmerman, G. Hendrix, J. Moeser, & D. W. Roush (Eds.), *Desktop guide to reentry for juvenile confinement facilities,* (pp. 21-42). Annapolis, MD: American Correctional Association.

National Council on Crime and Delinquency. (2008). *Juvenile assessment and intervention system.* Retrieved May 18, 2008, from http://www.nccd-crc.org/nccd/n_cj_jabout.html

Platt, J. (2007). *JJETSTREAM.* Unpublished document.

Rapp Zimmerman, C. (2007). Marketing reentry: Agenda setting and the media. In C. Rapp Zimmerman, G. Hendrix, J. Moeser, & D. W. Roush, (Eds.). *Desktop guide to reentry for juvenile confinement facilities,* (pp. 94-100). Annapolis, MD: American Correctional Association.

Robinson, K. M., Haupt-Hoffman, D., Stewart, B., Schneider, F., Hamm, N., & Garrison, V. (2007). Is obesity a problem in a juvenile correctional facility? *Journal of Correctional Health Care, 12,* 175-180.

Rosenbaum, D. P. (2007). Just say no to D.A.R.E. *Criminology & Public Policy, 6,* 815-824.

Ruddell, R., & Tomita, M. (2008). *Issues in correctional health.* Richmond, KY: Newgate.

Sherman, L. W., Gottfredson, D. C., MacKenzie, D. L., Eck, J., Reuter, P., & Bushway, S. D. (1998). *Preventing crime: What works, what doesn't, what's promising*. Washington, DC: National Institute of Justice Research in Brief.

Sickmund, M., Sladky, T. J., & Kang, W. (2008). *Census of juveniles in residential placement datebook*. Retrieved October 12, 2008, from http://ojjdp.ncjrs.org/ojstatbb/cjrp/

Snyder, H. N. (2008b). *Juvenile arrests, 2006*. Washington, DC: Office of Juvenile Justice and Delinquency Prevention.

Steffensmeier, D. (2008, March). *Trends in girls' violence and the gender gap: Analysis of diverse longitudinal sources*. Presented at the Blueprints Conference, Denver, CO.

Teplin, L. A., Abram, K. M., McClelland, G. M., Mericle, A. A., Dulcan, M. K., & Washburn, J. J. (2006). *Psychiatric disorders of youth in detention*. Washington, DC: Office of Juvenile Justice and Delinquency Prevention.

Tyler, T. (2006). *Why people obey the law*. Princeton, NJ: Princeton University Press.

Welsh, B. C., & Farrington, D. P. (2007). Save children from a life of crime. *Criminology & Public Policy, 6*, 871-880.

Uggen, C. (2008). *Ginormous question for juvenile justice*. Retrieved June 28, 2008, from http://chrisuggen.blogspot.com

Underwood, L. A., Robinson, S. B., Mosholder, E., & Warren, K. M. (2008). Sex offender care for adolescents in secure care: Critical factors and counseling strategies. *Clinical Psychology Review, 28*, 917-932.

Urban, L. S. (2008). Issues in juvenile program implementation: A case study. *American Journal of Criminal Justice, 33*, 99-112.

Vanyur, J. M., Nink, C. E., Upchurch, J. R., Bodman, J., & Greenwald, D. (2009). Investigating violence in prison. In N. E. Fearn & R. Ruddell (Eds.), *Understanding correctional violence*, (pp. 143-176). Richmond, KY: Newgate.

Zahn, M. A. (2008, March). *Girls study group*. Presented at the Blueprints Conference, Denver, CO.

Zahn, M. A., Brumbaugh, S., Steffensmeier, D., Feld, B. C., Morash, M., Chesney-Lind, M., Miller, J., Payne, A. A., Gottfredson, D. C., & Kruttschnitt, C. (2008). *Violence by teenage girls: Context and consequences*. Washington, DC: Office of Juvenile Justice and Delinquency Prevention.

SUBJECT INDEX

D

E

O

Office of Juvenile Justice and
Delinquency Prevention, 33, 79,
98, 106, 140, 265, 343,
ombudsman, 316, 321-323,
overcrowding – *see crowding*
oversight and accountability
accreditation, ii, 231, 238, 257, 316,
323-325, 329,
CRIPA, i, 319-321, 330,
litigation, 317-319,
ombudsman, 316, 321-323,

P

parens patriae, 23, 27, 201, 215, 217,
parental involvement
aftercare, 307,
case management, 289,
detention reform, 105,
educational programs, 269-270,
historical perspective, 27,
therapeutic foster homes, 70,
participant observer research, 203-204,
Performance-based Standards (PbS)
goals, 326,
outcomes and standards, 327-328,
violence reduction, 164,
performance monitoring – *see
Performance-based Standards*
post-traumatic stress disorder, ii, 188,
341,
predisposition reports (PDR), 248,
301, 304,
prison – *see jails (juveniles in jails and
prisons)*
Prison Rape Elimination Act (PREA),
146, 162,
prisoners' rights – *see litigation*
privately operated corrections – *see
corporate corrections*
public opinion toward juveniles, 3-6,
334-335,

R

recidivism
aftercare, 300-302,
boot camps, 9, 78-81, 87-88, 305,
case management (reducing
recidivism), 247-249,
correctional education, 274-275,
detention, 94-96,
evidence-based practices, 340,
juveniles in adult facilities, 126-
128,
Missouri, 294-295,
wilderness experience programs,
53,
reentry (community)
detention reentry, 302-303,
educational programs, 273,
from adult jails and prisons, 126-
128,
importance, 340-342,
Serious and Violent Offender
Reentry Initiative, 303,
rehabilitative programs
educational, 264-265, 274-275, 290,
evidence-based, 52, 339-340,
girls, 122-124,
measuring effectiveness, 326,
moral reconation therapy, 301,
new generation boot camps, 87-88,
166,
programs (types), 249-251,
public support, 5,
sex offender, 250,
relationships (staff-residents)
adult facilities, 121-122,
cottage institutions, 28-29,
girls, 147-148, 158,
therapeutic, 201-202, 207-210,
restorative justice, 142-143, 335,
riots/disturbances, 170,
risk assessments, 15, 101, 283, 337-338,
343,
rural detention reform, 105-106,

CPSIA information can be obtained at www.ICGtesting.com
Printed in the USA
BVOW040326181111

276393BV00007B/34/P